WOUNDED LEADERS

By the same author

The Making of Them
The British Attitude to Children and the Boarding School System
LONE ARROW PRESS 2000 & 2010

If the Church of England is the Tory Party at prayer, the Public School system may be called the Tory Party in the nursery. Here are set out the traumas, deformations and truncations of character that explain the British Establishment from the appalling Doctor Arnold to the Thatcher Matronocracy. The British are known to be mad. In the maiming of their privileged young, they are criminally insane.

John le Carré

A worthy and valuable aid in controlling the problem, not only by analysing its psychological components but also by pointing out ways to manage them, well-written, personally direct, and based on extensive study of the hundreds of 'boarding school survivors.' I can highly recommend it.

The British Medical Journal

A clear-sighted, frightening book about what we might call the institutionalized child abandonment - heartbreaking, thoughtful, lively and convincing.

Robert Bly

A powerful book.

The Scientific and Medical Review

Elegantly reasoned and passionately argued, it will serve humanity by driving a well-placed nail into the coffin of the misguided mythology of British boarding school education.

Jean Liedloff

A tender and ruthless analysis of the effect of boarding school life on girls and boys, both at the time and later in life, will strike many painful chords and unlock many painful memories. On almost every page one encounters a sentence, a quotation or an incident that prompts a mental, "Oh my God, yes!"

Angela Lambert

Read a chapter online at www.boardingschoolsurvivors.co.uk

WOUNDED LEADERS

BRITISH ELITISM
AND
THE ENTITLEMENT ILLUSION

A PSYCHOHISTORY BY

NICK DUFFELL

First published in 2014 by
LONE ARROW PRESS
London NW5 1LY, UK.

ISBN 9780953790432

The moral right of the author has been asserted.
A catalogue record for this book is available from the British Library

Printed by
Martins the Printers
Berwick upon Tweed
www.martins-the-printers.com

Set in 11 on 14 point Galliard.
Concept, text design and layout by Lone Arrow Productions.

Cover graphics by SJDesign
Cover painting by Mark Duffell

Orders: **LONE ARROW PRESS** Distribution,
257 St Andrews Road, Bridport, Dorset DT6 3DU, UK.
lonearrowpress@btinternet.com
tel: + 44 (0)1308 425684

WOUNDED LEADERS blog and additional information on:
www.woundedleaders.co.uk
woundedleaders@btinternet.com

BOARDING SCHOOL SURVIVORS workshops:
www.boardingschoolsurvivors.co.uk
info@boardingschoolsurvivors.co.uk

Permission to quote from Iain McGilchrist's
The Master and his Emissary: The Divided Brain and the Making of the Western World,
New Haven & London: Yale University Press (2010) is gratefully acknowledged.

Excerpts from *Recovering Sanity: A Compassionate Approach to
Understanding the Treating Psychosis*, © 1990 by Edward M. Podvoll,
reprinted by arrangement with The Permissions Company, Inc.,
on behalf of Shambhala Publications Inc., Boston, MA. www.shambhala.com.

Contents

Acknowledgements

First, appreciation to my wonderful production team: thanks to my expert and patient editor, Grace Fairley, to my pivotal reader Dave Shortt, to Mark Duffell for the extraordinary cover painting, to Steve Jones for creating the lively cover design, to Sue Amaradivekara for her creative promotion, to Kristen Harrison for her energy, skill and enthusiasm for the website, to my train-riding indexer Ed Emery, and to my accommodating printer, Andrew Harvey.

I much appreciate the encouragement from Hilde Bland, John Bunzl, Simon Cohen, Jeremy Cullen, Nick Dawson, Nick Hedley, Will Hammond of the Penguin Group, Leo Hollis of Verso Books, Jakob Horstmann, Adam Jukes, Brett Kahr, Reinhard Kowalski, Sten Linnander, Mark Smalley, Katherine Stroud, John Perkins, Anne Winchester and Felicity de Zulueta. John Bunzl, Andrew Mullis and Mark Smalley need a second round of thanks for their comments on the manuscript.

I want to express enormous gratitude to Bernie Dean, Colin Luke, Lyn Lidiard and Andrew Mullis. Thurstine Basset, Pippa Foster, James Foucar, Darel Hunneybell, Margaret Laughton, Nicola Miller, Simon Partridge, Joy Schaverien and Allison Ujeski have carried on the arduous work informing the world about boarding and its wounds to the soul; from these allies I have received extraordinary trust and loyalty, over many years, for which I am profoundly grateful.

I have also benefited from the support of the some intellectual giants: Lloyd DeMause, David Cornwell, Sue Gerhardt, Michael Goldfarb, Ronald Hyam, Oliver James, Iain McGilchrist, Alastair McIntosh, George Monbiot, Stephen Porges and Andrew Samuels, to whom much thanks is due. I owe undying thanks to three people who died much too soon: Rob Bland, Petruska Clarkson and Angela Lambert; without these visionaries my first book would never have appeared let alone birthed the current one.

I could not have gone as far as I have, both personally and professionally, without the help of Helena Løvendal-Duffell, who was both willing to put up with me while also not putting up with my ex-boarder behaviours and still try to love me – to her own cost. She has been my first critic on all these ideas, has taught me what it is like to be a foreigner living among the English, and helped me keep faith in my direction. No thanks is big enough for her part in it all.

Preface

Wounded Leaders

Despite the complexities involved in explaining it fully and the controversy that it inspires, the chief point of this book is simple enough. Because our elite are raised in boarding schools – away from their families, out of the reach of love, far from the influence of any feminine values and so on – we have been perpetuating a situation in which a grave disservice is done to individuals and the whole of our society. For we have been replicating, by means of a perfected, 'industrialised' process, a type of *Wounded Leader*, no longer knowing why we are doing it or even that we are doing it.

Notwithstanding the costly privileges of such an education, it consistently turns out people who appear much more competent than they actually are, especially in terms of non-rational skills, such as those needed to sustain relationships. This is the principal reason I use the surprising word 'wounded.' This woundedness is compounded because these people are unaware of their own defects and carry on regardless.

British public life, especially politics, is overflowing with such types, and they are a familiar breed. Their dominant position in the second decade of the 21st century shows how resistant Britain is to real change, as novelist John Le Carré, who has closely observed and written about such men for more than half a century, complained in July 2013.

A classic example of such a Wounded Leader from literature is DH Lawrence's Clifford Chatterley, a paralysed landowner confined to a wheelchair as a result of injuries sustained during the First World War. Clifford's wounds are both real and metaphorical: it is his inability to love that drives his wife into the arms of another, more instinctual man. Even though *Lady Chatterley's Lover* first came out in 1928 and was eventually published in its full form in the UK in the sixties, (when it was famously the subject of a trial for obscenity), the type of wounded leader described in Lawrence's book is still very much with us. The kind of problems Clifford exhibits domestically – a tendency to overvalue work or achievements, a lack of empathy, an inability to grieve, and so on – are still today being induced by an education system unique to Britain and her ex-colonies. I first described the clinical evidence for this in my 2000 book, *The Making of Them: The British Attitude to Children and the Boarding School System*. The issues still remain only partly recognised because – for very complicated reasons – the British public has been loath to link them to their causes. In the current book, I focus on their origin and how they affect us politically.

The Entitlement Illusion

Since the major path to power in our society – via public school and the glories of 'Oxbridge' – is still desirable and well-trodden, it has been easy for us to normalise this tradition and remain seamlessly accustomed to the entitlement it affords. For the most part, our elite fail to recognise the degree and manner of their entitlement; some of today's politicians appear to suggest – even to believe – that they have got where they are by means of hard work alone. This is one reason I introduce the notion of the *Entitlement Illusion*. We are used to it: it goes largely unrecognised, in the way that fish do not notice water.

The Entitlement Illusion is not an isolated phenomenon but a systemic problem that affects the whole of our society: the place and self-esteem of the British working classes is directly conditioned by it, as well as the whole nation's political apathy. We joke about it but we find it hard to take seriously the notion that our elite may be wounded and that our cherished private education may be perpetuating those wounds. It then becomes very complex; even many of those who see themselves as being against the Establishment or against bullying, are tragically subject to these themselves. Le Carré's work shows that we cannot understand whistle-blowers or spies without addressing this conundrum.

The Entitlement Illusion has a long history in Britain. It is a very successful mental conjuring trick that accounts for how we managed our colonial and imperial project without being troubled by much of a conscience. Later in the text, I will show how this was done by describing the psychohistorical context in which it occurred and explaining the psychodynamics of the dissociative 'defence mechanisms' by which such mental feats were accomplished. I will show that the latter are still being taught to young boarders today, masquerading as values.

In its heyday in the 19th century, the Entitlement Illusion meant that when we abolished slavery we paid compensation to slave owners, but not to slaves, and then felt good about ourselves. The process of what psychotherapists call *dissociation* and *objectification* made slavery possible. This process is at the heart of the boarding culture, and conditions many aspects of our society to this day. We still enjoy the wealth accrued by the Empire, run by ex-boarder gentlemen. Colonialism's enduring legacy is that it pioneered the model for globalised capitalism, which shapes the current age. The Entitlement Illusion is alive and well: it ensures we cannot feel we belong to a communal project like Europe without imagining ourselves as its leader; and its deceptive familiarity means that we go on blindly investing in an education system that produces wounded leaders and in a politics that no longer serves us.

My earlier book revealed the price paid for the ex-boarder's passport to elitism: a defensively-organised personality that is durable, if brittle. I am now able to add findings from other disciplines, chiefly neuroscience, to obtain a much broader sense of the problems, particularly the long-term effects on the brain. The notion of the *Entitled Brain* is introduced in the second half of this book. The Entitled Brain is one that is over-trained in rationality, has turned away from empathy and has mastered and normalised dissociation in its most severe dimensions; it is consequently incapable of recognising the fault in its own system.

Schooled in the development of such a brittle mindset, British elitism supports an outdated leadership style that is unable to rise above its own interests, perceive the bigger picture and go beyond a familiar, entrenched and unhealthy system of adversarial politics. Such a leadership style is not to be recommended – it may well be dangerous. It is manifestly unfit for purpose, given the demands of the current world in which, increasingly, problems are communal – indeed global – and in which solutions urgently demand non-polarised cooperation and clear focus on the common good, in order to take effect on a worldwide scale.

Back to the simple point I started with. Socially privileged boarding children are forced into a deal they have not chosen. They trade access to a normal family-based childhood for the institutionalised hothousing of entitlement. Paradoxically, because they have to speedily reinvent themselves as self-reliant pseudo-adults, they struggle to mature. The child who has not been able to grow up organically, whom ex-boarders are unwilling to identify with, gets stranded, as it were, inside of them. As a psychological consequence, an abandoned child complex inside these leaders ends up running the show.

The political implications of this are huge, for it means that it's the children inside the men running the country who are effectively in charge. In other words, my analysis shows that – to quote the title of Part II – we are being run by "the boys in the men who run things."

Jouqueviel, January 2014

Prologue

Commons' anxiety

On 27 April 2011, less than a year into his new job as Prime Minister, David Cameron robustly defended himself in the House of Commons with his now infamous remark, "Calm down, dear." This was hardly an event of international significance and yet, in Britain, with the emergence of such unveiled, casual misogyny, it was as if "the mirror crack'd."[1] Suddenly, the true face of a particular attitude, one that is rather well known on this island but not really mentionable, became visible. The incident would quickly be witnessed around the world, thanks to YouTube and news websites, before being overtaken by events of greater interest. I believe it is worth recalling that lunchtime event, for it reveals much about the British, their politics, their elite and their future.

The incident occurred during Prime Minister's Questions, a weekly half-hour during which Members of Parliament are able to submit questions to the incumbent for an answer, and for which the public pack the Strangers' Gallery. The spectators are there for the drama and the event has become national entertainment, a kind of legalised blood sport in which the confrontational style of British politics has a good outing, after which things soon return to how they were before.

If it is a gladiatorial spectacle for the viewers, Prime Minister's Questions is considered a test of nerve for the government and a trial of strength for the opposition; both sides understand how the game is supposed to be played. On this occasion, however, the man in the highest office seemed disproportionably rattled and resorted to a bludgeoning kind of tactic hardly associated with steady statesmanship; this was not really playing the game right. Cameron made his famous remarks as he faced pressure over hospital waiting times. As he attempted to read a quote from a former Labour MP, backing the government's National Health Service reforms, he had been heckled by a woman, the Shadow Chief Secretary to the Treasury. "Calm down, dear, calm down. Calm down and listen to the doctor!" the prime minister ranted at Angela Eagle.[2] The effect was electric, as *The Guardian* newspaper recounts:

> As the Labour benches erupted, the shadow chancellor, Ed Balls, angrily pointed to Eagle and to his wife, Yvette Cooper, apparently demanding to know to whom the PM had been referring. The Labour leader, Ed Miliband, appeared to call for an apology. But Cameron told them: "I said calm down, calm down, dear. I'll say it to you, if you like ... I'm not going to apologize. You do need to calm down."[3]

Finally, the Speaker, whose job it is to choreograph the proceedings and make sure that the House's internal traditions are adhered to, had to interrupt proceedings in order to properly calm things down. He told the excited MPs: "There's far too much noise in this chamber, which makes a very bad impression on the public as a whole," and directed the prime minister to sit down.[4]

Why had Cameron let his *sang-froid* slip? The Labour Party believes that Cameron betrays an arrogance when under pressure: Labour MP John Woodcock suggested that the prime minister was "losing his rag because he is losing the argument" and Labour's official spokesman branded Cameron's remarks as "sexist, insulting and patronizing." The party called on Cameron to apologise, saying his comments had not been prime ministerial but arrogant. The opposition's deputy leader, Harriet Harman, implied that Cameron's

> ... contemptuous response to Angela Eagle MP at Prime Minister's Questions today shows his patronising and outdated attitude to women.[5]

Caroline Flint, famously one of 'Blair's Babes,' accused Cameron of using the word 'dear' to "put women down," and said that she had experienced being similarly spoken to by

Cameron's colleague Eric Pickles in the past. When questioned about her own response to the onslaught, and seemingly determined to give as good as she got, Eagle sardonically told the BBC that she had been "patronised by better people than the prime minister," and that she didn't think "any modern man would have expressed himself in that way."[6] Her comments reveal both how deep-seated this kind of attitude must be and how she has had to learn to 'play the game' to survive at Westminster.

In reply, a spokesman for 'Number 10', the Prime Minister's Office, brushed the incident aside, saying that Cameron's remarks had been intended to be "light-hearted" and were but a reference to a well known advertising slogan from the celebrity ex-film director and *bon viveur*, Michael Winner. It may well have been this advertising slogan that had stuck in his brain, but what was plain for all to see was that the first among equals was clearly rattled by a woman telling him he had got it wrong. Worse, once started, he was evidently unable to stop himself. Many politically liberal observers noted that this was a definitive moment" one when Cameron's "carefully cultivated persona of a caring, sharing, socially up-to-date conservative was stripped away," as *The Guardian*'s Aida Edemariam noted.[7] Or, as Labour backbencher Chuka Umunna elegantly tweeted: "The mask slips." Others went further, noticing "Cameron's modern facade cracking under pressure to reveal the Eton-entitled, habitually sexist Bullingdon bully beneath."[8] Eagle and her leader Ed Miliband were quick to jump on this bandwagon and pointed out that what lies beneath Cameron's nice exterior is a bully. A month earlier, Miliband had commented on Cameron's "Flashman Routine," suggesting that the prime minister resorted too easily to bullying or cheap shots. "When he doesn't have an argument, he'll throw an insult."[9]

Such comments are hardly new news, for they exemplify the adversarial character of British parliamentary politics: the Opposition are expected to make massive political capital of any mistake made by a prime minister. But beyond this, there are important questions to consider here. I think it best to start with the following:

• Does it matter what is said about Cameron's bullying 'routine'?

• To what extent is bullying endemic in British life, and why?

• Why should the spectre of Flashman, a fictional public school bully from the 1857 best-seller *Tom Brown's Schooldays*, be alive and well more than a century and a half later?

• Why are the British people, so politically apathetic, still so keen to elect men whose inner personality seems to be so backward-looking, so fearful of challenge and so contemptuous of women?

The bully tradition and the Knife of Humiliation

Questions such as the above have intrigued me for a great part of my life, and I believe they are absolutely critical for understanding Britain's culture, our place in the modern world and our politics. I recognise Cameron's knee-jerk reactions as something I have seen many times before, chiefly from well-educated, powerful Englishmen who have had all the social advantages money can buy. The upper classes, in particular, can exhibit a lasting sense of entitlement if they are not crushed by their social burden. They themselves would not recognise this entitlement, so well established is it, like the landscape of the British countryside where villages still gather round the twin centres of authority established by the Norman conquest in the 11th century: the squire's mansion and the church. Even though the old aristocracy is no longer uniquely the governing class, the enclaves of money, business, church, army and politics are still the expected destinations for the grandsons of Empire. Their secure, elite, entitled positions would seem not to warrant such a degree of insecure aggression and defensiveness. But I am afraid it is a common enough story – it's the Entitlement Illusion.

Beginning in 1989, I pioneered psychotherapeutic work with a specific section of British society: male ex-boarders, who until that time had received no attention from the psychological professions, despite the fact that sending children away to board from frighteningly early ages was a common and uniquely British habit that had permeated all Britain's colonies. This study, and my numerous subsequent interactions with the public and the media, led to my writing the first psychological study of the effects of public school education on children and the adults they become, *The Making of Them: The British Attitude to Children and the Boarding School System*, which appeared in 2000.[10] When I watch the video clip of that Wednesday lunchtime in the Commons, probably now long forgotten in the swift moving world of politics, I observe something very familiar. Accustomed to reading the body language of ex-boarders, this is what I see.

There is a line of young men with puffy, self-satisfied cheeks. They are looking rather serious, as if looking serious is what they are supposed to be doing. They have the air of those who were born to be in power. They are sitting defiantly on green leather benches in an elegant fake replica of a medieval hall; it looks to me rather like a comfortable version of a chapel in a prestigious Victorian boarding school. These young men are – for now – sitting on the side that always belongs to the winners: the Government. This side always faces the current losers but the future potential winners: the Opposition. The winners and losers always sit on the same side, whoever is in power. This simplistic and unchanging structure of the room, unlike most other modern horseshoe shaped chambers, is thought by the British to be 'tradition'; but it is designed to facilitate a polarised way of doing business, where the winners hang onto their position and seek any means to put down their pursuers.

Now David Cameron stands up, looking rather pleased with himself, and starts declaiming. But straight away he is interrupted; he has been caught out having altered a very minor fact to his advantage. He is challenged and then panics.[11] I guess that Cameron is scared, so he lashes out. Instantly, his knee-jerk self-protection kicks in. No desire to have a dialogue with his interlocutor interrupts his lightening reaction. No sense of inner authority restrains him.

I suspect that, the very instant he senses the possibility of being attacked, a familiar heightened anxiety grips him. Fearing attack, he reverts to an instinctive defence against being bullied, which he learned a long time ago. It is as if he recognises a knife coming his way – 'The Knife of Humiliation.' Instinctively and rapidly, he grabs this same knife and plunges it into his opponent before it can be used on him. It is a knife that he knows well, I would guess. He knows the bullying arts backwards. He has been brought up with them and got used to them as a child, for they were normalised in the institutions in which was raised. By now, he has honed the blade of this knife and mastered its subtle use, as do so many middle and upper-class British, so that its employment is second nature and it appears completely and utterly innocent. "Simply light-hearted remarks." "It's just a joke!" "Only joking." "Did it hurt? Oh dear, you *are* over-sensitive," are the sort of things one usually hears after the knife has gone in.

Cameron's so-called 'light-hearted remarks' exemplify a familiar and rarely named problem in Britain. It is one that foreigners have to get used to and survive when they settle in England; similarly, 'foreigners' in the Commons – such as women and those from the 'other ranks' – have to get used its public school ways. Such bullying is normalised in the regular use of critical or humiliating remarks delivered in a style that declares the bully's innocence through recourse to the hallowed British conversational art form, humour: "What's the matter with you? Can't you take a joke? Only joking, don't you know?"

But make no mistake, bullying is bullying. I watch George Osborne, Cameron's Number Two, laughing a satisfied but cruel laugh, joining in – glad not to be on the receiving end, I would think. I see Nick Clegg, Cameron's additional (and unpredicted) Number Two, instantly recognise the immature attack. "Oh no," I imagine he is thinking, for he recognises these tones too, "...what now...?" But he sits frozen, perhaps in embarrassment, perhaps wondering how to respond to this when he is inevitably questioned about it later on.

Over the years I have become used to the signs of this kind of bullying. I have seen the way it is passed over as normal in the UK, and how inexplicable it is to foreigners, who discover that their natural innocence ends up betraying them in the face of it. I have made it my business to find out why this bullying style has been learned in the first place. Worse still, I have heard myself do it too and have tried to train it out of me. Looking deeper into these bullying tactics, there lies fear and profound insecurity, a brittleness of character that I have seen many times before. Bullies are scared, and so they adopt scare tactics to prevent the smell of fear from sticking to them. Cameron got scared, and I could clearly see the scared boy in him. In a clinical session I would greet this one – the frightened boy in him – with compassion. But he is not in treatment; he is in power and 'acting out,' as we psychotherapists say when someone behaves without recognising what internal conflicts are driving them, what is really stressing them, preferring to sacrifice someone else rather than look inside.

Bullying exerts terrible force on others and it kicks in under a peculiar and consistent internal logic. This logic is based on the perception of vulnerability as weakness, and the fear that weakness will lead to annihilation under hostile or uncontrollable conditions. That, I imagine, was behind Cameron's anxiety in the Commons: he thought he was going to be ridiculed, told that he was wrong, in trouble because he had told a lie. To someone who is not at all secure, deep within himself, these anxieties are swiftly and unwittingly interpreted as the threat of annihilation; they prompt an instinctual defensive counterattack. Such a reaction is especially the case if he hasn't developed any sense of internal reflection on his learned responses and behaviours, particularly those learned in childhood. It is categorically and specifically the case if he grew up having to fend for himself at an expensive boarding school. I am not suggesting David Cameron to be an insecure person, but I know from experience that those who I call *Boarding School Survivors* regularly cause themselves enormous stress by misinterpreting tiny challenges as profound threats and then overreacting.

I was not alone in spotting the PM's stress. Britain's best-known psychotherapist, Susie Orbach, was onto his anxiety when asked to comment on the 'Calm Down Dear' affair:

> What this portrays, or betrays, is that he's flustered, not her. You don't say that kind of thing unless you're flustered. He's trying to silence her, because he's got all shook up.[12]

Orbach is absolutely right, but why was the most powerful man in the land so 'shook up'? I am certain that the answer does not lie in Cameron, the man. We will need to go much, much further, to where such attitudes are learned, in order to get right to the heart of this problem. For this kind of bullying, this kind of survive-at-all-costs strategy and the kind of institution that the Commons represents – with its barely concealed misogyny, pathological fear of foreigners and reluctance to embrace change via a politics of consensus – all have their origins in the same place: the British attitude to vulnerability that is learned and perpetuated through our unique private, and usually boarding education known as *public schools*.

Privileged duplicity

At the same time as David Cameron was trying to calm his challenger down, the rest of the world was busy with massive changes. The Middle East was entering an age of revolutions, whose outcomes were too uncertain to predict but were shaped by popular will. The United States had its first black president; confidence in an economic fight-back and growth in the developed world had morphed into renewed fears of economic meltdown, with Europe looking likely to be the first major catastrophe.

Britain, however, had returned to the habits of a bygone age. The British people had just elected and agreed to be governed by a familiar breed, new packaging notwithstanding. The 2010 cabinet was massively represented by ex-public schoolboys whom the British public seem strangely content to put back in power over them. It is as if, despite the odd historical hiccough, we take for granted that our leaders should be drawn from a recognisable elite: those who bear the accent and demeanour of the privately educated. The majority of them boarded at our famous public schools; they embody a recognisable veneer of confidence and often a notable, if disguised, sense of entitlement. It is as if somehow we feel comfortable with them, like warm beer and bitter marmalade, like wet summers and losing at international sport.

On closer examination, the familiar qualities associated with an old-fashioned notion of leadership come with darker aspects. These include an ability to suggest caring sincerity while disregarding feelings; the habit of bullying each other at work (or better still, those who seem to be getting away with not working); the maintenance of the illusion that if he has to be involved in Europe at all, a Brit would naturally be a leader rather than a team-player. These attitudes come with a seamless skill in duplicity and a reluctance to self-reflect.[13] They are the fundaments of a kind of politics that we have come to expect and seem loath to change. But since we fail to take note of, let alone reject them, despite our amazing and enviable civil liberties, we remain enslaved to the most craven kind of conservatism and destined for increasing isolation abroad and fragmentation within our borders.

Bestselling novelist John Le Carré, who joined MI6 after Sherborne, Oxford and teaching at Eton, knows the shadow side of our political life extremely well, in particular the place of the ex-public school man's qualities therein. Le Carré has spent a long working life documenting a similar story in each of his 22 novels since 'coming in from the cold', or giving up his spying career. Le Carré's theme is the English ex-boarder as the 'Perfect Spy,' and sometimes spymaster. His characters live lonely, secretive lives, preoccupied with loyalty and betrayal. Between the lines, his fiction reveals how public school men develop an unconsciously defensive personality that equips them with the political and diplomatic skills of duplicity, even as this hinders them in domestic life. Here is his (anti-)hero Tim from *Our Game*:

> In the world where Larry and I did our growing up it would be quite wrong to presume that, merely because the right hand is bestowing consolation, the left hand is not considering covert action of its own.[14]

I shall say more later about how the ex-boarder acquires his skill in duplicity and how, perversely, he himself is regularly its first but not final victim, since a privileged start and the skills of self-reliance, forcibly learned at a very early age, do not only give social benefit. For every person in public life who seems to reap the advantage of this privileged education, there are countless others who suffer a kind of displacement in domestic non-institutional life. They find authenticity and intimate relationships beyond them, and their suffering goes quite unacknowledged. Boarding children, despite the advantage of their prestigious schools, grow up amongst their peers and never really come home again.[15]

The clinical name I have chosen for the specific and defensively organised personality structure, rooted in dissociation and typical of the ex-boarder, is the *Strategic Survival Personality*. I use the word 'strategic' because this personality style has a protective and adaptive function dedicated to avoiding trouble and surviving at all costs. It develops under duress, as a protective mantle, often in the very first moments the child has to survive alone at boarding school and adapt to the conditions he finds there.[16] Its main features include the instant employment of aggression as the best form of defence – as in the Cameron instance – or, alternatively, a 'duck-dive and freeze' conflict-avoidance style. In times of perceived stress, this person may overreact really fast because the 'flight-or-fight' mechanism of their autonomic nervous system gets engaged before the slower processes of the neo-cortex have had time to evaluate the context. Watching a clip of the 'Calm Down Dear' incident, it is not the substance of Cameron's attack that impresses most, although it is hard to ignore the unpleasantness of his patronising and misogynistic tone.[17] It is its speed and the PM's inability to stop himself that is really frightening, when I think of him as my elected leader-in-chief.

Aside from its defensive aspect, the Strategic Survival Personality's most common symptoms are the maintenance of a façade of confidence and success, masking (sometimes barely masking) a rigid emotional illiteracy and intimacy avoidance. And yet, his confident, apparently successful façade frequently has a quality of brittleness about it. When unchecked, this personality style has a tendency to crystallise over time into grandiosity, masochism or pathological rebellion – and occasionally a bewildering combination of all three.[18]

Despite its brittleness, the Strategic Survival Personality is amazingly durable. This is partly due to social reasons: amongst the British it is normalised as a kind of national character style. In point of fact, *normalisation* is a very successful and subtle defence mechanism used by an individual or group not wishing to be associated with qualities that might challenge a well-constructed sense of identity. Besides, even if an ex-boarder does recognise that he has this character style, it is very hard to shed. In those (rare) cases where an ex-boarder presents for therapy, the Strategic Survival Personality is extremely resistant to deconstruction by any therapeutic approaches. Moreover, it is unlikely to be recognised by most counsellors, psychotherapists, and psychiatrists who, more often than not, may be ignorant of the syndrome or intimidated by the client – or both. When ex-boarders do end up in therapy they are notoriously difficult to treat, for they have a tendency to desert as soon as the immediate crisis has calmed down.[19]

If the adult ex-boarder's personality structure is a challenge, one would imagine that the conditions that cause it to arise – children being sent away from home for their schooling – would be easier to rectify. Unfortunately, this is not the case. Having spent two and a half decades studying and working therapeutically with ex-boarders (and being one myself), I am no longer astonished at how resistant our nation is to acknowledging the problems inevitably associated with the uniquely British habit of sending children away from home to be brought up in residential institutions. To imagine that children who grow up in institutions will turn out to be fully fledged human beings without any psychological damage, able to function within the sort of loving families that they have barely experienced themselves, manifestly defies logic. Yet, as a nation, we seem reluctant to recognise it, let alone begin to shed this addiction. Why should this be so?

First, we have come to believe that the public schools are part of the traditional 'fabric of society,' and Britain is a genuinely conservative nation. Second, there is an awful lot of money and politics at play here. With the current debate in British education centring on schools that are 'independent' of local authorities, could be run by corporations like supermarkets and could make profits, the problem is likely to get worse unless we can find the will to stop it.

Even Labour governments, including Harold Wilson's in the sixties, have avoided dismantling the public schools, basically because they cost the government nothing, unlike other European countries where private schools receive a *per capita* payment for each pupil. Nationalising the public schools would require enormous political muscle and a confidence in public coffers beyond anything known in recent history; it will never be considered in times of austerity.[20] It follows that the public school lobby, having long ago succeeded in achieving charity status for their private businesses, is far too powerful for any politician to take on. Certainly no ex-Etonian (such as David Cameron or Boris Johnson) would even dream of it and risk betraying his class.

Even the therapeutic community in Britain has been slow to criticise the practice of private boarding; much of it normalises the issue by agreeing that it does not 'suit' everyone. In this respect, it is in line with most of the British middle class world in which educational opportunities for children remain polarised between two sectors, state and so-called 'independent', as if the condition of the former has nothing to do with that of the latter, which, as I shall show, it clearly does.

In the long run, despite their small classes and wonderful facilities, these institutions do not necessarily supply their society with the best leaders; quite the opposite, is the argument of this book. Even as some observers saw Cameron's brittle aggressiveness as a mark of his pugnacious leadership, very few realised that it actually points to a giant weakness – not just located *in him* but in the whole system of educating our elite. The wholesale disowning of vulnerability brings about enormous psychological perils. It is an elementary assertion of depth psychology that in chronically eschewing vulnerability, the fear of falling, or fear of failing, becomes acute and then chronic, because psychological aspects not brought under conscious regard will end up controlling the entire personality. Any psychotherapist would expect the symptoms to continue as long the problems remain unrecognised.

Subsequent losses in the PM's composure followed the 'Calm Down Dear' incident. In Prime Minister's Questions on 23 May 2012, for example, David Cameron rose to repeated and deliberate taunting by Ed Balls, in which Balls linked the poor state of the economy to a newspaper revelation about the prime minister's apparent fondness for wine. Cameron lashed out at the grammar school educated Shadow Chancellor and branded him a "muttering idiot," to riotous cheers from Osborne and others around him – no sign of Clegg that day – and a rebuke from the Speaker. There were cries of "Flashman! Flashman!" from the Labour benches, jubilant at having rattled Cameron once again.

Here's how entrenched the political problem is: the Opposition will readily make a link to Cameron's public school elite background, for the sake of returning the bullying, but no one is prepared to really address the causes of the problem.

A divided society

Despite two world wars, the establishment of a welfare state and now the information revolution, the traditional breeding grounds of British elitism and the consequent Entitlement Illusion – the major public schools and subsequently Oxford or Cambridge – remain consistent and undisturbed. More than half the 2010–12 cabinet went through this hothousing process. We are still failing to challenge it, and our educational system is becoming increasingly privatised and fee-paying. Britain is still structured by class in a way that none of our neighbouring countries are. If this meant that the society we live in was able to deliver excellent results in terms of health and general life satisfaction, as well as the quality of our leadership, it might be worth arguing for it. But realistically, this is not the case.

According to recent UNICEF reports, Britain has the lowest general health and satisfaction levels amongst her youth in the developed world.[21] The schools for the elite belong to this self-same society, whose ex-pupils then go on to govern. Perhaps it would be worth it if we had excellent leadership?

By any historical analysis, the last 50 years in Britain have produced a remarkable lack of noteworthy political leadership. Only Margaret Thatcher stands out, and mostly it is her obstinate wilfulness that impresses. Her legacy is a more divided and divisive society than she inherited. Thatcher, who did not go to public school but reinvented herself as someone who might have done, stood for its chief values of self-reliance and rugged individualism. She famously pronounced that there was no such thing as society, which became the battle cry against the hated indulgence of the 'nanny state,' a contemptuous term invented by her public school educated Tory colleagues, all forced to forego sufficient mothering in their own childhoods.

Tony Blair, who spent his childhood boarding at Fettes College – Edinburgh's Eton – used the word 'community' repeatedly on his way up the ranks of the Labour party. But when he was in power he abandoned it altogether as a concept and seemed not to notice how he was rebranding his New Labour project in the direction of a familiar rigid conservatism. Far from being at the helm of Europe – our stated attitude towards the Continent since the Second World War – we risk getting left behind. Nor have we produced any consensus makers on the scale of an Angela Merkel.

Although we grumble, especially about things like MPs fiddling their expenses, at heart most people in Britain do not think we have much reason to complain about our politics, if we even take it seriously at all. Rightly proud of our civil liberties, we have not had a tradition of tyrants in power. One view is that, though free on the outside, we are already tyrannised from the inside. The tyrant is our society's embedded elitism and entitlement, its hold over the whole society, and the seemingly innocent way it presents itself ("What *will* people think?"). What is still important is *who* you know, not *what* you know; politeness, not politics. This is much more the British way.

It usually takes an outsider to properly take account of such things, and this was certainly the opinion of Alexander Herzen, a high-born Russian revolutionary philosopher exiled more than 150 years ago to London. Despite his admiration for the liberty of British institutions, his already broken heart was finished off by English polite society. Writing in the mid-1850s, he celebrated how free from laws and police and government he felt, but declared:

> The freer a country is from government interference, [he cites England] the more fully recognised its right to speak, the more intolerant grows the mob: your neighbour, your butcher, your tailor, your family, club, parish keep you under supervision and perform the duties of a policeman.

> On the Continent people are powerless before authority; they endure their chains but they do not respect them. The Englishman's freedom is more in his institutions than in himself or in his conscience. His freedom is in the 'common law', in habeas corpus, not in his morals or in his way of thinking. Before the prejudices of society the proud Brit inclines without a murmur, with an appearance of respect.[22]

Bizarrely, Herzen's observations ring many bells even today. For the instrument of internal policing is "the prejudices of society," which in Britain means her class system, still securely in place, barely noticeable to us but shocking to outsiders. It is accepted by us and internally enforced – our internal Common Law.

Structurally, it is both dynamic (in its ability to recruit from below) and strongly conservative, remaining firmly top-down in tone. This is very important and very different to the social democratic systems of northern Europe, which regularly feature in the UNICEF reports as the most advanced and contented societies. Those societies are fundamentally different because they are not modelled on a top-down structure.

In Britain, 'top-down' means that even those who haven't been to boarding public school try to behave as if they have, and make sure they get their children into one if they possibly can. For, having your children at a private boarding school remains the one enduring sure way to move your whole family up the class system.

The publishing baron and billionaire Robert Maxwell, who in his day inspired the kind of loathing we now reserve for Rupert Murdoch, used to complain that high society never accepted him because of his lowly and foreign origins. Despite being a socialist and one-time Labour MP under Wilson, he sent his three sons to top public schools, so they would not have a similar problem.

The position and role of the public schools is considered traditional and immutable. All strata of society go along with this and, in their day, state schools would ordinarily take their cue from the public schools. Someone born on rougher streets who has since hung out with aristocrats and millionaires aplenty is Rolling Stone Keith Richards. He attended a technical school, the lowest (behind secondary modern and grammar schools) of a three-tier system created by the 1944 Education Act. Here he is, from his autobiography, reminiscing about his school in the early fifties:

> The ludicrous side to Dartford Tech was its pretensions to being a public school. The prefects had little gold tassels on their caps; there was East House and West House. It was trying to recapture a lost world, as if the war hadn't happened, of cricket, cups and prizes, schoolboy glory. All of the masters were totally substandard, but they were still aiming for this ideal as if it were Eton or Winchester, as if it were the 20s or 30s or even the 1890s.[23]

Our class structure, with its anachronism and elitism, remains stable and unchallenged partly because of the political apathy of those at the bottom of society (what Herzen calls 'the mob') and partly because of their tendency to ape those at the top. In the fifties, every children's comic aimed at the working classes used to have a cartoon about little rich kids and their public school antics.

Today, the sector of Britain whose voice is heard least continues to be fed on a media diet draped in 'bling' that aims for the very lowest common denominator and of which its highly educated creators might under different circumstances be ashamed. Occasionally there is an outburst of thuggery around football stadia or in overheated inner-city high streets, which produce a half-hearted debate about whether Britain is a broken society – a sentiment that a Wounded Leader will take when it suits him – or whether it is a symptom of wider causes. But nothing really changes.

Leadership in retreat

I should say from the start that this book is not 'about' David Cameron *per se*, although I do refer to some of his actions and statements, as well as those of some of his colleagues. It is about the phenomenon of British elitism of which Cameron is but one rather visible example; it is about the kind of behaviour that can emanate from someone of his background when in a position of power; it is about the hold that the Entitlement Illusion has on us and our addiction to it.

In subsequent pages I shall attempt to demonstrate how and why the kind of personality bred in our elite institutions is not good for British society as a whole, as a community rather than a series of self-interest groups. One reason will immediately become clear: in our world of increasing populations and multiplying global interests, such a personality will never be able to tackle complex social problems because of his inability to understand the reality of the communal.

Why should he be able to? He has had ten years of learning from the public school authorities that autonomy is strength and dependence is weakness; he has learned within a peer group, that has been watching him 24/7 for any signs of vulnerability, not to express his needs and to play what John Le Carré calls a 'game of one' when in company. He will, therefore, never be able to go forward and lead community approaches based on relationships, the understanding of the needs of others, making compromises or achieving consensus.

The world is increasingly a global community and its leaders have to be experts in such skills. The chief principle for the future has to be our fragile interdependence, but this is not something that is properly understood by someone trained since childhood to do without home and belonging, and to eschew all forms of vulnerability and all forms of dependence. A personality forged at an elite boarding school is unlikely to be able to make genuine compromises in the trust that a new synthesis will emerge, as is demanded by modern European politics, because he is likely to be dominated by an unconscious fear of belonging to a community. The communal is based on the principles of interdependent belonging.

Having had to do without loving parents as children and being thrust into a false community – a single-sex institution with a narrow age-range – most ex-boarders develop a very complex relationship with groups and communities, characterised by a mixture of suspicion and unfulfilled longing. Despite their intentions, those with an overriding thirst for power seem to end up suspicious of Continental values, backing self-reliance and prolonging a deep conservatism that keeps the old for the old's sake and robs the country of the benefits of its natural dynamism. This, of course, affects the whole society from top to bottom.

I shall try to show some of the reasons for this. I hope to explain how, from an early age, people whose psyches are dedicated to survival develop the habit of employing what today's cognitive neuroscientists call 'motivated reasoning' but what Freud's daughter Anna called *defence mechanisms*, since their basic stance to life, despite their privileges, is a defensive one.[24] Psychoanalysis proposed that when anxiety becomes overwhelming, the psyche's organising centre, the ego, deploys defence mechanisms to protect the individual. Psychologists say we are trying to avoid 'cognitive dissonance' – the fit between who we feel ourselves to be and who we are.

When the personality has no option but to keep surviving or face the *imagined* threat of annihilation then it may use one of the strongest defence mechanisms: the psyche's 'weapon of mass destruction,' – *dissociation*. Such an imaginary threat of annihilation is what I think gripped Cameron – for a nanosecond – before the phrase "Calm down, dear!" emerged to protect him. He had disowned his anxiety and projected it onto Angela Eagle, thereby dissociated for the vulnerable state that was threatening to overcome him. Did that reveal him as a bully who had learned his tricks at Eton? It is possible. Does it mean that he is a misogynist who learned his attitudes there? Also possible. These judgements would still avoid the crucial point. This is that the resort to the premise, "I am not the one who is flustered and needs to calm down – Angela Eagle is," precisely reveals the attitude of a Boarding School Survivor whose survival technique is strategic, dissociative, and immature.

I will go on to show that the side effects of the unconscious control that come from the disowned parts of the psyche, including the fear of their aggressive return, mean that someone else is always needed to embody the hated vulnerability of the self. This means that some kind of over-emotional Angela Eagle figure or other incarnation of vulnerability is an *indispensable* totem in all relationship situations.

I will show how the crystallisation of the Strategic Survival Personality means that our elite are not moved by inner authority but governed above all by fear. The bluff and bluster of these schoolboy leaders is rooted in the fear of being found out, unmasked, exposed, of not getting away with it. This is what made Cameron so anxious and makes his kind such poor statesmen, since all their actions become in the end defensive, their manoeuvres strategic, their style duplicitous.

There are times when even the Establishment recognises this, although it is usually dismissed if they seem to be able to sway the mob. In a clever television documentary in March 2013, Boris Johnson – at the time widely tipped to become Conservative leader and perhaps prime minister one day – was described by Conrad Black, who employed Johnson when Black was proprietor of *The Telegraph*, as "a sly fox disguised as a teddy bear."[25] In the same programme, Lord Sebastian Coe, who worked with Johnson on the London Olympics, observed his strategic personality at work close hand, saying there was "… not a moment of his day that is not choreographed."

I maintain that such a leadership style is, in the end, very dangerous. From the perspective of psychology informed by neuroscience, it leads to a hyper-rational and hyper-masculine stance (although a woman can also adopt it), which becomes dominated by excessive left-hemisphere brain activity that can fail to take account of context and prefers material things and ideas over living persons. I suggest that this actively works against our society since it is built on premises that go against the long-term interests of women, children and the emotional centres of men. It contributes to the maintenance of a false hierarchy in society that rewards sociopathic qualities while devaluing all that comes from the heart, including authentic inner authority.

In my first book, I made the case that the interruption of attachment formation and subsequent enforced self-control seriously affects children who suffer the best education money can buy. Perversely, as adults, it is their ability to function as if everything were fine that prevents them from getting the kind of help they need. Until now, I have confined myself mostly to the psychology, although manifestly it is a socio-political problem. In the current volume I will show how this situation can and does affect a whole nation. Previously, I devoted the last part of the first book to suggesting how, with good professional help and persistence, ex-boarders could stop *surviving* and start *living*. In the current book, which focuses on the wider implications, I am outside my sphere of influence but I am convinced that my earlier findings have relevance for the future.

In this book, I argue that understanding and changing the way the British breed their elites is an endeavour that is long overdue and may be the only long-term route to changing their lamentable politics into something more realistic and sustainable.

Introduction

British elitism and the effects of the boarding school system

British elitism is alive and flourishing, despite any reservations about its assets or desirability. It is principally fostered in the hothouses of the British 'public' schools. This private education system, which takes children from the age of seven or eight (and sometimes much younger) out of their families to board in institutions, was successfully reinvented as an industrial process with a militaristic ethic during the 19th century, in order to turn out reliable managers of the Empire. Since then, it has remained popular and, with few significant changes, is currently enjoying a revival. My case is that it is out of date and harmful. I maintain that the cost of the model of masculine leadership on sale here has been too high for the British – men, women and children – for far too long.[1] However, we British have accepted it, because we normalise private boarding and its elite products and, in a way that is hardly credible to outsiders, we deny that it has disastrous side effects.

The 2010 British general election brought public school and Oxbridge educated men back into the forefront of political life, as if the whole post-war period had been but a temporary illusion. This re-emergence was made all the more extraordinary because it occurred at a time when the rest of the world was keenly watching popular uprisings in the Middle East and worrying about the severest world economic crisis since the Great Depression.

In July 2013, the veteran spy-novelist and Brit-watcher John Le Carré commented:

When I ran away from my public school, I was being told that I
was the last generation; and it was the Attlee government [1945],
and we were only going to have only one kind of school in
Britain, were going to be like other countries. Now we have an
Old Etonian London mayor, an Old Etonian prime minister and
they're scattered across the cabinet just as they used to be.[2]

The raising up of David Cameron and company happened
to coincide with a personal anniversary: I was taking stock of
more than two decades of psychotherapeutic research into the
problems of elite education. I had been the first psychotherapist
to specialise in mapping the *psychodynamics* – the structure
of the internal psychological world that influences behaviour
– of adults who had been sent away as children to board. I
had published my initial findings in 2000 in *The Making of
Them: The British Attitude to Children and the Boarding School
System*.[3] The book investigated the history and causes behind
the uniquely British habit of educating the children of the most
well-off away from home. I explored the prevailing underlying
attitudes behind this cult and how these impacted individuals in
particular, and British life in general. I did no more than hint at
the political ramifications, not because they were not apparent
but, mostly, because of a convention in the psychotherapy
profession that this arena was to be avoided in order to remain
positioned within the apparently neutral territory of science.

Instead, I concentrated on elaborating on the specific kind
of defensive personality structures that ex-boarder adults tended
to develop – the *Strategic Survival Personality*. I argued that
enforced separation from loved ones at an early age, over very
long periods, in an institution in which they were surrounded
by an equally unparented peer group whose presence day and
night constituted a threat, would mean that boarders would
inevitably be thrown back on their own lonely resources to find
immature ways of reinventing themselves in order to survive.
At the same time, the benefits of privilege from such a very
expensive education could result in a brittle sense of entitlement,
or a crippling but secret inner shame. Because nothing had
been written about this in the psychological world, I looked
for parallels in British literature and illustrated my hypotheses
with the actual words of many ex-boarders who had managed
to find me. The publicity my work received meant that many

did. I then had to pioneer therapeutic approaches to solving the problem of what I called *surviving* the 'privilege' of boarding and the classic ex-boarder's profound but understandable difficulties with relationships, love and intimacy. In my book, I described my theory and casework in these uncharted waters.

Gratifyingly, the book was well received, initially by ex-boarders but gradually also by health professionals and writers, and was favourably reviewed in the *British Medical Journal*.[4] Many well-wishers have asked me to follow it up, perhaps with something in a more popular format, and until now I have been reluctant to revisit it. But when Cameron's coalition government became a reality and I found myself so frequently exposed to the psychological phenomena I had been trying to articulate, right in front of me on my television screen, something stirred in me. I decided to pursue the risky topic of combining what I had discovered clinically about specific psychological traits with what I could see in contemporary politics. My hope was that if people understood the problems inherent in how the British elite are brought up, they would be better placed to insist on changes to the education system that produces this kind of leadership, and thus the nation might make some needed changes. Hence this book.

The Wounded Leader syndrome

In the Prologue, I introduced a real life event that featured the leader at the time of writing, Prime Minister David Cameron. Readers will forgive my reminder, I hope, that the current book is not about any individual: it is about the systemic problem. I have neither met Cameron nor do I wish him any ill. His background simply exemplifies a classic phenomenon of British elitism of which my clinical experience enables me to make some very specific predictions. A man may have had an extensive training at Eton and Oxford for a public life at the top, but if his formative years were spent in an elite boarding school and his life has been unexamined, then his patterns of behaviour will most likely be defensively organised and *outside his conscious control*.

As an unreconstructed ex-boarder – what I call a *Boarding School Survivor* – such a leader will be unconsciously trapped somewhere between a childhood he never properly had and a maturity obscured by his pseudo-adult personality structure. I will explain this in detail in what follows but, for now, suffice it to say that this is a condition in which it is hard to be a genuinely creative politician, a responsive husband or a present father – although given awareness and will, it is not impossible. When this is added to his inexperience of family life and consequent lack of skill in relationships, the resulting character structure is one I call 'wounded.'

Paradoxically, this character structure is reinforced and rendered almost invisible by a cultural norm, which the British call tradition, that I introduce here and call the *Entitlement Illusion*. The combined syndrome has been extremely hard to name, let alone challenge. Not until 2011 did the appellation *Boarding School Syndrome* appear in the *British Journal of Psychotherapy*, introduced by Professor Joy Schaverien, accompanied by considerable debate in the psychological and mainstream media.[5] My professional assertion, as a psychotherapist, is that this is a most dangerous psychological foundation from which to run a country. With this awareness, as a citizen, I would be disinclined to elect such a *Wounded Leader*. But the Entitlement Illusion still prevents this awareness from spreading.

Britain has had generations of such wounded people, because this psychic state has trans-generational implications – in other words, unless challenged, it replicates itself over time. It leads to the passing down of a selection of undesirable psychological traits such as immaturity and lack of empathy. The resulting behavioural patterns can exhibit selfishness, duplicity, misogyny, bullying; they may be adversarial or alternatively placatory, sometimes accompanied by extreme self-deprecation and shyness. Above all, an unfamiliarity with emotional states and an anxiety rooted in having developed self-reliance too early at the expense of satisfying and valuing belonging needs will be unwittingly motivating these behaviours and crystallised by a sense of entitlement. The culturally normalised inhibition about self-reflection and ignorance about the syndrome means that the status quo remains unquestioned.

My professional work has helped me to understand the nature and origin of such characteristics and the attitudes that drive them. I then add a personal bias that runs explicitly through this book: I know I do not want such characteristics and attitudes in myself and, as an ex-boarder myself, I have tried hard to root them out; nor do I want them in those I care about. I certainly do not want them in my nation's leaders. I believe that all children deserve better care than the elite are getting. Now that I have become accustomed to looking at the issues in this way, I see the entire British education system as tainted by the elitist system, which affects its inbuilt unequal social spectrum from top to bottom.

Opinions aside, there are hard reasons why ex-boarders, particularly early boarders, do not develop qualities necessary for good leadership, even though they expect to be part of a governing elite and can 'talk the talk' with confidence. Below, I outline five of them, which are inevitably interlinked, and which I will take up again in much greater detail later.

1. My own clinical practice over nearly a quarter of a century – informed by a hunger for new and old psychotherapeutic models and methods and supported by colleagues – has repeatedly confirmed the problems for adult ex-boarders who have not examined their chronic Boarding School Survivor personalities. Having to disown feelings, softness, in fact all forms of vulnerability, so severely during childhood means that all vulnerability is seen as threatening. Consequently, the personality organises itself in a hyper-defensive way: creating stress but unable to deal with it; being incapable of admitting mistakes or making long-term decisions for the common good; in favour of a preponderance of short-term, survival-based and self-interest dominated solutions.

In summary: short-term survival-based and self-interest dominated solutions are the direct opposite of the qualities that today's leaders need.

2. The most easily recognised symptom of an ex-boarder is a difficulty with emotions. Over the last twenty years, the emerging discipline of neuroscience has confirmed much of what psychotherapists always assumed. Chiefly, this is that humans cannot take good decisions when, as a result of either physical lesion or psychological dissociation processes, their feelings and emotions are not fully accessible to them. Unsurprisingly, regardless of personal charm and attractiveness, maintaining authentic relationships is also difficult under those conditions.

Here we have a prescient problem, because the necessary skills for leadership in today's world are essentially relational and decision-making ones rather than analytic and rational.

3. Through the study of stroke victims, neuroscientists have demonstrated that the ability to conceive the world from a purely left-brain hemisphere bias presents a person with a conceptual world in which people may easily be treated as if they were objects, and wider contexts are ignored in favour of compartmentalised thinking. I shall show how it is precisely this kind of thinking that the boarding public school boy is encouraged to learn in his secretive self-reliant world. This way of seeing the world limits perspectives, tends toward 'them and us' contexts, and makes authentic relationships very difficult.

The politics of consensus, in which multiple views from different parties have to be integrated, now common in all Northern European democracies, is beyond the capability of this mindset, for it usually experiences consensus as a weakness – counterintuitive and abhorrent.

4. The combination of all these thinking, feeling and behaviour impediments crystallise into an excessively defensive attitude to life. This has long-term structural problems in the psyche, for it necessitates the construction of an outwardly competent but, in fact, defensive and *strategic* version of what the famous clinician D.W. Winnicott called the *False Self*, called here the *Strategic Survival Personality*. Such a personality inevitably fears attack and unmasking, both consciously, as in its strategic manoeuvres, and unconsciously, as frequently revealed in dreams and anxiety attacks. It predicts threat where there may be none, closes the door to intimate approaches – in case they may be threats – and handles the resultant stress very badly. When this personality type senses challenge to its survival it reacts instantly with aggression, and frequently bullying, rather than with calmness, curiosity or self-reflection. And because this personality type is the forerunner of what I call the *Entitled Brain*, it cannot conceive that there might a problem within itself. Clearly, politics can be an attractive arena for such personalities.

However, while narcissistically self-preserving leaders may charm at the beginning, they inevitably become politically harmful and cannot deliver value-driven leadership.

5. Finally, the public schools are a product of what I call the *Rational Man Project*. This is my name for the extremist Cartesian view of the world, which achieved enormous gains for Western civilisations and became the dominant cultural mindset. Though well documented in the history of science and philosophy, it has rarely been examined psychologically. I believe that it actually produces weakness rather than strength in the long run. Rationalism benefits its exponents – up to a point. But when it becomes extreme or excessive, as in the British Establishment version, there is a profound psychological distancing problem. Whatever does not count as rational – women, children and foreigners, especially indigenous peoples – is made into an object of derision and loathing. It subsequently morphs into an object of fear because it is unfamiliar and unworthy of curiosity; in consequence, these objects lose their subjectivity and then have to be dominated rather than related to. I suggest that the dominant values of this attitude are in fact what today psychotherapists call *defence mechanisms,* chiefly dissociation, objectification, compartmentalisation and normalisation.

The British version of extreme rationality – what I call hyper-rationality – affects all our social institutions, for better or worse. Hyper-rationality is increasingly out of step in a world that has to embrace difference, complexity and connectivity; leaders schooled in an outdated, over-rational approach will, at best, miss the point.

Psychology and politics as bedfellows

I am very aware of the risks of the kind of approach I am attempting: the difficulties inherent in the project are great. Linking psychology and politics is not encouraged in Britain, especially not by the professional psychological press, which bans it. Making national generalisations is also frowned upon: psychotherapists know that it takes many hours to really get to know someone and, while some acknowledge the notion of personality types, others are profoundly sceptical of any generalisation at all. Politics is an even more impressionable discipline than psychotherapy because it is so directly influenced by the zeitgeist and what people want to hear. It has an opposite agenda, of course, for generally it holds at its base an acceptance of the importance of strategy over reflection. So politics and psychology have not yet found an easy mutual cooperation.

There is also a third element that needs to be considered: that peculiar phenomenon the British media, mostly very conservative in tone. The tabloid papers tend to be full of pseudo-psychology, and often use it in a trivial way or to support party-political ends. A sizeable section of the general public is increasingly apathetic and content with gross generalisations along the lines of "all politicians are corrupt." Besides, politicians are geared to focus on outer realities rather than inner ones; those on the right are especially dubious of anything that smacks of 'navel gazing.' In serious 'broadsheets', journalists trace every move of our political heavyweights, whose memoirs in turn tend to be published with increasing speed, presumably so they can have their say before they get analysed by others.

We end up with politics without psychology and psychology without politics. I propose that with these two major forces of human endeavour still not talking to each other, we remain in the realm of black and white, them and us. So this book is also an attempt to address that balance. If I am right that the kind of politics we have – including the nature of our leaders, the entry of women into parliament, the class structure of our society, the shape of our education system, the attitudes to children and parenting, the embedded drive to privatisation, and even the design of the House of Commons – is shaped by an elitist and uniquely British system of private education that favours taking children out of the home, then a psychological approach to our politics is inescapable. In fact it is long overdue.

I prefer to call my own psycho-political approach *psychohistorical*. Some readers may wonder: "What is psychohistory, and is it really a genuine discipline?"[6] Here is a description by Maurice Isserman, the James L. Ferguson professor of history at Hamilton College, New York, reviewing the autobiography of leading psychohistorian Robert Jay Lifton in 2011:

Psychohistory is the field of inquiry that explores the psychological motives of individuals and groups of historical actors, as well as the psychological impact of historical events.[7]

There is an Institute for Psychohistory in New York, which offers this definition:

Psychohistory, the science of historical motivations, combines the insights of psychotherapy with the research methodology of the social sciences to understand the emotional origin of the social and political behavior of groups and nations, past and present.[8]

I would add that psychohistory also explores how shifts in consciousness and national mindsets create ways of thinking about the world in which people frequently collude to avoid 'inconvenient truths' or protect a favourable identity. But what sealed the choice of term for me was coming across the following quotation in a 1994 *New Yorker* interview with founder of the Institute for Psychohistory, Lloyd deMause, now currently in his eighties, in which the interviewer wrote:

To buy into psychohistory, you have to subscribe to some fairly woolly assumptions, for instance, that a nation's child-rearing techniques affect its foreign policy.[9]

Ironic as it is, I find this statement precise and correct. It is exactly the kind of argument you have to take exceedingly seriously, even if it is not always a popular view. I see the persistence of the kind of scepticism shown by the reviewer as a recognisable side-effect of Enlightenment thinking, where all disciplines become separated and out of dialogue with each other, which dominates the Rational Man Project. I will have more to say about this later when tracing the history of hyper-rationality.

I shall build on this further to suggest that new interdisciplinary approaches (this book is one tiny example) are essential to think one's self out of the trap of hyper-rationality, which is anachronistic and therefore anti-evolutionary. My claim is that psychohistory can become a missing piece in the puzzle, an evolutionary and crucial tool, and, in these days, a political necessity.

The (British) emperor's new clothes

As far as the phenomenon of elitist boarding is concerned, it is hardly 'rocket science,' as the British like to say these days, to recognise its faults. And yet, in the national debate, outside the anecdotal field of literature and entertainment, there have been few voices ready to stick their necks out sufficiently in protest. Any time the matter raises its head in the British media, there are hundreds ready to fill the online blogs with passionately aggressive remarks of the "It never did me any harm!" kind. I suspect that this is partly because British society, with its inbuilt conservatism, is extraordinarily good at self-policing, as Alexander Herzen suggested long ago.[10]

In 1998, radical columnist George Monbiot named the practice of boarding school "Britain's most overt form of child abuse," and suggested it offended "no fewer than eleven articles of the UN convention on the rights of the child, which Britain signed in 1991, yet it attracts scarcely a murmur of concern."[11] But Monbiot also seemed to wilt under an odd inner hesitancy, which is a peculiar feature of this self-policing. "I hope this doesn't sound like special pleading from a poor little no-longer-rich boy," is how he ended his piece. In 2012, however, he was much more forthright:

> It should be obvious that this system could also inflict wider damage. A repressed, traumatised elite, unable to connect emotionally with others, is a danger to society: look at the men who started the First World War.[12]

Monbiot is absolutely right: the problem of sending our most favoured sons and daughters out of their families to board should be obvious and the effects can be catastrophic. Looking beyond the 'winners,' like Cameron, it is not difficult to see that this has been the case for many individuals, and that this practice continues to place our nation anachronistically out of step with our neighbours. We should not need books like this one. But we have to remember that we are the nation that had to be advised in radio broadcasts by the good Dr Winnicott that holding babies was good for both mothers and children; in most places in the world, this would be self-evident. From the perspective of a society with such entrenched national attitudes, the socio-political arguments inevitably need deconstruction and analysis by means of psycho-political and psychohistorical awareness.

One of the obstacles towards getting a fresh perspective is the need to think 'outside the box.' In the case of British elitism, I think informed observers from other cultures offer the best chance to help us do so, sometimes by questioning things that are national institutions and sometimes by unpicking the language. This is particularly important when we come to the kind of covert hostility that passes notice or is taken for granted. A potent example here is the normalised style of bullying that passes for humour or banter in Britain – the 'Calm Down Dear' episode is just one incidence. This is regularly experienced as hurtful by outsiders or foreigners, or it is simply not picked up at all, and it may be shocking for native English speakers to discover this.

Like no other language, the middle-class use of English is frequently laden with hidden coercion. A veiled way of expressing a wish, for example, may allow a speaker to risk asking for something while not seeming to. The Dutch wife of a friend of mine would get irritated when asked: "Would you like to do the washing up?" Under the psychological microscope, this request turned out not to be a genuine or 'open' question. It wasn't at all about whether she had a desire for kitchen work; it left it up to her to deal with the duplicity in the question and, probably, the washing up. Psychotherapists recognise that asking for something (including asking some-one to do something for you) makes you vulnerable, in a sense, because you might not get it. So asking for something in a hidden way, using conditional tenses that the English language does so well, can be a way of avoiding vulnerability. Such use of the English language is almost exclusive to Brits.

The role of the outsider, one who can employ what Zen Buddhists call 'Beginner's Mind' – one who can see that the emperor has turned up without his clothes on – may in the final analysis turn out to be the most prescient one. In formulating my own arguments over the years, I have been extremely reliant on the views from those just outside British culture – those who are close enough to it to be in the market but not of it. I have had most of my own major insights from outside the island or in transition to and from it, which has been the shape of much of my own life. As someone who went to public schools and Oxford, I have also been horrified to discover the extent to which the problem I was describing was also present inside me. I have had to follow another path to recover my own humanity.

Sociologically, Britain is a unique case for this study, just as the one-family, one-child phenomenon is now being seriously studied in mainland China, the country where it has been practised most extensively since 1979.[13] Both China and Britain provide perfect sampling groups where wide-ranging and socially normalised examples of these syndromes can be observed. From understanding the psychohistory and psychopathology of the syndrome, I maintain we thereby find ourselves in a much better position to understand and evaluate the problems of hyper-rationality in general and in the world at large, and its consequences on the challenges for leadership universally. This is important in a world in which the social, political, economic and climate threats are on a much greater scale than humanity has ever had to cope with before, and therefore in which a much greater responsibility is placed on leaders. So while the present book is concerned with an extremely narrow and minor arena of human affairs, it is also a kind of hologram.

In the wider world, those with the perspective to think fully outside the box of Western culture are becoming fewer. I am thinking of the tiny remnants of indigenous cultures living in what is left of our wildernesses in a condition that can help us understand what the pre-industrial, pre-hyper-rational world may have been like. Those peoples who are still embedded in the old ways have a tendency to comment in a remarkably uniform way, no matter what continent they still huddle upon. They suggest that although the advances of progress bring undeniable material advantages, they have blinded its beneficiaries to wider and deeper values. To indigenous peoples, we appear like Gadarene Swine, driven as if drunk on materialism towards a self-inflicted grim future.

In 1925 the Swiss psychic explorer Carl Jung visited the Pueblo Indians of New Mexico. Why, he asked a middle-aged chief, did he "think the whites were all mad?"

"They say that they think with their heads," he replied. "We think here," he said, indicating his heart.[14]

In retrospect, it seems tragic that such voices were not given more attention. The hyper-rational mind – the Entitled Brain –

cannot hear such things. Our hearts, however, understand. Our hearts want to keep our children with us when they are young; our hearts want good education for all children.

About this book

The book is divided into five parts, like five acts in a play. Each chapter comes at the issues from a slightly different perspective and sometimes with a different voice, with themes which sometimes reappear, like characters in a play. Each chapter is a complete whole in itself and may be read in isolation but, naturally, chapters also build on one another. In order to cope with the density of material, each chapter is divided into subsections that can be read separately but will hopefully be read in sequence.

Notes to chapters are at the end; they include bibliographical references, website links and sundry remarks deemed unnecessary to the text.

I have tried to avoid too much psychological jargon by explaining terms as I go along in order to create a book accessible to the general intelligent reader. Sometimes I come at the material rather personally and not without emotion, from a narrow perspective; at other times I approach it with greater dispassion and from a broader perspective. This dual approach mirrors how our brains work, with a different attention (or in this case a different voice) between the two hemispheres, in order to come up with a synthesis. In this respect, I run the risk of disappointing those who would prefer an entirely academic approach as well as those who prefer the approach to be entirely personal. I sincerely hope that the strength of the 'story' may carry both sets of readers through.

In the first part, *The Golden Path up the Divided Isle*, I have taken the liberty of telling some of my own story of uncovering the previously unspoken downside of British elite education. The story throws a light on the prevailing social attitudes, in particular the defensive normalisation of the practice of sending children to boarding school. I do not discuss my own boarding days and only briefly mention my time as a boarding school teacher. Rather, I concentrate on the process of 'coming out' about the problems of boarding as well as my dealings with the public and the media as a so-called 'expert' on a subject that wanted to stay in hiding. The story illustrates how pervasive and subtle the culture of bullying learned in boarding schools remains in British life, how we have taken it for granted and normalised it, and how it maintains the denial about what we do to our privileged children.

In the second part, *The Boys in the Men who Run Things*, I describe in more detail the psychodynamics of the immaturity, the defensiveness, the bullying, the sexual ignorance and the duplicity that we are building into our elites through private boarding education. I describe its effect in creating an anachronistic mindset – the Entitlement Illusion – that is a very poor qualification for leadership. This section is illustrated by many references to recent political journalism and attempts to translate complex psychological phenomena into readily accessible language

In the third part, *The Rational Man Project*, I offer a sweeping view of the psychohistory of British hyper-rationality, an outline description of this history and an interpretation of it as I see it, in particular in terms of its effect on the social class system. This section rests on the psychological ideas explained in the second section, but is chiefly illustrated by references to literature of the 18th, 19th and 20th centuries, as well as by the views of some contemporary historians and critics.

In the fourth part, *Inside the Entitled Brain*, I refer mostly to philosophical and scientific developments. I collate evidence from the latest, fascinating research in neuroscience, to formulate pointers to explain the functioning of what I am calling the Entitled Brain, and explore why its development is such a mistake. The bringing together of these findings from neuroscience with philosophy, sociology and politics is in itself a radical step.

Finally, in the *Epilogue*, alongside my conclusions about hyper-rationality, I offer some possible directions concerning aspects of leadership and education that apply beyond the British case as well as some suggestions about the future of boarding in Britain.

ACT I

THE GOLDEN PATH
UP THE DIVIDED ISLE

A hidden problem emerges

To write is to fight.

Dr Nawal el Saadawi,
Egyptian fighter for women's rights, born 1931.

CHAPTER 1

Scholars from Oxford

Fortress fantasies ~ Dreaming amongst spires
Who's the British Establishment for, actually? ~ Falling away from spires

Fortress fantasies

From the top of the ramparts the edge of the city was visible, and then a great featureless plain spread before my eyes, hot, dry and dusty, disappearing into a blur on the horizon, threatening to cover the whole of the earth. Yards from where I gazed out, the huge scruffy vultures that wheeled in the daily sky far above head height could now be seen in close-up, unperturbed by my presence. Turning around, I could see the road that dropped from the proud Mughal fort, lined with giant, partly defaced statues of Jain Thirthankaras carved into the golden sandstone, towards the chaos of the sprawling Indian city safely below.

It was 1972 and I was in my early twenties. Sometimes I could take in this vista and sometimes I had to shut it out. Often I wondered what I was doing here at all. Officially, I was the new teacher at a prestigious boarding school housed in an ex-British Raj barracks within a fortified military complex that dated back to the 8th century. Built on an extraordinary outcrop of rock in the middle of the sweltering plain of central India, the site had been a religious centre since at least the first century before Christ. It had been almost too easy to get the job. I had wanted to get to India, but not just as a tourist. So I had written to the Indian High Commission in London to say I was about to leave Oxford with a 2.2 degree in Oriental

Languages, and could they find me something? Within weeks, I received offers of jobs from two different schools. Having made my way overland to present my entirely untrained self to one of them that I selected at random and had not even researched, I was warmly welcomed and introduced with the illustrious title of 'a scholar from Oxford.'

I certainly did not think of myself in this way – in fact, I felt rather embarrassed. In retrospect it must have been my Oxford credentials that got me the job but at the time I thought it was just luck. What's more, I am afraid I must have been a big disappointment to my trusting employers and colleagues, starting from day one when, to my horror, I found myself selected to represent the staff in the annual cricket match against the boys. I had never been a cricketer, though it was impossible to convince anyone of that – I had been to Oxford, after all: I had to be good at cricket! In the event, I was immediately dismissed – out 'for a duck' – when it was my turn to bat.[1] Despite this evident disgrace, everyone pretended not to have noticed. I did not have much more skill in teaching, either, and even less in dealing with young teenage boys. I was so freshly out of boarding school and Oxford myself that I felt more identified with the pupils than the staff. My only real achievement was eventually managing the cheekier of the spoiled boys I had under my care by getting them involved in a pantomime that we put on for the school. I found the staff room much more difficult.

Nevertheless, I was astonished how they accepted me, and how even the people in the town below seemed to welcome my young wife and me whenever we wandered around down there. When we bought a new bicycle we were treated to tea and free puncture repairs for life, so proud was the shopkeeper of having us as his customers. Only once in a year and a half did we meet any hostility and that was when we strayed into a poor area where foreigners were never seen. Mounted Indian style on the same cycle, me standing on the pedals and she side-saddle on the carrier, we were pelted with small stones. Otherwise, the kindness to us as English people was overwhelming. I wondered how it was justified. I saw us Brits as recent colonial masters and I found that hard to be proud of. We had left them the railway and our useful language, but we built our Empire on their wealth, enrolled them to die in our European wars and then abandoned the continent to civil war when we decided it was time to quit, leaving their educated classes feeling second rate, ashamed of their own extraordinary civilisation that I had studied at Oxford.

Frequently, as I walked back towards the old barracks from the ramparts, along avenues lined with shady trees colonised by screeching monkeys, I reflected on why on earth they seemed to love us still. I would wonder how the British had managed to overrun, control and live in India at all. I knew some of the military and trading history, but I didn't mean that; I meant that India itself was so huge, so foreign, so seething with life, so full of colour, people, activity, poverty, squalor and wildlife, that it was like an assault on the senses, a shock to the entire psyche for Westerners. One seventies' writer's take on it was that it felt:

> ... like walking into a [rock] concert that had been playing for five thousand years with seven hundred million people in the band.[2]

You either were enchanted by India or loathed it. My father, stationed there for part of the Second World War, remembered only dirt, chaos and upset tummies. So how did the British, I regularly asked myself, manage to dominate India and not succumb to complete overwhelm?

I knew that the Raj had principally been run by young men from stiff Victorian English families. Less than seventy years earlier, the forty-year-old Viceroy Lord Curzon ruled a land of 300 million Indians with a staff of only 150,000 Brits. Presumably, most of them stepped straight out of public school and into imperial service – a bit like me in my current job, I supposed. But I *knew* I was bluffing it, and I wondered how I was getting away with it. So how on earth did they get away with ruling over this massive, enchanting but chaotic and bizarre land? All I could imagine was that by serving in the Raj they would never really have needed to leave school, for the institutions they passed through would have been run on very similar lines. They could have remained public-schoolboy-gentlemen and bumble through as if the whole thing were a debating club, like our Parliament, as if the Indians were unruly new boys and they the privileged prefects. It took me a long time to find more of an answer.

Later on, I discovered that I was not alone in such speculation: the travel writer Bruce Chatwin had called the

British Empire "a world run by overgrown boys."[3] And all the while, these overgrown schoolboys maintained that the natives, heirs to one of the world's most profound philosophic systems, were not competent to look after themselves. Though the history of the British domination of India did not lack brutality, sheer force was not its prime feature; and military might alone could not account for the success, I reckoned. Was it gargantuan self-control, monumental ignorance or simply luck that led them to succeed in India in the way that they did? I just could not figure it out.

Neither Oxford nor my eventual studies of Indian culture had prepared me to answer such questions. In the second part of this book I set out my eventual findings but, for now, over this chapter and the next two, I shall be telling the story of how the extent of the problem revealed itself to me.

Dreaming amongst spires

In retrospect, I now recognise that my reception in India was due to my arrival on a well-established route of privilege leading from public school and Oxford, and I was undoubtedly expected to go on to greater things than teaching school. The golden path straight from Oxford to high office, notably government, is as sure today as it was in 1970, as it was a century earlier. It was recently subject to analysis by the American journalist and seasoned Brit-watcher, Michael Goldfarb, in an authoritative BBC World Service radio documentary, broadcast in October 2011, called *The British Establishment: Who For?*[4] Goldfarb's observations are insightful, not least because all systems are best observed by the interested person who is placed just outside the system they are watching. An informed foreigner is probably essential for the task of thinking 'outside the box' of the British scene.

Goldfarb, who, like Clinton in his youth, spent a year at an Oxford college, begins by trying to answer whether the British establishment actually exists and, if so, what it is:

> There is something about how British society works that gives people a sense that there is a group at the top who have in some way got their influence not by the sweat of their brows; even those who are in that group are aware that they are slightly separate from the rest.

Goldfarb is an excellent interviewer and pursues several unusual avenues to the subject, even managing to get good sense out of the maverick Toby Young, renowned broadcaster and columnist of 'robust' conservative persuasion, who usually plays it for laughs, and author of *How to Lose Friends and Alienate People*. Goldfarb recognises Young as an important if not iconic figure and one placed *just* outside the system of the current Establishment. Young's father, Michael, was a major Establishment figure of a different hue – a Liberal peer. He was at the centre of the educational policy of the early welfare state, founded the Open University and is said to have invented the word 'meritocracy.' Because his father's conscience went against educational elitism, Young the younger had to attend state schools, though he did manage to get to Oxford. In late 2011 he was in the public eye for co-founding a new so-called 'free school,' albeit one based on very old-fashioned principles. A keen observer of all matters elitist and educational, Young told Goldfarb:

> The curious thing about the English Establishment is that it survives in spite of having almost no defenders. I mean, politically, it has no defenders at all.

Goldfarb, however, suggests that the reason the Establishment survives is that it has proved very adaptable, which, as we have seen, is a prime feature of the art of survival:

> Once it was located in the hierarchy of the church, the military, the Empire, but as Britain became more secular and the Empire disappeared it shifted towards the corporate world. Now in my travels around the country for this BBC documentary, looking to see what the Establishment is and who it benefits, I find it's changing again. But the constant in its evolution is the importance of one institution: the University of Oxford.

I had 'gone up' (as you are supposed to say) to this most elite of universities in 1968. Among my contemporaries were John Redwood, Gyles Brandreth, Martin Amis and Bill Clinton. I was enrolled to 'read' the classic Oxford degree course, PPE (Politics, Philosophy and Economics). This was more my public school housemaster's choice than my own, for these were not yet the days of indulging the wishes of teenagers. Besides, if I could pass the exams and interviews, the government – amazing as it seems today – would foot the entire bill, less £40 per term, for which I had to submit accounts to my father, whose own background was far from elitist. I knew I was getting a privilege, but I still found Oxford a real puzzle. There was something going on there that I did not understand.

If the teaching style was designed to produce an intellectual elite, I remember it as particularly poor, and the academic regime as staggeringly lax. In the first two terms undergraduates were left largely to their own devices. We had to attend at the most one lecture a week and once a fortnight a tutorial in which we were supposed to present written work based on our reading. There were some obligations: it was important to be dressed in our gowns for these events, and we eventually had to pass the Preliminary Examinations at the end of the two terms. Tutorials, the most intimate of the teaching arrangements, had an unfailing rhythm to them. My economics tutor liked to make himself tea while his two tutees in turn read their essays out aloud. I can still hear his comments issuing from the kitchenette of his oak-panelled quarters that looked out on the perfect lawn contained by the elegant mediaeval quadrangle.

"*Mister* Duffell…," he would begin, savouring the title and surname with which we were always pompously addressed and relishing the pause with exquisite, well-honed timing.

"You write an elegant essay but you know *ab… so… lute… ly nothing* about economics," evidently enjoying to the full all four syllables.

It may have been an uninspiring teaching style, but he was certainly right on the last point. What I learned of economics, with its insistence on an optimum degree of permanent unemployment to feed the labour market, struck me as callous. Philosophy consisted of nothing but mind-numbing formal logic and epistemology, when I had imagined it was going to be about Life with a capital L. Politics was going to be delayed until after the examinations. I was disenchanted. So, after scraping through the exams, I changed course to study Sanskrit, in defiance of my career prospects but in an attempt to follow my developing interest in all things oriental and thereby my heart. The teaching wasn't always much better though. I remember sitting in a bored circle of students in the rooms of renowned Professor Zaehner within the hallowed confines of All Souls College, translating in turn stanzas of the *Bhagavad-*

Gita. Zaehner had just published his acclaimed translation of this religious masterpiece, but his guidance was confined to the grammatical niceties rather than the spiritual significance. What an opportunity missed, it seemed to me.

How could I be so ungrateful as to be disappointed in Oxford? I was bewildered that it did not have the primary goal of filling me with knowledge or teaching me to think. At least, that *appeared* to be the case and I never quite understood in those days what it was supposed to be about. I *needed* to be taught to think. I was no scholar and I seemed to have emerged from public school filled with an inner fog. But were others disappointed? It seemed not, apart from those who cracked up when the final exams drew close and they realised they had not yet done any work. In late spring, the psychiatric hospital, affectionately known as 'Warnforde College,' regularly welcomed more of the educated than one would imagine, and the River Cherwell accepted more than was decent.

In general, when I looked around, Oxford seemed to me to be a kind of 'public school part two;' at my public school the masters had even called themselves 'Dons,' as the Oxford Fellows did. I had still to understand the nature of this preceding educational privilege, which, due to my father's ability to save money and want the best for me, had presented me with huge social advantages while also causing me to lose touch with my family from an early age. It now had me walking through honey-stoned medieval cloisters next to smooth young men who assumed the privilege to be naturally theirs. I could not fathom its purpose. That, however, was before I had come across the famous Victorian novel, *Tom Brown's Schooldays*, in which the elitist ambitions are plain to see through Tom's father's self-reflections:

> Shall I tell him he's sent to [Rugby] to make himself a good scholar? I don't care a straw for Greek particles or for the digamma, no more than does his mother ... If he'll only turn out to be a brave, helpful, truth-telling Englishman, and a gentleman, ... that's all I want.[5]

For my part, I found the gentlemanly public-school atmosphere I encountered at Oxford disturbing. Like a boarding school, it featured an endless store of special terminology, self-referring traditions and bizarre rules and rituals, like climbing in over walls after gates were closed at night and needing permission to enter a college that housed those of the other sex. Such rules seemed to represent the institutionalised shame of carnality on behalf of the Oxford Fellows rather than the real world of 1968. Worse: I was mortally embarrassed to have a manservant – called a 'scout' – to clean up my room for me. I was appalled by the immaturity of what passed for fun, like the crude custom of 'sconcing.' This was the tradition of accusing someone of breaking one of the unfathomable rules of table etiquette during 'Hall' (mealtime taken in the great college dining hall), such as talking about your work or the portraits hanging on the walls. If the senior presiding peer approved the sconce, the accused had forthwith to drain in one go a large tankard filled with several pints of beer, or pay a fine. I can now imagine that all this was small beer compared to what went on in the Bullingdon Club, where several of the 2010 Conservative ministers enjoyed their gilded youth.[6]

Many of the state school students – there were a number in attendance in those liberal days – seemed too entranced by the glamour and too taken up with drink and freedom on their first time away from home to share my doubts. So I felt quite alone, which I was also used to, and out of synch. I teetered between contempt for it all, at one moment, and the next, imagining that the problem was all in me.

Who's the British Establishment for, actually?

For the majority of my fellow undergraduates, I imagine Oxford to have been a delightful stepping-stone on a sure career road, as it will also have been in David Cameron's day. Michael Goldfarb declares that 62% of the 2011 British cabinet went to public schools and 69% attended Oxbridge, with public school and Oxford as the background to most of the main players.[7] He sees Oxford as a completely non-partisan training ground for the governing elite of whatever political hue. It can thus be thought of as the ultimate social network in Britain, where those in the know and who are going to be in power get chummy with each other. Often the most successful people there are those who as boys attended the major public schools, where they were already versed in the rituals of self-promotion and election to various bodies and societies before their facial hair had grown. Eton's exclusive club 'Pop' is the quintessential version of such a junior Establishment clique. The teenagers who are elected to Pop are the most popular and powerful boys in their peer group at Eton – in short, those who are deemed to be natural or entitled leaders.

The skill people ultimately learn at Oxford, Goldfarb concludes, is not so much to understand the world or the various disciplines that they are supposed to be studying, but to develop their way with *words*. At least, this is what he discovers via another long-time observer of the British establishment, Thomas Kielinger, esteemed columnist of German daily newspaper, *Die Welt*. Fluent public speaking rather than real intellectual ability is what is on offer here, says Kielinger, and it is what differentiates the British elite from the German. He is not being ironic; he says that this skill is very impressive, even to a German intellectual and top reporter.

So is Oxford just a glorified talking shop, a finishing school for the chattering classes? This may not be so far from the mark as it first sounds. Could it be that reading out your essay and fielding the ironic comments *was* the training, rather than the subjects you read? Was the fact that I knew nothing about economics an irrelevance – was it the *style* of the observation that was everything? Is that why I, the son of a pragmatic man who had worked his way up from the bottom, just didn't get it? Maybe Oxford's aim simply was to teach you how to *talk* rather than how to think. Perhaps learning to declaim and argue was the real training for future leaderships, presenting a view and despatching those who disagree with you the real skill. It is certainly what is at the heart of Prime Minister's Questions. It is not so much *what* you say as *how* you say it. And in that arena, you have to be able to say it in a way that lands like a punch on someone's nose. Was this why Cameron, Boris and Co. bounced back into power as if their whole lives had been a preparation for it – because they knew in their bones that *how* you say things matters far more at the top than *what* you say?

Of course! Britain is *all* about how you speak. No other nation is so obsessed with every whiff of accent, every nuance. The one thing that all prep schools make sure they do before they send a child to public school at thirteen is rid him of any trace of a regional accent and equip him with the ability to speak in the tones that suggest leadership. These can only come naturally from the upper or upper-middle classes in Britain:

the same tones that Edward Heath, Margaret Thatcher and John Major could manage but a parody of. The 'right' kind of talking seems to fall into a nationwide self-regulated style, which in each age has its slightly different timbre, according to fashion, but has no true name. It has various minute subtleties: some experts claim they can spot an Eton accent, for example. Unofficially it is simply known as 'well spoken,' particularly when applied to children. Officially it is known variously as Received Pronunciation, the Queen's English, and sometimes, Oxford English. This is the English you need to speak in order that no one can trace your regional provenance, that no one will think you are 'trade,' as people used to say, before 'traders' became the wealthy gambling gladiators who dominate the financial industry.

And speaking well in public is exceedingly important at Oxford. Traditionally, the royal road to power is open to those who make President of the Union, who thereafter have a strong chance of high office, like at least three former prime ministers as well as Michael Gove and Boris Johnson. The Oxford Union, it should be said – for those who don't know – is not actually a *union*, just as the pubic schools are not actually *public* (they are proud to be private); nor is it like a 'red-brick' university's Union bar, where students hang out, drink beer and play too much pool. It has no connection to union representation – such as the ill-fated National Union of Mineworkers, trounced by Thatcher in the eighties, or even the National Union of Students. The Oxford Union is a super-posh debating society that holds two-sided discussions about world issues, or, more accurately, issues of concern to its members, and frequently invites celebrity speakers from other elite worlds. Over the years, the Oxford Union has regularly put up motions such as "This House Would Abolish Private School." Oddly enough, exactly this topic was last contested on 27 October 2011, when Toby Young and others spoke *against* it. Unsurprisingly, the motion was defeated two to one.

The top six boarding public schools, then Oxford and the Oxford Union remain the best-trodden route, the shortest high-speed line to the top. Should we assume that such fast-track streaming of the privileged is a sure bet to engender quality leadership and a healthy society? Is that what brought the British success in India? Kielinger's account of his native Germany would not make us imagine so. Germany is much more of a realistic meritocracy than the Britain of Toby Young or the earlier one of his father. There, we find neither elite schools nor elitist universities, and yet their society is unquestionably flourishing, with superior economic performance, responsive social systems, adequate social housing and no noticeable class system, despite a greater population. Educationally, Switzerland is similar, but additionally has the highest number of Nobel Laureates and registered scientific patents per capita of anywhere in the world. However, only 20% of those who achieved this success went to the *Gymnasium* even, the top educational stream, which is without real correspondence in Britain but is perhaps comparable to what used to be state-run grammar schools.

Toby Young is no 'wet';[8] he turns out to be a staunch defender of private education, which he did not himself receive and about which he seems somewhat piqued. In the Oxford Union debate, to which he was an invited celebrity, he defended private education on the grounds that it does not cost the taxpayer a cent. Although Young likes to present himself as a champion of competition and elitism, he nevertheless seems to have been overwhelmed by what he saw at Oxford during his time there in the mid-eighties. This is how he recounted it to Goldfarb:

> I remember being shocked when I first arrived at Oxford at the kind of extraordinary sense of entitlement of these public school boys who I had never really encountered before. They effectively ran everything by kind of droit de seigneur, and the people around me running the place were people like Boris Johnson, who was in my year, David Cameron who was two years below me at Brasenose College. And lo and behold, 25 years later Boris Johnson is the mayor of London and David Cameron is the prime minister.[9]

Young just cannot hide his Tory backbone, but at the same time he is troubled that the real top echelon in Britain attended top public schools before Oxford, where, like Boris, they often rose to prominence in the Oxford Union, and whence they moved effortlessly, like Cameron and Osborne, into junior political advisory roles without any other life experience:

> I mean, the route to the top is even narrower … It is not enough merely to go to Oxford or Cambridge; generally speaking, it's the people at Oxford or Cambridge from hugely privileged

backgrounds who have received fantastic educations at some of the best schools in the world that only the very, very rich can afford to send their children to – it's those children who go on to run the country.

This lack of experience through privilege is worth noting, as is Young's crucial phrase: "It's those *children* who go on to run the country." Later on I shall have more to say about how the children inside the men actually *are* running the country, and that this *is* the problem. For now let us briefly consider their lack of experience. In a 2012 TV documentary, the veteran broadcaster and naturalist David Attenborough reminisced about what it was like being a grammar school boy at Cambridge just after the war. Discussing a fellow undergraduate from a semi-aristocratic background, who had been on a seamless path from Eton to Oxbridge, Attenbrough had been profoundly shocked. The fellow didn't seem to know anything about life, reasoned the young biologist, but couldn't imagine, with his privileged start, that he had anything to learn.[10]

For the winners' clique, the path of privilege is well worn, even if its presentation in the 21st century has been through some unpredictable and surreal changes. Young suggests that:

> Osborne, I'm sure, thinks of himself as wholly deserving of his extraordinary status because he had to work damn hard to get there, but at the same time the pool of people from which he could have emerged is tiny.

Going with the flow of modernism, says Young, Eton and Oxford have reinvented themselves by means of an illusion, into what he wittily calls "chimaeratocracies." Interesting idea. Young has a point, for the really odd thing is that Cameron, Osborne and Co. do seem as if they really *believe* they got where they are by their *own efforts* alone. They don't need a big CV when they can pull off such an extraordinary conjuring trick. Exuding confidence, they manage to ignore their entitlement, their being 'to the manor born,' and proudly present themselves as ordinary folk of the common-sense, meritocratic, aspirant middle-classes, who form the bulk of those to whom their party appeals.

I am sure I wasn't alone amongst observers who couldn't help note how odd it was that, during the 2010 election campaign, David Cameron played the part of 'Good Ol' Dave,' ordinary bloke, compassionate conservative, just like you or I – despite the fact that his father was a stockbroker, he had attended Eton and Oxford, and his ambition was to become prime minister! It was a fabulous piece of self-invention by a master of disguise and it meshed with the fabulous piece of self-deception that our electorate seemed ready and willing to buy into. But it wasn't simply that he was pulling an election stunt – we are used to that. The really, really worrying thing – exactly as John Le Carré warned about in his novels of ex-public school men and their seamless duplicity – was that Cameron *himself* seemed to believe it.

Falling away from spires

What makes someone like Cameron seem to believe in his own illusion? Could it be the same phenomenon as Tony Blair's unshakeable faith in his 'conviction politics,' assertively fiddling to the tune of his Iraq war folly while his New Labour experiment was in flames, doggedly refusing to shed his self-belief even in the eventual public enquiry? Could it be a similar conjuring trick that the British Raj seemed to have performed on India for over a century? Was its simply that those ex-public school men believed in their own entitlement and superiority?

It was to take me many years to get close to answering those kinds of questions satisfactorily for myself, and many more before I could name the Entitlement Illusion. All I knew then, from my gut, was that there was something rotten in the state of elite Britain and that I couldn't bear to be part of it. I did not know then how much of my life I would be dedicating – consciously or unconsciously – to the search for answers, or in many ways *acting* them *out*, as we psychotherapists say. But I did eventually find what I was looking for and begin to articulate it, at about the time Cameron would have been leaving Oxford, at the end of the eighties.

But before then, and after India, I returned to Britain and headed for the hills. With a tiny amount of money, I acquired a ruin on a mountaintop in mid-Wales and set about trying to restore it. I was delighted to be raising children who I knew would stay at home for their education. I tried to head full-speed down the opposite road, towards what I thought was freedom, away from the world of Oxford. It was a rebellion in which I set myself the task of learning to use my hands rather than my head and in doing so probably broke my father's heart. Certainly he had no way of understanding what I was up to; he had done all he could in his life not to have to use his hands for work. I worked in factories and care-homes; I immersed myself in carpentry and self-sufficiency. I was the most qualified person ever to attend the government-funded (thanks again) joinery course, which was run by ex-army personnel, and probably the only trainee who had ever asked for special leave when his goat was expecting twins. In fact, they were so taken aback, they granted it.

I learned a lot during those years but I eventually ran out of steam, ran out of my marriage and had just enough of a breakdown to lead me towards the world of psychotherapy. I entered first as a patient and then, once I discovered the true freedom in finding a way of talking about things that could not normally talked about, I became an enthusiast, eventually a trainee, and finally a practitioner. One of the important lessons I learned, while picking myself up from the fall, was that rebellion was not the freedom it seemed; since you always had something to rebel against, you could hardly do without an enemy and therefore you weren't free at all. Some of that journey is documented in my first book, to which I refer interested readers.[11] It was at the beginning of my own reinvention of myself as a psychotherapist that I finally pieced together an understanding of what might be happening in the mind – and eventually the brain – of men like David Cameron in the split second before they launch something like a 'Calm Down Dear' missile, and why they do it.

I was also to discover what a poisoned chalice this understanding was, as I began to realise how few wanted to hear this story and how many definitely did not.

CHAPTER 2

Boarding on the Couch

Privileged silence ~ Loadsamoney! ~ Inner and outer politics
Keeping a straight bat ~The Cameron Test

Privileged silence

It was the late 1980s. David Cameron had left Eton and was nearing the end of his time at Brasenose College, Oxford, and Mrs Thatcher was beginning to run out of steam. Maggie's great coup, the buying and reselling of social housing that released billions of pounds and addicted the nation to the euphoria of easy borrowing, had transformed Britain; but the boom had just peaked. I was getting divorced and living in a flat in London's Crouch End – later wittily known as 'Couch End' because of the number of therapists who made their beds there. I was completing two training courses and getting as much and as wide experience as I could, with the manic enthusiasm of someone whose mind had been asleep for many years and was now allowing himself to pursue a career rather than rebel. I had finally, and joyously, encountered a teaching style that recognised the valid place of both intellect and feelings. I had begun to flourish and I was keen to make up for lost time.

I had started working as a counsellor and family mediator and was a member of the systemic family therapy unit at a suburban social service department. Next I got asked by the man who had been my first therapist whether I would like to assist him on a programme of therapeutic workshops for men. It was during my involvement with these groups that something struck me very hard: I became aware that they included representatives of a specific kind of man with whom I felt more in tune than the others. I sensed that these men might benefit from a different approach to the one we were using; they seemed to recognise and gravitate toward each other. What they had in common was that they had all been sent away to board as children and would casually let on that it had impacted their lives for the worse. They retained a discernible but vague quality of what I then called 'woundedness' about them. Although they seemed comfortable in each other's presence, they were reticent about having been boarders or about what boarding had been like for them without a lot of prompting. I had to dig it out of them, trying to discover what the common themes might be.

Of course, it all rang bells in me too, because boarding had been my own background. I had done a full ten years, starting from the age of eight in a rather benign European school that catered for the sons of officers and NCOs of the American forces, who were all over Europe during the 1950s. Then I was moved to a small English prep school yards from where Dickens wrote *Bleak House* to take my 'Common Entrance' exams. Finally, and shockingly, I arrived at a major public school with a very upbeat take on 'muscular Christianity' and a good record in producing Oxford entrants. Nothing particularly bad happened to me there but I hated the plethora of rules and restrictions, brutally enforced, and the manic timetable that left us no with free time at all, as if free time was something essentially dangerous to us boys. It meant that I collapsed when I returned home for holidays, out of synch, dreading the new term, irritating my father with my seeming ingratitude for his massive investment in my future. I was the first in my paternal family to have such a privilege, and the fees were paid by dint of hard saving and judicious investment, so my not liking it did not go down well at home. My major problem was that I already knew from my initial American-style experience of boarding that it did not have to be done like that. Boys did not need to be over-disciplined, mistrusted and feared – we had been allowed to hang out and play a bit and it hadn't ruined us. I had already seen something else, so I was never a convert to public school life and never believed in it, even if I was rather a timid rebel.

So in the late 1980s I knew I was onto something, although I barely suspected how those ten years had affected my own behaviour as an adult. I knew how they had guided my life choices so far but it had never come up in my individual therapy. None of the therapists I saw (who knew I had boarded) seemed to think it was worth investigating, and I was too embarrassed to bring up my privileged education as any kind of problem. Perhaps it was because they themselves had not been boarders. Besides, boarding had never featured in any of my psychological reading; it was never referred to as an environment in which children suffer difficulties because of living away from home from a very young age or behave oddly because of a lack of parenting.

In fact, the only thing I had ever read that came close was William Golding's 1954 novel *Lord of the Flies*, which fictionalises the brutality that can occur when children without adults are left to their own devices. Golding set his tale in the aftermath of a nuclear war, mirroring the fears of the age. Marooned on a desert island, the children descend into savagery: they attack and scapegoat each other with astonishing ferocity. With staggering irony, this famous book was required reading for O-level preparation at my public school. No one ever even obliquely alluded to the possibility that it might have referred to boarding school, but to us boys it seemed oddly familiar. We understood it instinctively. Before he went up to Oxford, Golding had attended Marlborough Grammar School, where his father, a committed socialist, was a science master. The author seems always to have felt a little inferior for not having had a public school education. I can well imagine that he would have been familiar with accounts of life at the nearby famous Marlborough College boarding school. Perhaps he became obsessed with them, since that school dominates Marlborough town centre and, when I was at public school in the early 1960s, its distinct reputation for brutality had travelled far beyond the market town's borders.

This absence of therapeutic enquiry about boarding remains a very singular situation in boarding-obsessed Britain. At the time I felt utterly alone with this, although much later I discovered that I was not the only one to have noticed it. In a paper published in the scholarly *British Journal of Psychotherapy* in 2011, the Jungian analyst Professor Joy Schaverien quotes examples of famous psychoanalysts such as Wilfred Bion, John Bowlby and Patrick Casement, whose therapists had missed the significance of their boarding experiences in their own analyses.[1]

What I did apprehend then was that ignorance or denial about the effects of boarding was a near universal situation in Britain. Despite frequent references in literature to the agonies experienced by children at boarding schools, the long-term effects of a boarding education had remained entirely unnoticed by the medical and psychological professions, with nothing written on the psychological effects. So I began to realise that a powerful syndrome affected many people without it having been properly identified. I felt sure that this contributed to the shame that many ex-boarders felt about what they had experienced as trauma but rarely felt able to openly discuss.

I therefore set about making a study of the issues and wrote a qualifying thesis on it. In the summer of 1989 I collaborated with a colleague, Andrew Mullis, to design a therapeutic workshop for male ex-boarders, aimed at helping them recognise the issues, talk about them in a safe environment and be freer to move on in their lives. Provocatively, I named my target group 'Boarding School Survivors.'

The aim of this designation was a deliberate attempt to shock. I wanted to say: "Look, there is no doubting the privilege of a private education, but what is not acknowledged is that you actually have to survive boarding school, and that this survival is achieved at a cost." I hoped the provocation would startle people into understanding that such survival is unrecognised because the shame of having such an expensive privilege ensures that ex-boarders are silenced about its effects.

I knew also that people would challenge the notion that these privileged children had to *survive* an education that others might long for, so I had to carefully articulate what I meant by a *survivor*. I had to explain that there are situations where children feel so unsafe that they have to adopt certain strategies and mechanisms of behaviour and self-presentation out of a fear of non-survival. Later, as adults, they betray themselves as survivors to the informed eye, because they cling to these behaviours even when the original traumatic environment has been left behind long ago. They do not feel safe in themselves.

The definition of psychic health as one of being safe *within yourself* was something the radical Scottish psychiatrist Ronnie Laing pointed to in the 1960s; he called it being *ontologically* safe.[2] Deeply unsafe people do not trust themselves to be able to manage their present environment without the use of a survival personality, constructed long ago, that had worked well enough at the time. The most basic of these survival mechanisms I identified as repressing feelings and becoming excessively private, even secretive, while carrying on as if everything is perfectly fine. Many of the areas of life where these individuals run into problems involve situations in which emotions shouldn't be repressed, situations that involve being the opposite of private, such as being a husband or a father.

I wanted to make people think carefully about the hidden costs of boarding, universally regarded as desirable in Britain due to the extraordinary facilities offered by the schools and the high social status such an education provides. I wanted to suggest that this was not simply an individual psychological problem but a systemic one: also a political one, since boarding school survivors regularly occupy positions of the highest national influence in all spheres, including government. I was not then implying that Britain was traditionally led by people who were psychological casualties and misfits, but I already suspected that many of those in power were survivors who happened to be part of the elite, rather than organically emerging leaders.

It was becoming clear to me that in surviving long periods away from loving parents in the hothouse atmosphere of public schools, boarding school survivors had in common that they had needed to adapt themselves by means of a variety of defensive personality manoeuvres that limited their emotional range and the ultimate development of their full potential. In exchange for the undeniable privilege of the small classes, the intensively competitive atmosphere, the social perks of the old school tie and the right accent, they would have had to sacrifice something of their *inner* selves. In the absence of normal parental support they might have been bullied or abused but even if they were not they would have had to construct a defensive personality structure to keep them safe. For the dangers at boarding school were not imaginary; they would have included the attempts of other frightened lonely children to bully or scapegoat them, the assault of humiliating teaching styles as well as the abuses of predatory staff members.

Perversely, the walls of this protective structure invariably, in the end, also keep out that which is not a danger, like intimate approaches of love, care and friendship. As those walls remain unacknowledged they are defended as manfully as the ramparts of any Crusader castle, and sometimes attack appears the best form of defence. Once these defensive personality structures are in place, they are extremely difficult to recognise and deconstruct; they stand firm to protect the inhabitant, even in later life when the dangers are no longer there. Relying on such defences means ex-boarders become partial people, compensating for low *emotional intelligence* with over-developed intellects, their acquired status, their irony and their covert hostility – all dedicated to survival – and unwittingly adopting the defensive illusion of entitlement.[3]

This is why Cameron can react so fast and turn his anxiety round into a bullying offensive before even he knows what is going on. It takes enormous insight and courage to live without these walls. To confound the problems, while the syndrome and character style remains unrecognised, there is no motivation to unlearn such behaviour.

Loadsamoney!

I knew I was onto something big but I had no idea how big or how to develop it. How was a novice therapist going to help anyone recognise such an issue when he had barely begun to articulate it himself? I would have been limited to testing it out on myself and the few boarding school survivors who were within my sphere of influence, were it not for an ironic twist of fate: news of my workshops came to the attention of a columnist for the recently launched, very successful newspaper *The Independent*.

I'd first met Angela Lambert in the early Eighties when she was a chief reporter at ITN television news.[4] She had hired me to work on the roof of her late Victorian house, when I was still making a living as a carpenter, before my rebel Boarding School Survivor personality crashed and led me towards the couch. Angela passed me round most of her colleagues in the same news office and I worked on all their homes. I guess I hadn't been able to sufficiently hide my Oxford accent, and this – along with my shyness about money – must have helped those educated property owners feel they could trust me, caught as they were between their desire to improve their investments and their terror of London builders. They weren't wrong to be mistrustful: in those days of booming property prices and high-flying estate agents, the revenge of the working classes on the London gentry was impressive.

The inner suburbs of London were becoming gentrified almost as fast as the Russian Empire expanded in the mid-19th century. There was hardly a road without a cluster of skips and For Sale signs. Genteel Victorian streets, which either had never fulfilled their speculative promise or had fallen into shabbiness, were rapidly stripped of their bedsits and 'converted' into apartments bursting with 'period features' for the confident, tasteful, youthful and, above all, flush bourgeoisie. They colonised seedy Clapham and Stroud Green and turned them into New Posh, for which new roofs and alcove bookshelves were rapidly required. Even if feared, builders were in high demand. The needed but terrifying artisan was soon to be hilariously immortalised on primetime television by public-school educated comedian Harry Enfield as 'Loadsamoney,' the shamelessly money-grubbing plasterer in his tasteless shell-suit.

Working in Angela's welcoming home I savoured real ground coffee (still a luxury in those days) in strong mugs before work in the morning to the background of her formidable intellectual conversation. She is best known for her novel *A Rather English Marriage*, which became a film starring Albert Finney and Tom Courtney, and for a history of the sensitive group of Edwardian aristocrats known as 'the Souls.' In early 1990, I was invited to a party at her new home and, simply to amuse her, I took along the leaflet for my *Boarding School Survivors* workshops. At that time, as I now know, she was just completing her fictionalised account of her own boarding experience, which she said was "beastly." *No Talking After Lights* is a tour de force that describes the stifling world of competition for love and popularity in girl's boarding school.[5] Angela was excited by the timing of our meeting; she had been looking in vain for someone to write a serious anti-boarding piece for *The Independent's* dialectical column Free Speech, which she edited. To my enormous surprise, she commissioned a thousand words on how I saw the problem of boarding: a gift that even carried a fee – my first white-collar earning since leaving India!

I wrote the piece in the August holiday, with paper and pencil on a cliff-top in St David's Bay, South Wales, the Irish Sea bashing the beach far below me. Entitled *An Edifice which can Crush the Soul*, it appeared on 1 September and created a sensation.[6] A huge mailbag from readers followed – apparently the largest *The Independent* had ever received. Piles of letters began to arrive on my doormat, kindly forwarded by the newspaper. Those letters changed everything for me. I suddenly had complete strangers pouring out their hearts about their boarding experience and describing how it had affected the adults they became. The letters confirmed everything I had suspected and more.

Most correspondents were desperately appreciative that at last someone had publicly aired a subject that until now had been strictly taboo. Most imagined they were the only ones suffering and concluded it to be their own fault – that they had been over-sensitive or weak. Many letters were from wives or girlfriends in despair about problems with their spouses, which they could now identify for the first time as being due to the partner having being sent away to school. So, quite unexpectedly, I had the astonishing and unprecedented good fortune to receive, unsolicited on my doormat, a mass of evidence in the form of autobiographical case studies of the syndrome I had been tentatively proposing – undeniable evidence that there had been a bubble waiting to burst.[7]

A psychological, social and political volcano had erupted. Before I could pause for breath, my article spawned pieces from other newspapers. In the first months I was interviewed by *The Guardian, The Times, The Telegraph, The Mail, The Wall Street Journal* and many other national, local and international titles, in a knock-on effect. From that day on I was suddenly I was a media 'expert' – a 'talking head' – and had to deal with frequent enquiries and invitations from the media to speak on the topic on radio, TV and in newspapers. I was entirely unprepared for this. I had to find how to respond to journalists' interest while not exposing my clients, or over-exposing myself, and to represent counselling and therapy in a good light. I was obliged to engage with the wider educational arguments as well as deal with strident opposition to my views. It was like being dropped in at the deep end.

Just as there were many who were mightily relieved to hear my voice on the subject of the psychological problems associated with the boarding school system, there were many others who were not, and many who had vested interests in leaving the subject of boarding unexamined. When it came to public debate, many of them spoke with vociferous denial of the problem in a most aggressive way, which shocked me. I also received a few hostile letters suggesting I was trying to create a "cult of victims." These defenders claimed boarding was "character forming," summarised in clichés such as "It never did me any harm," or "It was the making of me." There were others who suggested more insidiously: "Not everyone is cut out for boarding."

This apparently logical statement reveals far more about the issue than immediately appears. There is a tone in such a sentence that I think is worth unpacking because it is perhaps one that the innocent reader and non-Brits do not pick up on, but is integral to understanding how the establishment attitudes to boarding and to children operate in Britain. "Not everyone is cut out for boarding" sounds very reasonable, as if it is offering a level of tolerance; but this is not, in fact, the case. Instead, it is the voice of the covert bully, a feature deeply embedded in British life, for it implies there are weak or oversensitive people – "not myself, don't you know" – who just can't take it. These weaklings are just not made of the right stuff. They should not be in the elite anyway and just as well, as this sorts the wheat out from the chaff.

In the end, my opponents served as my greatest teachers – even more so, perhaps, than those who agreed with me. Facing the critics of my work, I found out that there were many traps to avoid. Principally, I had to resist the tendency to identify with the implied flaw of weakness, that I simply represented those "not cut out for boarding." It was as if I was regularly being told to 'calm down, dear.' To make sense of this aggressive defence, I had to try to imagine the 'weakness' in those who opposed me so strongly that they themselves could not accept, the vulnerability that they so seemed to fear, the childishness they seemed to despise and wanted to distance themselves from. I imagined that perhaps they needed to protect their own survival personality, to ring-fence any idea that an abandoned child still inhabited them. Thus any discussion about the problems associated with boarding would be very threatening to them indeed; any talk of therapy would produce a huge and conflicting threat to the notion of self-reliance heavily promoted by the boarding schools, which they had duly tried to embody.

In order to keep a firm grasp on reality when discussing boarding in Britain, it is important to fix firmly in the mind that we are talking about young defenceless children. It is especially important if they later grow up to be winners and robust defenders of the status quo, like Boris Johnson and David Cameron; they too started on a route to self-reliance when they were only very, very little. In exchange for the privilege of this expensive education, boarders lose a lot. It starts with their homes and the sense of it being okay to be child. Often they lose touch with something that is their human birthright – the sense of being embodied as a feeling, relating and sexual human being. To get a feel of this, I refer the interested to the selection of *Independent* readers letters in my previous book.[8]

The loss can occur very early. The letters reveal a small minority of children who went away to board from four onwards. Some who came from the colonies did not see their parents for a year or more. More conventionally, they are despatched from about the age of eight, or in other cases at eleven or thirteen. These are all vulnerable and impressionable ages, and the impact of this loss has gone underground in British society. To my mind, the nearest literary rendering of this is ex-boarder Philip Pullman's recent masterful trilogy, *His Dark Materials.* In Pullman's story, children are captured by adults and separated from their *daimon,* an animal representing their animated soul.[9] Even though the author does not expressly acknowledge the connection, many ex-boarders describe a similar feeling of having been robbed of something.

Inner and outer politics

Increasingly, I began to understand that taking my psychological position on boarding meant engaging in the political arena in which personal issues are secondary. Although therapists generally seek to keep these two spheres apart in this case it seemed impossible, since I had inadvertently touched on a national sore spot. In fact, the social and psychological dimensions of ex-boarders' paralysing secretive shame and aggressive self-defence are tightly interwoven. There is a boarding industry lobby that represents a lot of money – some several billion pounds in annual turnover – and it surely did not want some crank of a psychotherapist telling people that their product was bad for them. In fact, I would regularly be trotted out for a debate on national or local radio to find I was up against a spokesperson of the Boarding Schools Association

(BSA), whose mission it was to discredit me as swiftly and as 'reasonably' as possible. I was now involved in media politics, British style, whether I liked it or not.

The debating style practised by the British media is profoundly adversarial. The name of the game is to try to find two absolutely opposing viewpoints whose supporters tear into each other and deliver blows to the other's argument in the shortest number of words, whilst at the same time seeming perfectly rational. There is always the sense that interviewees must be dealt with in a great hurry, as if there are far more important things to talk about coming up next. But the reality is that it is always more of the same. As I began to be treated as if I myself were in politics, I started to experience how this style encourages defensiveness in politicians. Any notion that an argument is already false, when delivered in aggressive soundbites rather than deeply worked debate, never arises. The idea that someone invited onto a programme might have something of value to share is rarely conveyed on British news or magazine programmes. Very few interviewees manage to get round this problem, unless they are foreigners who don't understand the rules, which is perhaps why so many Germany politicians acquitted themselves so well when they came in for a grilling about the Eurozone crisis on British TV. In the anxious days of spring 2012, German politicians and economists interviewed by British presenters simply sidestepped the traps and remained as calm as Spanish footballers, probably because they were unaccustomed to the style.

In Britain, the way of doing such business derives from the same adversarial structure as the House of Commons, and before that Oxford and public school, where the need to ridicule your opposition is taken as read. It is the complete opposite to the cultural style I discovered when I started to listen to public broadcast radio in France. On *France Culture*, and even on the more popular *France Inter*, speakers are given time to expound on their topic; interviewers use exploratory questioning to help them build their arguments, and programmes regularly last ninety minutes.

How different it was on British radio, where I waited for what seemed hours in the secret windowless corridors of Broadcasting House only to be whipped in and whipped out again once the quick thrusting fray was over. Has this to do with why some say the British make bad lovers? On one occasion it went completely wrong for the producers: I was left to wait with my opposition, a kindly headmaster with whom I got on well, and we went on air disappointingly agreeing on many things. The *Today* presenter looked completely flat. More often than not, however, being interviewed meant that before I was deemed worthy of being listened to I had to protect myself from being rubbished. The apotheosis of this style is the Jeremy Paxman (Malvern and Cambridge) interviewing technique. Fortunately, I never had to face Paxman's charisma, wit and, some might say, bullying tactics.

Being set up against the vested interests of the BSA was challenging enough and sometimes intimidating. Before I could have a hope of landing my argument I first had to prove that I was not simply another pathetic axe-grinder endlessly whinging on about my own past when it should have been put to bed years ago. Naming the boarding issue as a problem was a major task. On the one hand, I was now regularly receiving plaudits from the public, thanking me for naming issues that individuals had previously felt alone with and somehow wrong to be feeling, whilst on the other, in the public debate, I had to deal repeatedly with the challenge of naming what had up to then been unnameable, and that did not want to be named. In saying that boarding was a problem I risked condemning a beloved national habit and in outlining the character of the ex-boarder I risked denouncing what passed as an accepted national character style.

I faced resistance from two different sources, first my opponents, and worse – my own internal self-criticism. This came in the form of strange attacks of shame, hinting that I was simply recycling my old childhood issues that I should be over by now. At times, an inner voice tried to cast me a 'pathetic' person who would never disprove the BSA claim, that I was one of the weak ones. And then, most irrationally, a fear would erupt, as if it really weren't over, as if I had never left school, as if I was still boarding and the old punishments were still around – being humiliated, bullied, 'sent to Coventry,'[10] beaten and expelled. The external attacks simply hurt sometimes, but the internal pressure was deadly. I had to recognise it as the real enemy and therefore the real learning ground. It was probably a similar inner attack of feelings that constrained the normally forthright George Monbiot, quoted earlier, when, at the end of listing the horrors of boarding, he excused himself with: "I hope this doesn't sound like special pleading from a poor little no-longer-rich boy."[11]

Eventually, I began to recognise such feelings as typical internal constraints that keep many boarding school survivors from speaking out about the system. I named this the *Boarding Effect*. I now understood that the pressure to deny and normalise the issues operated at three levels, frequently enforced through covert bullying:

> 1. First, on the *macro level, in society*, the practice was thoroughly normalised and linked with tradition, even if the tradition was mostly nurtured in the cradle of ersatz and fake Victorian Britain.[12]

> 2. Secondly, on the *micro level, interpersonally*, you faced being attacked and accused of being a wimp and a failure or past your sell-by date. If you hadn't enjoyed boarding when at large it was so seemingly acceptable you may have already been whispering this in your own ear for many years, so:

> 3. Thirdly, again on the micro level but this time *intra-personally*, you beat yourself up.

When I was back in my right mind, not staggering under the accusations or, worse, believing them myself, understanding the Boarding Effect helped enormously in that it allowed me to sharpen my mind on the psycho-political points and try out my case in the soundbite brevity that broadcasting demanded. It meant I had to maintain a wide perspective, to adopt a meta-view. I realised I had to get into training.

Keeping a straight bat

Perhaps the love of what the British media call 'lively debate' derives from that mysterious game of cricket (that I had failed to master) where you have to learn to take a rapidly moving hard leather ball (that hurts like hell if it hits you) on the 'back' foot and play it elegantly away for your own side to score. You have to defend and attack with an equal display of motion, but with restrained emotion. If done well, it is a seamless blend of relaxation, mastery and aggression that features in no sport other than this quintessentially English one. I had to learn to take the BSA's bowling and aim for the boundary. Even if I could never knock them right out of the ground, I had to get good at spotting what kind of ball was being bowled.

The primary conservative approach to private education emphasises the consumer's right to choose – a big topic in England and usually an excuse for saying that cash should always win. This is taken as read, so the boarding lobby generally favours a three-pronged attack. Surprisingly, they do not lead with the macro reality that a private elitist education will open doors in the corridors of power and wealth – this is taken for granted, I suppose, built in to the Entitlement Illusion. They prefer to pitch their argument in the micro (interpersonal) realm. They like to open the bowling by rubbishing the opponent, asserting that the issues that Duffell (and other misguided detractors) raise relate only to the distant past and not the carpeted, phone-equipped present. In today's world, parents are reassured to see that dormitories proudly boast radiators, toilets always have doors and the smaller children are confidently allowed their teddies, so that they can relax in the knowledge that their precious offspring are receiving really first class treatment.

Actually, this is not a difficult ball to hit. The customers of the BSA are, of course, the parents, who no doubt want the best for their children. But in their cosy TV-commercial presentation of the environmental side of modern boarding there is one thing missing: parents. This may suit some parents who have uncomfortably discovered that it demands considerable personal effort to bring up a child, but the argument itself attempts to deny the self-evident value of a loving, tactile family. A teddy bear is not a realistic substitute for the love of a parent for more than a few hours – it never has been and it never will be. Nor will telephone access ever suffice as parenting. It is therefore easy enough to rebuff these points with basic common sense.

Next, the BSA despatch a bit of spin[13] by proposing that boarding schools help busy parents to offer their offspring 'quality time', pointing out that we all know how busy we are today and, besides, working parents with children at home have very little opportunity for quality time. I am sure this argument strikes a chord for some, and that the BSA felt very modern and pleased with themselves when they came up with it. However, if you have been a divorced parent – and many now have – you will know that trying to squeeze in a bit of quality time to order when you finally see your child is a recipe for failure. The argument is clearly nonsense. What children actually need is the opposite – let's call it 'quantity time.' This includes time moping around and just knowing your parents are there, sometimes interacting with them and sometimes not, frequently not even wanting even to talk to them but knowing that they are there when you need them. It's about experiencing *belonging*, and this is mostly an unknown feeling for boarding school survivors, and thereby the promoters of boarding.

The quality time argument denies a self-evident value of bonding and attachments in general. It misses a crucial fact that parents *themselves* benefit from hands-on parenting. It is *good* for you to be a parent. Actually, most European parents say they enjoy it! It is without doubt a skill to learn, frequently a challenge, sometimes a course in self-development. It helps you to learn to love, to think about another soul, to create realistic boundaries, to develop real authority. I hear a common response from continental Europeans who are not familiar with boarding culture. When they hear about the British practice they invariably say: "Why have children if you are going to send them away for someone else to bring up?"

At this point, the BSA bowlers get a little frustrated and decide it is high time for a few well-aimed 'bouncers', designed to intimidate and then hurt the opposition.[14] For there remains the third point, the thorny question of whether all children are affected by boarding or only some. This gets confounded by the implication, as I pointed out above, that only the weaker kind of child may be 'damaged' – a subtle continuation of a typical bullying style. It can still hit home and hurt.

A quarter of a century from the first workshop for ex-boarders, although I understand it, I am still sometimes shocked by the ongoing normalisation and denial of the issue, both socially and psychologically. Those of us who campaign against boarding regularly come up against the same brick wall. Those who contribute to the online debates – where such things are mostly conducted these days, safely out of the way in the blogosphere – can feel quite hurt by the level of vitriol written in defence of boarding.

The Cameron Test

The most common and understandable challenge from the non-converted runs something like this: "Surely not everyone is damaged by boarding?" This may be accompanied by some anecdotal evidence, like: "My nephew, Justin, absolutely loved it, and now he's an account executive for ..." etc., etc. It is a question that demands an answer. Whilst the question "Should we be sending young children away to school?" needs only a bit of common sense, this one is more complicated and needs some psychology. Here psychotherapists may have an advantage, but they must be very clearly focused and take a meta-view, a wide perspective. In responding to this, it is crucially important to use the right words. It is the second reason, apart from the desire to provoke, that I chose the term Boarding School Survivor in the first place.

This is how I see it: from the perspective of *damage* we will always have an ambiguous answer, but from the perspective of *survival* we will not. For it is not a question of everyone being damaged or not. The issue is that every child has to *survive* it. Every child is obliged to endure long periods without love and affection amongst other similarly isolated and scared children, and this has to be survived. Unlike their parents, who have exercised their consumer choice to opt for private education, the children have *no choice* but to survive. And they do it by negating part of themselves and getting good at reinventing themselves. The psychological issue is *how* they survived, whether they are still doing it as adults and what the *cost* of this is on their lives and families. The political issue is what the cost of this survival is on a macro (societal) level.

Let's put this frame of reference to the test. I propose using 'The Cameron Test,' which I designed in late 2010. It goes like this: can we argue that David Cameron seems a damaged individual? Hardly, he is the top man in the country, which sees itself as the top country – especially in Europe. He is one of the youngest people ever to get the job; he has a good salary and a pretty wife. He is a Winner. No question. But that he had to survive boarding as a child is not in doubt for me. To the trained eye, Cameron, like Tony Blair before him, can be spotted acting with behaviours typical of a boarding school survivor. I have alluded to these already and will go on to describe in more detail. They may include a seamlessly smooth duplicity, an apparent unshakeable faith in his own ego, a tendency to bully when he feels cornered and a barely concealed contempt for being told what is what by women and foreigners and so forth – in other words, by those not part of what I call the *Rational Man Project*, which I'll explain at great length in the third section.

I am not saying that such behaviours are evil – I just don't want my leaders to be acting like that. I am not saying that they are unpredictable, either. If you send a child away from his mother and family before puberty, along with a lot of other scared children to an institution where you regiment them, overwork them and tell them what a tremendous privilege it is, you are likely to produce adults who may be very civilised but do have some odd behaviours. If they become national leaders there is a strong chance that the country's foreign policy might be affected, to come back to that *New Yorker* reporter's disbelief, quoted in the Introduction.[15]

In the final analysis, you don't need very much psychology to get this argument: you just have to be able to *feel*, and not be governed by your own fear – either of guilt as a parent, or of not surviving if you are an ex-boarder. Common sense suggests that it cannot be right to send young children off to school on their own and make them learn to fend for themselves. When they are fifteen or sixteen, it is a different matter. Sometimes I have had to abandon all psychological arguments and speak to my interviewer in a very simple way. I will remind them with a basic physical demonstration, my hand hovering over the floor, just how big (or rather how little) an eight-year-old child is.

To me, it feels a bit like reinventing the wheel. I regret that the discoveries of 100 years of psychotherapy seem hardly to have affected our national life. Meanwhile, we keep sending little children off to school and electing them as leaders when they grow up; although growing up when you have not been allowed to have a childhood is not straightforward, as we shall see.

CHAPTER 3

British Bulldogs:
The story of covert bullying

Surviving on camera ~ The first brick in the wall
The British attitude to children ~ "Only joking!"
Nice English covert bullying ~ A monstrous regiment of toffs

Surviving on camera

"The thing is, I'm completely neutral myself, otherwise the
schools would never give me access," said the tall, elegant
man, lowering himself into one of my well-used consulting
room chairs and looking me straight in the eye.

"Actually, my brother went away to school, but I didn't,"
he said, taking in the surroundings, perhaps already looking for
camera angles, I thought to myself.

It was spring 1993 and Colin Luke, the founder of an
independent film company, *Mosaic Pictures*, who had just
made a celebrated BBC television documentary about heart
surgery, was researching a new project.[1] As in the earlier film,
which had been acclaimed for its sensitivity, the proposed
one, also aimed at the BBC, would use a new technique with
unobtrusive cameras to follow a group of small boys and their
families through the boys' first term at prep school. I would
be interviewed and would give my views of what the children
might be experiencing, alongside the commentaries of parents,
teachers and the boys themselves.

In the flurry of excitement that the idea of boarding school
survivors had created, I had already had a few approaches from

would-be documentary makers. Of all the media people I had come across, these were the ones who scared me most. I found them more like estate agents than journalists, and instinctively distrusted them. I had approached the American poet and speaker Robert Bly, who had already taken a favourable interest in my work and had himself experienced being mocked by the British media, and asked him for advice.

"My advice is to not let the cameras in," he growled at me.

And yet, there was something about Colin that I immediately felt I could trust. His approach was neutral, he knew exactly what he wanted to do and at the same time was open about what he expected to find. A rare combination of artistry and scientific enquiry had allowed him to enlist the cooperation of both parents and schools, and I was intrigued. However, I was not convinced that such a film would be able to show what I considered the problems to be, because I had spoken to many journalists who had already visited boarding schools and failed to spot unhappy children. I knew why: the kids would have fastened their Happy Masks on pretty quickly and would be at pains not to show the signs of the problems ex-boarders might report many years later. Nor was I sure that I wanted to expose the children to any more pressure.

In the event we went ahead, and Colin's team were remarkably sensitive. They obtained extraordinarily intimate footage, using unobtrusive one-man crews equipped with tiny professional video cameras, similar to the camcorders available to the general public at the time. The finished documentary was a landmark work, for it revealed direct visual and incontrovertible evidence of children adopting what I had identified as a Strategic Survival Personality.[2] We now had filmed examples to go alongside the public letters and, taken together, this evidence was very striking. You can see the children putting on their false selves, constructing their Strategic Survival Personalities right in front of your eyes. At one point, you see a nine-year-old boy go through the rigours of presenting himself as a self-sufficient little adult and then, almost by accident, slipping back into his natural spontaneous child-self: it is heartbreaking to watch. He has begun to abandon himself, and he will never trust his mother – or perhaps any woman – again.

The process of making the film had an unusual impact on the normally hard-headed film crew. They became increasingly distressed as they witnessed the parents' attitudes to their children and then the children's noticeable loss of spontaneity as, cut off from the comfort of their families and homes for weeks at a time, they suddenly had to adapt to an alien, male and all-encompassing institutional environment. While filming, many of the cameramen became close with the children, who clearly made attachments to them. I'll return to this strange bonding process in the next chapter. The remarkable thing was that camera crews in general to tend adopt a pretty *realpolitik* view of the world, but, watching the rushes in the cutting-room, my wife Helena and I were struck by the sight of these hard-nosed guys in tears, in fury and in disbelief, watching what they themselves had filmed.

The Making of Them was first shown on the BBC's *40 Minutes* slot in January 1994 and had a considerable national impact. It is still gripping viewing today and is now freely available on the internet.[3] Colin is still rightly proud of it, using extracts from it in the masterclasses he now gives on filmmaking. One man wrote to tell me that when it was shown (a year later) in First Class on a British Airways flight, he was so affected that he got on the next plane home and immediately took his son out of boarding school. The documentary was widely reviewed the day after its first broadcast and temporarily brought the boarding debate back into the public eye. Several reviewers virtually overlooked the film itself because their own boarding experiences had been re-energised by what they saw, and consequently used their reviews to express their own outrage and distress. Over the years I have to come recognise this strange phenomenon: a professional person, whether in the media or the helping professions, is invited to think psychologically about boarding, and a whole host of unprocessed feelings and memories get evoked, because this is the first time they have had the opportunity to take the subject seriously.

Here's one example, surprisingly from that bastion of tradition, *The Telegraph*. David Thomas, in the guise of television reviewer, shares thoughts on his own boarding experience, triggered by Colin Luke's film:

The first lesson I learned about boarding school life is that if you want to survive being deprived of your parents' affection then you have to persuade yourself that you did not need it in the first place. Herein lies the great flaw in the public school system. In many ways prep schools are idyllic places. They are usually in the country. You can play football and cricket and make huts in the woods. But what you cannot do is love. You can't love your parents because it hurts too much. And you most certainly can't love your fellow-pupils because there is an overriding taboo against any hint of homosexuality. So, after a while, you just get out of the habit of loving. As I dare to say many of those Boarding School Survivors – not to mention their wives – will testify, getting back into the habit can be a very difficult task.[4]

The first brick in the wall

My role in the film was as a 'talking-head,' trying to describe what I thought the little boys were going through and how this might affect them later in life as adults. For me it was poignant to see those tiny children after I had spoken to so many adult ex-boarders, as I tried not to frighten away viewers with too much anti-Establishment rhetoric or psychobabble, but to articulate for them how I saw the boarding child's great *double bind*. A double bind is a conflict that results from having to negotiate impossible situations, often with little power.[5] It is a psychological trap, rooted in a lose-lose mindset, which results in a kind of internal conflict in which you are damned if you do, as well as damned if you don't.

The typical boarding child's double bind is exceptionally vicious, as I shall try to explain. Firstly, it steels the ex-boarder against future loving – it is no longer safe to trust that he won't get abandoned again in the future. Secondly, it puts in place an important protectively designed inner structure that can remain both friend and tormentor for life. This structure is in the form of an internal bully whose function is to make sure the boy's suffering remains opaque. But it actually has twin applications. On the inside, the internal bully keeps him shamefully feeling that he is not good enough and may never be. But on the outside, he prevents the whole boarding process from being condemned by the adults by acting as if everything is just as the parents want it to be, thereby keeping his parents onside. As soon as the boy has the double bind in place, he begins his career as a survivor, but becomes lost to himself. He has fallen from a great height, as it were, and his innocence is gone.

There is a painfully ironic camera angle in the part of the film where I introduce this concept. We follow a shot of the boys going down an enormous staircase that has been fitted with extra railings – to stop them falling, or jumping, one imagines – and my voice is heard over the clattering of little feet going down the steps, as I try to explain the boarder's double bind. I suggest that, unconsciously, the eight-year old boarder's inner dialogue goes something like this:

> I know Mummy and Daddy love me, because they told me so. I know it's important to them to send me away to school and it costs a lot of money and I should be grateful. But I hate it. If they love me, why did they send me away? Either they don't love me or there's something wrong with me.

And so he figures it out with childish logic and explains to himself why he is feeling like this:

> If they don't really love me it must be because there is something wrong with me. If they do, and I feel like this, it must be because I am wrong.

This is, in essence, the first brick in the wall that the boarder puts in place to make sense of his experience. It is the first time that the Boarding Effect, described earlier, kicks in intrapsychically. It is too much for him to live with; he will have to defend against it. And because it is so central to him, he will be defending against something that he feels is at his core but that is hidden in a kind of a fog. Thereafter, this little boy is more than likely to be desperate to show that he is not wrong. In this desperation he will be aggressively on guard, quick to put down anyone he thinks might be 'wrong', and especially anyone who might suggest that he is. This is the little boy who lives inside the boarding school survivor and is unlikely, like Peter Pan, ever to grow up.

This is the origin of Cameron's 'Calm Down Dear' panic button: he must never be the one who is 'wrong.' It lays the foundation stone for the cult of bullying, which is why the bullying sticks so readily. It is how the British Bulldog is let out of his cage, why the two sides of the House of Commons roar and rage at each other that the other side is the one that has got it wrong. It is why Britain cannot do coalition politics.

The British attitude to children

Eventually, co-opting Colin's title, I completed my book, *The Making of Them: The British Attitude to Children and the Boarding School System*, which appeared in 2000.[6] In the process of writing it, I made a fairly exhaustive survey of the literature, which confirmed my suspicions that despite an abundance of fictional and autographical accounts of boarding school that recounted its various horrors, such as corporal punishment and predatory sexuality, this was the first psychological study of the subject. Even the fictional treatment, I thought, did more to normalise boarding than highlight its problems. Best-selling novelist William Boyd, who is one of the few people to have written convincingly about it, commented on this in an interview with Mariella Frostrup in February 2012:

> Of all the fictional terrains that a writer can explore, the boarding school experience is the experience least honestly portrayed ... it's generally seen through rose coloured spectacles.[7]

He is right: it cannot be honest, because the whole society can joke about it but still colludes with keeping the brave faces on. After all, our public schools are the 'envy of the world' or so we like to think, because all nouveau riche foreigners are busy getting their children into them. So we are left with lots of novelistic accounts that go into what I call the 'only joking' category (more about this below), and no serious enquiry.

The only document I could find that came anywhere near to a rigorous approach to boarding was an extraordinary sociological survey of public schools[8] and some other writings that emerged from the burgeoning (but soon to be all but ignored) field of academic sociology in the late sixties.[9] Royston Lambert's unique study, *The Hothouse Society*, was hampered by academic impartiality and the confidentiality enshrined in his interviewing method, so nothing came of it. He received hundreds of anonymous sexual abuse confessions – none of which were followed up, which says much about the context of the day. In the end, Lambert, a prodigious intellect and fiercely independent thinker, seems to have been bought out: he was removed from any position of possible criticism by being offered the headmastership of the most 'progressive' boarding school of the day, Dartington. 'Progressive boarding,' being another short-lived fashion of the late sixties culture of openness, did not survive the decade; besides, the idea rested on a contradiction in terms.

Interest in the psychology of boarding began to gather some momentum with a further stroke of good fortune: in March 2001, my book was favourably reviewed in the *British Medical Journal*. It meant that every GP in the country had a review of the book on their desk. The idea of recovering from boarding was taking tiny steps to ease itself out of the margins. Having the book in print took the work a little beyond the attention of journalists wanting but a for-and-against controversy. More importantly, I now began to hear from other therapists and academics who were working on their own papers on the psychology of boarding and needed to have something to quote. These were to include Professor Joy Schaverien, who has written many respected articles and has since become a colleague. Later, my wife and I joined forces with her to train other therapists in understanding the complicated issues of this syndrome. We now had to articulate what was specific to this newly identified client group and develop effective theory and methodology.

Over the years I have continued to pursue the topic in a variety of ways. Boarding is alive and well and yet it seems that the term boarding school survivor is becoming increasingly known. The workshops have continued to the present day and are also now offered for women. Correspondence from the public keeps arriving, nowadays by email, especially at times when the subject is featured in the press or television when a sudden deluge of correspondence arrives, only to dry up again in time. Of course, the internet has changed the nature of feedback in so many ways: readers get in touch with authors more easily and can publish their reviews on booksellers' websites. In general, the tone of the readers' reviews of *The Making of Them* is one of enormous relief: "I thought it was just me," "I am so glad that someone is finally speaking about this in public," and so on. But there still are the occasional robust responses from those challenged by the notion of someone suggesting they may have had to survive boarding.

These writers, I imagine, don't want to upset their internal applecart; they fear waking the little one inside. But their remarks are usually aggressive, framed in what I now recognise as standard-issue bullying tone. Rather than a discussion of the content, it is all in the delivery – 'Calm Down Dear' style. The notable feature is a self-satisfied smugness that betrays a contemptuous delight that someone else – not them – has identified themselves as a sufferer of boarding. In other words, someone else has been found to represent the vulnerability or incompetence that any 'normal' ex-boarder (with double bind, internal bully and Strategic Survival Personality firmly in place) refuses to identify with. Here is one review that appeared on Amazon in December 2011:

> If you didn't fit in at boarding school and you were a bit of an outsider and now want something to blame for your miserable life; then this book is most definitely for you. If on the other hand you were in the 90% and you were not a misfit/oddball; then this book is utter tosh.[10]

Happily, these are the exceptions, because few who speak in these voices would bother to read the book unless driven to prove that they are not 'wrong' and not misfits, or perhaps to take compensatory delight in rubbishing it. But it would be disingenuous to suggest that these rebukes have no sting, especially, I imagine, for the many readers who are in a delicate state having just dared to 'come out' as boarding school survivors. Such attacks are designed to hurt and are sure to get under someone's skin. If it doesn't hurt, then it makes you furiously angry, which is another victory because you have lost your sang froid, and have shown you can't take it. It is classic British bullying and, I am ashamed to say, it sits right at the heart of our national character.

"Only joking!"

Can it be true that the British – perhaps better the English – are a race of bullies?

Surely not, with our famous love of 'fair play', our cricket, our gentlemen, our gardening, our kindness to animals, our politics that bends over backwards to avoid extremism, our common sense, our legendary niceness. But we are certainly busy with the word. The 'bull' element is strong, like in bully beef, in 'British Bulldogs,'[11] the childhood game where you roughhouse each other and all become British in the end, and the archetypal Englishman, bluff-speaking John Bull from the 18th century, with his comfortable mistrust of Johnny Foreigner. What is absolutely certain is that we definitely do not think of ourselves as bullies; we are more used to thinking of ourselves as the ones who'll stand up to the bullies – always foreign – whether Napoleon, Kaiser Bill or Hitler, the 'Argies' or more recently, Saddam, whom *we* certainly did *not* bully.

I propose – and with some nervousness – that there is a seam of hostility that is quite remarkable on this island, and that it is organised and policed collectively and individually with a great deal of false innocence and denial. Some great literary figures have recognised this: D.H. Lawrence, for example, who was an outsider because he had crossed the class barrier, and James Joyce, the Irish genius. Here is Joyce describing what he called "the whole Anglo-Saxon spirit," in an essay on Robinson Crusoe and colonialism:

> .... the manly independence, the unconscious cruelty, the persistence, the slow yet efficient intelligence, the sexual apathy, the calculating taciturnity.[12]

But for those who are not yet convinced, we perhaps need some more current examples. Let's take cricket to start with. Actually, while cricket may appear boring to the uninitiated it is in fact a pretty tough game, full of strategy, rife with humiliation tactics, designed around an extremely hard ball that is hurled at speeds up to 100 mph. A particularly vicious form of bowling, known as 'Bodyline,' was invented by Douglas Jardine in the 1932–33 Ashes Series against the Australians, whom he was said to have loathed both as players and spectators, presumably because they were foreigners. Jardine, who attended Winchester and Oxford, was an old-school bully type and is remembered as Test team captain for his intimidating style of bowling, his defensive batsmanship and his poor people-management skills. Strangely enough, English cricketers objected to Australian and West Indian aggressive bowling so much in the postwar days that extra protective clothing was introduced for batsmen. These days, batsmen wear hard helmets with visors, where previously they had only cotton caps to shield them from the effects of being struck on the head by the ball, a lethal missile made of leather over a wooden core.

A Jardine-style character would hardly be acceptable these days as the captain of an international team, because of the amount of public relations and media interviewing required. We can no longer publicly tolerate any unsubtle forms of bullying or racism. It could be argued, however, that a certain lack of deference to authority or established norms that sometimes teeters on the edge of bullying is justifiable. Jeremy Paxman and John Humphries give British politicians a much harder time than their obsequious French counterparts, like famous TV anchor Patrick Poivre d'Arvor, give to theirs. Whether that helps in the long run is another question, but it surely contributes to our politicians becoming increasingly devious. And there are other areas in public life where we still relish a boyish bully.

The broadcaster Jeremy Clarkson, whose boarding career, ironically, was financed by his parents marketing a stuffed toy of the children's fictional character Paddington Bear, is someone who has made a living out of being a politically non-correct, reactionary Peter Pan. *The Telegraph* once wittily ran as an ongoing feature a 'Clarkson for Prime Minister' campaign, so closely did he seem to speak for a John Bullish heartland of 'hang'em and flog'em and drink-plenty-of-beer' opinion. His great achievement is the TV show *Top Gear*, a boys-love-cars-and-jokes fest, known for its repetitive and self-referring teasing. But Clarkson also likes to talk up his bulldog style on any show that will have him. Introduced with patent irony on the BBC's prime time *The One Show* on the last day of November 2011 as someone "with balanced, uncontroversial opinions, who makes great effort not to offend," Clarkson was asked to comment on Britain's biggest public sector strikes in 30 years, which had been triggered by the stringent cuts and redundancies that the coalition government was introducing to pay for the vast deficit following the prime-mortgage banking collapse in 2008.[13] Clarkson said of the strikers:

> I'd have them all shot. I would take them outside and execute them in front of their families. I mean, how dare they go on strike when they've got these gilt-edged pensions that are going to be guaranteed while the rest of us have to work for a living?

The presenters had got a bit more than they bargained for and quickly moved on. Of course there was a huge fuss. The programme's producers were roundly criticised. Newspapers led with headlines like 'Should Jeremy Clarkson apologise?' The Labour leader said Clarkson's comments were "disgraceful and disgusting." The BBC were loath to apologise; they acknowledged that Clarkson had made a 'misjudgement' but had not infringe the Broadcasting Code. The BBC know that the bulk of the British public adore this kind of thing, variously tut-tutting or approving of the bullying in secret, while in public tending the usual innocent excuse: "Only joking. Can't you take a joke?" Finally, the issue was apparently put to bed by the prime minister, no less. David Cameron managed to reassure the public on breakfast TV, telling *This Morning* that the *Top Gear* presenter was 'only joking':

> It was a silly thing to say and he obviously didn't mean that.

At the time of writing, Simon Cohen, a school teacher writing a fascinating book on the rise and dominance of public school humour over more working class styles, is still trying to get a proper apology from the BBC for the Clarkson incident, and is making efforts to interest his local MP in getting the Ombudsman on the case. It is an uphill struggle. The consensus in Britain is that if you are offended or hurt by something that is 'only joking' you should relax and not take life so seriously. Generally, the disguised bully tactics that both Clarkson and some politicians employ with casual charisma get dismissed without reference to the content – to what is actually being said.

Seen in cold blood, Clarkson's statement is a deliberate and profoundly hypnotic declaration of political war. With "the rest of us have to work for a living," Clarkson positions himself shoulder-to-shoulder alongside Cameron, Osborne and Boris in the new Entitlement Illusion. His clever syntax asserts that Clarkson and similar worthies have got where they are by hard work alone and that the public sector workers are scrounging animals who serve only their own self-interest. Not only does it legitimise the government's austerity regime, but, in true John Bull style, it strikes at the liberal middle classes who oppose it. Its deceptive humour hypnotically reinforces the class barrier better than any defined rules, and here I recall the Russian émigré Alexander Herzen, who must have experienced this himself. The humour is directed at an audience that secretly shares Clarkson's contempt for industrial action as the weapon of the terrifying disowned mob.[14] Once said, it has already done its work, apology or not. It is very finely-honed covert bullying, learned over many years of confinement and dog-eat-dog strategies at boarding school and exercised with adult confidence in British public life.

Humour, whether innocent, malign or an uncomfortable mixture of the two, has been and remains at the centre of British life. Nor is it any coincidence that the superbly creative pool of satirical comedians that Britain can be justly proud of draws on public school and Oxbridge credentials, from the Cambridge Footlights through Monty Python and onwards. In my first book I showed how the boarding school boy humorist could find a survival mechanism that worked for life – and even made him rich – and I shared some of the early memories of Tim Brooke-Taylor and others. People like John Cleese and Peter Cook were masters of turning the frustration and loneliness of their childhoods into surreal hilarity. It may have been the spirit of the age, or it may simply be that the men in question were of my own generation, but the next batch of public school satirists appeared to be less accomplished at hiding the bitterness apparently brewing in them.

Best known is perhaps Ian Hislop (born 1960, made Head Boy of Ardingly College, followed up by Magdalen, Oxford), team captain of the BBC quiz show *Have I Got News for You* and editor of the magazine *Private Eye*. Hislop has made a career of a delivery appearing to overflow with repressed bile, mocking all sides of the political spectrum. For Christmas 2012, he fronted a rather a limp attempt at analysing British emotions in a lavish three-part TV documentary.[15] Then there is Craig Brown (born 1957, Eton and Bristol University), columnist, satirist, creator of over-the-top political characters Bel Littlejohn, an ultra-trendy New Labour type, and Wallace Arnold, reactionary conservative. Brown has dissatisfaction pouring through his cultivated middle-way tone.

To those who can ignore their hostile edges, such men can be very amusing. But they are highly complex personalities, I would suspect. It is as if they have dedicated their lives to fighting extremists and bullies with humour as their weapon;

but, at the same time, they seem blind to the style of covert bullying they themselves employ.

Nice English covert bullying

The secret of employing overt as well as *covert bullying* in Britain is in the language. It's not the words or grammar, it's how we use it. It's in the understatement, innocently leaving the other person to guess what your real meaning is; it's in the vague, amused distance, implying a superior position without asserting it. The English, as opposed to the rest of the British and others who speak it but were not really born into it, are the masters of this style. And what a marvellous language English is! Having lived in several lands, spent many years cooperating with European psychotherapy colleagues on professional training and conferences and translating documents into English, I am enamoured of the flexibility, nuanced precision and economy of the language over any other I have yet come across. And yet I have also taught large training groups of Europeans, all studying in English, in which I, the native speaker, was the only person some of them could not understand. Perhaps that is because as an Englishman I tend not just to *speak* it but to *use* it. What a language! I love and respect it; it is a superb tool – but also a formidable weapon.

The English language is fine-tuned for hyperbole as well as minimisation. Professional journalists feast off this abundance and delight in the use of their prose. The media's use of words is regularly cynical, and subtly done. British newspapers blazon a style that ranges from ironic faultfinding to almost imperceptible ridicule. For example, debating the psychology of boarding issue in the press I have always to deal with the claim that I apparently assert that ex-boarders are "scarred for life." This turn of phrase makes a mockery of a notion of the casual process involved and of the human spirit's own resilience. It presents the bearer of the epithet as a complete failure – just in the 'innocent' choice of words. No other language is quite so tuned in to this art, as far as I am aware.

The English language is also highly exclusive in that non-native speakers are unlikely to respond to the level of sarcasm and irony involved in our humour. This even includes Americans, who deploy the language in a more straightforward way, which leads me to imagine that it is something developed uniquely in post-Enlightenment Britain.

Not only does the English language offer a secret code for bullying but it clearly supports the class divide, for it is only really the upper section of society who know how to deploy it properly. BBC Radio 4, that instrument of comfort and quality that A.A. Gill once likened to the very sound of the English countryside, with all its wonders and common sense, can do it perfectly.[16] Dozens of cheaply produced programmes fete the British middle classes, especially at the weekend. None did it more successfully than Ned Sherrin's lively guest show *Loose Ends*. Sherrin, boarding school and Oxford educated – of course – continued to present his programme right up until he died aged 76 in 2007. The spell he cast was as if from another age, however. His charming style and rampant wit could delude the listener into imagining the thirties or forties were still with us and we were all upper class, Catholic, gay and rich, hanging around Soho but retiring to the Savoy for supper as if "trying to survive in London on three million a year" (Sherrin quoting from Noel Coward's play *Private Lives*). His programme would have been completely and utterly inexplicable to a foreigner.

Sherrin's Saturday evening show was a feast of literate celebrities who would giggle and complain in the same lazy, mocking voice that I remember hearing in late 2006: "Oh, you know what it's like having the builders in and to have to choose taps and endless decisions ..." Having lived on both sides of the middle class and builder divide, I am rather rare in being able to speak both languages. I know what it's like doing the building work, so when I hear statements like this, I don't giggle – I recoil in annoyance, thinking: "It's someone doing your dirty work for you, madam – be glad!" I know very well why London builders are feared. They demand such outrageous sums, chiefly because of the way the middle classes alternately look down on them and try to charm them, and respond in the only and obvious way, by taking from them what they obviously have (but claim never to mention because it's too impolite) – their money. Then the builders depart, leaving the chattering classes to enjoy their gentrified residences. But if you don't speak any of these 'languages' you can just not get the allusions.

I remember my wife, Helena, well-used to speaking and even thinking in the English language, but in her Scandinavian innocence just not understanding how middle class English women talked about 'doing up' their houses. Having lived with me and taken part in restoring marginal houses for many years, she knew how much work was involved in restoring houses. She would wonder how these women had the time to do so much 'doing up'. Eventually she realised that they hadn't been shovelling and scraping but choosing colours and curtains. The English language in its glory again!

This coded language means that foreigners in Britain can end up feeling more foreign than they had expected, more foreign than their command of the language would suggest they should feel. Sometimes they lose their confidence, especially given that, through natural innocence or by giving people the benefit of the doubt, they can end up feeling as if they are being foolish. Sometimes it seems as if that's exactly what is intended. D.H. Lawrence was a man who experienced both sides of the class divide and seems to have had his finger on exactly how this worked in his day. Here is a poem from the Roaring Twenties:

> The English are so nice
> so awfully nice
> they're the nicest people in the world.
> Americans and French and Germans and so on
> they're all very well
> but they're not really nice, you know.
> That's why one doesn't have to take them seriously.
> But it doesn't really matter what you say to them,
> they don't really understand –
> you can just say anything to them:
> be nice, you know, just be nice –
> but you must never take them seriously, they wouldn't understand
> just be nice, you know! Oh, fairly nice,
> but not too nice of course, they take advantage –
> but nice enough, just nice enough
> to let them feel they're not quite as nice as they might be.[17]

Hostility and niceness are hand-in-hand here. You can be bullied in Britain and not even notice it if you are not alert to all the cues in the language. If you do notice and go "Ouch!" there is a standard reply, beloved of the Clarkson Cameron brigade: "Only joking. Can't you take a joke?" In other words, "You *are* over-sensitive and I am *innocent*." Game, set and match.

Should we imagine that these attitudes are safely in the past now that we all travel all over the globe on cheap airlines? Unlikely. We love going abroad but enjoy wincing at foreigners mangling the Bard's tongue in their in-flight announcements. My Danish wife says it is still tricky living in Britain: "People never speak their mind in England and always pretend that they do – I always get caught out." Unless you are 100% tuned in, you just don't know whether Jeremy Clarkson was making a provocative joke about shooting the strikers, or not. It is such powerful code that you are beaten in your attempts to try to come to terms with it. In the face of unrecognised (covert) verbal bullying it can take a lot to argue your case. This is a powerful subtle way of controlling people.

Back to Herzen, who loved our freedoms but living amongst the British broke his heart, even when Tsarist repression had failed to break his soul. We don't need a police state, he suggested, because we police it ourselves. This policing is embedded in the language. The fact that I knew nothing about economics at Oxford was perhaps an irrelevance, after all, as my tutor intimated, it is the style of observation in the UK that is everything. Perhaps learning to speak cleverly and nuance your bullying is the real training for future leaderships. Perhaps presenting a view and despatching those who disagree is the real skill – it is certainly still at the heart of Prime Minister's Questions.

Not quite saying what you mean – the other skill that is generally fine-tuned at boarding school – is a socially accepted form of duplicity, often known as 'good manners.'[18] In British public life, the really 'clever' thing seems to be to say something duplicitous in the *right* way, to show that you belong, and belong in the *right* place. In order to be taken seriously, those few women in parliament have to get used to a certain way of speaking and learn to give and take the banter. Even then, women are unlikely to be able to deliver like the big old patriarchal bulls who know the ropes – for starters because they can never have been to Eton, because that is for boys only.

A monstrous regiment of toffs

In his mastery at linking his spoken, normalised, bullying point of view with the great old traditions of state and religion

– learned at places like Eton – you've got to hand it Boris Johnson, Mayor of London. I remember a free moment in October 2011; I was skimming a copy of the *Evening Standard*, London's now free daily newspaper noted for its establishment and celebrity sympathies. And there he was, 'Boris' (as all Londoners call him), larger than life, wearing his delighted-to-be-outraged look on his substantial face, looking like he had just stepped out of the pages of the *Beano*.[19] Hearken the words of Boris, pontificating on the Occupy protest campaign outside St Paul's, calling for new laws to prevent "tent cities ... erupting like boils" across London and telling the activists: "In the name of God and Mammon, go!"[20]

Boris's message is clear to those who can hear it. Just between the lines, with his choice of language, he is telling those people something very definite about who he is, how he thinks and who he is addressing. There is a biblical reference, but Boris is not suggesting he is a religious man, as an innocent foreigner might imagine. No – a Christian in the UK these days would play his style down and use a secular, milder metaphor. Boris is actually telling us that he is someone who spent a good ten years listening to the language of the King James' Bible in a chapel at an expensive boarding school – in his case *the* school, Eton. If you don't immediately recognise that, then it just shows how much you can be taken seriously. It is a bit like the old Gentlemen's Clubs in central London. Once, they didn't have name-plates outside them (and some still don't) because if you didn't know where the club was, you didn't belong there. New boys at public school regularly spend many painful hours mugging up on little details to do with names and places that apply to in-school traditions and have to be learned very quickly.

What Boris wants you to know, through his sarcastic declaration, is that he is an authority figure, one of the Establishment, one who belongs. This is the Entitlement Illusion in full flow. This is how 'top people' talk, and Boris's branch of the top have a kind of divine right. Now we arrive at what he *really* means, which is that this is *their* language, *their* cathedral, *their* city, *their* country, *their* money, perhaps even their *God*... so the rest of us can just f*** off back to 'Prolesville'[21] and stay there!

Those few words from Boris, with all their packed messages, had me reeling. This was worse than all of Ned Sherrin's guests put together. I began to feel sick and badly in need of some fresh air, so I headed out of my consulting room, walked up the road and climbed to the top of Parliament Hill on Hampstead Heath, a favourite spot for countless Londoners. There, in the extraordinary panorama of the capital's best view, was a new and shocking sight. Venerable St Paul's Cathedral, untouched by the Blitz, usually sharply visible even among the high rises of the banker's towers in the entitled enclave of our financial services industry, was now lost to the skyline. From my vantage point, I could see that directly behind St Paul's, obscuring the perfect outlines of Wren's dome – a symbol of real value in the City – had risen another new tower, grey and phallic. I did not know its name then but I had little doubt whether this one was in service of God or of Boris's M-word.[22]

Looking down on the city, I knew I had come full circle. This must be it – the answer to the question that had come to me as I stood on the parapets in India. This was how the British had ruled India. We flattered their leaders, the Rajas, to imagine they could become part of the British Establishment, and got them to send their sons to Eton. We hardly ever intermarried with Indians but discreetly bought sex from them, the resulting children – known as 'Tommies' – being universally despised by Indians and British alike. We exploited India's wealth, its natural resources, its labour and even its markets by reselling its own textiles back to it, finished by home-grown slaves in our dark Satanic northern mills.

But worse, much worse, we undermined the people *from the inside* to make them feel inferior – wrong at core, just like the little boarder, with a bully on the inside – to police themselves, as Herzen would say. We did not need so many acts of outward cruelty – one Black Hole of Calcutta was quite enough – because we ruled India from *inside* the people, by getting them to believe they were inferior. We got them to do the job for us. We had the whole of India 'fagging' for us, as it were.[23] We got them to install their own internal bully, meaning they were top-down bullied by parts of their own selves and the Brits could safely remain top dogs. It is a breathtaking achievement, the most efficient imperial method ever devised, and one that I'll explain in more detail as we go on.

The 2011 version of Boris would have been just as much of a success in 1911 or even 1871. He is not only steeped in the language and unconscious habits of bullying but completely cut off from the consciousness of it, and thereby from the responsibility *for* it and any motivation to change it. It is not hard to imagine how, in similar tones to his 'God and Mammon' proclamation, public school officers were able to lead millions to their deaths in the First World War and carry on doing it for years, despite the self-evident suicidal hopelessness of the endeavour. The Duke of Wellington is sometimes rumoured to have said that the great slaughter of his day, the Battle of Waterloo, was won on the playing fields of Eton, although this quote is doubtful given that he had apparently hated Eton in particular and sports in general. Adolf Hitler, however, was convinced that Britain owed its victory over Germany in the First World War to the military ethos of Eton, as he told Anthony Eden when they met in Berchtesgaden in the months before Munich. Eden, an Old Etonian himself, and not getting the point, attempted to set the Führer right and charmingly reassured him that the Eton cadet force was "a shambles."

Unfortunately, this entitlement attitude – bullying and the disowning of it – is all over top British life still. The whole denial of boarding school problems is reinforced by the same mechanism: subtle bullying, which is ever-present, and inner shame as a result of the internalised fear of bullying, the internal bully. That mechanism certainly got to me when I first started writing about boarding and was trying to name it, as it did George Monbiot too, at first. It was what Cameron was trying to use on European leaders in early December 2011 with his famous 'veto,' but it seems that the politicians in question weren't sufficiently intimidated for it to work. The then French President Sarkozy refused to shake Cameron's hand, we are told, and is rumoured to have said that Cameron wasn't really at the conference and had been behaving like a spoiled child. Cameron must have got under his skin, however, even across the language barrier.

So much resides in the use of the language, in the tone of the voice. An American colleague tells me how he hears something disdainful and superior in the way his English wife speaks to him in any kind of minor conflict. After ten years in this country he is still not comfortable with it; he has never heard it in the States. It doesn't mean that people in the US aren't cruel or don't try to put other people down – they can and do, sometimes. But it doesn't have the same feeling of reasonableness, the same implication that if you were to object you could not *reasonably* have a case, so you might as well shut up.

It's time to go deeper into the psychopathology of the Entitlement Illusion and consider its product, the Entitled Brain. First we must consider in greater detail the internal setup of the Strategic Survival Personality structure and the psychodynamics of the bullying. Then we can return to the political implications of this in political leadership. Despite an ability to reinvent itself with up-to-date spin, a similar style of leadership that took us into the folly of the First World War is still on offer today. Those who have developed it may have levered themselves into top positions, but our political leadership remains hollow. They will have got where they have by a staunch belief in themselves and will never imagine the need to deconstruct their personalities; rather, they are still dedicated to building them up.

I will return to this hypothesis with evidence from different vantage points in what follows.

ACT II

THE BOYS IN THE MEN
WHO RUN THINGS

Inside elite British ex-boarders

When innocence has been deprived of its entitlement,
it becomes a diabolical spirit.

J Grotstein, *Forgery of the Soul*, 1984

CHAPTER 4

Strategies and Dissociations

Born to Run: the Strategic Survival Personality

Before we return to politics we need to establish a psychological profile for the Wounded Leader. This will involve introducing the complex psychodynamics of the Boarding School Syndrome, which I hope to do in plain language. By the end of this part of the book, readers should be able to recognise the boys in the men who run things.

Perhaps the most deceptive feature of the syndrome that I have been outlining is that ex-boarders hide their emotional and relational dysfunction behind a façade that usually projects confident functioning and resembles a classic national character ideal. Attempts to approach the subject therefore demand an added delicacy, as if they were attempts to deconstruct the beloved British national psyche. The character ideal is one that is well known and regularly celebrated in our letters, theatre and film. Mostly, it appears as the self-effacing, conflict-avoiding, intimacy-shy, gentlemanly type so classically represented in the late 20th century by the actor Hugh Grant.

Its other face – the hostile, sarcastic bullying type – is also known, usually in the form of a 'Flashman' sort of character. Although this is not one that we British care much to identify with, I will focus on it more. As we have seen, in England, the efficient bully with his smooth, sarcastic humour is either normalised or too cloaked in innocence to be named as such. We make do with words like 'robust,' which describes for us admirable aggression. As far as identification goes, we prefer the niceness. But common sense reveals that there are two sides to any coin, and D.H. Lawrence's poem, quoted in the previous chapter, makes the other side of our famous niceness very clear. Psychologically thinking, a bully is only ever one facet of a character, for bullying inevitably arises out of fear, and there is plenty of fear around whenever children are herded together over long periods without anyone to love them.

The key to understanding ex-boarders is to understand the institutional conditions in which they grew up and the fear that is engendered there. In my research, I came to realise that boarding produces a specific personality type, or style of *False Self*[1] (in the terminology of the famous British expert on childhood D.W. Winnicott), which I named the *Strategic Survival Personality*.[2] The name came to me in my practice one day. A high-flying corporate lawyer in his late forties had sought psychotherapy to explore the sudden unexplained fits of panic he developed when making presentations. At a certain point he described himself as 'strategic,' and explained why. Despite his outward success, all his life he had been trying to stay out of trouble. It had ruined his personal relationships, because he tended to mistake any approach to him – even an intimate one – as a potential threat. He had always led what he described as a 'double life.' This man was describing the essence of the Strategic Survival Personality.

Living in rule-bound institutions where they are unable to show their feelings, constantly surrounded by their peers who are scared and on the lookout to scapegoat any signs of vulnerability in others, boarders, needing to survive, quickly develop a strategic way of life. This means becoming Machiavellian, trying to stay one step ahead, staying out of trouble, anticipating danger, promoting the false selves they are selling, sometimes self-effacing, sometimes bullying. They develop a personality that is born to rule but also "Born to Run."[3]

The plethora of incomprehensible rules in the boarding system and the ease with which they can be broken is retained in the memory of all ex-boarders. It certainly astonished me as a twelve-year-old when I transferred from my American school to an English prep school. My previous school had its rules, of course, but it was not obsessed with them like this one, which itself was a rank beginner compared to my public school. Nor were the American school's rules deemed necessary of enforcement by means of corporal punishment – a lesson that British private schools took another 43 years to learn.[4] Whereas at my earlier school we played ball games for fun and by-the-by learned to cooperate, at public school we were obliged to play 'Games' and had to learn to compete and stop talking. Having to negotiate that transition was confusing, intimidating and – luckily, for my own sanity – infuriating. As a young man just out of school, I consequently became obsessed with breaking all rules and not getting caught, out of reaction to the life that had been forced on me. I now think that the obsession with rules was far more deliberate than first appears and I see three reasons for it.

First, it was to give a sense of a miniature society bound by internal self-referring codes, as if society itself was an institution, which was the British model, as Alexander Herzen pointed out so vividly. Second, and more darkly, it was to break the loyalty of the child to any prior rules about conduct learned in earlier belonging groups – family, culture or class. This was especially important since boarding school is the highway that opens up the hierarchy to the classes below, whose inferior cultural ties, according to the grim logic that prevails, must be severed. In the colonies, boarding schools would be the prime tool for breaking the ties to native languages and religions, as we shall see in Chapters 8 and 9.

Astonishingly, according to one researcher, a third reason may have been to protect boys against the 'depravity' – in other words, homosexuality, or sexuality in general. I'll say more about sex later, but first here's how *The Independent's* Roger Clarke, in typical ex-public school broadsheet style, reported this impressive, if unusual, piece of research in April 1995:

> Sociologist and writer Alisdare Hickson has inadvertently compiled the funniest book of the year. He wrote to 5,000 distinguished personages trawled from the pages of Debrett's and Who's Who, asking for their memories of homosexual encounters at public school. Some returned the letters defaced with remarks like "bugger off" and "you prurient shit . . . at my school you would have been done." Others were happy to reminisce.[5]

Hickson draws many interesting conclusions from his courageous feat of anecdotal history-gathering. His idea is that the rule obsession was a deliberate policy of the disciplinarian movement to reform the public schools that kicked off in the puritanical 1860s. The chief motive was to counteract the boys' tendency towards 'beastliness.' The extraordinary idea ran like this: the less the boys met each other – especially those of different age groups – the less they would be tempted to have sex with each other. This left only the vice of 'self-abuse' to be policed.[6] In consequence, every second of the day was regimented with volumes of pointless tasks, codes, rules and regulations invented to limit the boarder's freedom – always something on the timetable. The result of this was not wholly successful. Unsurprisingly, breaking rules for the sake of it appealed to teenagers, while sexual experimentation during adolescence in single sex institutions was given the extra flavour of forbidden fruit, serving freedom as a realisable vote of protest against institutionalisation. However, the process did have some long-lasting effects: most ex-boarders find it difficult not to be self-scheduled on a permanent timetable; many are still tormented about their sexuality.

Raised in the overcharged atmosphere of multiple rules and the consequent hunting down of transgressors means that boarders strategically develop one of two obsessions, depending on their individual proclivity: either keeping their heads down, or breaking the rules without getting caught. How might this affect them psychologically? It is clearly a dangerous cocktail. Adding the rule issue to the double bind about being wrong (explained earlier), plus the need to maintain a brave face without any emotion, plus the inner shame of privilege, it is not difficult to see how evasive secrecy becomes a way of life at school and extremely hard to shed in later life, because the ex-boarder is unaware of doing it.

The main behavioural feature of the Strategic Survival Personality, then, is action to avoid trouble, before reflection. Sometimes, as in 'Calm Down Dear,' an ex-boarder will lash out when a simple pause and qualification might suffice. The confidence of his false self does not extend below the skin, so an assured pause is most unlikely. Furthermore, the strategic habit has a very dark side because in the strategic way of life, anything – or more pertinently any*one* – may get sacrificed through a variety of face-saving behaviours, including betrayal, bullying or simply being dropped. The latter is very prevalent in intimate relationship situations and causes enormous hurt, even if unintentionally done. It is extremely difficult both for the victim to name it and for the ex-boarder to recognise it, let alone lose the habit, precisely because the self he formed is not used to being in situations of loving mutuality. He has had to look after Number One for as long as he can remember.

Over the years, many things confirmed the strategic hypothesis. For example, boarding school survivors in psychotherapy frequently recounted dreams with similar elements: they are on the run from something or someone, or about to get caught and be unmasked, or are up for trial and facing the death penalty. The novels of John Le Carré, the famous spy author, repeatedly feature dilemmas of ex-public school men caught between belonging to and being against the establishment, living lives full of duplicity, subject to repeated acts of betrayal. Personal communications with the author confirmed my hypotheses. I had therefore to discover a way of working with ex-boarders that could give them the confidence to stop 'surviving,' without them fearing that they were being unmasked, stripped naked, as it were. Originally, I was influenced by the sexual abuse recovery work that I was professionally engaged with at the time. The appellation 'survivor' derives from this but it has an additional and crucial dimension, one that even some therapists, who recognised the trauma of children away from home for very long periods, found very difficult to see.

Any psychotherapist's daily practice includes work around early deprivation and family of origin, so the client with what is known as 'attachment problems' is familiar – especially as Attachment Theory regains popularity.[7] Less understood, and needing emphasis when introducing the syndrome, is the sophistication of the ex-boarder's strategic survival self and the widespread devastation it can bring to individuals, couples and families over generations. It starts with the loss of connection to parents. It may never be recovered, the distance never repaired, as emotional repression often turns into what could best be described as amputation, especially for those starting to board at the six- to nine-years-old age range. Children are not able to make informed choices; they trust their parents to know what is best for them and don't want to disappoint them. Being sent away, they learn expertly to put on their brave faces, unaware of the problems this will cause them later in life. Then the normalisation really begins to bite, for, the syndrome being barely recognised, adult ex-boarders take their experience to be normal and easily discount problems in intimate relationships and family life. They frequently retreat into workaholism, ill-equipped to heal from something they don't know they suffer from.

Dissociation

"I was born in Lebanon and my childhood was pretty idyllic, apart from the war," began comedian Dom Joly in a weekend newspaper column called My Family Values.[8] He continued in a sad clown's voice:

> When I was seven I was sent to boarding school in Oxford. I'd spend term time talking to people about pony club and then I'd go back to the war zone. But I much preferred the war zone. I hated boarding school. It was just a horrible place; everyone was bullying everyone. My dad hated school and yet he sent me to the same sort of place. I never quite understood why.

Joly is not alone. One of the most puzzling things for many ex-boarders is how a parent may admit to having hated his time at school but will nevertheless send his own children away. The father knows very well how he suffered; but any empathy to the child inside him is still dangerous in case it awakens his own vulnerable side, so his survival personality has made it taboo.

Like all boarders, the father has had to survive by means of dissociation or *splitting*, the therapist's everyday word for this defence mechanism and the foundation stone of self-protective personality structures.[9] Dissociation begins as a self-saving mental trick that any of us may instinctively perform when we are ashamed or embarrassed to make something known, to accept or integrate something. We put it to one side, think of something else; we use forgetting, not referring to, compartmentalising or denial in order to assist us in maintaining our internal composure. The ex-boarder father cannot afford too much empathy for the actual child about to be sent away to school, his son, otherwise he could have his own history triggered. This would make the splitting fail and the whole house of cards would come down: all that investment in surviving will then have been wasted. So he disowns the problem and passes it down the generation line. The son is forced to pick this up too, along with his own need to survive. It's a tradition in Britain.

Dissociation is the original 'divide and rule' strategy in its individual and pre-political form. Joly's story shows how it easily divides a family, but at school it is a crucial tool. As rule-bound institution and the psychology of the strategic boarder collide, the preoccupation with rules and the imperative to not be wrong create a further and mind-numbingly perfect but poisonous twist inside the boarder's mind. Here's how it works: it's as plain as milk that not everyone can make it. Someone has to be 'The Pathetic One;' someone has to be 'The Stupid Child' who gets it wrong; someone has to be 'The One Who Gets Into Trouble.' The boarder knows this in his bones. "It had better not be me!" runs the inevitable internal logic. Hence the boarder, who learns to live a solitary life in a 24/7 'total institution' with zero privacy (sometimes not even in bed or in the toilets, for the reasons explained by Hickson's careful collection of data), psychodynamically *needs* others around him to embody the roles that he wants to avoid.

Dissociation operates at increasing degrees of severity. There can be a conscious and deliberate use of dissociation in order to emphasise a required context and detract from another, and here we may employ the mental tactics of deletion, false blame, abrogation and wilful blindness.[10] Technically, dissociation's function is to protect the individual from realities too difficult to identify with or to integrate, and thereby avoid the problem of a kind of a meltdown in the brain known as cognitive dissonance. Here is the very readable Stephen Grosz's elegant explanation:

> Splitting is an unconscious strategy that aims to keep us ignorant of feelings in ourselves that we're unable to tolerate. Typically, we want to see ourselves as good, and put those aspects of ourselves that we find shameful into another person or group. Splitting is one way we have of getting rid of self-knowledge.[11]

Psychoanalytic scholars regard dissociation as a primitive defence mechanism, and their bible, the American Psychiatric Association's Diagnostic and Statistical Manual of Mental Disorders (DSM), classifies it as an indicator of pathology. But in its most basic form it simply involves withdrawing attention from a mental process or object. It is said that South Sea Islanders were unable to see the white man's sailing vessels when they first appeared, and this may be why: they had no known category for mentally storing the image, so they deleted it in order to keep functioning as before. We now know that dissociation involves highly compartmentalised mental processes depending on the activities of the left hemisphere of the brain in its function of inhibiting the right hemisphere, which has a greater aptitude for larger contexts and relational realities.[12]

Where dissociation becomes habitual, as when it is used to maintain identity and combat perceived threats of annihilation, such as when a child has to fend for itself over long periods without protecting parents, it can become a chronic mental state. This extreme degree is *unconscious* dissociation, which employs the psychological mechanisms of *disowning* and *projection*. Splitting as a defence of the fragile or invaded self is well known in psychoanalysis. The most severe cases involve people whose consciousness seems to be utterly detached from their bodies and *in extremis* results in cases of *multiple personality disorder*. Much less is known about dissociation in better functioning individuals,[13] since the focus has been on what has been considered pathological, and, as we saw above, ex-boarders put on a good show of conforming to the national character ideal.[14]

When a child, needing to survive long periods without love, touch or parental guidance, is encouraged to cut off from his primary emotions and bodily reality and taught instead a form of emotional *un*-intelligence (to paraphrase Daniel Stern's famous term[15]), he will need to employ dissociation extensively. The resulting adult cannot avoid being in deep psychic trouble, for he will have developed a defensively organised psyche built on disowning and projection. This means his stance in the world will be quite rigid and precarious, despite what it looks like from the outside. He will have difficulties distinguishing between friend or foe and therefore in maintaining authentic relationships. Remaining sexually immature and severely challenged by the demands of emotional intimacy and parenting, he will be eternally on guard.

In the context of an elitist education, the awareness of privilege instils an additional and rather unique problem: an unrealistic and unconscious dose of either entitlement or shame, and sometimes a combination of the two. Entitlement inflates the brittle veneer of confidence that functions as a smokescreen to such an adult's pathology, and a society that values hyper-rational competition over authenticity colludes. Alternatively, where shame is primary, it may sabotage an individual from ever assuming genuine authority.

I see three differing and distinct levels of extremity of dissociation that apply to ex-boarders, who I believe constitute a distinct case. I hope thereby to show how boarders and ex-boarders organise their inner and outer worlds. Let us start by seeing what the process I call Level I Dissociation looks like.

The 'I am not The One' imperative

It is evident that human beings are born with much greater vulnerability and consequent dependence needs than other mammals, due to our large heads that house our complex, self-reflective brains, our evolutionary triumph. For many years, as we grow, we look to others to protect and nurture us. If through circumstance we find ourselves without protection from others then we have to protect ourselves or we won't survive. We attempt to do that by controlling the environment in which we find ourselves and, if that is not possible, we turn that function of control upon ourselves, forcing ourselves to adapt by compromising our needs and expectations. So far, so good.

In practice, we can well imagine that a little boy who has experienced his parents' care every day of his life so far may go into shock when being left by them in the confines of a huge, unfamiliar institution. This *Threshold Experience*, aptly described by Simon Partridge, means that the little boy soon realises that he cannot in any way control his new environment.[16] The next logical step is to control himself. The first thing to deal with is his evident fear at being alone and his sad feelings that go along with it, commonly known as homesickness. He has no other choice but to repress these feelings and to refuse to identify himself as one who has such emotions, because to be seen feeling these things would make him vulnerable amongst the other little boys who are busy toughening up.

Near the beginning of the Colin Luke's film I spoke about in Chapter 3, we see a little boy of eight on his first or second day, finding a place in the playground where he can be alone and let his tears run. Then we see some other boys approach him, probably in their first year rather than their first term. "Are you homesick?" they ask him, in what seems quite a tender manner. "No," he immediately responds. "*NO–O*," he says again, more emphatic in his denial. This is the deliberate beginning of a mechanism that will soon become unconscious. He has tried to control his feelings and he refuses to identify as one who is homesick. He is now, as it were, writing the line over and over again in his brain: "I am not The One Who Is Homesick/Vulnerable/Needy, etc." It really helps him now, but he will find it difficult to erase over time.

The disowning process can become quite complete. Here's one example: "I hope you're not missing me because I'm certainly not missing you," lied one boy in a letter home to his mother.[17] The needed proposition develops in the child's mind: "I am not The One Who Is Homesick (Vulnerable/Dependent/Wrong, etc., etc.)." It soon becomes a structure with which he must now identify, a territory he must now defend. At the same time, whenever feelings do arise, he tries to think of something else and compartmentalise them, to lock the door on them. It is the most basic form of dissociation. Such manoeuvres do help him to function, to keep going; in boarding school language it is known as 'settling in.' He can now get on with his job of being a boarder, just like a soldier who has to override his natural feelings to be able to function and do his job in battle. The boy becomes a little soldier, practised in the art of dissociation, dedicated to staying alive – a survivor.

Avoiding being The One Who Feels Homesick and sticking to "I am not The One …etc.," means relief at hand but trouble up ahead. The side effect is an internal conflict that becomes a structural difficulty. It takes energy to keep what is disowned out of consciousness and to sustain identification with the owned. Structurally and dynamically, the dissociating mind now exists in two halves or identities, like Government and Opposition, as it were, on their discrete benches on different sides of the House. The House of Commons embodies this psychic structure in tangible form. One side stands for the competent self, frequently identified as adult – albeit a pseudo-adult – sometimes known as an *inner parent*. This side tries to control, keep down and prevent identification with its opposite, the incompetent, vulnerable *inner child* part.[18]

The pseudo-adult is encouraged in the normal growing up process but kicked into over-drive by the ethos of self-reliance actively promoted by *all* parties – by the schools, of course, who are selling trained minds and independence, and by their customers, the parents, who do not want to feel guilty. Worse still, it is welcomed by the child himself, dealing as he is with the painful distant memory of home, now associated with all forms of vulnerability and dependence which need to be disowned, beginning with homesickness. This need to keep the two conflicting poles apart keeps the survivor's brave face on at school and helps it morph into a functioning false self in later life. The fear of not being able to do so gives the brittle quality.

This internal tension may be the reason for the kind of dreams I referred to, in which the psyche is warning of the collapse of the defensive structure.[19] It is further exacerbated by the double bind around having been sent away from home – feeling unlovable but subject to high expectations of achievement. The dissociation by which the Strategic Survival Personality 'resolves' the original split between home and school keeps independence and dependent vulnerability locked up in quite separate parts of the psyche. The result of such an approach to life may give an outward appearance of self-sufficiency or even leadership, as promoted by the boarding school ethos, but in fact it involves a desperate need to keep control.

Level I dissociation operates through a process that keeps the disowned part fairly close at hand, but in inner conflict. An internal war – between independence and dependence, for example – consumes resources, like any war, but nevertheless it has a reasonable chance of coming into consciousness and being integrated as part of the identified whole. It is as if the psyche wants us integrate all aspects of our life, but not to be overwhelmed by having to face what it has decided not to identify with.

An internal conflict between that which is owned and that which is disowned serves survival and avoids cognitive dissonance, but not without cost. It may add up to a profound self-betrayal for the sake of survival, akin to what writer Leonard Shengold calls *soul murder*.[20]

It's you!

Disowning has further gears for use when an environment is severely hostile, when a person is barely supported, or when the qualities being repressed are even more taboo. The next process involves exporting the disowned problem outside the psyche. It is then no longer part of *me* but assumed be part of *you*. It is rather like the English in the 18th century exporting the Lowland Scots to divide Northern Ireland so they could establish formal rule. In psychology, this form of exporting is commonly known as *projection*.

Projection answers the ensuing problem of disowning something, which is this: if I am not 'The Stupid Child' then where *is* he and *who* is he? He has to be somewhere. At Level II, the further escalation in degree of dissociation means that I can disown something and comfortably see it turn up somewhere else, which supports the apparent reality of the dissociation process. "I am not The Foolish Child" works brilliantly well when a Stupid Child is shown to have turned up somewhere else, close at hand – it's you! No wonder we all loved to hear Captain Mainwaring in the popular late-Sixties TV series *Dad's Army* repeatedly calling Pike, "Stupid boy!" Pike's 'uncle' was Mainwaring's posh second-in-command, to whom he felt socially inferior (because he had not been to public school) and in whose presence he felt his own confidence frustratingly undermined. A Stupid Boy was necessary to help the Captain rebalance himself. Viewers all registered the joke, even if they did not quite know why, so seamlessly is this situation woven into British society.

This is the precisely the process at work during the 'Calm Down Dear' incident, where the finely tuned radar of David Cameron's defence mechanism detects a threat to him and he instantly registers, "I am not The One Who Is Flustered (Emotional/Wrong, etc.) – it's Angela Eagle who needs to calm down." The Incompetent One has been satisfyingly transferred onto Ms Eagle and the PM feels better, even if he'll have to clear up the mess later. This export/projection process takes two players and regularly turns up in intimate relationships, especially marriages.[21] It is crucial to the foundation of public school bullying.

It frequently occurs in the beginnings of a romantic relationship where, for example, someone who does not wish to acknowledge his vulnerability becomes attracted to someone who seems overtly vulnerable. Later on, he will invariably find this same quality irksome and hateful.[22] For, this Level II dissociation would seem an incredibly successful technique – but for one problem. The human psyche is a marvellous thing and is entirely ecological. This means we cannot actually throw anything away: if we try, it tends to come back in a strange way, to haunt us, as it were. The impulse to self-protect can now have consequences, as Grosz explains:

> In denying and projecting a part of ourselves into another, we come to regard these negative aspects as outside of our control. At its extreme, splitting renders the world an unsettling, even dangerous place.[23]

The disowned part sometimes feels like it wants to attack the disowner, as if to overthrow its inner balance, which of course it would, were it recognised and identified with. Making friends with it could lead to a Level I inner conflict, which offers hope of integration if the two polarised parts were to get into dialogue.[24] But dialogue is unlikely. The internal atmosphere resembles rather a rowdy Opposition bench that wants to overthrow the government, or at least table a 'No Confidence' motion.

In adult life, the ex-boarder's disowned complex around incompetence and vulnerability will often be projected onto a life partner. The relationship dynamics of ex-boarders are rife with the projection and denigration game, and can be very hurtful for the unwitting partner. This partner now becomes the location for The Foolish One, The Angry One, The Stupid One, The Messy One, The Dependent One – all the Ones that the ex-boarder has refused to identify with as a child and now as an adult projects out to sustain the bad dissociation and the good identification. If the partner is able to reject these projections there will be trouble in the marriage, but ultimately more hope of them being re-owned and integrated and thereby of real relationship. If they really stick, then the trouble gets much deeper.

Before we turn to Level III dissociation let's see how an ex-boarder's dissociation and projection can turn into bullying that masquerades as innocence.

An example of masterful covert bullying

I have already hinted that beneath an ex-boarder bully there hides a fearful and vulnerable boy and a lifelong struggle with love, power and the acknowledgement of vulnerability. Appearing charming and cultivated to the world at large, his self-protective bullying may be consistent and brutal but reserved for domestic consumption only. But public bullying can be achieved with a light and delicate touch, so unconscious and subtle as to be almost imperceptible. The uncomfortable aggression is disowned (Level I dissociation) and the uncomfortable identity, The Foolish/ The Vulnerable One, is projected (Level II).

What does this look like in practice? Below I quote an example of a masterfully cryptic version of covert bullying and analyse the steps minutely. It comes from an email to my website from someone who had just finished reading my first book. The bullying tool is the subtle use of the English language, as we saw in the last chapter. It could easily pass unnoticed because of the innocent content and the unbearable lightness of touch. It may sound perfectly straightforward to the untutored ear, but on closer analysis it reveals a dance in which The Angry One and The Foolish Child are both disowned and projected. The letter starts with unreserved praise but ends up in a game of emotional musical chairs:

> I finished reading Nick's excellent and eye-opening book, the revised 3rd edition 2010. On the way through I noticed several typos, but unfortunately did not make note of them. They do tend to detract rather from the otherwise very professional writing. Is he aware that there are typos?

Here's how things can land in a relationship – in this case it is in relationship with me, someone the reader has never met, and to whom he is initially grateful. Being grateful is problematic because gratitude would make him dependent, and boarding school has taught him that dependence is a no-no. Luckily, I have indeed committed several typos, and typos are sins against perfection, against the English language and against the altar of pedantry where worships many an ex-public school man or woman, because they have suffered there as children. So The Foolish Child archetype begins to fly and lands on me.

I immediately get irked when I read these lines. Not because of the typos – only Allah is perfect – and I know by now that reading that book is a rollercoaster ride for many people. No, I get caught in irritation because of his curious innocent style: "Is he aware…?" What this really means is that I have been selected to be The Foolish One who hasn't spotted the typos – although, in reality, if I had spotted them and had not corrected them I would indeed be a fool, wouldn't I? So the question is not a real one – a bit like the washing-up incident quoted in the Introduction.

But this is not reality – it is an export drive. It is projection. Luckily, I don't take it too personally because I have met this dynamic over and over again and I have an idea what it means. It is a game, but a horrible game, none the less. If he gives full praise then I become The Competent One, meaning he then has to take The Incompetent/Dependent One role. But, happily, he can focus on the typos thereby remaining The Competent One, while I take the position of The Incompetent One. Although I have an idea what is going on, I have to confess that it still does work a bit: it does make me a wee bit angry.

So in the end he wins: I have to claim The Angry One seat (as well as The Foolish One) and he, by definition, happily takes the I Am Not The Angry One spot. Nor can he "unfortunately" help me out in my predicament, because he did not make a note of the errors. Game, set and match – in three innocent and subtle lines. It's quite brilliant really, in its chilling precision, in its well aimed, controlled passive aggression. I suspect this man to be unconsciously preoccupied with all these qualities and feelings: vulnerability, incompetence, dependence and anger. Giving me unqualified praise would have made him terrifyingly dependent. I suspect that, in particular, his anger is leaking out, since I begin to soak it up like a sponge.

Perhaps the reader is thinking, "Hang on a minute, aren't you being a little oversensitive here to someone who has just praised your book? What do you expect of your readers – utter capitulation? Full, spread-eagled obeisance?" I can understand such a reaction. But, trust me, it's a complicated process and the problem *has* to be transferred to someone else. This kind of bullying serves survival by splitting, duplicity and denial before fully exporting the problem in order to confirm the exporter's rational sense of sense. It is an unconscious rollercoaster, and one so normalised (he will have had schoolmasters who spoke in exactly this way to him) that were it to be named it would be dismissed, as usual, as "only joking" or "you are so sensitive." The covert bully would be deeply offended at having been accused of anything beyond his identified innocence. The English are so nice, as Lawrence said.

This brings us to my Level III, which can get pretty violent. For, here, not only does the person project onto a second person and make them carry all the qualities and feelings that he has disowned by exporting them, but this second person also actually feels all these things themselves, as if they were theirs all along.

Dump truck ethics

My earlier example of the letter to my website was a tiny, unimportant vignette. It can get much, much worse. A partner may end up experiencing the actual feelings of shame, despair and loneliness that the boarding school survivor has not let himself feel. These feelings can be debilitating, and their source can be a mystery to the partner, who somehow feels that she (the partner could be a he) is not strong enough or that she herself is wrong, as in the boarder's original double bind. This can do catastrophic harm in a family. At this level, the practice of so-called self-sufficiency tends to exploit and feed off others. It becomes a predatory trading situation: the worse the importing partner tends to feel, the better the exporting partner feels.[25]

In cases where dissociation has been acute, or has been going on chronically, undiscovered over many years, then the level of export becomes extreme, shrouded in secrecy and the pathological fear of being found out. This process has a different quality and is known in the trade as *projective identification*, as opposed to simple *projection*. Projective identification is where a second person actually experiences and fully embodies all the feelings that the first cannot tolerate and mistakes them for their own.[26] Real harm can be done in such cases and the hope of integration in the one who is projecting is much slimmer. It is as if the Opposition is now neutralised and living under a dictatorship where there is no hope until the dictator dies or is overthrown by forces outside the realm. But generally, there is not enough psychic energy to stage a revolt, because the partner has become pathologically depressed.

In 1991 a very interesting experiment was set up to compare the effectiveness of antidepressant drugs, cognitive behaviour therapy (CBT) and systemic couple therapy. In the London Depression Intervention Trial patients diagnosed as 'depressed' by NHS psychiatrists were randomly assigned to one of these three treatment modalities, after which results were compared. One of the major findings was that depressed people seen in systemic couple therapy did significantly better than those treated with CBT or antidepressant medication. The eventual report showed that chronic non-empathic behaviour in an intimate relationship or disowned or unrecognised depression on behalf of one of the partners may clearly result in the other partner presenting themselves as clinically depressed.[27] Similarly, these findings support what a leading American marital therapist Terrance Real concluded in 2002. Real encountered multiple cases of what he called *covert depression* among male partners presenting problems with their either over-angry or depressed spouses.[28] As in the London trial, the mental health of the partners studied by Real consistently improved when the hidden cause of suffering became revealed. Those partners can be understood to have been suffering from the effects of projective identification, and they needed a third party to free them.

I believe the incidence of this problem in marriages with ex-boarders in Britain to be in epidemic but as yet unrecognised proportions, so that many partners regularly think they are going crazy for unknown reasons. Currently, even if the couple is in marriage counselling, the likelihood of the therapist recognising the ex-boarder problem is unfortunately quite low. While the splitting and projection may be unconscious, the ex-boarder's drive to survive, to not be found out, to not be wrong, is near the forefront of his mental agenda, so his Strategic Survival Personality will go into overdrive not to give the game away. His greatest defence is being a normal, functional, middle class British man with all the associated characteristics. The therapist may be intimidated by his confidence, or, being of the same middle class ilk she may readily normalise this character style. She may even have her own children at boarding school, never imagining what a dangerous training for intimate relationships this can be.

Sometimes one half of a couple can explode with the realisation of what has been going on. We frequently receive cries for help from spouses or girlfriends for whom the light has just gone on about why they have been feeling so alone, so isolated, so fearful for so long. Here is an example from 2011:

> I am about to reach 15 years of marriage to a very corporate high flier, ex-public school, man and am not sure if I can take any more of it. I found your site after listening to something on Radio 4 about boarding school survivors and I realised that that is exactly what I have been dealing with all these years. I have a husband who has no concept of or apparent need for relationships of any kind other than those which can bring short term business benefit.
>
> He has no ability for intimacy, and no perceptible sex drive. Despite the destruction and unhappiness this causes, he also has never willingly sought help for it. It is my problem rather than his. I want so much to resolve some of this and not ruin the lives of my children by blighting them with a divorce. I feel that his issues are so specifically English (the public school system and repression). Can you help?

The painful reality is that nothing much can help unless the ex-boarder himself wakes up to the problem. This may never happen but if there is to be any chance, his partner may need to find her bottom line, find her No. Sometimes it takes something drastic to make this happen, such as the threat of divorce or an affair, probably with someone who is able to extend a little kindness. Here is another example, from 2013:

> I attended the lecture at the Tavistock in March this year and was relieved to find that much of what you and Joy Schaverein spoke about chimed so totally with what I had experienced with my ex-partner. My ex-partner was sent to 'X' school when he was six and then to 'Y' school after that. I never understood why I had felt so crazy to the point of wanting to section myself.

I suspect such problems are endemic in British life, for our elite are seamlessly versed in splitting and projecting and any challenge is automatically treated with bullying. But are the victims of this bullying only domestic? How does it happen at the very top of British society, where the entitlement, the dissociation and the projection can be most severe? We will never know whether Diana, Princess of Wales had to suffer unnameable hurts at the butt end of projective identification, under the effect of dump truck politics. It is certain that things went powerfully wrong for her and she was trying to get out. I find it hard not to speculate that her efforts to rid the world of those hidden death traps, military landmines, may have had some extra personal symbolism that she was unable to speak about.

How might this affect the other end of society? Could it be that the British working class as an entire group have been suffering projective identification from the upper classes? Have they been standing in for the stupid, messy, incompetent children the latter wish to distance themselves from in their own collective psyche? Could this explain some of the unhappiness, the lack of self-respect, the grimness that sometimes marks the British working class as distinct from their counterparts in Europe? Could this explain the discrepancy between football's glittering Premier League, full of fluent foreigners, and the struggling national teams, full with depressed British men?

Compliers, Rebels and the Crushed

In our quest to understand the psychological problems unconsciously acted out in the elite circles of British politics, there remains, after the three levels of dissociation, one further aspect of the ex-boarder's profile to consider. I want to briefly introduce a further tripartite typology, *Survivor Types*. These I categorise as *Compliers*, *Rebels* and the *Crushed*. The types apply to adult ex-boarders, though they may well have been practising for the role as children in school. They are rough guides rather than determined categories and an individual can sometimes combine aspects of more than one type.

1. Compliers
Compliers survive by denial of the problems of boarding and have identified with the values of the school – better to be on the winning side! Their motto is: "It never did me any harm." They are likely to put any defects down to the checks and balances of 'character building.' They thrive in institutions after school and are fond of the word 'robust.' This is the class that is naturally most represented in the public world of business and politics. Compliers are the main defenders of the status quo

and the upholders of the system and are embedded in it. Such characters do not tend to appear in therapy, but on the rare occasions they do it is usually as a result of a sudden unpredicted problem that threatens to break down their functioning level. They will leave as soon as the problem is fixed.

Sometimes they may discover a chink in their armour when a child is born or reaches boarding age. Now the Complier suddenly connects to some of the unrecognised needs in the child from which he has distanced himself. The dissociative process then suffers a failure, which may be permanent or temporary, according to how the individual deals with it.

The determined Complier type will maintain his dissociation at all costs, even if there may be the odd hiccough. Compliers are above all things loyal, especially to institutions and ideals. Like the party whip, which is so often successful in the Conservative party, they have a strong tendency to support each other's compliancy. The complier is deeply conservative in the original sense of the word. Some have a touch of rebel in them, like Tony Blair, which gives them some charisma and energy, but in the end their establishment loyalties come to the rescue and they stay true to form.

2. Rebels

Rebels have not been able to practice complete dissociation: they know they've suffered at school but tend to reject their own potential, often along with the whole of the established order, and 'throw baby out with the bathwater.' They tend to be loners, avoiding joining groups at all costs, particularly that mother of all groups, the Establishment, because it is in group life that they have suffered. They are often to be found in solitary professions where skill and hard work are necessary, and where the casual observer would not realise that they had 'benefited' from an elite private education – such as being a carpenter. I met many such men before I took up my psychological studies and have been among their number. They can be charming in terms of their friendliness, their preoccupation with freedom and their liberality. But Rebels, in particular, adopt a masochistic stance to the world and are shy of real intimacy. Their survival defence preserves healthy outrage but is constructed along rigidly self-negating lines, endlessly snatching defeat from the jaws of victory. Their Strategic Survival Personalities put up serious resistance to any attempts of deconstruction, and masochistic styles are well known to be challenging for the psychological practitioner.

3. The Crushed

By the Crushed, I mean those who really do not function at all well as adults. Here we are in the realms of *personality disorder*, defined by the DSM as:

> A deeply ingrained and maladaptive pattern of behavior of a specified kind, typically manifest by the time one reaches adolescence and causing long-term difficulties in personal relationships or in functioning in society.

The visibly wounded boarding school type may differ from the standard definition of personality disorder because the problem rarely shows up in adolescence. As we know, the outward face of the Strategic Survival Personality tends to exhibit high, if brittle, functioning. Some of the Crushed may have been able to put on their brave faces just enough to avoid annihilation. Others may have been sufficiently damaged at home not to be able to erect a Strategic Survival Personality at all, and are in consequence badly picked on by staff and children alike. In these cases, bullying leave its mark ineradicably.

While some struggle to function for the rest of their lives, others may commit suicide. Included on this grim list are those who may have come from good enough homes but whose attractiveness subjected them to unwanted attentions in the hothouse atmosphere during puberty. In such cases, the disowning and projection is unbelievably cruel. A beautiful child can unwittingly stir the longings of others, which will be a complex mix of the sexual impulses aroused in adolescence, the need for affection and touch, and even normal friendship. Such a boy is regularly called a 'tart' or some other pejorative slang name by his fellows, who avoid and torment him. Hickson quotes one anonymous contributor to his research who, as a boy, went against the current because his own sexual longings were irresistible:

> While no one else was prepared to carry the stigma of sharing a study with the house tart, I welcomed any opportunity to get close to Andrew.[29]

He will, of course, have kept all his feelings secret, which may have given an added boost to his desire. The other boys, being ashamed of theirs and afraid of being punished for acting on it (usually expulsion, entailing the ultimate disgrace for parents), disown it and project it out: "I am not the One who is the cause of these homosexual longings – it's him," runs the thought. And then, as we have seen, the dissociation produces an external threat in place of the inner one and so, while the fear is hidden, the object can be justifiably scorned and attacked as a danger.[30] It is very cruel.

Survivor types are not the same as levels of dissociation: the first two of these types can do the splitting steps perfectly well. This is especially true of Rebels, who deceptively may seem very aware of themselves, versed in politics or psychology, but can be extremely and subtly passive aggressive. The problem with the Crushed is that, unable to put sufficient resources into survival to be credible, they may not have been able to split enough.

The upshot of all these forms of splitting and defensive personality organisation is that boarding school survivors tend to resist their psyche's own inbuilt tendencies towards integration and maturity. This strain of immaturity has a cumulative and negative impact on the whole, especially our politics, to which we must now return.

CHAPTER 5

The Man in the Boy: The Boy in the Man

Forever young ~ Peter Pan and the Lost Boys ~The armoured boys
Growing up too fast ~ The Blair factor ~ Surviving betrayal

Forever young

How the internet has changed everything. One of its marvels is that you just have to type in the words 'Blair' or 'Cameron' to be able immediately to watch video clips of these men speaking, meeting, walking, from their earliest arrival in the public eye right up to the present day. Where we used to have the television news – and before that the Pathé newsreels – to remind us whom we had elected, we can now pretend a certain intimacy with our leaders, should we want it, that never before has been available.

When I watch David Cameron, George Osborne, Michael Gove or Tony Blair, my overriding impression is that they look so young, so youngish, so youthful ... I am sorry, but I just can't find the right word. What can one say about the ever-smiling, 'it-wasn't-me-sir' face of Jeremy Hunt (Head Boy at Charterhouse before Oxford), 'promoted' in Cameron's first reshuffle to the prestigious but unenviable job of Secretary of State for Health, in the wake of the Murdoch scandal?[1] What would be the right word for him?

Then there is the puckish Andrew Mitchell (Rugby, Royal Tank Regiment and President of the Cambridge Union), famous for being very 'upset' with police officers who made him get off his bicycle at the gates to Downing Street, while he was still International Development Minister and Tory

Chief Whip. At the time the *Daily Mail* alleged that he had denounced the police officers as "f***ing plebs."[2] The truth of what happened is highly disputed, vehemently denied by Mitchell, and, at the time of writing, the subject of much media and legal interest. We may never get to the full truth of this incident but it certainly highlights our class divisions. The latest allegation is that the police came up with the word 'plebs.' Strange. But why would the police feel the need to retaliate? Did they feel like 'plebs' around him? And why use that word? It's one I've not heard since I was a schoolboy, when it was a special term reserved for new boys and 'other ranks' in the nearby town. 'Pleb' is a real public school insult, a favourite weapon in the boarder's arsenal, rife with insults informed by the rational diet he is fed while away from his family. The word signifies a kind of contemptuous lower order, but comes from the Latin 'Plebian,' meaning lower class, as distinct from the Roman elite, the 'Patricians.'

But one thing is certain: Mitchell was not *wrong*. According to a cabinet colleague, in a masterful piece of strategy, the Minister was apparently "*right* to feel sorry for what he may have said [my italics]." Not wrong, then; for the ex-boarder's Strategic Survival Personality invented in childhood cannot be wrong – ever. With his boyishly parted hair, determined to survive being 'out of bounds,' as it were, Mitchell, nicknamed 'Thrasher'[3] at Rugby, does seem like a schoolboy.

What is the right word for these men and their odd youthfulness? Dare I say 'immature'? Could it be that my feeling is purely subjective, simply because John Major was the last prime minister to be older than me? It is possible, but I really think not. Certainly the passage of time means that age seems more and more relative. Popular wisdom suggests that it starts when you notice how young the policemen are getting: perhaps next it switches to prime ministers. A third milestone has to be the profoundly shocking revelation of someone standing up and kindly offering you a seat on the tube. Maybe it is simply that we see more of them, more *into* them, with today's ubiquitous media coverage, which Blair & Co., in particular, courted and tried to tame.

No, I'll stick to my guns. Once you begin to notice the phenomenon of ex-boarders in positions of power and start to understand what surviving boarding school was like, however, you can imagine, if not see, how young they are on the inside.

I don't mean 'young inside', as in the popular phrase, "You're as young as you feel". Nor am I quite referring to Ogden Nash's witty quip: "You are only young once, but you can stay immature forever". I am talking about sensing the presence of something that is not *congruent* with the person's biological age. It is as if you can see the boy *inside* the man. It is as if they will always stay young and then perhaps suddenly turn into old men. The Swiss psychologist Carl Jung had a name for this phenomenon: the *Puer Aeternus* – an eternal boy trapped within a man, refusing to grow up. The American poet and post-Jungian, Robert Bly, developed this idea and called it the *Flying Boy*, emphasising such a tendency in a man to be unrealistically out of touch with the world around him – 'ungrounded,' as therapists say. Bly reckoned it to be one of the most dangerous complexes for a man to get caught in.[4]

When we think of the boys within men in British public life, we must not forget that other prominent Etonian – I hardly dare use the usual phrase 'Old' Etonian – Boris Johnson, who seems to trade off his youthfulness, to play at being an overgrown schoolboy with his unruly mop of fair hair and his bicycle. One wonders what happened to his cap, blazer and satchel. What a magic trick to disguise ruthless ambition behind boyish buffoonery! Where did he learn it, and why can't we call his bluff? If it is a gimmick for Boris – the public don't need him to have a surname – it was certainly not intentional on the part of Tony Blair or David Cameron. Neither man wanted to be a boyish figure of fun; quite the opposite, their cultivated image was one of very serious concern. Towards the end of his reign, Blair began to look increasingly worn out and aged by the burdens of the job, whilst remaining strangely young.

Fascinatingly, Michael Sheen, the Welsh actor who has now played Blair in three films, seems also to be preoccupied with the politician's youthfulness. Sheen has never met him but based his performances on the study of video clips. In Peter Morgan's 2006 film *The Queen*, which portrays a horrible coldness in the Royal Family, Sheen's Blair tussles with Her Majesty, who is the same age as his deceased mother, in a peculiarly intimate way. Asked by interviewer Rebecca Murray what was most difficult about playing Blair in the film, Sheen replied:

> Just to have the kind of gravitas of a Prime Minister the same time as having the kind of youthful energy that he had when he

came into power in '97. So getting the combination of that and hoping the people would accept me as him and accept me as Prime Minister, because I think I look about 12 in the film.[5]

The *Puer Aeternus* complex, or the tendency to remain incongruently young, happens to be one of the classic features of boarding school survivors. There is a logic to it. Having to grow up too fast and being encouraged to throw off childish things too soon, perversely means that something immature incvitably remains alive in them. It is as if the boy has been preserved in aspic. This means that they stay young, not like aging rock stars with their absurd greying adolescent looks on late-night documentaries about the Seventies but, rather, as if they have not yet had enough of their mothers to care for them and worship them – which, of course, they haven't. Psychologically, we could say that the presence of various aspects of their selves that they had had to disown, and therefore failed to integrate, contributes to their immaturity. It means that something of the child will still be alive, as it were, hiding but peeping out, showing through.

In the popular psychology of the last thirty years, the notion that we all retain parts of our personality that are still young is well enough known. This phenomenon is called the *inner child*. There is much written about how the inner child can unconsciously influence our thoughts, feelings and motivations as well as choice of intimate partners, and so on. In the last chapter we saw how an inner figure is frequently regulated by an opposite pole in the psyche, an *inner parent* figure, composed of apparently more powerful and grown-up aspects that boarders were supposed to identify with and embody, which can end up as an *inner bully*. This conflict is quite near the surface in ex-boarders, so we can sense the presence of this child. Not surprisingly, considering their hothouse education, boarding school survivors do not wear their hearts on their sleeves, but they do tend to wear their survival children quite prominently.

The presence of this child is not necessarily an unattractive feature. It can be the source of considerable charm, especially when it comes along with the good manners and veneer of self-effacement taught at public school. When combined with the gift of good genes and the skill of great acting, the popularity of character actors like Hugh Grant, Hugh Laurie and, before them, John Le Mesurier and Ian Carmichael is assured. These men, who all boarded at public schools, made a career out of portraying a well-known English type, a bumbling figure who flees responsibility and abhors conflict, sometimes with a Bertie Woosterish innocence, the positive side of the British character ideal. It is not the same charm as carried by other male actors known for their attractiveness, like Michael Caine, George Clooney, Sean Connery or Cary Grant, for example, who are more famous for their relaxed style and not taking themselves too seriously, which heightens the appeal of their obvious good looks. None of the latter, incidentally, were boarders.

This boyish charm has its dangerous side too, however. Couples therapy often reveals cases where a woman has fallen in love with an ex-boarder's heady mixture of sophistication and youthfulness, confidence and safety, intelligence and innocence, richly coloured by the little boy inside him, whom she (unconsciously) imagined she could save, rescue – love him back to full humanity. This frequently proves too much for the woman in the end, because it is a major task and it is not really hers. If he wants to fully embody his mature adult self, each boarding school survivor has to take himself on, become aware and monitor his own survival patterns.

There is a principle at work here. Perhaps I can oversimplify it:

You can put the man into the boy but you cannot take the boy out of the man.

Not without considerable effort and willingness, that is.

Peter Pan and the Lost Boys

Boys are always destined to become men, but if the process is interrupted or speeded up there can be consequences – and making boys into men in quick-march, double-time is what these militaristic boarding schools were designed to do. With this goal, they have had a peculiar effect on the whole of British life, including our families, schools, literature and institutions. The side effect is that in some sense many of the boys who went through the process never really grew up and never really came home again, just like J.M. Barrie's Peter Pan and the Lost Boys.

For generation upon generation, Britain's traditional elite have been boys from 'Never-Never Land' dressed in men's bodies. Prime ministers used to try to look as grown up as they could, like headmasters with their stiff collars, pipes and cigars. But now, as today's technology allows us to see much more of them, as they become increasingly true to type and as we see more *into* things, they are starting to look like Peter Pan again, in their open-necked shirts, swinging cricket bats for the camera, trying very hard to look interested while touring factories and *extremely* serious when meeting foreign leaders. Peter Pan, the boy who never grew up, is alive and well and, horror of horrors, running the nation. How did we let it happen?

Barrie's seminal myth of English boy-in-manhood first appeared as the Victorian dream was about to fade and the playing fields of Edwardian Eton were about to be transposed to the killing fields of Belgium.[6] The stories of Peter and his chums' eternal childhood, his adventures with Captain Hook, the crocodile, the coquettish mischief of Tinkerbell the fairy and his need for Wendy to be his substitute mother have been a perennial favourite in Britain, surviving a Disney treatment as well as countless amateur dramatic pantomime productions. For Peter is a classic *Puer Aeternus*. His abode is Never-Never Land, the name later adopted for the ranch retreat of that reclusive gender-free 'Über-Puer' of indeterminate race, Michael Jackson. But the original home in the story is of course a posh London S.W.1 address, Kensington Gardens, where, now cast in bronze, he can be seen, forever young.

The jumping off point of the story is that Peter has gone away and has become an orphan, like all boarders do. His family home is strangely quiet; his mother and the dog are touched with a faraway sadness. Like all boarders, Peter uses mental processes to compensate, flying away in his imagination to faraway lands with fairies. Peter categorically refuses to grow up. Crucially, he feels *entitled* to the mothering he never had and demands it unselfconsciously from the main female in his life, Wendy – something that will probably ring bells for wives of ex-boarders but seems to have passed unnoticed into the myth that this story became. The myth of British elite entitlement, however, is still going strong, busy compensating for what should have belonged to the boys to begin with: a safe loving home with good-enough parents.

And there is a further twist to Peter's ethereal boyishness, for Barrie's take on sexuality appears to have been particularly immature. He boarded as a child – of course – and then grew into a professional socialite and eventual baronet. Hanging out with all the literary figures of the day, he eventually made what seems to have been a short marriage of convenience, while he poured his regressed homoerotic imagination into his eternal youth. In the first manifestation of his story as a stage play, *Peter and Wendy*, his hero is described in the stage directions as a beautiful boy with a beautiful smile, still having all his baby teeth, "clad in skeleton leaves and the juices that flow from trees." Peter Pan still bewitches us, for he represents, I believe, an archetypal resistance to growing up, understandable in boys sent away from home too young. But this resistance also encompasses an unconscious renunciation of responsibility, a revolution against a marriage of equals with the kind of British woman who could send her child away to the kind of school where boys have to become men much too fast.

As readers may well imagine, I have heard many heart-wrenching stories over my years of conducting psychotherapy sessions and facilitating workshops with boarding school survivors. One I shall never forget is of a man who told me how his father had yelled at him, "Be a man!" when he was upset about having to go away to boarding school for the first time, at the tender age of four. Yes, four. Because growing up fast and not needing others is traditionally the prime aim in a boarding public school, designed to produce robust self-sufficient administrators of the Empire. The briefest sketch of the history of these schools is worth considering at this point, to understand how it is built into the system. For those readers who wish to know more about this history, there is plenty available, including some in my own previous book.

The armoured boys

Although boarding schools in Britain derive from the great monastic and ecclesiastical traditions, their heyday was the 19th century. Public schools, originally meant 'for the public,' meaning open to all who could pass the exams and pay the fees, as opposed to reserved for the sons of clergy or guildsmen, thrived and multiplied. Britain needed thousands of new gentlemen who could run the developing Empire as officers and senior administrators, and these schools were fit for the purpose of producing them. By the mid-19th century there were many new schools and existing ones had undergone a revolution in ethos. Turning away from the leisurely, platonic enclaves, they were transformed into the current fashion: boot-camps, economically policed by senior boys, with stringent timetables, systematic corporal punishment, and diets that consisted of more chapel than food, more sport than academia.

Their chief rigour was to be ever-alert to the terror of sex and the dangers of comfort and laziness; their no-nonsense militaristic regimes were intended to get boys away from the influence of their mothers, to toughen them up, to form their characters and develop their backbones. The process was guaranteed to turn them rapidly into rational men who had loyalty to their institutions rather than their families. They would turn their backs on childhood and, remembering their old school, would dedicate themselves to work, play, fight or die for their class, their country and the values enshrined therein, uninhibited by any sentimental attachments to comfort, to home, to family. Only in this way would the boys later be able to survive and thrive in the brutal environs of the North West Frontier (present day Eastern Afghanistan), for example. This is precisely where the bully Flashman (of whom some of Cameron's opponents say he reminds them) turns up in George MacDonald Fraser's extraordinary mock sequels to *Tom Brown's Schooldays*, which appeared from the end of the Sixties.

The products of these schools would be intrepid and successful – never mind if they tended to be partial people "with well-developed bodies, fairly developed minds, and underdeveloped hearts," as described by the great English novelist E.M. Forster. And as such they tended to become quintessential Englishmen, ready to serve their country but strangers in their own homes. For, as Rudyard Kipling reminisced in his last work, written after the death of his only son and four years before his own in 1936, the boys who were to run the Empire had been very well trained:

> Then they taught with palm and toe —
> Then I learned with yelps and tears —
> All the Armoured Man should know
> Through his seven secret years.[7]

And it worked. It was an ideal of manhood sold to the British that they held dear over many years. It is still with us, successfully integrated into the top-down values and ideals of national life and character to this very day. Kipling's "armour" explains why, when he leaves school and finds himself in a modern domestic environment rather than an empire, an ex-boarder will more often than not find genuine intimate relationships and parenting extremely challenging. You cannot engage in those activities in any convincing way if you have been brought up to be an "Armoured Man." This is because of obvious reasons of unfamiliarity but, paradoxically, it also inevitably means that your disowned inner child has been running your life since you went away as a young boy to boarding school. You will most likely be looking for a Wendy to mother you, or a fantasy sex-goddess, like the boys in Lindsay Anderson's 1968 public-school fantasy romp film *If*, or, better still, both in one package, rather than a real live woman. Let alone the fact that your partner will have an uphill job trying to live with and love someone who is trained to be a pathologically private person after his "seven secret years" – or more commonly, ten years of three-month terms of 24-hour days, being surrounded by other self-protecting boarders and having to stay on guard.

The armoured layers of protection can be very durable. Besides, the psyche has its own timing, which seems not to favour youth in terms of self-reflection. Most of the people who have made the choice to come into therapy in the wish to stop surviving and embrace living are in their forties or fifties. Some form of crisis usually precipitates it, whether that be losing a job or a partner, or the sudden rush of feelings that can occur when a survivor becomes a parent for the first time or his child reaches prep school age. It often needs some gap in the schedule of an over-busy life for the opportunity to concentrate on such feelings to occur, which is perhaps why it often takes a personal fall before people attend to them. One can well imagine that our busy young prime ministers have not had the time for the luxury of much self-reflection, even if they were to have the inclination.

Even when a survivor is drawn to the task of taking himself on to try to recover and come back to life so that he can become an authentic adult, it is not easy. These men have been through a process they now look back on with horror, and this is very difficult; it can be unedifying for them to acknowledge that they have become a product of one of these institutions. One man who was in therapy with me described his dilemma perfectly, recognising that he was *both* the child who had been sent away *and* the adult result. He was able to say what it must be like for his partner:

> It is easy to love the nine-year old, but it's hard to love the survivor with his inability to touch or be touched.

For those who do not wish to question the mix of advantage and disadvantage this educational privilege affords – the Compliers – British society is well supplied with institutions that can be an attractive destination after school and university. Much of the ethos in British institutions resembles public school, whether at the bar, in medicine, the church, the army and the City (at least until very recently), and most especially in politics. Outsiders have to force their way in, for these institutions are made to measure for the boys in the men, as are the boys for the institutions. It is, as it were, an arranged marriage: they are perfectly suited and wedded to each other.

Growing up too fast

Observing boarding school survivors who have not yet seen how their inner child still drives their current lives, you may sometimes get the flavour of both the boy and the pseudo-adult at work in him. Sometimes you can see how the inner child inside the survivor puffs himself up to be grown up, as it were. To see this process in action and formation in the early days, it is really worth looking at Colin Luke's film *The Making of Them*, which is a remarkable and unique record of capturing this process (we encountered this film first in Chapter 3).

I suggest watching the nine-year-old little boy, Freddy, who switches between puffing himself up to be grown up and reverting back to the child he actually is. You can see it on You Tube.[8] What you don't see on the film is that these children are being followed around by cameramen with tiny video cameras, so that the boys got used to being filmed and in the end hardly noticed the process, as the filmmakers told me.

"Boarding school," begins Freddy,

… has changed me, and the one thing I can do now is "get used," and when I'm older, and when I'm something like twenty, and if I become a businessman, I am going to have to be able to manage by myself, and so being at boarding school is quite a lot about being able to manage and handle yourself without help from other people…

In a voice that is not quite his, Freddy is repeating what he has learned so far. You can hear it in the stress he places on the grown-up sounding words. But, then, perhaps seeing the face of the cameraman or just remembering who he really is, he changes tack once and then double-backs once more:

Well, everyone needs help from other people, sometimes in their life, but …

And then, remembering who he is supposed to be once more:

… but, for me going to boarding school is a real achievement. It's made me more grown up, it makes you more grown up and it gives you a better education, and you might become a prefect, prefect in Division One, and it then gives you a RESPONSIBILITY [the upper case is my attempt to show how he puffs right up on this word]. And it really has changed me quite a lot, and I'm able to manage by myself now.

"How old are you?" asks the cameraman, who may well have been the boy's best friend by this time. It sounds like he is putting in some reality testing but, Colin told me some years later, he was actually shocked and broke the rules. It is the only time in the film we hear a voice off. Its effect is to allow the boy to become calm and become a child again:

I'm nine… well, I'll be ten on November 3rd, 'cause I'm nine at the moment, and I had clown birthday cake last time, and it was really nice, and on the nose was that really yummy stuff and it was red and I had the nose all to myself and it was really nice and I ate all of it, because I went: "Right, that nose is mine!"

It is a heartbreaking experience watching Freddy trying to embody the self-sufficient grown-up he imagines the school and his parents want him to become. But it is a revelation for the psychologically minded observer to see how a young child constructs a Strategic Survival Personality to become the apparent child-adult he is expected to be. In the rapidity of this juvenile process, we can observe how it involves betraying the self he really is and substituting a kind of pseudo-adulthood. We can imagine how he may be in danger of never really growing up in an organic way. As he grows up, Freddy will probably come to fear being thought childish, or vulnerable, or weak, so that those around him who seem to express or stand for these qualities will unconsciously become threats to him. Then he will have to puff himself up to deal with them, to dissociate from them, to control them, to calm them down.

This process is what is so unique about the formation of the boarder's strategic survival personality – it keeps his child, as it were, in aspic. This is precisely why Cameron and Blair seem so young. When you begin to get a sense of it, you notice the puffing up, the pseudo-adult coming out in them, as it were, in their desperation to look sincere, or serious, or important, or truthful – anything as long as it is not foolish, childish or dependent. That has to be someone else, as we know, for "I am not The Stupid One." The puffing up process is painfully evident in Cameron, especially when he has his serious face on. At those moments I can almost hear little Freddy saying, "when I become a *business*man, I am going to have to be able to *manage* by myself".

The Blair factor

In Blair, I often thought the puffed-up boy was noticeable in how he walked, with his suit buttons determinedly fastened. It was most apparent when he was indulging in the act that led to his losing the confidence of the electorate – his 'Yo, Blair!' camaraderie with George W. Bush. This was especially puzzling for many observers, as he had seemed to have a real 'special relationship' with Bill Clinton, ideologically a much more natural bedfellow and whose advice he had regularly followed in the early days. Peter Morgan's third film in his Blair trilogy, *The Special Relationship*, shows him beginning as an acolyte to Clinton; then, when the President is weakened by the Lewinsky scandal and Blair is strengthened by success in Kosovo, dropping him altogether.[9] Morally superior, Blair abandoned the no longer useful Clinton, switched allegiance to

Bush and, like the Pied Piper, marched the country off to war in a trance. It was the unpopular invasion of Iraq in 2003 that alienated and infuriated the British public, who had loved him to death six years earlier.

The cartoonist Steve Bell famously lampooned Blair as Bush's poodle. Understandable, though I thought it a bit harsh. I saw him slightly differently, more like a head boy sucking up to the headmaster, the one who really had the power. The poodle metaphor suggests blind allegiance with no will, whereas the head boy metaphor seems much more likely to me because it embodies the rigid sense of duty that seemed to move Blair and the double role he ended up playing. Actually, Blair did not make head boy at Fettes nor did he take part in Union debates at Oxford – a touch of the Rebel Survivor Type, perhaps. It may be one of the reasons he seemed to take on the part of Bush's sidekick with such relish. He certainly seems to have had an abiding fascination with power, which extended to his early love life.

Blair's time at Fettes receives little prominence in his breathless autobiography, *A Journey*, although it includes interviews with some masters who said he was known for flouting authority.[10] But Blair does recall the fellow pupil who was his first love. Amanda Mackenzie Stuart was the first female pupil to be admitted to Fettes and the only girl in the school at the time – poor lass – and Blair, in a feat of his now well-known staggering willpower and confidence, beat the other 450 boys to her. "She was the daughter of the chairman of the governors. They were an amazing family," he writes. Conveniently, he later used a flat owned by her parents in Edinburgh to plot out his political future.[11] Blair seems to have been preparing for power – not a characteristic of a poodle personality, I suspect.

If Blair did not get the job of head boy at his boarding school, he did end up with an even more prestigious and delicate job. By acting as head boy to Bush (seven years his senior) under the pretext of the special relationship – always more special to the Brits than the Americans – he took enormous risks while perhaps imagining that he was playing safe. A public school head boy or senior prefect has to manage quite a difficult role, in fact. He has the power of the position to enjoy but he has to pull off the duty of being the chief representative of the school and mouthpiece of its government, the masters, while at the same time being the first amongst his peers, with whom he will have been popular.[12] Betrayals are inevitable. It is a bit like being the wife of a patriarch, who ends up betraying the children she loves through her loyalty to the chief.

But if Blair was caught in an illusion, and 'acting something out,' then it was experienced by others as an extremely dangerous delusion. However you saw it, his stance was catastrophic for the nation as a whole, leading us into a second Gulf War. Blair marched us resolutely on, despite enormous public opposition, despite the evident duplicity of the non-evidence of weapons of mass destruction, despite the exposure of the dubiously cobbled-together sources. The decision to invade Iraq, without a UN mandate and in the teeth of bitter opposition at home and abroad, would link the two leaders together in the public mind forever and would herald Blair's downfall some years later. He had been given the benefit of the doubt in his shadowy rivalry with Gordon Brown, who on the way had rescued him from adopting the Euro, but this undemocratic lurch to an unprovoked and illegal attack on Iraq convinced the public that he relied too much on spin and was not to be trusted.

The aftermath of this has yet to be integrated by the British. It was certainly terminal for many innocent people, including David Kelly, scientist and expert on biological warfare, employed by the British Ministry of Defence, and formerly a United Nations weapons inspector in Iraq. Lord Hutton decided that evidence related to Kelly's unexplained death, including the post-mortem report and photographs of the body, should remain classified for 70 years.[13] A Le Carré story if there ever was one.

How Blair was loved and welcomed and then went on to throw it all away is one of the great mysteries of modern politics. I recall the extraordinary optimism on that night in May 1997. I remember how many people stayed up all night for that election. I can still hear the vast cheer that went up from Alexander Palace, a mile or so from my flat, when the announcement was made that the Conservative MP Michael Portillo had (unexpectedly) lost his seat. At that time, we thought Portillo the advance guard of the Right, though today he seems like the very voice of reason in his new career as broadcaster and commentator. Despite the great faith in a new order we invested in him, Blair betrayed his followers like no other politician in living memory. It was the first time in Britain, in the wake of Clinton and his Third Way in the US, that we had someone in power who seemed to have been a product of the revolution in ideas of the Sixties and Seventies. How he managed to let the betrayal happen, with his tight command of the media, defies belief.

Was it simply that they were trying too hard? Or could he never really resist the lure of the Establishment? Whatever the reasons, in October 2011 it led to the absurdity of David Cameron, no less, acting the revolutionary in a further belief-defying fit of self-righteousness, suggesting that the Chilcot Inquiry (the public inquiry into the war in Iraq) was "an Establishment stitch-up."[14] Before becoming Conservative leader, Cameron had of course voted in favour of the war, confirming his stance to no less a bastion of sincerity than the popular TV show host, Jonathan Ross. The future PM, wearing his most serious Freddy-like face, declared, perhaps reading from Blair's script:

> You've got to do what you think is right even if it's unpopular, that's the only thing you can do.

The reader who has been with me so far will not be surprised if I propose that there are several recognisable features of an ex-boarder's Strategic Survival Personality at work here, albeit advanced ones, that can throw light on Blair's extraordinary journey – not quite the story he tells in his best-selling memoirs. They have to with masochism, betrayal and self-betrayal. We'll start with the masochism.

In 2004, Blair was struggling to stay credible but, while he was persuaded to carry on by supporters, he surprised everyone in October by announcing he would not seek a fourth term in office if he won the next election. The announcement had been designed to end speculation about his health; he had undergone an operation to correct an irregular heartbeat. But the announcement backfired on him, giving opponents the opportunity to brand him a 'lame duck.' So, for the 2005 general election campaign, that Machiavellian maestro, Alastair Campbell, came up with what was called the 'masochism strategy.' In a planned series of TV debates, Blair would permit voters to vent their anger about Iraq at him.[15]

Masochism, the reader may remember, is a feature of the Rebel survivor type, and Blair had a fair measure of that in him during his boyhood at Fettes. Perhaps the unconscious masochism, if not the rebellion, was still in the man – for you can put the man into the boy but it is harder to take the boy out of the man. Blair, however, was a phenomenal performer on live debates: he could give the appearance of transparency while still being virtually invulnerable. Even veteran cynical journalists are still amazed at his composure,[16] apart from those who had already given up on believing him and increasingly saw him as a master of deception – even self-deception. For upbeat performance in adversity is the chief value of the strategic survival personality.

So Blair marched blithely on and eventually dumped Brown in the mess he had made by betraying his former supporters. How could such a bright man be so blind to the betrayal he was committing?

Surviving betrayal

Betrayal has been a national obsession since long before Tony and Gordon argued over who was betraying whom, at least since Shakespeare gave us Othello. And betrayal is another of the great unrecognised but cherished blood sports in British boarding life. I am not saying the British are by nature perfidious, but a boarding child has certainly been steeped in betrayal. First he gets betrayed by his parents, dumped away from home in an institution for what is apparently going to be 'the best years of your life;' then he gets betrayed by the boarder's double bind, which goes like this:

> If they love me, why do they send me away? And if it is so important to them and I don't like it, there must be something wrong with me.

Next, in order to survive, he has to practice a profound self-betrayal: he must cut off parts of himself that get him into trouble or are unwanted; and these parts are those that are closest to his humanity – his feelings, his vulnerability, his childishness, his trust in others, his innocence, his sexuality. To maintain survival he has to reinvent himself as someone who does not need love and therefore cannot be betrayed. Most boarding children make this sacrifice instinctively and unconsciously; it is profoundly masochistic.

Betrayal is a wound to love, to trust, which often features in the corridors of power. John Le Carré's books are apparently about spying, but I think they are all about betrayal. Le Carré, ex-boarder as he was, was obsessed with it, and underwent his own lengthy writing therapy, both honouring the boy inside of him, I imagine, and exposing the menace of the world just under the political facade. His stories feature betrayal and self-betrayal going hand in hand, and I have learned enormously from him in this area. In *The Making of Them*, I concentrated very much on this connection and here I'll re-quote an abridged extract from his early masterpiece and semi-autobiography, *A Perfect Spy*. "Betrayal can only happen if you still love," writes the central character, double agent Magnus Pym. In the book's *denouement* Pym's controller from East Germany, Axel, who has been the counterpart of Pym's British mentor in the service since he left school, puts his finger on the centrality of betrayal. "Sir Magnus," Axel ironically begins,

> You have in the past betrayed me but more important, you have betrayed yourself. Even when you are telling the truth, you lie. You have loyalty and affection. But to what? To whom? Yet you also have morality. You search. For once nature has produced a perfect match. You are a *perfect spy* [italics mine]. All you need is a cause.[17]

Sometimes I think it could have been written about Blair. He certainly espoused morality. He was unquestionably a man with a cause, to which he has never shown disloyalty. The nation might have taken him back into their hearts had he but found it in himself to say: "I made a mistake about Iraq." But no. This was not just the usual U-turn phobia, I suspect: his self-belief had pathological dimensions. He would never allow himself to turn back.

I have heard many stories of new boarders choosing the road to self-betrayal at a particular moment, sometimes on their first day at school, and there being no road back from then on. I like to wonder whether there was an equivalent single moment when Blair made his political act of self-betrayal from which there was no return. One idea occurred to me while watching the movie *The Queen*, which I thought was much more about Blair than the Queen. The scene is a pivotal moment in recent history: the nation's dumped sweetheart, Princess Di, has just been killed, and the railings of Buckingham Palace are becoming a flower-strewn altar to grief – grief that the Royal Family is failing to show to their subjects, who urgently demand it. As the monarchy appears increasingly bankrupt, Blair's popularity rises, to the delight of his republican wife and advisers. He is shown meeting the Queen, trying to convince her that her response to the death of the People's Princess is insufficient. But she will not be reminded of her *annus horribilis* and instead she makes a speech to her first minister about the values of tradition and duty.

Perhaps this could have been Blair's 'tipping point', his power moment, his ultimate head-boy scoop. He begins to develop an admiration for her, almost a *mother transference* in psychoanalytical terms, as if his place at her side has mesmerised him.[18] Blair described his own mother, who died when he was 22, as an "almost saintly woman" whose death changed his life forever.[19] It was in this new role at the Queen's side as advisor and saviour that – at least in Peter Morgan's script – Blair seems to abandon all his Rebel part and transform into a thorough Complier and bastion of the Establishment. There is an echo here of his father Leo, who lost his mother at an even younger age and was later adopted. Blair senior was a self-made man who had been Secretary of the Scottish Young Communist League in 1938 but became chairman of the Durham Conservative Party in the Sixties and would have stood for election if he had not suffered a stroke.

The movie now shows a Blair renewed, invigorated, confident where he had once been hesitant. He dismisses the views of his pushy wife Cherie, telling her that a republican Britain is ludicrous, denouncing the anti-royal stance of his New Labour advisors. He phones the Queen at Balmoral and recommends measures to regain public confidence in the monarchy, and she agrees that lessons have to be learned from the way things were handled after Diana's death. It becomes a crucial relationship, most likely a relief to Her Majesty, who had apparently found Mrs Thatcher insufferable. How odd then that when out of office (in real life), Blair went on publicly to reveal his attitude to this seminal relationship with the Queen and betray her. Tim Walker of *The Telegraph* was astonished at how Blair wrote about her:

He claims that at their first meeting, the Queen had told him: "You are my tenth prime minister. The first was Winston. That was before you were born." In a remarkable example of *lèse majesté*, Blair writes, too, of how the Queen occasionally exhibited hauteur towards him.[20]

What was Blair thinking of, writing in public about such intimacies when he was out of office? Was it revenge for his moment of self-betrayal by committing an unprecedented betrayal of the monarch? Was it a moment of return to his crowd-pleasing Rebel? Was it a moment of masochism by the confused boy inside the confident man? Whatever it was, he is unlikely to be forgiven, one imagines. His non-inclusion among the 1,900 guests invited to her grandson's wedding in spring 2011 was perhaps payback considering that all surviving PMs had been invited to the wedding of Charles and Diana exactly 30 years earlier. Gordon Brown was also dragged into the list of the omitted with him. In the end, the palace seems to have had the last word, even if the flavour is of so much sour grapes. Walker continues:

> "Her Majesty has to be able to talk to her chief minister in confidence, without any sense of trepidation that her words might some day be retailed in a cheap and cheerful volume of memoirs," one courtier tells me. "No prime minister before has ever done this and we can only hope that it will never happen again."

David Cameron, who at the time was doubtless already making notes for his memoirs, is unlikely to make a similar mistake. But if Blair makes his expected return to politics – and surely that prodigious talent, self-belief and speaking ability has not yet been used up – I am certain he won't be troubled by it at all. He will have done only what he believed was right.

Le Carré would recognise this as the principle quality of the *perfect* spy.

CHAPTER 6

Johnny Foreigner

Cry V for Veto! ~ The ghastly swot ~ Tabloid nation
Born to rule, not to belong ~ Conservative Britain
A view from the High Road

Cry V for Veto!

If it was a moment of temporary triumph for British
xenophobes, the beginning of December 2011 marked a
very bad spell both for our politics and for the reputation
of the UK in the wider world. Even seasoned foreign observers
must have been hard put to understand what was going on. But
it was a window into the astounding psycho-political world of
British elitism and a free seminar on attitudes that feel way out
of place in the early 21st century. The timetable ran something
like this.

On the evening of Saturday 3 December, Tory MP Aidan
Burley, 32, (Eton and Oxford), was spotted in a posh ski resort
in the French Alps with a bunch of inebriated chums, dressed
in jolly Nazi uniforms, drinking and *Sieg-Heiling* to celebrate
the stag night of another Oxford man. These worthies were also
witnessed taunting a waiter for being French – 'Only joking,'
we imagine. Sky News reported:

> One guest, sitting beside the MP in a restaurant, was filmed raising
> a toast to "the ideology and thought process of the Third Reich".
> Later, after moving on to a British-themed pub, some of the group
> chanted: "Mein Fuhrer! Mein Fuhrer! Mein Fuhrer!", "Himmler!
> Himmler! Himmler!" and "Eichmann! Eichmann! Eichmann!"
> Mr Burley, who has been sacked from his post as a parliamentary

private secretary but remains an MP, this week apologised for his "crass and insensitive" behaviour. But Mr Burley would not directly address claims that he hired the SS uniform for the stag night.[1]

Next, on the night of Thursday 8 December, at a meeting in Brussels to create new fiscal measures designed to halt the economic meltdown of Europe, Prime Minister David Cameron had his very serious face on as he attempted to intimidate his European leader colleagues by dissenting from the initiative. Although this ploy was a spectacular failure at the meeting, at home the right wing of his party and the tabloid press were in full victory celebration over what became known as 'Cameron's Veto.' Their St. George had poked the monster of Brussels right in the eye in defence of John Bull's inalienable right to make money as and how he wished.

That same weekend, economist Will Hutton, author of the masterly *The State We're In*, principal of Hertford College, Oxford, and Chair of the Big Innovation Centre, recognised this as a big moment for the Right and described its triumph as follows:

> Cameron's circle is the hedge fund managers who payroll his party, rightwing media executives and the demi-monde of Tory dining clubs, Notting Hill salons and country house weekends, all of whom he knew could be relied to cheer him for his alleged bulldog spirit and Thatcher-like courage in saying No to European 'plots.'[2]

And then, probably late on Sunday 11 December, the *Daily Mail's* Simon Heffer, a journalist who in August had come up with "Where Hitler failed by military means to conquer Europe, modern Germans are succeeding through trade and financial discipline. Welcome to the Fourth Reich,"[3] was at his desk. Presumably having already read that most of the more responsible press were horrified, Heffer sounded the air-raid warning siren in the nostalgic recesses of the jingoistic islander's mentality and addressed those not at a country house weekend (but wishing they were) by announcing:

> German and French politicians, in particular, are making dark threats about bombarding the City with new regulations as a punishment for Mr Cameron's veto.[4]

In actuality, Cameron's so-called veto was a misnomer. He was neither asked to vote on anything nor present when anything significantly precise was proposed. But 'veto' sounds better in the politics of gesture, designed to reassure his own party and perhaps give himself the feeling that he was doing something while the country was sliding further into austerity, recession and gloom. Andrew Rawnsley of the *Observer* is much better qualified to explain this than I:

> Veto is a powerful word. It sounds presidential. It smacks of decisiveness. It rings with defiance. So in every interview he has given since the Brussels summit, David Cameron has boasted of wielding 'the veto'. For a day or two, it might just gull the more simple-minded Eurosceptics in his party that their prime minister did something tremendously strong when he left himself and his country in a minority of one. Yet in all the dictionaries that I am familiar with, 'to veto' is to prevent something from happening. While it is technically true that he 'vetoed' an EU-wide treaty, the prime minister did not actually stop anything meaningful at all. The only thing he has blocked is British influence over negotiations vital to this country's future.[5]

Not only was Cameron's 'veto' a non-event, but the whole financial and economic reading of his mission also seems to have been recognised as misguided. I don't mean that in the way that an opposition party might, in order to make political capital: right across the spectrum of serious intellectual assessment and comment, even British observers were baffled and shocked. Hutton, barely concealing his frustration, explains the economics of it:

> There was no threat that could not have been resisted if Britain really was committed to defending the casino dimension of the City. Our entire relationship with the member states of the EU, along with our capacity to shape policies that may influence a far higher share of our GDP, has been put at risk for nothing. At worst, a dozen foreign investment banks and a couple of dozen hedge funds, along with their bonuses, might have been affected. But now the capacity to defend them, even if we wanted to, has been thrown away. As an act of self-defeating, crass stupidity, this has rarely been equalled in British foreign policy.[6]

I am quoting Hutton and others at length because that December week was a crucial time for seeing the darker side of

British elitism at work and I want to let the professional political observers, who are the experts here, explain the facts before I attempt any psychological interpretations.

Hutton, who went to a Grammar school, is an especially important voice, I believe. A phenomenally bright advocate of restrained benevolent capitalism, he has written intelligently about the ills of what he calls 'gentlemanly capitalism.'[7] He is an opponent of private education and the entitlement mentality that Michael Goldfarb pointed to in his radio documentary *The British Establishment: Who For*.[8] He is highly critical of this strand of parasitic and self-congratulatory politics, called the "Chimaeratocracy" by Toby Young, [9] in which:

> ...the rich believe they deserve their status. They're not lucky; they've worked hard and owe nothing to any public institution or society. Wealth is seen as a sign of worth in itself and to be so deserved that if menaced with taxation you threaten to leave the country.[10]

Hutton has done very well, but he could have played a more central role in national politics had he been listened to or, paradoxically, been more afraid to make his case. But significantly, he has been a consistent critic of the over-rich and a backer of the idea that Britain serves both her own and the world's best interests by full engagement with Europe. He also has pretty good intellectual credentials. All of these aspects work against him in the long run. In his commentary on the December 2011 campaign, he spots the kind of policies that he has been trying to warn against for many years. For Hutton, Cameron's actions are an unmitigated disaster:

> We have made it significantly harder for the 17 members of the eurozone rapidly to put in place the cluster of policies needed to save the euro. Chancellor Merkel said the compromise was workable – to widespread German scepticism; the European Central Bank warmly welcomed the progress, but announced no new measures. If the euro breaks up because its members have to move clumsily and slowly outside the formal EU treaties and institutions because of Cameron's veto, the resulting series of bank collapses and consequent depression will hurt Britain badly. What's more, fellow Europeans will not forgive us for a generation. This is a catastrophic moment in British and European affairs. Today, once again, the Conservative right, indulging its atavistic instincts

and egged on by a no less atavistic right-of-centre press, is landing the country in the soup.[11]

Hutton knows too well that Cameron is not an isolated voice trying to please only his party's right wing. The tabloid press, directed by the great media barons who represent forces that operate at supranational level, are sufficiently anti-European not to need much encouragement. One only needs the barest sense of history to note the allusion to the Blitz in Simon Heffer's jackbooted rant or the ease with which the chauvinistic Brit bolts on a Frenchman to Aidan Burley's 'only joking' Nazi night out just a week earlier. One might innocently wonder why serious politicians want the support of papers such as the *Sun* or the *Mail*, which trade on the lowest possible common denominator, and in which a political article is immediately followed by a full-page feature on the delights of *The X-Factor* and *Strictly Come Dancing*. But, unfortunately, courting the popular vote will inevitably remain high on the menu for all politicians in the bread and circus mentality that is the downside of all democratic systems.

The ghastly swot

The British tabloid press is staffed by highly professional people who dumb down their commentary for the sake of sales. This goes without comment, because anti-intellectualism is both acute and chronic in British public life, and, perhaps surprisingly to those who do not understand the British scene, is a key feature even of our elite education. Excepting perhaps Winchester, where an intellectual tradition is carefully groomed, one of the most hated public schools figures is the *swot*: the boy who takes the academic side of things seriously. Anti-intellectualism is a characteristic of the traditional public school boarding bully type and in politics it can grant success to a politician like Boris Johnson.

Psychologically, anti-intellectualism is based on unacknowledged fear, like most forms of bullying. The view of the classic conservative, especially the ex-boarder Complier type, is that an intellectual is someone who thinks too much – perhaps feels too much. He is therefore unlikely to be an asset to British society at large, which as Alexander Herzen proposed, polices its values from the inside out. Readers may recall the father in *Tom Brown's Schooldays*, who wants his son to be nothing but a 'Gentleman.' Traditionally gentlemen relish the manly pursuits of hunting, fishing and shooting, and, if there has to be an employment of mind or spirit, prefer 'muscular Christianity' to navel-gazing.

Even when we do have intellectuals, they tend to the ironic, effete and chauvinistic end of the spectrum. W.H. Auden, for example, railed against the "cult of salads" and warned that before very long the south of England would resemble "the Continong."[12] More recently, lavishly opinionated television super-pundit Jonathan Meades guided viewers on an "exhilaratingly sullen" grand tour of sarcasm around France and the French.[13] Meades informs and entertains but, in a *tour de force* of sophisticated irony, lets us know he stands on a higher plane.

Those who see themselves within a European tradition may be alarmed to see the anti-foreigner spirit still alive and well, more attractive to the anxious than the apparently 'soft' politics of Johnny Foreigner's 'Continong.' The tabloid Right love to get behind and jeer, lacking the healthy doubt that the aversion to compromise in Cameron's attitude will lead to lose-lose solutions, them-or-us dialectics, with-us-or-against-us politics, and later I will show how such a mindset gets crystallised within the human nervous system. Charged up and unaware they accept Cameron's attempt to abandon and punish The Messy Stupid Children in Europe for not accepting British leadership. Yet, with psychological eyes, we clearly see his gesture as the act of a man who is desperate to prove he is not The Foolish One. In photos taken of him at the time, a childish desperation screams out at those who can see the boy inside the man. Claiming to be the big protector the financial industry, he dissociates from the knowledge that he has in another part of his mind, that the over-protection of the financial industry was the cause of the 2007 economic disaster in the first place.

As an organism, the tabloid press is terrified of anything that passes for weakness, softness or intellectualism, and remains obsessed with the shining falseness of celebrity. Thus it bears uncanny similarity to qualities I have ascribed to the ex-boarder's Strategic Survival Personality. Europe provides a very useful function for the tabloids and the Conservative Right, for it furnishes them with something to despise, thereby giving them something to feel superior to, project onto, so they can feel safe and block out their anxiety. This is exactly the same process at work in a public school bully, so it is familiar ground for many. Happily for them, Europe supplies them with both the French, 'the ones we can feel good about mocking' and the Germans, 'the ones we can feel good about hating.' Anyone who does not join in with this bullying becomes a threat and therefore a class traitor for this group. It is classic dissociation and projection on a very primitive scale and highly visible to the psychological eye.

The splitting operates just as well within the Coalition as anywhere else, and the degree of vitriol employed is a sure sign of a disowning process at work. So, just as Cameron earns the right to become the *Daily Mail*'s reliable son, Nick Clegg *must* become the dark brother. In fact, Clegg comes in not just for criticism but for rank hatred for daring to voice his contrary opinion over the euro veto, not joining in with the game of foreigner bashing. According to Heffer, Clegg is

> … a fully-subscribed euro-obsessive, unable to see any wrong in the misjudgements, corruptions of the EU blinded by a fanatical obsession with the EU.[14]

Heffer then proceeds to supply:

Ten good reasons why he [Clegg] likes Brussels so:
1. His Mother is Dutch, his father half-Russian
2. Apart from English he also speaks Dutch, French, German and Spanish.

I will spare readers the next seven; suffice it to say he continues in this vein of idiocy until his final devastating point number ten:

10. He was a ski-instructor in Austria during his gap year.

I can imagine some readers might have a John MacEnroe moment while reading this. Can it be serious? Is it 'only joking' again? It is almost impossible to know. Perhaps it is a bit of both. But one can hardly make fun of it or satirise it because it is so hysterical that it is difficult to imagine anyone taking it seriously. Yet, it is pieces such as this that enflame and motivate the electorate's choices, and are therefore extremely bad for democracy in the long run. At the heart of this irrational hatred of Clegg is something rather simple: he is far too intellectual, I suspect, for British tastes, and likes foreigners too much. He plays right into the tabloids' hands by having a Spanish wife and by suggesting that almost everything in Europe works better than in Britain. Those of use who visit Europe regularly know that, apart from traffic lights, paperwork and tea (which deserves boiling water), there is some mileage in this claim.

Tabloid nation

It may be better for one's overall mental health to roll over and adopt an only-joking attitude to the whole of the British press. What better to teach us this than the late Eighties' hugely popular, too close for comfort TV series, *Yes, Prime Minister*:

> Jim Hacker:
> Don't tell me about the press. I know exactly who reads the papers: the *Daily Mirror* is read by people who think they run the country; the *Guardian* is read by people who think they ought to run the country; the *Times* is read by people who actually do run the country; the *Daily Mail* is read by the wives of the people who run the country; the *Financial Times* is read by people who own the country; the *Morning Star* is read by people who think the country ought to be run by another country; and the *Daily Telegraph* is read by people who think it already is.
>
> Sir Humphrey:
> Prime Minister, what about the people who read the *Sun*?
>
> Bernard Woolley:
> *Sun* readers don't care who runs the country, as long as she's got big tits.[15]

How are we to understand this British tabloid phenomenon, with its particularly xenophobic and vitriolic character, that seems to be reasserting itself rather than diminishing? I don't think it is simply explainable by the 'island race, Britain-stood-alone' mentality of some Brits, though this represents a rich and acceptable seam. If it were not so extreme, it would be tempting to imagine that there are strong forces that wish to invoke the politics of black and white, of them and us, of

"You're either with us or against us." The British generally despised such attitudes when they came across the Atlantic with George W. Bush, but they are less easy to spot closer to home. Perhaps it is better to divide and rule in Europe by enflaming a hatred for Brussels rather than risk protesting about the status quo at home, or about our inability to do anything but support the financial system that brought the world to its knees. Certainly the rise of the fear-driven and fear-driving UK Independence Party in the spring of 2013 is a clear indication of this unconscious motivator. Perhaps there are similar forces that prefer not to have a Will Hutton too close to power.

Most Americans, especially those who understand that Britain and Europe are distinct but connected entities, are puzzled by the strength of this Europhobia too, thank goodness. Even President Obama felt it necessary to phone Cameron in January 2013 to caution him against a proposed speech about pulling away from Europe. Here is the ever sensible Michael Goldfarb, reporting on the Conservative party conference in early October 2011, weeks before Cameron's heralded advance into Europe:

> It is hard to explain just how ingrained hatred of the European Union is in the Conservative grassroots. The EU symbolizes all that is wicked in social democracy; it also symbolizes the resurgence of France and Germany, the two nations whose wars Britain was drawn into and bankrupted by (most Tories today were not alive for either World War, but no matter).[16]

From the perspective of the *New York Times'* Roger Cohen, who is well used to right wing politics and the home-grown lunacy of the Tea Party, and is no particular fan of Europe, Cameron's mission to Europe was equally incomprehensible:

> The British mistrust of what lies beyond the Channel has always been fathomless. There across the sea, on a suspect Continent, lay lands of constitutions, Napoleonic legal codes, defeated armies, imperfect freedom, rabies, wife-swapping and garlic. The Tory Euro-sceptic, the pinstripe effluence of an ex-imperial nation [...] wants less Europe not more. In his [...] heart beats the spirit of Britain's "finest hour" [...] holding out against the Luftwaffe. Only now the object of resistance is Germany's glum Frau Merkel. Since Cameron's "No," there's been much chatter about the return of Britain's "bulldog spirit."[17]

The German perspective, however, sees Britain as lost in the habits of the past. In an interview with the editors of *Der Spiegel*'s January 2013 history special, entitled *The British Empire 1600–1947: When England Ruled the World*, the renowned Frankfurt historian Peter Wende explained that the British Empire arose without any master plan, but rather from a chain of chance events. A crucial perspective for the British, he maintained, was that their overseas empire should cost them as little as possible, which seems fairly consistent, considering the current drastic cuts to the welfare state. That London still insists on a special role in Europe is because: "The idea still anchored in political consciousness is: 'we are a leading world power.'"[18]

Closer to home, Lord Ashdown, who in his time failed to achieve the highest office in the land but worked diligently for a peaceful Europe, seems to have given up all hope of his country's emergence from the bulldog trance. Ashdown begins his comment on the Cameron 'veto' with an historical perspective. He recalls Hugh Gaitskell, having just delivered his speech opposing Britain's joining Europe in 1962, remarking to his wife how many people were clapping. She replied: "Yes, dear, but it's the wrong people who are clapping." Ashdown seems to know how she was feeling:

> This weekend, it's the Eurosceptics who are clapping. Many British newspapers are clapping Mr Cameron for "standing up for Britain" – at last. French ones are clapping M Sarkozy for sticking it up "la perfide Albion" – at last. But those of us who believe our island's greatness has been about taking the risks of engagement rather than the false security of isolation, feel bereft, sad and depressed. Beneath the tragedy of last Thursday night, lies a deeper and more disturbing fact than Sarkozy's pique. Long years of anti-European prejudice from the Tory Eurosceptics, laced with downright insults from their supporting press, have now generated a growing anti-British prejudice in many European capitals, not just Paris.[19]

Ashdown supplies no explanation for this regressive move but is forthright in his condemnation and certain that it will backfire. He takes the press attitudes as read:

> This will have consequences not just for Britain's influence in Europe, but its standing in the world. A Britain with reduced clout

in the European Union is a Britain of less interest to the United States, China or any other important global power.

Andrew Rawnsley also despairs at the short-termism of Cameron's anti-European gesture:

> He may get a hero's welcome from some of the Tory Eurosceptics who are exulting in Britain's isolation and celebrating this as the most magnificent performance since Margaret Thatcher wielded the handbag. But that is likely to prove to be very short-lived. They forget that Mrs T never made the mistake of leaving an empty chair where Britain ought to be sitting. Once their initial euphoria has worn off, Tory sceptics will discover that this outcome does not advance their ambition to repatriate powers from Brussels – it has made it even harder to achieve.[20]

Roger Cohen, while he agrees with these sentiments, is commenting from just a little further outside the British box, in America. First, this means he takes a broader historical view, suggesting:

> Self-delusion is a lingering attribute of former imperial nations adjusting to a lesser reality.[21]

Secondly, he cannot fail to comment on the utterly surreal atmosphere of Cameron's tactics and the role of the tabloids:

> In fact, Cameron, playing the wrong chips without partners or preparation, was not so much opposed on grand principle as eyeing an opportunity to extract concessions for the very City of London financial institutions seen as the villains of the 2008 meltdown and its dire aftermath. That was politically inept – less the fighting spirit of the Normandy hedgerows than the self-regarding hypocrisy of the giant offshore hedge fund that Britain often resembles these days.

> Even without an election five months away, Nicolas Sarkozy, the French president, would have been tempted to avoid shaking Cameron's hand. With an election the snub for perfidious Albion was too good to pass up. Of course *The Sun*, the British tabloid whose dislike of Gauls is exceeded only by its disdain for Germans, shot back at Sarko: "Who do you think E.U. are?"

Born to rule, not to belong

The self-delusion that Cohen recognises as undermining our politics and relationship with the wider world is a highly significant feature here in Britain. I believe it is chiefly due to the prevalence of boarding school survivors at the helm of things for so long. For they are experts in the art of self-delusion and the repression of genuine feeling and, therefore, beginners at empathy, which is a fundamental quality for skilful politics. A Cameron, with his confrontational and brittle Strategic Survival Personality, cannot do what President Obama achieved in Russia in 2009, when to everyone's surprise he made friends with President Medvedev and gained much headway on a difficult disarmament treaty. His infectious relationship with the American enthused the Russian with reforming zeal, which must have worried his colleague, Prime Minister Putin.

Next, Obama faced a difficult meeting with Putin himself, the real power behind the throne, who was likely to be miffed by the American's influence over his president. Obama's strategy was to take the game to him by sincerely asking him to explain what had worked and what hadn't worked in recent Russian-American relations. Putin talked for an hour and Obama listened then asked to extend the meeting so that he could respond.[22] Whatever the outcome, this was statesmanship based on cultivating relationships.

Obama's strategy was the opposite of Cameron's in Brussels, which gave the impression that he was simply trying to bully his colleagues in order to excite his supporters, regardless of the widely accepted opinion that Britain lacks sufficient influence to follow through. Back home, confronted by the reaction from outside the Eurosceptic circle, Cameron became defensive, maintaining that "Britain will still have influence in Europe." He was unable to say Britain will "be part of," "belong to," "be contained within," or "work together with." An Obama could have said and meant such things, but these phrases have far too much 'belonging' in them for an ex-boarder to even utter them.

I am not surprised: countless ex-boarders have told me about their difficulties in belonging. Belonging is not part of the Strategic Survival Personality's agenda; to him it smacks too much of being still attached to his mother's apron strings. And then there is what might happen if he joined a new group. As an ex-boarder motivated to recover, it took me years to get the courage to join a tennis club, for example. For boarding school survivors have had perforce to become autonomous at the expense of their belonging needs. Those who are Compliers, who have not even begun to examine themselves, do not even realise that they can't *do* belonging. Phrases implying belonging are too associated with femininity, too claustrophobic, with too few escape routes.

Perhaps an ex-boarder PM's unconscious deep fear and horror of the feminine prevents such concepts from seeming feasible. Obama, on the other hand, credits his mother as his foremost teacher.[23] Instead of belonging, the public school and Oxford way is a compensation via *entitlement*. The Entitlement Illusion is to celebrate and triumph British leadership, regularly repeating the cliché that Britain's role is to influence and lead in Europe – more self-delusion, a hyper-conservative refusal to admit that times have changed. Or more simply, to re-quote Roger Cohen from above: "the lingering attribute of former imperial nations adjusting to a lesser reality."

Yet, to make communal politics work, a sense of belonging is a first and necessary step. It's common sense: if you want to become a leader you have to belong to the gang first. Next you have to prove your capacity for leadership. But we can never lead if we are not prepared first to belong, and all Europeans know that. It is something that people regularly rub in my face, as an Englishman in l'Europe, where the other non-Eurozone distinctions of European membership are no longer discussed.

I am not qualified to judge the arguments concerning a single currency – readers will remember that my Oxford tutor said: "Mr. Duffell, you know nothing about economics" – but in my heart, I feel that the idea of union is important, after the ghastly slaughter of young men during the 21st century. I am certain, however, that with the likes of Cameron – let alone the likes of John Redwood – at the helm of British leadership we are *incapable* of joining, let alone leading. Furthermore, the other glaring problem is that the British lead in hardly anything these days, with the exception of gardening, binge-drinking and unhappy children – witness the 2007 Unicef report.[24] Perhaps we might add to that list, general conservativeness. Our world ranking in terms of representation of women in parliament, for example, is number 52 – equal to Uzbekistan, the Czech Republic and Eritrea.[25]

Conservative Britain

The UK is at heart conservative (small c), even if some say it is insufficiently conservative about what needs preserving and too afraid to change that which needs changing. Conservatism, in its pragmatism and mistrust of extremes, has value, and where it involves stewardship and the questioning of change for change's sake, it may be desirable. But where it seeks to conserve self-interest or to return to policies that were anachronistic, divisive or unethical when they fell out of favour, it becomes dangerous. It is socially dangerous because, without sound leadership and resistance to knee-jerk survivalist fears, conservatism can get hijacked by inflammatory rhetoric, as Europe witnessed to huge cost in the Thirties.

Psychologically, conservatism is risky because of blindness to larger contexts, such as global belonging issues, while being satisfied with the most primitive defences of splitting and projecting. In this, it fosters the conceptual reality dominated by left-hemisphere brain activity at the expense of that of the right hemisphere, which sees the larger picture and the web of relationships, as is clearly described by Iain McGilchrist in his ground-breaking analysis, *The Master and his Emissary: the Divided Brain and the Making of the Western World*.[26] I shall return to this point in depth in the fourth part. In the meantime, let us hear from Will Hutton again:

> The Tories are one of the world's most enduring political parties. But this long life is built on its cultural attractiveness to parts of the English middle class, especially in the home counties, rather than on its political judgments, which have, over the centuries, been almost continuously wrong, especially in foreign policy. It was wrong to resist revolutions in France and the US; wrong to go slow over abolishing the slave trade; wrong to champion the Corn Laws; wrong to embrace appeasement in the 1930s; wrong to contest the decolonisation of India. The British right's instincts – jingoistic, imperialistic, anti-progressive and isolationist – have consistently led this country into calamities. [27]

Does anything underpin Hutton's perception that British conservatism has consistently bad judgement? I think so. Here is one psychohistorical view, building on the hypotheses so far put forward.

British society is extraordinarily free, but the price is internal self-policing and class conflict. It is rooted in a more complex problem within its elite concerning the most basic psychological issues: the internal regulation of emotions. On the one hand, I see a disproportionate and chronic reaction to the most primitive emotion of all – fear. Britain's hyper-conservatism arises directly from an attitude of fear and loathing – towards children, vulnerability, foreigners, women, intellectuals. This attitude is due to the dissociation and failure to integrate all of those elements into the mainstream identity over two centuries, despite our other successes, including comparatively good race relations in the capital. The normalised repression of feelings means, as I shall show in Chapters 11 and 12, in which I review new evidence from neuroscience, that areas of the brain become starved of emotional information and impeded in the decision-making process.

This mindset reinforces the habit of residential education for children even as it arises from it. Historically, over a very short time, the boarding/bullying entitlement ethos won social prominence at the expense of many other sensible and sensitive realities. Politically, no real opposition to the consensus reality in the UK exists because there is hardly any established tradition of liberal intellectualism as there is in Europe – at least since the days of Wilfred Owen, long gone. Perhaps Michael Foot was the last wisp of Fabianism in the Commons, a tender and timid shoot thereof, anyhow. The current brand of political opposition, to whom the public are most exposed, are mostly right of centre with few philosophical leanings towards notions of holism. This amounts to a one-way street towards the regressive attitudes of tribalism.

Will Hutton now stops pulling any punches as he reaches his inevitable conclusion:

> For him [Cameron], politics is not about statecraft in the pursuit of a national vision that embraces all the British. It is an enjoyable game to be played for a few years, in which the task is to get his set in and look after them and hand the baton on to the next chap who will do the same. The over-riding preoccupation was to manage his tribe, now in thrall to the worst of ancient Tory instincts that have been so consistently wrong.[28]

A view from the High Road

The one place in Britain where politics is really on the edge, where identity and leadership is being reviewed in a creative way, is just across the border. Here is a land where there exist more than five million semi-foreigners, 89% of whom were described in the 2011 census as Scottish. They now have a fine new Assembly building and a majority nationalist party. Where once it was a gesture of wishful disdain, Scotland is taking the idea of independence from the UK very seriously, and thinking of setting itself up as a kind of Scandinavian nation – Scotland's populations and weather are rather similar to some parts of Scandinavia.

As is the case with Europe, David Cameron, as an ex-boarder who has not had enough of belonging at home, again fails to understand what is going on and what such deep movements in community feeling might mean. For strangely enough – or predictably enough, once you have developed the psychological eyes to see with – the very same people who appear to fear and loathe foreigners are also fervently committed to the so-called 'traditions' of the Union. Here's Paddy Ashdown, again, wrestling with this problem:

> The Eurosceptics are now in control of the referendum agenda. And Mr Cameron has given them a much more powerful argument: if being in results in such isolation, then why not be out? Alex Salmond, too, has been given an un-covenanted gift. If England is to be out of Europe, why should Scotland not be in?[29]

Here we see the limits of British elite leadership: drowning in the Entitlement Illusion, they can only come up with fear-driven reactions to change, rather than hold a broad picture that encompasses history and the future. It has to do with the kind of wounded leadership that the British have come to take for granted and that is currently being challenged in Scotland.

I hinted earlier that I hold it as important that conservatism is not to be discounted *per se*, for that risks moving into the adversarial ground of party politics. A notion of leadership that 'conserves' is not to be roundly dismissed if it is demonstratively in service of some wider whole or more important truth, rather than simply the maintenance of the economic status quo or bogus tradition. In search of this, in my previous book, I began a meditation about the origins of the notion of the 'gentleman' and its function in leadership. I would like here to add a further step in that discussion because it has bearing, I believe, on the emergent nature of Scottish politics from the stagnation of Westminster. I begin with some remarks about the function of internal leadership from the perspective of depth psychology.

Many psychotherapists suggest that the psyche's leadership can come from one of two posited organisational centres, depending on its self-awareness and maturity: the *ego* or the *self*. Of course there is much debate as to the nature of these structural concepts, since neither yields to Cartesian measurement, and there are as many psychological schools as there are religious sects. In general, the ego is more like the state: it is understood as having responsibility for the survival and defence of the realm (or organism), and sometimes as the one who primarily wants things to be seen to be done. In ultra-protective mode, it is the creator of the *false self* (which includes our Strategic Survival Personality), as we have seen.

The self, by contrast, concerns itself with values beyond statehood, as it were. Recognising that survival has been achieved, is a more mature locus of intrapsychic governance that assesses choice, direction and values by which to live, often for the good of more than just the individual organism. Pushing the metaphor towards its limits, one might say that the self is concerned with what in current political terms would be called its 'legacy.' The shift from the earlier organising centre to the riper one is what Carl Jung meant by his idea of *individuation*.

Just as such movements can occur in an individual, psychohistory argues that they also take place in our collective, in human history, over time. The arising of the ideas of courtly love and chivalry in the early Middle Ages is possibly one of those times when the self took over from the ego. (It may be that it coincides with the right hemisphere conceptualisation coming into balance with the left, according to Ian McGilchrist's neuro-cultural analysis.) I see this as a shift in focus from the cult of the warrior – which had gone about as far as it could go – to a focus on power and will being put in service of the feminine principle of within life, and thereby of a greater whole. This purposive dimension is accessible within the deepest archetypes of masculinity to those who are interested in pursuing it.

One of these masculine archetypes is the *gentle-man*, as opposed to the out and out warrior. The gentle-man is one who *con-serves*, meaning 'serves together,' or rather, serves for the sake of the whole, as opposed to simply for himself. In *The Making of Them*, I traced the origin of the iconic English gentleman to the local squire, whose creation was an integral part of the territorial reward system of the Norman Conquest. I suggested that this might account for the historical basis of the Establishment's entitlement mentality. The situating of those French-speaking gents in their big houses, I suggested, has been the dominant feature of the English social and geographical landscape and is the basis of our social system and deep divisions, including the polarised classes and types of newspaper. Again, we may need to be slightly outside the box to see it: a German colleague tells me that he hates the English countryside because he can see only feudalism whenever he travels in it.

Over the years, as wealth spread, the status of gentleman became increasingly available to the rising middle classes. In the 18th century, what Noel Annan called the 'gospel of the gentleman' developed as an attainable ideal beyond the landed gentry.[30] As this ideal grew, it became increasingly suffused with ideals of sacrifice and loyalty to the evolving Empire. In the industrial age, the ideal invented the public schools to manufacture gentlemen to order. The result was impossible high standards that Annan called 'the insufferable ideal.'

And yet, despite all the rigidity and fear, which I have been at pains to explain, the ideal itself was still touched by strands of influence coming from an aspirational cult of service inherited from chivalry and courtly love, where there is a core 'conservatism' in the sense of self-dedication and responsible custodianship. Such motivation tends to evoke and be rooted in an individual leader's self or soul, rather than his ego. It is therefore part of an individuating and potentially generative process. In contrast, an *egoic* movement would tend instead towards defence or regression, as in the ex-boarder's Strategic Survival Personality, dedicated only to stasis and survival.

I imagine such an ideal of leaderships to be closer to the Celtic ideal of chieftainship than the Norman. The Celtic ideal may derive from yet another, earlier root, now only hinted at through myth and legend, as well as tales like those told by Tolkien, which still have enormous appeal to our unconscious. In this ideal, the leader saw himself (or herself, as in the case of Boudicca and Jeanne d'Arc) as *identified* with his or her people and the land. Such identification necessitates a profound responsibility to subjects. It is the source of a concept of leadership as a sacred duty, in return for the power and privilege held. Over the years, these notions have become blurred, lost, exploited, overridden in modern ideals of the nation state, forgotten in national politics. In a post-modern world they may sound archaic and naive. But it is just possible that some of them may currently be re-emerging in Scotland.

Whatever the outcome – and a move away from the Union will be highly complicated if it were to happen – the Scots are surely being reinvigorated in the independence debate. Stewart Maxwell represents the West of Scotland for the Scottish National Party and is Convener of the Scottish Parliament. In his Wikepedia entry, he is refreshingly pictured wearing a handsome blue *cagoule* – already very Scandinavian in his disdain for the dark suit demanded by London. In a revealing interview with Michael Goldfarb about the role of the Establishment north of the border, Maxwell goes straight and bluntly towards an historical leadership perspective:

> I think one of the differences comes from the history of the two countries, where, certainly in terms of being a leader in battle in the past, being a chieftain of a clan meant that you had to lead from the front. If you didn't lead your men into battle, then your own men would have killed you – they had no respect for you. In England there's a kind of history of leading from behind, where you sent your men into battle because you were a noble, you were a lord, you were someone who should just gain respect from your title and your birthright. So there must be a difference in the way the cultures have developed, and perhaps that still exists somewhere in the psyche.[31]

This is precisely the difference between the two psychological organising centres we have been discussing and it makes a huge difference to a people to have these differing archetypes in the psyche.

There are two other main areas, perhaps more prosaic, that make Scotland radically different from England. First, there is something noteworthy about the *indigenous* nature of Scotland. An indigenous culture rests on an emotional and cultural reality of a people belonging in their *soil*, in their *identification with place*. Despite having been overrun and annexed by their southern neighbours, Scotland retains a huge, live and authentic well of belonging, visible in the clan system, in the cultural traditions of music and poetry, in dress, in local legend and in landscape, all of which have a unifying function. Alastair McIntosh, political activist and academic, founder of the Centre for Human Ecology at the University of Strathclyde, calls this "ensoulment of people and place." In an introduction to an extraordinary compilation of interdisciplinary ideas that make up what he calls 'radical (i.e. to do with roots) human ecology,' McIntosh says:

> The ideas [...] are consistent with what I think of as 'the Scottish School of Human Ecology' as part of an implicit worldwide Indigenous School – one that takes its bearings from the perennial ensoulment of people and place. They arise from a grounding that is cultural in the lives of the people in my land who have either been born with, or have come through adoption to acquire, footholds in its bio-regionally bounded communities of place. Some of these people are figures of international repute; others are little known firth of [beyond] their native soil. What melds them into the semi-homogenous compost of a worldview that I would see as Human Ecology of the Scottish School is the essential relationship between people and their place, their ecology: the experience of being and/or becoming what the Isle of Lewis poet Iain Crichton Smith described as "real people in a real place."[32]

This grounded reality principle is very much in evidence in the Scottish question. It can lead toward a politics that takes its cue from the community and the land and results in a pragmatic set of desires and aspirations differentiated from the English entitlement mentality. There is a clear direction, according to McIntosh, who quotes Patrick Geddes' saying: our place is to "act local – think global." Although this maxim may already be a bit out of date as the time for global action bears down upon us, Stewart Maxwell would probably concur with it. Pressed by Goldfarb on whether the Scots envy the establishment clique, Maxwell continues pragmatically, insisting that the Scots only "want it to be fair," that there should be good schools, and so on:

> In Scotland there's a kind of disrespect of the establishment, whereas in England, I think, there's an admiration of it. There's a very aspirant middle class who are desperate to be part of it, who

want to send their children to private schools, whereas in Scotland there are some people like that, but it's not the norm here.

How this plain speech contrasts with the bombastic rhetoric of Unionist Conservatism, in which history is selectively used to downgrade the appeal of independence! At the same time, it tends to pass over the darker facts of the annexation of Scotland enforced by English brutality, the divide and rule strategies involving still remembered inter-clan betrayals, the employment of Lowlanders to break the spirit of the Northern Irish, the degrading of the dignity of the lairds through their effeminising presence at the London court, and the resulting enclosures and abandonment of the peasantry.

In case the reader should imagine that the bullying of the Scots only happened in the past, here is how the UK Prime Minister, during Prime Minister's Questions on 11 January 2012, displayed his exasperation that Scotland's First Minister wanted to announce the date of the referendum in his own time:

Its not a referendum it's a neverendum![33]

Such an 'only-joking' attempt to humiliate Alex Salmond is expected in Britain; it is certain to rouse the tabloids to bellow something like "PM lambasts Scotland!" But, in reality, it is rhetoric from a Never-Never Land mindset, from Peter Pan's country of immature desperation. A wounded leader like Cameron cannot rise to say something like: "I understand your important aspirations, Scotland, but I do not want to lose you because I care about you." No, he can only muster a false assumption of hollow authority coming from an inner parent figure trying to silence an imagined Foolish Child.

This tone is one of patent immaturity. It just won't do in the world of grown-ups; it wouldn't wash in a business meeting in the corporate world. It does not approach statecraft. It is not fitting to the seriousness of the subject. But in the grip of the Entitlement Illusion, we normalise such regressive bullying as politics as usual.

Can readers imagine Obama talking about a 'neverendum' or making a similarly childishly aggressive remark?

"No way, José," you might want to say.

CHAPTER 7

Relationships, Sex and the Prince's Tale

Political empathy ~ Puberty in the dorm
Growing up with sex in the dark ~ Puberty needs to be 'mirrored'
Adolescents for life ~ The Prince of Errors and the Game of One
She who must be obeyed

Political empathy

David Cameron's difficulties in Europe show up something fundamental about the value of relationships in politics. Really successful leadership always entails the management of differing and often complex relationships. For this reason, a good leader has to understand the value of relationships in general and have developed a minimum of skill in the art of relating. This is taken for granted in Europe, where Cameron's deficiencies therein were revealed. The wariness of his colleagues exceed their usual suspicion of Britain's commitment to the European project, rooted in a communal ambition never to repeat the mistakes that led to centuries of continental warfare. Those highly experienced political observers I quoted in Chapter 6 seem to agree that Cameron's actions were politically reprehensible because they ignored these deep European motives in favour of playing the bully for short-term aims of satisfying his domestic right wing.

There is, however, a further way of looking at these facts: as a practitioner of depth psychology specialising in boarding school survivors, I see Cameron simply doing what he is capable of, expressing himself in ways familiar to him. In a clinical setting, a man faced with the difficulties that relationships present would not inspire condemnation; he would require compassion, lots of reparative re-parenting, some teaching about the nuances of relationships, and so on. But he is not in treatment, and I do not want my leaders to lack relationship abilities; I would prefer that we train them expressly in this skill and select those who are the best at it. Foreign affairs expressly require the careful cultivation of relationships, so I would be unlikely to want an old-Etonian to represent my relationships abroad. For that matter, neither would I want a would-be patrician, like Michael Gove, to be in charge of the welfare of children in state schools, unless I imagined the most important criterion to be saving money by attracting corporations into the education sector. Ex-boarder politicians may have a certain clout by projecting their confident selves, but they are highly unlikely to be good at relationships.

Should readers be surprised by the premise that boarding school survivors lack relating abilities? Don't the schools promise that living in a community is a way of developing interpersonal skills? We need to bear in mind that, in the love-free institutions where they reside, boarders have to learn one primary and indispensable skill before all others: survival. They have no choice but to learn to survive, and even if they appear confident and charming – as if they *seem* like they are relating – this may simply be part of an adopted charisma. However, relating is not something that can be bluffed indefinitely. Adult ex-boarders can be charming, witty and entertaining and talk extremely knowledgably; but as boarding school survivors they have been avoiding authentic relating like the plague since their schooldays. And there are many good reasons why this should be so: originally to get over the loss of their parents, then in case they were suspected of homosexuality, and evermore, in case their false selves should be seen through for what they are.

Many ex-boarders are attracted to the *idea* of intimate relationships and, consciously or unconsciously, have their hopes on being saved when they leave school by being reintegrated into the world of women, although 'woman' is frequently represented by a sex-goddess fantasy, like the charming fantasy scene in Lindsey Andersons's well-known film *If*, where the boarding school boys escape to a café in the town, whose pretty young attendant offers them delightfully playful sex. But the women with whom the ex-boarder attempts relationships in later life regularly – and exasperatingly – turn out to be *real* people. And real people have *needs*.

This is a very complicated situation for the boarding school survivor. First, it is bad news if he has decided, as part of his strategy to avoid being vulnerable, "I am *not* the one who has needs" because a crucial part of relating involves knowing that is okay to have needs and being ready to take those of other people into account. And, second, because another feature of the Entitlement Illusion kicks in here. The normalised experience of not being cared for, over many years in boarding school, coupled with the disowning of needs, means that the boarder (and therefore ex-boarder) may well develop an inner and unconscious entitlement that someone *ought* to be responsible for taking care of him, making it *their* business to discover and satisfy his needs. The illusion is that the ex-boarder is then frequently busy with an internal and largely fantasy relationship rather than a real one.

In the world we live in today, knowing how to relate to people as real people with real needs is not just defined to the domestic sphere: it is a *sine qua non* of high office. Andrew Rawnsley, *The Observer*'s Chief Political Commentator and Associate Editor, also seems to consider Cameron's difficulty in relating as crucial. Rawnsley suggests that it went pear-shaped in Brussels on 8 December 2011 because of:

> ... a personal failure by David Cameron: his complete lack of friends in Brussels starkly reveals that he has not nurtured vital relationships with other key actors. It is usual at such summits for leaders to be quite understanding of each other's needs to have 'wins' that they can take back home to please their parties and voters. During the very difficult negotiation of the Maastricht treaty, John Major extracted crucial concessions, including the opt-out from the single currency, for Britain because he had cultivated a relationship with Helmut Kohl. The then German chancellor persuaded other reluctant European leaders to agree by telling them: "John needs this."[1]

Will Hutton comes to a similar conclusion:

> David Cameron is the best and worst of upper-middle class, home counties England – decent enough but saturated with prejudices he has never cared to challenge. He understands his own party and its instincts, but beyond that his touch is uncertain and his capacity to empathise with others close to non-existent.[2]

These are not lone voices, nor those of men with particular axes to grind; they do not hail from some new-age subculture. Here is another. Even though he boarded himself, Jeremy John Durham Ashdown, Baron of Norton-sub-Hamdon, GCMG, KBE, PC, better known as Paddy Ashdown, comes of solid soldier stock and knows how to call a spade a spade:

> It wasn't because Mr Cameron's demands were immodest that we are here: they had been negotiated down within the coalition to very little indeed (and preceded by dozens of smoothing European calls from Nick Clegg). Almost nothing was unique for Britain except the right to have stronger regulation for the City.[3]

Even from such a background, and even if Cameron is technically his commanding officer these days, Ashdown, who was deeply instrumental in trying to rescue the tragic debacle in the former Yugoslavia in the Nineties, understands that establishing relationships in modern politics is more than crucial – it is the norm. He also knows that bullying your allies just won't do and that the French President's refusal to shake hands was not only due to petulance:

> Mr Cameron's 'asks' were rejected, not because they were too great – but because it was he who made them. No other British prime minister of recent years would have had difficulty getting this package through. This was Gallic pay-back time for all that unwise Cameron lecturing – and sometimes worse – from the sidelines these last months. I suspect that if he had asked for a cup of tea, Sarkozy would not have lost the opportunity to refuse it. Not a statesmanlike reaction from Sarkozy to be sure; but a human one.

There is something so fundamental here and so obvious that it seems beyond belief that Cameron & Co just don't – or won't – understand it. It can be very depressing to dwell on. A month after Cameron's euro veto, veteran feminist Germaine Greer was asked about the British attitude to European-style political relationships on the BBC's popular programme *Question Time*. Seeming to lose the wind in her sails, as if bored to death that we still hadn't got it, she wearily mustered only the briefest of replies:

Coalition politics is something the English are going to have to *learn*.[4]

Greer has been in Britain for long enough to know how bad its natives can be at relationships. Already in 1970 she was writing about the splits and ambiguities that run through our attitudes to sex, gender and relationships.[5] Doubtless she knows that this is another thing that the British learn from the top down, and that those educated at our elite schools are likely to be the most uneducated in these basic matters. So how would the public school elite of Britain learn how to relate at all, let alone understand the subtleties of give and take that have determined continental coalition politics for many years now? In this, once more, we have to go back to the basics – developmental ones.

To recap: up until now I have been considering how the British elite are raised and conditioned, and the pathology that results. My aim is to suggest that a nation might want a better start for those who go on to become their leaders. My compassion is self-interested, so that we eventually get leaders who are not defensive, not bullies, not afraid to belong, but who understand that empathy and relationships are important. In this context, public school boarding scores close to being the worst possible psychological start for the development of such qualities, as behind the times as imagining that the best leader would be the most accomplished fist-fighter or swordsman we can raise.

Puberty in the dorm

So far, we have seen how children left alone at an early age follow the impetus to survive and how their resulting survival personality inevitably turns into a brittle and hollow shell. We have observed how a boarder has to forgo his attachment needs, disown and project out undesirable vulnerable and dependent qualities, and make an over-reliance on his compensated false self, his Strategic Survival Personality. When we begin to consider relationships and sexuality, we have to change gear a little and think of children aged twelve and over and how they fare in the elite environment of a British boarding school.

With the arrival of puberty, everything changes for a child. By now the boarder may have become used to the separation, but at puberty children's needs are changing. At puberty children need more than just parents – they need *parenting*. And parenting means that parents have to *do* something; it is not enough for them just to be there. At puberty, the tasks for parents are more complicated than before, and more hands-on, and demand a level of reality. Virtual parenting does not work.

Precisely what is that children need their parents to do at this time?

• Parents need to be *setting realistic boundaries* as their children become more autonomous with lives that increasingly encompass both the outside world and home. Sometimes this means getting into arguments.

• They need to *engage fully with their children about life* and values, society and religion. Teenagers will not accept untruthful parenting. Sometimes this means engaging in arguments.

• But most of all – and this is vital and irreplaceable – parents have to *guide their teenage children in becoming sexual human beings*, for that is precisely what is happening to teenagers, inside their bodies, whether they like it or not and whether they are prepared for it or not.

The boarder has no parents available, either to argue with or to confide in. They are just not around, by definition. For sexual guidance, he has only an ever-present paranoia about sexual exploration with self or others, inherited from the 19th century, and the risible and delayed sex instruction usually known as the 'leavers' talk' – a ritual of mutual embarrassment that enlightens no one. In the place of living boundaries, when he reaches puberty the boarding child has the enormous edifice of the public school rule book, which, according to Alisdare Hickson, is chiefly designed to protect children from having mutual sexual contact. "For the last 150 years," he proposes,

> ... it has been the fear of homosexuality, more than any concerns about children's education or health, which has shaped the

experience of boarding school life. It initiated the move towards smaller, single-aged dormitories and changed the layout of beds, it brought about the introduction of phased going-to-bed times, it enhanced the importance of the housemaster in regulating leisure time activities, it gave rise to the night-time torch rounds, it affected the layout of pews in the school chapel, it was reflected in the regulations and taboos that grew up around friendships between boys of disparate ages, it swayed decisions concerning the content of the curriculum and the Sunday sermon, it spawned modifications to existing school uniforms, it was the raison d'etre of the cold shower and it dictated the acceptable bounds of art classes and dramatics societies.[6]

The absurdity and horror built into this system would never have produced grounded individuals. Rebelling against it was only logical, and adolescents are made for rebellion. Critic and jazzman George Melly, who died in 2007, colourfully failed to hide his feelings about this:

> ... wicked and potentially damaging form of institution which has indeed turned out many thousands of inhibited, reactionary, pathetic alumni during the last hundred and fifty years or so. What prevented total disaster was the boys' natural instinct to revolt. Sex, like smoking and drinking, was anathema to authority and therefore an excellent form of protest. To be surrounded only by one's sex at the height of puberty is to ensure homosexual activity.[7]

Melly, an early unashamed 'out' gay man, is not saying that boarding is a recipe for homosexually, but rather a route towards general sexual disaster. He retains, he says,

> ... a reinforced loathing for the cruelty and hypocrisy of the public schools in general and admiration for those boys who defied the status quo. I feel that while caning and whipping may well have worked for the benefit of certain severe ladies given to leaving their card in telephone boxes, few or none of those boys who turned out to be homosexual did so because of their sexual quarantine at school.

For the Victorian authorities, homosexuality, or even innocent exploration, was not the only problem; there was equal fear and horror that boys should be masturbating. It takes only the barest knowledge of adolescent boys to realise that stopping their bodies from this impulse would be like persuading water to run uphill. Their bodies could not be controlled, so the only avenue left, once the rules and the architecture were in place, was their minds – through the instilling of shame. In this endeavour, the public schools have been extremely successful, drawing on Victorian tradition and the great sexual problem at the heart of Christianity.

Hickson, does not tackle the issue of the boys' resulting relationship skills at all, staying simply with the issue of sexual expression. He based his account on the memoirs of those in positions of power in the 1990s, which implies that their memories came from a period between the Thirties and the Seventies. What a pity he did not extend his research into later years. He would have been surprised how relevant his remarks still were. Even Hickson seems to have fallen into a familiar trap, baited by the Boarding Schools Association, of thinking that the introduction of carpets, radiators, phones and a handful of girls into the boys' schools, will have changed anything substantial. Unfortunately, this is not the case. With surprise, he quotes what he calls:

> ... a grim and solemn prayer Christ's Hospital boys were still repeating nightly before bed in the late nineteenth century, "Preserve us, O merciful God, from all evil dreams, from all affrighting and distracting fancies, from the horror of the night, and the works of darkness," written by Henry Compton (Bishop of London 1675–1713).[8]

It may have surprised him to know that, a century later than his interviewee heard it, at a time when Hickson was no doubt busy with his own project, this very same prayer can be heard recited by prepubescent prep school boys in Colin Luke's film *The Making of Them*, shot in autumn 1993. I am confident that there are little eight-year-olds puzzling over the prayer's message this very evening.

Growing up with sex in the dark

One fact established over the past century of psychotherapy is that whenever sexuality is regarded as a problem rather than a part of life, then its problematic nature, perversely, becomes aggravated. This is because, paradoxically, ignorance tends always to create more ignorance, and repression creates over-excitement.

All physical contact – affection, hugs, cuddling and sex – is likely to be mixed up for those who boarded, sometimes with disastrous consequences, as we shall see later on. Going through adolescence in a single-sex institution is far from ideal, so some public schools have toyed with coeducation as an antidote to homosexuality and paedophilia or as a modernising move to enhance their customer reputation. Hickson quotes one headmaster of Harrow who acknowledges that the lack of contact with girls encouraged homosexuality, confessing that "the remedy for these evils will be in restoring life as far as possible, to its natural conditions."[9] This may be a good soundbite but it is clearly nonsense, for here we are immediately back to the same real problem: these conditions are not 'natural' in any way, shape or form. 'Natural conditions' would be children living in families with parents present, in normal environments with people of mixed ages and genders.

When parents are not on hand to provide guidance in puberty then the sexual parenting function is devolved to the peer group or the staff. Either way, this abrogation is problematic: the peer group is patently incapable of fulfilling a role of genuine guidance since it is composed of the uninitiated. The masters may ignore such *in loco parentis* responsibility. Worse, some may exploit a child by grooming and sexually abusing him, for, as Evelyn Waugh wrote in his unfinished auto-biography published just two years before his death:

Some liked little boys too little and some too much.[10]

There is ample opportunity for this, given the affection-starved condition of the children and the 24-hour institutionalised life. Waugh may have had a witty turn of phrase ('only joking') but the grim reality of such abuse has destroyed many lives. For an up-to-date account of grooming and abuse at boarding school, I recommend, for those readers who have the stomach for it, the 2008 documentary film *Chosen*, which comedian Billy Connolly, serious for once, recommends should be shown in every school in Britain.[11]

Despite the proliferation of sexual imagery and themes on the internet and in the media, the question of how parents can sexually guide their children in adolescence is one that still dogs us, particularly in Britain, where, according to a 2007 *Unicef* report, we have the least happy youngsters and the highest incidence of unwanted teenage pregnancy – to say nothing of the prevalence of child sexual abuse – in the developed world.[12] The problem is not by any means confined to boarding schools and is most visible at the other end of the economic spectrum, but Britain's top-down structure means that a connection cannot be ruled out. There is an unspoken but prevalent attitude here that adolescents no longer need parents and can be left to find their own way. It is easy to see how this attitude can be built on top of the normalised habit of sending the most privileged youngsters away from home for most of their childhood.

Puberty needs to be 'mirrored'

There is an entirely different attitude to adolescence in Holland, which is where my wife and I had to go to get the training we needed to work therapeutically with sexual and puberty issues. We went to Holland because the absence of focus on sexual and puberty issues in Britain is paralleled in the psychotherapy scene here. This lack of interest in puberty is quite remarkable, despite the fact that, anecdotally, many people view their adolescence as a time when everything was changing for them and they frequently felt out of control, alienated or unhappy. Unresolved adolescent issues regularly affect people's lives, even if unconscious early issues are traditionally more sought after in analysis.

This professional avoidance may have to do with the fact that while Freud's Oedipal theories never found much appeal here, both Object Relations and later Attachment Theory, which focus on mother-child issues in infancy, were British inventions and dealt with sexuality in a mainly symbolic way. Perhaps the renowned British embarrassment about sexuality meant that topics of earlier life were more wholesome, or perhaps it was that many influential British theorists were ex-boarders who did not want to stir up memories of those days.

Puberty, however, is anything but symbolic, signalling as it does the unavoidable announcement of procreative potential arriving in a child's body. The changes it brings in its wake are profound: the body grows with often alarming rapidity while it gets flooded with hormones and begins to secrete sexual fluids, menses and semen. For the first time, these fluids make their presence known by escaping from the bodies of the children and coming out into the world. Aroused by becoming newly visible and by new inner sensations, children become preoccupied about how they look, about their appeal to the other gender, about what their peer group are wearing, saying, thinking, listening to. All of these things are now uppermost in their minds, but at puberty, children need help from their parents in understanding, embodying and regulating them. Adults who fail to engage with them truthfully are immediately discounted; the way parents conduct their own intimate relationships is under constant scrutiny.

Sexual Grounding Therapy, evolved by Willem Poppeliers, whom my wife and I encountered in the Netherlands, provided an understanding of the nature of these needs and the way they can be met.[13] Space does not permit me to go into details here, and I have written elsewhere about parental guidance in adolescence.[14]

To curious parents I must say that I am both afraid and delighted to say that it is not about having a 'good talk' about the facts of life together. Briefly, in essence, boys and girls need to be *sexually mirrored*, to use Poppeliers's terminology. In other words, they need to have fed back to them that the changes in them have been recognised and approved of by their parents, who welcome their child's development into a becoming a sexual being.

In fact, puberty puts the parents somewhat on the spot, because how they behave is vitally important at this point. Opposite gender parents can help children build a good sense of self when they allow themselves to graciously notice and feed back that their child is becoming someone who has sexual attraction. Same gender parents do likewise when they embody non-stereotypic behaviour, showing that men can be emotionally sensitive and responsive and that women can be powerful and full of agency. By means of their authentic behaviour, the parents, cooperating together, have the power to show that intimate sexual relationships between the genders can be durable and satisfying, even if sometimes challenging.

These parental functions and acts are so powerful and so needed that, time after time, when my wife and I have made clinical demonstrations of them as part of professional training sessions, our mature students – particularly women ex-boarders – frequently experience powerful longings and emotions arising within them. This occurs while taking part, or even simply witnessing, all these years later, a role-play situation involving parents who respond properly to adolescent children concerning their emerging sexuality. For us, this is an indisputable indication of what boarding children have to forgo during adolescence. This kind of parenting and its lack has a huge effect on the adults that children become.

Adolescents for life

In the absence of sexual parenting we are mass-producing adults who have not learned how to regulate our sexuality and have not imbibed the values of relationship. Where such adults are at the pinnacle of our society, we are providing very poor role modelling to those who look up to them; this is often expressed individually in sexual problems. For boys, confusion about sexual orientation, internalised homophobia and shame are the results of missing a parental response to their development, and this can be worse at the hands of their peer group or unscrupulous staff, as we have seen. For girls, internalised misogyny can result. Preoccupations with right body shape, clothes and food make girls especially vulnerable anyway, while the claustrophobic and competitive atmosphere of crushes and friendships in boarding school can prove extremely stressful.[15]

N.B.
An important and not widely known issue is that children in puberty/adolescence need a *sexual response* from caring adults – and *not* to be involved in *sexual acts*.

This is why it can go so badly wrong when boarding staff exploit children who are in need of adults who can distinguish between these two crucial differences. An adolescent cannot distinguish between them, especially in the ignorant and overexcited hothouse conditions of an elite boarding school. This is how unparented children at puberty can get abused, just as younger children get abused in the terrible absence of parental presence. Child sexual abuse keeps its victims frozen in development, crippled with shame and full of unconscious rage.

At the time of writing, the Jimmy Savile case is inspiring many adults who were sexually abused as children to come forward and challenge the shame left with them by their abusers. In the cases I am involved with, the Crown Prosecution Service is now quite prepared to take retrospective action against boarding school masters who until now had gone undetected and protected in these institutions.

Adolescent sexuality needs to be supported, but, eventually, when the time is right, it needs to be outgrown. Boarding tends to keep development in an unfinished state, as we saw in Chapter 5. A lingering immaturity will affect the person sexually, emotionally and, of course, relationally. Ex-boarders' relationships, both in the private and public sphere, will be conditioned by this. Immature attitudes to sexuality are part of the whole hyper-rational cultural experience, however. Can the case be made that ex-boarding males are among the most backward in this area, when males in general are noted for an adolescent-style sexuality and lack of relationship skills, and when sexuality remains an ongoing issue for the whole world?

One entry on the highly democratic Amazon customer review facility, which enables anyone to have their say on any book, caught my eye, in this context. Entitled 'Now I know why I am so Weird', a review of my first book ended: "This book has the potential to scare you into realising who you are." Writing in 2007, the reader, from Cardiff, continued:

> I attended boarding school in England and my parents assured me it was a "privilege" and that a lot of sacrifices had been made to send me there. On reading this book I have realised why I do not form sustainable relationships, why I only cry if someone dies and why I am so critical of emotional actions. After reading this book I now know I owe a huge apology to all those former girlfriends and friends that I have treated like objects rather than people.[16]

It is an enormous breakthrough and a source of profound and potentially healing grief when someone realises just what British boarding school training has done to influence his relational behaviour towards those who have tried to love him and how he has remained stuck in a sexually adolescent state without knowing it.

The Prince of Errors and the Game of One

Living strategically, not being able to trust or be trusted and playing what, after John Le Carré, I call a 'Game of One' – in other words, being in a relationship as if it were a solo pursuit – are like trying to murder an intimate relationship. If a breakthrough like the one quoted above never happens, it can mean that a partner's love may be wasted in a fruitless pursuit. When relentless regular bullying, unnoticed by the outside world, is coupled with needing a partner for form's sake rather than for love, it may mean great unhappiness, even someone's complete destruction. The prognosis is grim and often tragic.

I have come across many such unhappy cases, and the British upper classes can be amongst the most cruel when it comes to the intimate life. I cannot, of course, share any case histories of those who have confided in me, but I can point to one well-known case and allow the reader to revisit it with different eyes. For an example of this in tragic proportions, let us turn to the most famous boarding school survivor in the land, whose love story became national history. I do not mean a prime minister, but the unfortunate Prince of Wales and the story of his disastrous threesome. The third partner, whose influence led this story towards catastrophe, was not, as one might expect, the other woman but, according to academic feminist Bea Campbell's magnificent speed-written account of Princess Di's downfall, it was Charles' great uncle Lord Mountbatten.[17]

Descended from the Prussian warrior caste of Battenberg (note the subtly anglicised change of name), Mountbatten was an ex-boarder and a very complex man. Military Man personified (in his case it was the Navy: he was First Lord of the Admiralty), he made it his duty to ensure that both Princes Philip and Charles joined too. Ironically, Mountbatten died in his own boat, blown up by an IRA bomb at the beginning of the Thatcher era. His role in this story is that the young Prince Charles looked to him as his mentor, to compensate for his distant parents. This excited and engaged the older man who only had daughters from his own unhappy and faithless marriage.

According to Sarah Bradford, author of *Elizabeth*, by the time the prince was twenty, Mountbatten had become Charles' refuge from his father's incessant bullying and his mother's coolness and became "his confidant and greatest single influence on his life."[18]

Mountbatten's life goals were the exorcism of his shame about his German origins and exaltation of the monarchy, which had also undergone a de-Teutonising makeover when its family name was changed to Windsor. The royal household had been reinvented in 1969 by means of a television documentary, *Royal Family*, which presented an ordinary family doing an extraordinary job. It was at Mountbatten's side that Charles seems to have received his only instruction in matters of women, relationship and sex; this was to prove catastrophic. Jonathan Dimbleby, a well-known royal-watcher and friend of the prince, recounts that by the time he was twenty-five, Charles was being urged by Mountbatten to "get on with sowing some wild oats." With classic understatement, Dimbleby puts his finger on the point:

> Mountbatten combined a traditional view of women with a worldly attitude to sex, but from the perspective of a later generation, Mountbatten's advice on matters of the heart may seem trapped in values of another age.[19]

It is doubtful whether his heart ever came into it, for by all accounts Mountbatten was a wily strategist, firmly rooted in his head and sympathetic to secretly indulging the male weakness in the loins. From most accounts of his character, we may imagine that the heart, that bridge and guide to real relationship, was firmly shut tight in him; he seems to have had no advice for Charles about how to keep his own heart open. Instead, the old man – who had a reputation amongst his colleagues as an obsessive (though often careless) and grandiose organiser, whose membership of the Establishment masked mistakes and a penchant for self-promotion – counselled the younger man to play the field and learn the arts of seduction, even when Charles was neither attracted by nor gifted in such a lifestyle.

Dimbleby was right to point out that Mountbatten's sexual attitudes looked backwards in time. In the Edwardian upper-middle-class English world, there was no shortage of men who idealised women or treated them badly, or a mixture of the two – Bertie Prince of Wales was a famous example. J.M. Barrie and C.S. Lewis are prime examples from the literary world. If unchecked, and not brought into consciousness and recognised as part of survival behaviour, this habit – a possible outcome of the classic ex-boarder's immature and entitled attitude to women – results in a destructive, if normalised, misogyny. As the novelist William Boyd said in a recent interview:

> Sex and power are the two elements in at boarding school life that really corrupt even to the extent that they can make people evil.[20]

As if it were one of Boyd's plot-twisting novels, the tragic element of such a legacy in the prince and princess's story was to take another turn. When it seemed that Charles should be picking himself a bride, Mountbatten's counsel became even more important. Campbell is convinced that Diana's downfall was specifically due to Mountbatten's counsel on women.[21] This was that Charles should take pains to keep what the elder man called the "two sides of womanhood" apart. In practice this meant one woman for marriage, the official outward-looking face, and another for sex, pleasure and possibly even as confidante.

This is classic military compartmentalised thinking, classic ex-boarder's left-brain in charge, classic splitting. When the subject of sex comes up, the unexamined Strategic Survival Personality is able to exile love, empathy and relationship to an internal foreign continent. If it were not so tragic it could almost be funny, along the lines of a *Rawlinson's End* comedy: "There's milady wife and then... here are the daughters of Satan..."[22]

Biographer Anthony Holden suggests that Charles initially resisted, for he did not want "like so many Princes of Wales before him, to watch a marriage of convenience slide into one of arrangement."[23] But as a young man under the heady influence of his great-uncle Mountbatten and his father Philip, famous in Europe (but, oddly, not in Britain) for rumoured extramarital affairs, Campbell suggests that the prince began

> ... to live the parallel life urged upon him by the royal community, which ultimately ruined his reputation.[24]

Then, in 1980, around the time of Mountbatten's funeral and not long after he had been refused by his granddaughter, Amanda Knatchbull, Charles fell for Diana at a barbecue. As Andrew Morton recounts in his celebrated biography of Diana, he seemed sad, and Diana empathised. Apparently, she uttered what to the lonely prince must have been a fatally attractive phrase: "You need someone to look after you."[25]

It is not hard to imagine that these must have been the words Charles had been longing to hear all his life. As for being looked after, the young prince had experienced what little looking after he got from his nanny, rather than his mother. Queen Elizabeth, mother and figurehead of the nation, is said to have watched without touching, while Nanny bathed him. So his inner child will have made an instant attachment to a woman whom seemed spontaneously to offer genuine care. Charles would have been hooked.

The prince had attended his father's former schools, including Gordonstoun, famous even amongst boarders for its Spartan, outward-bound ethos, cold-water regime and fear of sexuality – "Colditz in kilts," as Charles himself put it.[26] So a powerful physical hunger for love would be quite understandable.

It was into this background that Mountbatten had poured his sexual counselling. Dimbleby, Charles' chosen biographer, suggests that:

> Without any apparent surge in feeling, he began to think seriously of her as a potential bride.[27]

But Diana's account is somewhat different. What came next was probably the first of many shocks for the young woman, as the prince's inner child, now in the guise of the eternal adolescent – a familiar one in many adult ex-boarders – decided this was the moment to make his move. Here, from Morton's accont, is what Diana says she experienced:

> The next moment he leaped on me practically, and I thought this was very strange, too, and I wasn't sure how to cope with all this.[28]

Charles was making a classic boarding school survivor's mistake: the confusion of unfulfilled childhood attachment issues with sex and the wish to have an adult intimate partner. Like many young men from cold upper class families, Charles, whose personal story counts him among the extreme cases, had not experienced sufficient love and care from a mother to whom he could make a warm and stable attachment. His inner child was quite rightly full of craving for these things. As a boarder at Gordonstoun, he will have drawn a complete blank in attachment, parenting, sexual guidance and sexual mirroring.

Charles received no help with identifying this problem, and the young adult he had become would not have been able to articulate it consciously. Happily, he did have another mentor, Laurens Van der Post, who introduced him to a value-based psychology. But the South African's brand of mystical Jungianism would have been of little application at that time and most unlikely to either alert Charles to his lack of attachments or to afford any realistic idea of sexuality.[29]

Ideally, attachment should lead in time to an ability to love over and beyond the need to attach. It should provide a foundation to an active loving that is more than an unconscious, limpet-like possession of the other, so that the other can become a person held in empathic warmth. This is the true basis for intimacy: loving the other so that intimate exchange between equals can take place. If attachments have not been made then intimate loving is a great difficulty.

This is the hole, I imagine, that without warning, Diana fell into and tried tragically to get out of. By now, readers may have guessed that I have been using the story of the prince and princess as an allegory to learn from, as all stories of princes and princesses were ever meant to be used. It ended very badly in a tunnel in Paris, but the story for us in Britain is still far from closed because the lessons have still not been learned. Campbell is confident that Mountbatten was causal in the unfolding of this sexual disaster. I would add that the responsibility goes wider: the neglectful vacuum of parenting available to the young prince drew in such a false friend, and was later to pull him and his bride into hell.

She who must be obeyed

By reputation, public schools tend to produce homosexuals or misogynists, or at least cold lovers – but is this true? In the absence of having made good attachments, males are known to overcompensate through sex, to over-use sex for bonding and gratification rather than as intimate exchange. The boarding system has an added inbuilt and serious problem with females: they are utterly absent, except in a service role. As compensation, boarders readily make women, already becoming unfamiliar, into fantasy figures, whether goddesses or servants. Their absence is the greatest possible stimulus for fantasising, behind which there may lurk an unrecognised fear that women will always let them down. Le Carré, eloquently describes how a boarder may lose his trust in love along with the loss of his mother:

> Her demise entrenched him as a self-reliant person, confirming in him his knowledge that women were fickle and liable to sudden disappearances.[30]

Unrealistic ideas of women are to be expected, given their scarcity and the enforced Spartan manliness of the schools. Longings for rescue and comfort become mixed with those unaccountable stirrings in the loins. The official line that traditionally makes sex dirty and to be feared is mixed with the peer group attitude that it is a passport to heaven. This concoction has the combined effect of ensuring that boarders emerge without the slightest realistic idea of what a real woman might be. As mother goddesses they will inevitably disappoint, for marriage (or intimate relationship) actually means that you have to learn to get on with a real person, a real live woman, with her own feelings, wishes, moods and limitations, and who may not be entirely focused on serving you. As erotic tramps or eternally ready sex objects, the other favourite male fantasy, women will also disappoint, for exactly the same reason. The result is the same: a totally unrealistic notion of femininity, with women on pedestals or to be avoided at all costs.

Some ex-boarders resolve this problem by bypassing women for sex altogether. According to Cambridge researcher Professor Ronald Hyam, this tradition was established in the heyday of the Empire, when the white women were miles away, young, poor servants were everywhere, and very few complained.[31] Like being back at boarding school? When the *memsahibs* started to arrive *en masse* in India and Africa in the late 19th century, their prudish conservatism meant, according to Hyam, that their men retreated to an even remoter secrecy. Prostitution and pederasty began to boom as the ubiquitous shadow enterprise of the Raj. The Imperial trade routes, says Hyam, became the first global sex-business network, remaining until recently shrouded in secrecy – the untold story of the Empire. This was the world Mountbatten grew up in and in which he got his own sexual education, the world that he passed on, unadulterated, to the future king in the late 1970s.

Hyam's remarkable book *Empire and Sexuality* is hair-raising for those brought up on the literature of Kipling and Conan Doyle, with their images of fastidious chastity and brisk walks on the moor when tensions mount. Hyam studiously pored over British Imperial records to establish its sexual history. Cambridge wouldn't publish it, however, because, amongst other traumas, Hyam apparently scandalised his Alma Mater over revelations about the promiscuous conduct of its 17th century fellow Samuel Pepys, beloved historian and another Lord of the Admiralty. It is indispensable reading for anyone interested in this little known branch of colonial history and the sexual inheritance that still affects our nation – especially, I have to say, our poorly sexually-educated elite. The result of public school and Imperial attitudes to sex contributes unavoidably to a hard-to-acknowledge hallmark of British society: full-blown but unconscious misogyny.

This leads to countless unnameable horrors in relationships. Domestically, it means that even despite the challenges of intimacy that anyone has to face, marriage for or with an ex-boarder is inevitably going to be difficult. Unconscious misogyny will affect sexual 'performance' along with relational availability and is likely to erupt symptomatically in excessive irritability.[32] Socially and politically, misogyny in its softest normalised form results in an overvaluation of masculinity, an over-respect for the opinions of men higher up the hierarchy and the regarding of women as, at best, a necessary diversion. It is hardly surprising, therefore, that women in a Parliament that is clearly modelled on a boarding school tend to be an uncertain few – or a particular, hardened kind. For this unconscious misogyny is not just a male ex-boarder problem; it affects the women around them and, worse: it also takes root inside women themselves, not only, but especially women ex-boarders.

The implications are that there are generations of women growing up not rooted in a positive femininity. As mothers, they raise girls who do not have good femininity mirrored back to them and raise boys who look down on women. The boys learn to respect *only* the opinions of other men, but are dependent women for sex, and therefore secretly hate them for this dependence. In consequence, British middle-class women, I suggest, have been forced to grow up with and identify with a femininity whose true nature is ignored or despised and disowned. This is an incalculable problem for a society, and one that would horrify much of the indigenous world, where pride in female wisdom and traditions tends to be a corner stone of the community.

No wonder women ex-boarders suffer so much – sometimes I think more than the men; they have been forced through a mould designed on extreme male lines. And perhaps no wonder so many women were complicit in giving up their children to the fashion and demands of their epoch. The de-feminisation of women is rather unique in Britain and produces the kind of family in which natural instincts are gone against. It readily colludes with the banishing of children, femininity and the indigenous. I shall say more about this in the next chapter.

The only other route into sexuality for the British elite would be avoidance and repression. This has fostered trans-generational ignorance and shyness, and hence the repressed protagonists – across a very wide spectrum – from the classic Middle England movie *Brief Encounters* and the shocked judges in the *Lady Chatterley* obscenity case in 1963, to the *Carry On* films and Benny Hill. The reader may be wondering how this legacy sits with today's 'cappuccino classes,' the rampant working-class sexuality on display in any town centre at weekends and the highest rates of teenage pregnancies in Europe. The answer is that, sexually, we are a society that is at a complete loss about how to bring up our young and, like everything in Britain, it spreads from the top down.

But once the damage is done, the route for an individual ex-boarder, in my professional and personal experience, is in learning to love. I hope that this is what Prince Charles is doing now. Ultimately, we could say that the boarding school survivor's major issue is not sexual: the problem consists of wounded love. Boarding children suffer a surprising and normalised withdrawal of love. The adult problem consequently becomes: can they love, and can they let love in? Can they open the doors of their inner fortresses, designed to keep them safe in the absence of love, when love may be coming their way? Mostly, they mistrust love, and if love is indeed the greatest force on earth then this becomes the greatest crime.[33]

The application of this is relational, which means it affects relationships across the entire spectrum. The challenge is whether the elite ex-boarders can begin another education. Can they learn to love? Can they let the other love them, can they let another matter to them? Can they put their need for gratification aside and be capable of empathic loving? These are steps to maturity. There is no need to fear being seen as a victim, or staying as one, if these difficulties are recognised. It doesn't have to go against the inbuilt fear of navel-gazing that is still maintained by the conservative classes in the 21st century, for, as body-psychotherapist Stanley Keleman teaches, the potent position of the aware adult is not even to dwell on "how I was loved or not loved" but to reflect and act on "how I have difficulty in *loving*."[34]

ACT III

THE RATIONAL MAN PROJECT

The evolution and psychohistory
of British Elitism

One time we had a palaver with the 'laibon,' the old medicine man. When I asked him about his dreams, he answered with tears in his eyes:

"In the old days the *laibons* had dreams and knew whether there is war or sickness or whether rain comes and where the herds should be driven."

His grandfather, too, had still dreamed. But since the whites were in Africa, he said, no one had dreams any more. Dreams were no longer needed because now the English knew everything!

Carl G Jung, *Memories, Dreams, Reflections,* 1959

CHAPTER 8

Rational Man

A world afraid to turn upside down

One unseasonably hot and thundery autumn day in around 1850, an old woman's thoughts turned to the fateful events of more than half a century earlier.

"It was like this in the French revolution, I remember," she said.[1]

She remembered being a young woman in the 1790s, ironing her best muslin dress, when the news came of the beheading of the queen of France. She had put down the iron and stood utterly still at the hearing of this momentous event; she could still call up the exact pattern of the muslin in her mind's eye.

The woman in question was the grandmother of Thomas Hardy, one of the greatest figures in English literature. Born the son of a poor builder in rural Dorset, so successful was Hardy in his lifetime that, five years before his death in 1928, he was able to entertain Edward Prince of Wales to lunch at his home, just a short walk away from his humble birthplace. His biographer, Claire Tomalin, related how Hardy remembered his grandmother in the old cottage, recalling the execution of Marie Antoinette in October 1793.

This anecdote reminds me of a psychological truth that is sometimes hard to take in. We are influenced by more of the past than we care to think about; the great historical movements of thought, feeling and action take their own time to be integrated. Even though we think we live in an isolated and momentary present, two hundred years or so of history is well within our psychic span. In the ever-present flow of news we tend to overlook the impact events have on individual human lives, but our deep responses and attitudes towards them can have trans-generational significance. As Doris Lessing says:

> Great public disasters that mark the psyches of a people, a country, live in people's nightmares but take time to come out into consciousness – we do not deal easily with horror.[2]

We may have forgotten an event, but our collective unconscious psyche may still be trying to integrate it. I suspect that the French Revolution, remembered by this Victorian countrywoman, instigated as much worldwide fear and consequences that were as far reaching as 9/11, the assassination of JFK, and Pearl Harbour put together.

We do not know whether Hardy's grandmother was reflecting on that unprecedented act of rebellion or sympathising with the young Queen's fate out of womanly empathy. Her own poverty-stricken estate was hardly comparable to the life of wealth and rumoured excesses of the beautiful Queen of France who came to symbolise the wanton extravagance of the 18th century monarchy. But Tomalin tells us that Hardy's mother made no secret of her disdain of the institution of marriage, so it is possible that his grandmother was appalled at what can happen to women tied to their husband's fortunes, and that his mother had inherited her beliefs. The political and the personal can be heavily intertwined, and things that are deeply shocking stay in the collective unconscious to form the attitudes of generations.

The French Revolution caused ripples of trauma that influenced the entire character of 19th century Britain in ways that are not to be underestimated. It laid the foundations of what would eventually become the hyper-conservatism of Victorian England, which in some ways still holds today. A current parallel would be the way in which post-9/11 trauma gripped the whole of the USA and became crystallised into a culture of fear, under the influence of which the country was readily persuaded to accept the blatant excesses of George W. Bush's neoconservative administration.

The widespread fear of the late 1790s and early 1800s was considerable and understandable. Britain had just unnecessarily lost America through ignorant and unnecessarily belligerent statesmanship and now, less than 250 miles from London, the French monarchy and upper classes were losing their heads. It was already clear that the entitled foundations of class-based society were not invulnerable but could be uprooted by foreign political vandalism. The catastrophic fantasy was that it would soon spread across the channel.

Even though the architects of the uprising in France were middle-class Enlightenment intellectuals and the Emperor himself was a minor noble, the son of a diplomat and lawyer, the overriding fear was that revolutionary poison would tear apart the still feudal landscape of Britain, which had come through her own Civil War intact. As it turned out – and luckily for the British elite – Napoleon Bonaparte's imperial aspirations worked as a conservative force. The legitimate fear of his geopolitical ambition covered the underlying terror of losing the established order, rallying the lower orders of society to a unified defence of the realm. It meant fifteen years of what today would be called world war, in which countless young men died for a cause they believed was legitimate – the halting of Napoleon's drive for a pan-European French Empire.

Revolution had been averted this side of the Channel, but the potential for revolt in Regency Britain had been real enough. America had broken away to become a new kind of country; France had broken the mould and become a danger to the whole of Europe. Stopping Bonaparte united other European states for the first time, however, and eventually changed the political map. For the time being, a huge and concerted military effort was required, and the casualty rate from these wars, fought as they were by armies that were heavily equipped with state-of-the art firepower, was enormous. Despite eventual victory for the allies, the Napoleonic wars nearly bankrupted Britain and resulted in many years of economic depression, unemployment and grinding poverty. The ancient Holy Roman Empire finally collapsed, sowing the seeds of nascent nationalism in Germany and Italy. Spain imploded and lost its hold over its colonies. Britain, however, eventually emerged as the leading power for the next century and a half. Unchallenged at sea, she also led the field in a development that was to change the entire planet. But she did not lose her fear of revolution.

In combination with her growing imperial might, another sort of revolution was to provide Britain with staggering wealth and a sense of world domination for many years to come. This was the real revolution, the Industrial Revolution, which was fast changing the face of Britain's geographical and social landscape. The unstoppable triumph of industrialisation eventually developed into a worship of progress that would irredeemably transform the planet. Opposition to this tsunami of change came principally from two sources: the Romantic movement of artists and poets, who saw that nature was in danger of being abused, and, at the other end of the social scale, the landed peasantry, who saw that their way of life and livelihood was in danger. Sporadically, pockets of the landed peasantry dared to protest the unemployment caused by the increasing use of the new force – machinery. The Establishment's fear, which had been whipped up by the French Revolution, meant that these legitimate protests were controlled with astounding severity. Here's Thomas Hardy in his seventies, recalling his father telling him about an incident he had witness in the troubled 1830s:

> He had seen four men hanged only for being with some others who set fire to a [hay] rick, one of them a half-starved boy who had run up to see the blaze and weighed so little that they had to puts weights on his feet to break his neck.[3]

The old order reinforced

Hardy was born into a world of profound change in which the older order was fighting for its life. The young writer took it upon himself to document the changes he saw happening, in the form of serialised novels – the nearest thing to television at that time. His descriptions of a countryside and way of life that were rapidly changing are incomparable in the history of literature. My favourite example, not mentioned by Clair Tomalin in her admirable biography, is a short story called *Absent-Mindedness In A Parish Choir*, in which Hardy tells how the local squire gets his way and abolishes the lively and colourful church string band, replacing them with a machine – a harmonium.[4] Hardy's father was a fiddle player, much in demand at celebrations, and his son learned a great deal from him. Hardy quotes from life, as he does in many of his stories, which are as near to documentary footage as we can get.

Hardy occupied the unusual position of being born to the labouring classes but dedicated to an occupation that required him to cross the barriers of class in order to achieve status and financial independence. As a man who dared to raise himself out of the class into which he was born, Hardy was in a unique position to *see* and *feel* the combined effect of rampant change and class entrenchment. The irony was that at the same time he was relentlessly pursuing his personal aim of reinventing himself as an English country gentleman, an immense task for one who was neither born to it nor educated at a public school. Hardy is not the only British writer to have taken a journey through the apparently impenetrable barriers of social division. Some years later, D.H. Lawrence occupied an analogous position, while George Orwell experimented in the opposite direction on his way "down and out." Hardy's personal life, despite his writing, was also a testament to the dominant Victorian hyper-conservatism of the age; all his stories end tragically, as did his own loves.

Hardy was aware that the forces of progress could not be arrested and that the landed peasantry were a spent force. Even the newly created industrial working classes seemed doomed. What Hardy was hinting at was that peasantry, who, along with the artisan classes, were losing their feudal position to become disposable tools of capitalism, were fast becoming what in psychological terms would be called *objects*. That is to say, they were starting to become more like things than persons, to be squeezed for their labour or, as 'poor things,' to have charity bestowed upon them.

We will shortly examine how this psychological process of *objectification* had previously been perfected overseas as the principle mechanism for the success of the colonial project, allowing, as it did, the rank exploitation of indigenous peoples. As objects rather than subjects, their lands would be ripe for the taking without troubling the conscience of Rational Man. Later, in the fourth part, we shall follow the latest summaries of neuroscientific research, to examine how the hyper-rational mindset operating within individuals stimulates unbalanced left hemispheric brain activity, which 'prefers' to focus on inanimate objects rather than living subjects. But at this point it is enough to consider that the excessive anxiety about social revolution meant that the British elite's terror of their own common people underpinned their contempt for and bullying of them.

This only increased the dominant sense of entitlement that remained consistent throughout the 19th century and into the next – underlying Winston Churchill's despatching of troops to break protesting Welsh miners in 1910, and beyond.

But as the 19th century progressed, the social order was anyway subject to a dynamic and unpredicted internal shift: the middle classes were unstoppably on the rise and their sons were needed in numbers to run the expanding Empire. To meet this demand, and to short-circuit the cumbersome process of evolving the right kind of men capable of imperial service, a new piece of social engineering was needed. Enter the new 'public' schools. Then, as now, the surest way to cross the social divide was to be educated at one of the public schools ('public' as they were open to all who could pay the fees), which were soon churning out the requisite young men in droves.

I use the phrase 'churned out' quite deliberately, for this was a quasi-industrial process using human factory lines, and the industrial metaphor is not a coincidence. When I first began my study of boarding, I was astonished to discover that by far the most common complaint I heard from ex-boarders about their schooling was not the separation, not the beatings, not the wretched food, but the feeling of being objects put through what several correspondents called a kind of 'sausage machine' turning out uniform products in terms of accent, opinions and codes of behaviour. Remarkably, the objectification process was now operating at the top of the ladder as well as the bottom.

As the century progressed, the public schools became increasingly central to the imperial dream. Their reform and expansion in the 1860s marked an epoch of unshakeable national determination and confidence, bolstered by the continued success of this unique educational process. Originally intended exclusively for the sons of the landed gentry, the expansion of the public schools in order to turn out batches of games-playing gentlemen to rule the Empire (and thereby the world) was the most curious, unique, successful and durable of Victorian inventions, the most dynamic piece of social engineering Britain had ever devised. It broadened out the elite base and recreated an expanded society, explicitly divided for the duration, poised to survive the waning influence of the aristocracy that was fast becoming a feature of modern Europe.

Now Britain had a newly expanded and confident elite, and it was this new gentry that counted rather than the working man. The rights of man had been discussed and fought over during the English Civil War; they had inspired the inception of a whole new nation – America – and had been argued over in the abolition debates. Now, these rights swung firmly over to the side of privilege and stayed well put. The sensuality of the 18th century was a thing of the past; the ancient indigenous ground of life that Shakespeare immortalised would soon become a folk memory. Not until the 1950s did Britain attempt briefly to revise this pattern, toying with the idea of social democracy. The ready-made public school educated gentleman was the gold standard of the re-established divided society. His place and replication still goes unquestioned today. He remains crucial to the continuing success of Britain's class-based society and resistance to fundamental change.

Running on fear and confidence

Neither the French Revolution nor the Industrial Revolution would have been possible without a previous revolution that had begun more than a hundred years earlier. This one was not political: it was a revolution of thought. The Enlightenment introduced a major new way of thinking about the world that favoured the rise and pre-eminence of rationality over experience, of concept over matter. In *The Making of Them*, I discussed how the world-view that privileged Reason (or rationality) over all other approaches to life inspired and created the conditions in which the public schools were conceived and made possible the standardised production of rational gentlemen. I suggested that this way of thinking still underlies the boarding schools' championing of independence and competition at the expense of feeling, relating and all forms of perceived dependence. I argued that this way of thinking is out of date and puts intolerable strain on individuals.

I now propose to take things further and examine how Victorian hyper-conservatism and its public school ethos – the former rather widespread but the latter unique to us and our colonies – have been supported by what I like to call the *Rational Man Project*. My thesis is that Britain is still singularly in its grip, and therefore stuck in an outdated past, and that the addiction to the public school educated elite is an addiction to an outworn Rational Man Project. Let me explain.

In 19th century Britain, rationality had a unique spin, I believe, and became identified with a specifically British way of dealing with the world because of two contradictory overarching psychological pulls, the historical significance of which I have just alluded to. First, there was an *internal contraction* due to fear of revolution and chaos; secondly, there was an *external expansion* of Empire, propelled by the dynamism of the age of industry and its unstoppable confidence and appetite for new resources and markets. This dynamism was fuelled by greed and resulted in grandiosity. These two contrary forces – fearful internal contraction and grandiose external expansion – gave British society its particular character.

Despite vastly different world situations, we are still trying to regulate and balance these deep unconscious emotional drivers, I suggest. In our current world, therefore, I think it still makes sense to argue that the fallout from the British Rational Man Project is still with us. It causes our society grave problems in the following way:

- It maintains the inherited class structure with its entitlement-rich male elitism intact and is still strangely confident, despite a changing world.
- It impedes the maturation of the British political scene because of its outdated and self-referring character.
- It prevents the emerging new paradigm of thinking globally from finding fallow ground among our leaders – particularly the notion of thinking about the world as a communal issue – due to fear of foreigners and fear of losing the status quo.
- It continues to support the fee-paying, hyper-rational, love-free institutionalisation of the elite's children.
- We do not notice the Rational Man Project's grip on us because we are too close to it, like the fish who do not know the water; identified with it, we believe it to be our hallowed tradition.

To appreciate the extent of this problem, we must continue the story of its origin and heyday. Specifically, we must consider how 'Rational Man' – the generic specimen of the Rational Man Project – functioned internally. To that end, we must examine how Enlightenment thinking developed in the British case.

The foundations of the extraordinary expansive movements of the Enlightenment were dug by great pioneers, such as Galileo and Copernicus, at the end of the Middle Ages. The Renaissance had marvellously set Westerners free from the church's traditional stranglehold on thinking. It allowed European men to sally forth in boats and 'discover' the 'New World' and was the preparation, we can now say in hindsight, for the overturning of all previous conventions of thinking. Descartes and his colleagues created the next step towards mental freedom: the Enlightenment would change everything. With the new ability to be curious about the natural world as an objective phenomenon that could be measured and predicted, with laws that could be ascertained, natural science flowered and rational ingenuity blossomed. This revolution in curiosity built up a head of steam that boiled over into the invention of countless machines, devices, instruments and tools – the beginning of what today we would call 'technology'.

This technological and scientific revolution was the proud engine of the new god, Progress. Progress was to the Rational Man as reliable a divinity as Providence had been to the Puritans. Progress brought enormous wealth and fuelled the potential to analyse and classify the entire range of creation, hitherto considered the business only of God and his earthly representatives. According to this new logic, the non-European world was now destined to be fully harnessed, colonised and exploited (what today we would call 'developed') simply because it was there. In Britain, the visible benefits of this expansionism can clearly be seen. A short walk around the Clifton district of Bristol, with its oversized stone buildings, raised from the accrued wealth of colonies run by slavery, confirms the pragmatic advantages of the rational colonial project.

By the latter half of the 19th century, feasting on the wealth created by the biggest import-export business ever known, British grandiosity hardly knew any bounds. Now Darwin's theory of natural selection, rationalised as inbuilt competition, established the superiority of man – specifically white British man – according to the laws of nature. For, in his ability to cognitively map the world and dominate it, Rational Man's role as subjugator of existing indigenous populations was theoretically legitimised. This was masterfully achieved by means of a very convenient – but devious – logical process, which I shall explain. Once again, I will attempt this by analysing its psychological mechanisms.

The logic of Rational Man's Entitlement Illusion

Deprived, apparently, of the gift of abstract thought or the ability to form recognisable civilisations, the world's indigenous people and their lands were clearly there for the taking. In the eyes of Europeans, those faraway foreigners started to become more like things than persons. Symbolically, they stood for the direct opposite of the grand ideal – Rational Man – and thereby made him even more prestigious. By this inverse psychological principle, indigenous people fulfilled an inhuman role – mere objects – sometimes colourful, sometimes loathsome.

Rational Man, on the other hand, operated by measuring, classifying and compartmentalising the world. He was therefore identified with the *measurer*, not the measured. In order to keep his identity distinct and separate, he needed to employ various mental processes. The chief of these were *dissociation* and *compartmentalisation*, the same processes we observed when studying the psychodynamics of the *Strategic Survival Personality* in Chapter 4. From the mid-18th century onwards, we can observe dissociation operating on a massive, global scale. Dissociation became the unconscious driveshaft of the engine of colonialism. It becomes visible throughout the Rational Man Project the moment one develops the eyes to see it. In fact, it soon becomes evident that dissociation is the project's most prominent feature.

Rational Man's logic starts out fairly simply but soon becomes extremely complex. It runs as follows: the indigenous people encountered in the New World provided labour and servant material in abundance but could also be very useful in other subconscious ways. Not being white Europeans, they represented that which was 'Not-Rational Man.' As such they fulfilled a symbolic role, ranking as subhuman vessels that embodied all those qualities that Rational Man would not identify with and was therefore busy disowning. These qualities were all enemies of the great god Progress: laziness, childishness, vulnerability, ignorance, promiscuity and so on.

In his fervent wish to dissociate from anything that was not rational progress, the idea that in some cultures people might work during one season and then rest or conduct religious ceremonies during another was not considered significant to Rational Man. It simply meant that they were 'lazy savages' not wedded to the notion of *industry* or the Protestant work ethic, Rational Man's favourite themes. Britannia was well on the road to riches because of the New World. Economically, Rational Man needed natives to do the manual work; but he needed them psychologically, too – to stand beneath him.

Indigenous life was neither seen nor appreciated in its own context but entirely interpreted through the emergent excessively rational mind-set. The small minority of Rational Men who were curious about these other worlds had to disguise their interest in satirical fairy tales, as Jonathan Swift did in his *Gulliver's Travels*. Daniel Defoe's *Robinson Crusoe* was a much better depiction of Rational Man's psyche than Swift's novel, for Crusoe was a survivor who organised and developed his desert island, unselfconsciously taking Man Friday – his opposite – as his servant. Crusoe 'saves' Friday from being cannibalised and justifies his own superior status by virtue of the mental gymnastics emanating from his rational Protestant intellect and sense of entitlement. He rationalises Friday's unpaid service to him as a step forward in the black man's own betterment. Crusoe's Entitlement Illusion results directly from his widespread use of dissociation and compartmentalisation.[5] This trick became a crucial part of the popular and enduring narrative that allowed the white man's unquestioning motivation – his sense of entitlement, coupled with his charitable duty. For there is one more psychological function for indigenous man to fulfil: psychologically, this second role of Friday's is much more subtle and important than simply being a servant.

In the mid 20th century, psychoanalysts identified the principles of *objectification*. In its origin, this is a psychic process whereby an infant uses its mother as a platform for satisfying its own needs for safety and nourishment. In adults, the same psychic process can be used pathologically to promote narcissistic behaviour or as a defence. In short, it is the turning of people into objects so they can be used or exploited, either psychologically or economically. In the case of the early British colonists, both ways fitted miraculously well together.

Next, psychoanalysts recognised that the objectification of people can manifest in two apparently separate but interlocked forms: *denigration* or *idealisation*. In the former, the object is looked down upon, hated and despised; in the latter it is looked up to and even worshipped. But in both cases, it has little or nothing to do with external reality. The estimation of the object's value is entirely virtual, since all the referents are internal to the objectifier. In other words, they are all about the attitudes of the person who is doing the objectifying. What's more, in the end, denigration and idealisation turn out to be but different sides of the same coin. In clinical practice, psychoanalysts discovered that whenever they were idealised by their narcissistically wounded patients, they were likely to be denigrated quickly thereafter, so that both polarities were, in the end, meaningless.

Through this lens, we can see that the colonial denigration of the indigenous world had further possibilities of transformation into a kind of idealisation. Using other Enlightenment principles, this time libertarianism or utopianism, the savage could be idealised or romanticised. Or, maintaining good Quaker benevolence, one could have pity on these strange figures who were deemed so inferior. The wonderful thing about both these options was that the practitioner could feel better about himself, since both fitted his value system and helped him override the otherwise obvious excesses of exploitation.[6] He could emerge with his conscience wiped clean. Not that this psycho-conjuring did much for the indigenous world, since it was but another spin of the virtual merry-go-round.

Pitying the poor Indians

Enlightenment style pity needs a little defining. It is not an outpouring of empathic feeling or the joining in communal grief, as might be depicted in the scene of a medieval *Pieta* sculpture, belonging to a world of reference now abandoned. The Rational Man Project was based in a more Protestant ideal, abstract and yet pragmatic. It translated emotions into ideas or actions – preferably both. With Enlightenment Pity bolted onto the worship of Reason – as celebrated in Alexander Pope's pity for the "Poor Indian" – Rational Man could compensate his rank exploitation of the indigenous world with some moral balance.[7] Furthermore, according to Professor Laura M. Stevens of the University of Tulsa, the sentimental side of Protestantism would thrive on finding those "who must be lost in order to be found."[8] Such a version of pity went to the heart of the redemptive gospel of Protestant evangelism: the natives could become the lost sheep that the colonial shepherd would restore to the flock. It further legitimised an impassioned export drive in the form of the 'benefits' of Christianity and European languages.

Over time, this meant that the recipients of pity would have their own beliefs and tongues eradicated as a matter of policy. And here is where the British boarding school system suddenly came into its own as a valuable export item. The eradication of instinctual desires and customs learned at the mother's bosom had been perfected in the public schools at home. Applying these techniques in the colonies was a mission that was especially suited to the Victorian British educational ideal. The Victorians had learned how to break the will of their own children and they would now practise it abroad. So, towards the end of the 19th century, the establishment of native boarding schools in Australia and North America became the new gold rush. Civilising the savages was a project that went hand in hand with taking over their land, while the apparent need for the former would easily obscure the cunning of the latter.

Official records from the time concerning the legacy of these institutions are only now coming to light. In 2008, the Canadian government set up a truth and reconciliation commission, an official independent body, to look into the history and legacy of residential schools for aboriginal peoples in Canada. Initially, this was a response to numerous complaints from former students, represented by the Assembly of First Nations and other aboriginal organisations, against the government and the Church of Canada. The commission had a budget of C$60 million and was to complete its work by June 2015. In the spring of 2012, it published its interim report, *They Came for the Children*, and summarised the first principles of the residential school movement thus:

> First Nation leaders entered into the treaty making process for the purpose of establishing a relationship of respect that included an ongoing set of mutual obligations including land sharing based on kinship and cooperation. For its part, the Canadian government saw the treaties only as land transfer agreements. The government's policy was one of assimilation under which it sought to remove any First Nations legal interest in the land, while

reducing and ignoring its own treaty obligations. Schooling was expected to play a central role in achieving that policy goal.[9]

Remember, pitying did not actually mean *identifying* and *empathising* with the aboriginal residents; that was not part of the Rational Man Project. Rather, pity as a conceptual stance became a mechanism for Enlightened society as a whole to rationalise its superiority and take advantage over those who had lost their personhood and become objects. In fact, in the most rational of all languages, French, someone whom we pity or to whom we give charity becomes known as an *objet de pitié*, an *objet de charité*. In the final analysis, pitying meant fixing the 'poor Indian' in a subhuman category. Unconsciously, both idealisation and denigration had inevitably come full circle: dissociation, compartmentalisation and objectification had done their work.

Enlightenment Pity and human rights

The withholding of human rights, particularly from Africans, made it possible for Europe to gain extraordinary wealth from the New World, primarily by means of the Atlantic slave trade. From its beginnings in the 16th century, it is estimated that about 12 million Africans were transported across the Atlantic to the Americas.[10] Britain gained her enormous wealth and mastery of the oceans through perfecting what became known as the 'triangular trade,' in which her ships took arms, cloth and metal goods to West Africa to trade for captured Africans. Those who survived the voyage would be sold into slavery in the Caribbean for sugar and coffee to satisfy emerging tastes at home.

This was not the only trend emerging in the coffee houses of London. The great liberalising movements that had been released by the Enlightenment and had resulted in the American and French revolutions, also meant that some thinkers would take Enlightenment pity a step further – out from dissociation and into the reality of humane political action. Their chief focus was to try to wean Britain from the addiction to slavery that had fuelled the pre-industrial colonial world, first through pamphleteering and eventually through the reform of Parliament. Here is William Cowper, from his poem,

'A Pity for Poor Africans,' written in 1788 but not published till his death in 1800, ironically resonating on Pope's earlier piece:

> I own I am shocked at the purchase of slaves,
> And fear those who buy them and sell them are knaves;
> What I hear of their hardships, their tortures, and groans
> Is almost enough to draw pity from stones.
>
> I pity them greatly, but I must be mum,
> For how could we do without sugar and rum?
> Especially sugar, so needful we see;
> What, give up our desserts, our coffee, and tea?
>
> Besides, if we do, the French, Dutch, and Danes,
> Will heartily thank us, no doubt, for our pains:
> If we do not buy the poor creatures, they will:
> And tortures and groans will be multiplied still.

As Cowper sweetly hints, the slave trade had an immensely powerful lobby whose argument ran that slavery was indispensable to the success and wealth of Britain. Through their tame MPs, the merchants and planters warned that abolition would mean ruin for Britain, as the whole economy would collapse. If Britain ceased to trade in slaves with Africa, her commercial rivals would soon fill the gap. The Africans, to boot, would apparently be in a much worse situation if they were humiliated by Johnny Foreigner rather than by English gentlemen. As an aside, readers may note how the arguments against abolishing slavery summarised by Cowper are reminiscent of those used by the British government in the 21st century to avoid regulating or penalising banking and financial trading: "It's a no-brainer! We have to do everything to save our banks or we will lose our advantage and others will mop up the gains!"

Eventually, a collection of Romantic literary figures, Quaker activists and political reformers built up a head of steam and, having since 1787 bombarded Parliament with petitions, managed to get both Houses to take the human rights situation seriously. Alarmed by a violent revolt of slaves on the Caribbean island of Saint-Domingue (later Haiti) in which Napoleon lost more men than at Waterloo, Parliament passed the Slave Trade Act in 1807, which was an attempt to ban *slaving* rather than slavery itself. It took exactly fifty years, from the end of the War of American Independence to the Abolition of Slavery Act in

1833, to have the practice banned in the Empire's domain, and even then it excluded those lands governed by the East India Company.

The 1807 Act resulted in a payout of millions of pounds in compensation to some three thousand individuals, including several bishops, who had investments in the lucrative trade.[11] Amongst the compensated, as researchers at University College London revealed in 2013, were ancestors of David Cameron.[12] Shameful as it clearly was even then, such business was as common as people investing in stocks and shares today, for the objectification of those plucked out of their lives in West Africa had been fully and completely normalised. The slaves and their descendants have never been compensated. And, as Baldwin Spencer, Prime Minister of Antigua and Barbuda, argued in a Caricom (heads of government of the Caribbean Community) meeting in July 2013, much of the region is still suffering as a direct result of such exploitation.[13]

Important as the outlawing of slavery was for humanity, it was a further step of self-invention for the British. In *Bury the Chains: Prophets and Rebels in the Fight to Free* an Empire's Slaves, award-winning American historian Adam Hochschild suggests that after the 1807 Act, British self-congratulation knew no bounds.[14] In the late 1830s and 1840s, the imperial fleet, staffed mostly by press-gang, ruled the waves. At the same time, it saw itself as an international do-gooder – a police force with a duty to enforce a ban that was not yet agreed to by less evolved Continentals and Americans. For the British felt good about themselves; they were proud to be the world's leaders.

The project was sufficiently advanced that Rational Man was beginning to feel secure about his ordained place at the top of the tree; and so, out of *noblesse oblige*, he could direct his generosity towards those at the bottom. Much more importantly, however, Britain's industrialisation was in full swing. Bit by bit, the profit from the use of machines began to rival the profit from the exploitation of slaves abroad and the feudal classes at home; the latter would eventually – even happily – turn into consumers. Thus, some economic disincentives of slavery were beginning to arise. Drunk with greed and success, Rational Man marched unstoppably on, trying to exploit and control the world in the name of the grand new god, Progress.

Unconsciously, however, the side effects of Enlightenment dissociation remained active, even if they had yet to be recognised. Psychological forces drive behaviour whether they are acknowledged or not; and, by one of the first laws of psychology discovered by its founding fathers, while they are unconscious they do more than drive – they control. In its attempts to reintegrate, or recycle, as it were, the ecological nature of the psyche means that what is disowned eventually begins to oppress he who has disowned it. Rational Man needed to employ the powerful psychological forces of dissociation, compartmentalisation and objectification to cope with that which was 'Not-Rational Man' – women, children, 'natives' and, in Britain, foreigners and the working classes. But this meant that he had a serious psychological problem, because in his inability to integrate them as part of his identity, he was building psychological weakness into himself, even as he built himself up.

It is a problem that continues to this day for those raised in British boarding schools, those rational hothouses in which the inmates *are* in fact children, born of mothers; for the logic means they have to rapidly disidentify from and disown those aspects of themselves and are left with but their brittle defensive personalities hidden under rational perfection. It was from these schools, in less than ten years, that exquisitely manufactured Rational Men would emerge – as long as they had learned to practice the arts of dissociation, idealisation and objectification as tiny children and took these skills as normal. But they would leave with a built-in sense of entitlement that was as natural and unquestioned as anything they had known. It was breathlessly fast and almost perfect – except for one flaw.

What Rational Man had disidentified from was now felt as outside of him, specifically below him. It was threatening to the maintenance of his identity and existence and therefore fearful, at any moment it might rise up. What he dreaded was represented by real live people, so his weakness was unconsciously constantly being excited or provoked. As we saw earlier when we discussed the psychodynamics of the Strategic Survival Personality, when chronic dissociation from Level III is practised, that which is disowned is imagined to be capable of attack. This paranoiac phase of dissociation then legitimises keeping the original defence mechanism in place and supports the entire vicious circle. This, readers may recognise, is the psychological mechanism behind the recent so-called 'War on Terror.' The concept of 'terror' gets created and then has to be fought. The fight then becomes legitimate because it has been psychologically legitimised.

In fact, Rational Man was (and still is) permanently at war. He was at war with himself and with the world he had created. The self he was at war with was his own indigenous self, the natural, emotional, innocent, spontaneous, sometimes lazy, sometimes erotic self – the self the boarding school survivor had to send into exile. The expression of this forbidden self was restricted to secrecy and dreams, waiting for Freud to uncover this truth. The incongruity of Rational Man's outer grandiosity and inner war meant that, by the end of the 19th century, he ruled supreme in the outer world but was controlled in his inner world – and was about to enter the folly of ritual self-destruction that was the First World War. By then, the indigenous world, from Australia to India and from Africa to America, had been fully brutalised and subjugated: the natives, now fully objects and not persons had become unworthy of the fulfilment of any promise made to them. Thus, all promises were duly broken.

Safe rational boxes

The march of progress was unstoppable, Britain at its head, driving the 19th century on, to the extent that it has been called 'the British Century.' The dizzying advances in technology, trade and privilege would eventually melt down into the trauma of the Great War and the Great Depression that followed it. In Chapter 9, we will see how this coincided with the discovery of the unconscious mind and how the British public school entitlement mindset coped with it. But for now, I want to look at some of the other psychological effects of Enlightenment thinking and the legacy that is still with us. We have discussed dissociation and objectification; now we need to turn our attention towards compartmentalisation, which goes hand in hand with them.

At a macro level, the Rational Man Project has defined the entire structure of our environment. One of the most prominent ways this can be seen is in the different branches of science, art, justice, politics and so on, which are now very independent disciplines. This was not the case in the pre-modern era, when the religion's hold over human curiosity meant disciplines of thought were merged and held back from advancement. But the Enlightenment facilitated a process of differentiation in which disciplines were able to separate and specialise, thereby generating an enormous increase in detail and focus. The result was a revolution in the amount of knowledge and skills that humans amassed; the downside was that disciplines of thought became over-specialised and isolated from each other.

At the micro level, a prime example of this is the medical profession today. Its compartmentalisation is evident in a visit to any hospital, which will be clearly organised and structured according to its separate departments. What ties the whole thing together, in Britain at least, is the hierarchical structure, beginning with the elite pinstriped senior consultants and extending right down to the hospital porters.[15] Compartmentalisation has to rely on a clear hierarchical chain, otherwise its lack of connectivity will create structural problems. Of course, such division has its purpose and value in medicine, but it also has downsides. In cancer treatment, for example, the isolation of departments that do not talk to each other can mean that patients get different treatment plans and prognoses dependent on whether they are talking to an oncologist, a radiologist, a chemotherapist or a surgeon. In his magnificent book, *The Emperor of All Maladies*, subtitled 'A Biography of Cancer', Siddhartha Mukherjee describes this state of affairs from the perspective of a hospital clinician turned historian of the disease. Mukherjee suggests that the lack of joined-up thinking has contributed to the widespread terror of cancer and the failure of society to go beyond a mindset that sees itself at war with the disease.[16] We still know so little about the origin of cancer; is it beyond imagining that in future we might understand it as the disease of Rational Man?

On an anecdotal level, I remember the bewilderment of a dear friend who had been diagnosed with cancer in his lymph nodes. Told by his oncologist that this would mean his immune system would fail, he was prescribed chemotherapy, which in turn would have a detrimental effect on his immune system. When my friend asked how he might support his immune system in order to fight the cancer, the irritated response was that he should go and see an immunologist and ask there. Unpacking this unfortunate bedside manner, we may spot the Rational Man at work on his project, and it may help our comprehension to analyse it. Readers will, I hope, forgive me if I amplify the metaphors I am using for the sake of understanding.

The doctor in question, secure in his Rational Man identification, has to deal with and try to fix the patient's body, a frustrating and faulty piece of *matter*, which in Enlightenment thinking terms is inferior and inert. The owner of this body is now identified with this dead matter and as such is not really supposed to ask questions. He has become the *measured*, not the measurer. He is there to have things *done to* him by the clever specialist, Rational Man, by virtue of his status, and out of Enlightenment 'pity.' Of course, compartmentalising works well enough in terms of the allocation of resources, but without a good 'bed-side manner' it fails in terms of empathy and emotions, which are all at the human level. The patient may or may not get better, but sometimes he may have an experience of losing his personhood in his exchange with the doctor. He has to remain an object. Experience, empathy and emotions are all foreign items, which, in this case, Rational Man has had to disown in order to fully embody his godlike rationality.

A rational horror story: the psychologically needed underclass

As a present-day example of the severe limitations of Rational Man's thought and its dangers for our whole society, I would like to introduce readers to another doctor. Anthony Daniels worked for ten years as a psychiatrist in prisons and hospitals in Birmingham. His alter ego is Theodore Dalrymple, a specialist in elegant, angry prose that regularly features in the *Daily Telegraph*. His Birmingham experience inspired him to write *Life at the Bottom: The Worldview That Makes the Underclass*, a collection of essays and shocking case histories.[17]

A vociferous sceptic of all things 'wet' (including Europe), Daniels describes treating an 'underclass' of people addicted to chaotic lifestyles marked by violence, unwanted children, drunkenness, drug abuse and crime, for which the perpetrators lack all ability to sense even minimal accountability. As he relates it, murderers regularly describe how "the knife went in," battered girlfriends habitually say, "he just can't help himself," children are routinely abandoned. The commonest case seen on the psychiatric wards is the male overdose, which, according to Daniels, is intended to demonstrate that the man in question can't help beating up his girlfriend, needs treatment and shouldn't be prosecuted. Thousands of such cases have persuaded Daniels that society is in denial about a Britain bereft of values and in a catastrophic and rudderless state. Ignorance, brutality and fear rule inner-city life, he maintains; no one has outside interests or a sense of history or any notion of having a choice. All live for the present moment and for themselves only. Going against the grain is impossible: "the intelligent self-destruct; the sensitive despair."

Daniels firmly ascribes the cause of this malaise to "middle-class intellectuals and ideologues" who have spent the last fifty years deconstructing hierarchies so successfully that even the police, burdened by paperwork, quotas and mandatory attitudes, have given up and feel themselves part of the victim culture. I have some sympathy with Daniels' frustration at the excesses of postmodernism. I do not believe he is wrong to denounce the quota culture that comes out of political spin and I fear he is right about the extent of the problems. Crucially, he proposes that Britain, beyond and above all other nations in the world, is the place where the evils he names are most clearly manifested.

I agree with Daniels entirely – but not for any reasons that he would appreciate. For despite his classic hyper-conservative polemic, what he fails to say is that this situation is a systemic outgrowth of the Rational Man Project, root and branch. In Britain it was taken to extremes, as we have seen, by the twin multipliers of fear of revolution and grandiosity of Empire – inner contraction and outer expansion. The Rational Man Project's psychodynamics rested on distancing, compartmentalisation and dissociation. The British hyper-rational project added foreigners and home-grown working classes to the list of disowned and therefore abhorrent things to be distanced from. In consequence, there is a large section of the population who have felt worthless for a very long time, who feel they belong to a pariah class, a separate nation from the upper and middle-classes in a way that is completely unknown on the Continent. And, unsurprisingly, some behave accordingly; what is surprising, I think, is that there are so many who do not.

This is not to excuse the behaviours to which Daniels draws attention or to argue simplistically that those who display such behaviours are victims; rather, it is to place this as a *systemic issue* alongside British elitism. It is the same phenomenon as ex-boarders who have unhappy wives: as we have seen, a wife of an ex-boarder is likely to be unhappy because she is carrying all the disowned parts. The disowning of one 'problem' begets another in a different place, but in the same system. How does this work in a larger system, like the British class system? Throughout Europe, working-class Britain once had a deserved reputation for football hooliganism – until the game was cleaned up and monetised. These days, the variety of loathsome behaviour known as 'getting legless' is confined to town centre drinking sprees and European holidays. Today, the British drinking tourist – who can now be female or male – is universally despised. In France, even biker meetings or rock festivals are gentle events compared to a normal British weekend, and the difference is growing, not getting smaller.

This has nothing to do, as Daniels suggests, with post-modern intellectuals; it is simply a return to form after some years of extraordinary national unity produced by the Second World War. It is a psychohistorical problem: a simple but systemic example of the disidentified and disowned, the loathed and feared, coming back to haunt and attack the rational world of the middle classes, not in the form of phantoms but in the form of real people.[18] For the real tragedy is that the people who Daniels is talking about *do exist* and do frequently act the way he describes. But they are not doing it in isolation. The British working class have been left stranded by the Rational Man Project; they have picked up all the disowned material from the rigid endurance of the British class system that demands that someone has to be at the bottom, and that this won't be the elite. But now that the sun has gone down on the British Empire, there are no more natives for Rational Man to be above, save those immigrants at home, many of whom seem much more socially adaptable than he is.

We have worked the British Raj trick on our own people – they feel bad about themselves from the inside. This means that they have not been able to evolve like their counterparts in liberal Scandinavia and Holland, or in Germany or France, where there is a social democratic centrism to the culture. In these countries, the difficulty is more with recent arrivals. Not having had far-flung Empires, Northern Europeans don't quite know what to do with their Middle Eastern and Asian immigrants, since they are not used to positioning themselves in relation to them.

Despite our relative success at race relations in Britain, our elite strata of society are pretty consistent in how they place themselves in relation to immigrants and the other ranks. Daniels, for example, is very comfortable in his doctor/Rational Man identification. In his book he makes some worthwhile points, but it is clear that he is busy observing and measuring his underclass's activity with disdain, as if he was dealing with dead matter, as if he were measuring skulls in the early 19th century.[19] His conclusion is that it cannot be anything to do with *him*. It is therefore the 'Not-I.' It must be those others, those liberal "middle-class intellectuals and ideologues" that have produced this genuine horror. But the reader may remember that this is exactly how dissociation and compartmentalisation work. Besides, being an intellectual is banned under British Bulldog Rules. So intellectuals are also relegated to the disowned pile named 'Not-Daniels-the-Rational-Doctor-and-Observer'.

Dissociation rules OK, once more. The tragedy is that we British are still doing it in the 21st century.

CHAPTER 9

Reason's Catastrophe

Rationality – an altered state? ~Schools for imperial rationality
Playing the game ~ Shell-shock and the Great Unmentionable
Wounds to the deep emotional self ~ When will we ever learn?

Rationality – an altered state?

It was a sharp January morning in 1993. While John Major, the last British prime minister to date not to have been groomed in a public school, was struggling to keep his authority over a government riven by sex scandals and Euroscepticism, I was deep in the heart of old Europe. I was hurrying through the cobbled streets of Zurich's *Altstadt*, knowing that the tram I had to catch would leave not a moment earlier or later than the 08.18 that the timetable displayed – or boasted, as one began to imagine after a few days in Switzerland. I looked around at the square in which my cheap hotel stood, to my amazement already scrubbed back to a consistent Swiss cleanliness when last night it had been a scene of staggering revelry. Innumerable drunks had caroused the packed alleys, jostling with blatant prostitutes and flamboyant transvestites. Pedestrians had to beware of writhing chains of masked people of indeterminate sex practicing for the following month's *Fasching* (the Lenten carnival) celebrations. All through the night there had been sporadic cries and the sound of smashing bottles until finally a dead quiet fell, only to be broken, much too soon for my liking, by the din of motorised brushes and refuse lorries.

As I crossed the river and entered the financial district, it began to dawn on me that my home for the week's seminar I was attending, a hotel I'd thought was a respectable place for less well off tourists or travellers, in fact doubled as a bordello.

Even more surprisingly, I had to admit that it seemed to handle its twin roles with complete aplomb. The contrast between the two faces of the city was startling. Maybe it would have been less of a contrast if the authorities hadn't gone to such lengths to ensure it was all so clean and tidy by the time the morning's journeys to work began. Perhaps this could explain why Carl Jung had arrived at some of his theories here, especially that of the *shadow*, the name he used for the collection of aspects a person did not want to identify with, had disowned or had not yet faced, from the great well of psychic material that is called the unconscious in Jungian psychology. Our shadow, both literally and in Jung's apt metaphor, is something we have turned our back on but that we can never escape, for it is always with us.

The twin sides of respectability and revelry that dwelt side by side in old Zurich and that, due to the industry of the city authorities, never actually met, seemed to me a testimony to Jung's idea. In his memoirs, Jung explains that that the concept of the *persona* (meaning mask in Latin) had been inspired by the masked carnival processions he saw in Basel.[1] We all wear a mask, he proposes, behind which we hide the darker aspects of our personalities. As the tram clanked away from the super-smart Bahnhofstrasse, underneath which were said to be countless bank vaults in which were concealed profits from organised crime, I was glad that something had just clicked in me. After all, I had come to Zurich to study Jungian psychology and it looked like it was beginning to reveal itself to me. That was worth losing a bit of sleep for.

Minutes later this 'click' would go a notch further. To start the second day of our seminar, Dr Arnold Mindell, a former physicist and now a renowned American re-interpreter of Jungian themes who had made his own studies in Zurich, calmly but provocatively announced: "Rationality is an altered state." Rationality an 'altered state'? In other words, a hallucinatory or psychotic experience as in a drug-induced state or in serious madness? Is that what he was suggesting? In fact, he seemed to be proposing something quite different. He was not asserting that madness was the shadow of Age of Reason – not quite. Was he proposing that rationality as a monolithic way of viewing the world could become a blind trance? Could he be suggesting that, in the grip of what I now call *hyper-rationality* (which I was only then beginning to articulate for myself), self-evident truths – such as the assertions that children need families and indigenous people deserve respect – could easily be denied and overridden as if they did not exist? Yes, that made perfect sense to me. Taken to extremes, especially to the extreme British version of the Rational Man Project, rationality could be classed as downright crazy while maintaining perfect respectability. It was like the two sides of the Altstadt!

I began to consider those Victorian and Edwardian empire-builders and explorers who were role models for countless British schoolboys. Many of them were completely irrational in their behaviour but despite the often foolish context of their actions what we retain of them is their heroism. Even when they were clearly off their heads, we tend to think of them as loveable eccentrics. Take those 19th century explorers, Burton and Speke, for example, who sulked with each other over hundreds of miles of jungle, footslogging through malaria-ridden equatorial Africa, searching for the source of the Nile. Busy suppressing all weakness and feelings, they were run by their own tantrums and competitiveness, while they risked the lives of dozens of their native bearers. And then there was General Gordon, the masochistic megalomaniac hero of late Victorian tabloids, revelling in his own eccentric take on orders that resulted in a predictable bloodbath in which he and thousands of his men perished in unnecessary 'glory' on the walls of Khartoum.

These are just a few of many, and most were ex-boarders. The years leading up to the Great War witnessed the apotheosis of such a style, as in the brave but foolhardy amateurism of Scott of the Antarctic, hopelessly racing the (evidently more at-home and better equipped) Norwegians to the South Pole. The Brits, with insane Protestant masochism, chose to draw the sleds themselves rather than use dogs. These freezing Britons took the art of self-sacrifice to new depths; one of them, Titus Oates took the art of self-effacement to new heights with his immortal throw-away line: "I am just going outside and I may be some time." My own boyhood favourite – perhaps because he seemed so out of step with Western life – was T.E. Lawrence, given to prodigious feats of physical endurance and linguistic mastery, but tortured by his sexuality and his masochistic obsession with all kinds of flagellation, by himself and others. Lawrence of Arabia courted notoriety shamelessly, but when it arrived he fled it, twice reinventing himself as a private soldier with the full cognisance of the Ministry of Defence before carving himself up on his motorbike in postwar seclusion just round the corner from Thomas Hardy's Dorset home, Max Place, where, at the height of his fame, he had the Prince of Wales to lunch.

These men were Super-Brits; they have their place in history and are counted as part of what puts the Great into Britain, some would say. But despite their hyper-rational origins, they and countless other examples are so riddled with irrationality that by the late 1960s and early 1970s they had come to be seen as remote figures of fun to those of us who were growing up then. I remember for a brief period owning one of those scarlet military tunics that were all the rage in Carnaby Street. I would appear at parties wearing it, thinking it was a great joke and delighting in the fact that my generation had escaped National Service, before I realised that it was very hard indeed to breathe inside it. Those internally constricted heroes of the British Empire seemed absurd to us then; they were absolute gifts for the public school and Cambridge humourists, such as the Monty Python gang, who dominated our television sets with an abandon that had never been seen before, poking merciless fun at the evident madness of classic imperial self-importance.

Schools for imperial rationality

It is March 2012, nearly twenty years after my 'click' moment in Zurich and a hundred years since Captain Oates went outside for a while. I am sitting by my fire, watching the loved but feared TV anchor, Jeremy Paxman, trying to come to terms with the good, the bad and the mad of the British Empire in a lavish five-part BBC documentary.[2] It is one of those series where the presenter wears the same shirt all over the world, designed, I suppose, to relay a reassuring continuity, although I find it uncommonly distracting. I watch him with interest as he flits around the globe and then in whimsical mood pursues an interview with Python's own Michael Palin about the surreal 1970s series *Ripping Yarns*, in which the comedian delightfully satirised the decent chaps and eccentric explorers of Britain's heyday.

Paxman is on the trail of the imperial madness but, disappointingly, it is an interview that he does not really develop; in fact, the whole documentary seems to miss the legendary determination of his "Can you just answer the question!" interviewing style. He seems to take a rather 'bewildered of the Home Counties' attitude to the Empire, as if he himself might be a man torn by conflicting attitudes. I can sympathise. It can be hard to be a product of the British Rational Man Project, let alone an Establishment success figure, and at the same time be a man who is of his time, one who recognises the degree of folly built into it. The result seems to be that in his 2011 book, which the series cunningly promotes, Paxman repeatedly confesses his own puzzlement at the madness therein but pulls back from outright condemnation:

> There was something inherently nonsensical about it [the British Empire]. How could the ultimate purpose of colonisation be freedom?[3]

No such qualms beset journalist and historian Richard Gott, however, who published his *Britain's Empire* within days of the Newsnight presenter's book appearing. Speaking with an authority that eludes Paxman, Gott sees the Empire as "the fruit of military conquest and brutal wars involving physical and cultural extermination of subject people."[4] Gott's book, which has received wide acclaim, is an assault on the sort of neo-jingoism promoted by Cameron's Education Minister and well-known friend and employee of Rupert Murdoch, Michael Gove. It powerfully debunks "the kind of glorious narrative history" that Gove, no doubt backed by a wealthy lobby, has been calling to be reinstated in British schools. On a different occasion, I suspect that Paxman the pugnacious interviewer might want to rise up and join Gott in demolishing Gove's rosy radicalism that claims to be in the service of combatting privilege by promoting more schools outside of state control.

Where Paxman does rediscover his certainty is in stating that the breeding ground for the 'nonsensical' imperial attitudes, which we tend to lovingly normalise and underestimate as 'eccentricity,' was none other than the public school system. The Empire, he asserts, was run by "decent chaps, sturdy and self-reliant, ready to obey orders, all of which they learned at public school." They were, as it were, the prefects of the Empire, and it was for this purpose that the enormous expansion of public schools and residential education took place. "If you could survive a British public school," Paxman wryly proposes in the final episode, perhaps reflecting on his own time at Malvern, "you could survive anything."

The twin features of self-reliance, borne out of emotional restraint and physical hardship, and the structured hierarchy of privilege, deeply familiar to an ex-boarder, were the perfect training to become a district officer or governor of an indigenous population in a country that was not their own. It was a natural extension of their function that the public schools should evolve as a fast-track path, via Oxbridge, towards a seat at the Establishment's top table, towards wealth and privilege. Hence, the fact that an education minister from such a background can be promoting a return to jingoism is shocking in 2012, but it should not surprise us. That we should have such an education minister responsible for all policy in the state education sector that will educate more than 90% of the electorate is of questionable morality. Surreally, in Britain we just take it for granted.

The public schools have been extraordinarily successful at promoting their own kind, as we have seen earlier. They were designed to produce the boys to run the Empire and, through the nation's identification with Empire, they fostered a loyalty to their class that became identified with the nation itself. This extraordinary conjuring trick still works in the 21st century. The durability and success of these institutions is noteworthy, and it rests on the fact that they were perfectly adapted to their purpose of supporting the Rational Man Project.

In fact, they can be described as total institutions, in American sociologist Erving Goffman's famous term, mostly used to describe asylum and prison culture.[5] In essence, according to writer Simon Partridge, Goffman's theory suggests that: "The institutional experience served to make the recipient gradually less able to function in the outside world."[6] In the case of the public schools, this can be seen in the side effects affecting many of those who experienced this education but who did not go on to lead the Empire. It explains some of the retained madness, affectionately now known as 'tradition,' as Partridge points out:

> One way of coping with this is to seek out similar institutions
> – politics/law/banking – where the institutional tradition lives
> on and go into them. For example the House of Commons and
> House of Lords seem to be run pretty much like public schools.

Whenever parliaments in other countries are featured on the news they all seem quite modern with up-to-date technology aiding the communication, whereas the GB parliament resembles a cramped old-fashioned affair where everyone shouts and bays at each other.[7]

As total institutions, public schools can be thought of as production machines for the socialisation of boys, the perfect combination of industrial technology and imperial ambition. The first step, as Paxman rightly identifies, is that the boys who were going to run the Empire had to be "removed from the noxious influence of home." This was true whether it was for English boys whose home was near the school, for those who were to be sent miles overseas from the colonies or for native children who were never going to be in charge. Hector Langevin, Public Works Minister of Canada, said in 1883:

> In order to educate the children properly we must separate them from their families. Some people may say that this is hard but if we want to civilize them we must do that.[8]

This separation from family was (and remains) an essential step in the success of the heavily gendered British Rational Man Project. A boy child, after all, unlike his sister, was potentially a civilised rational being; it was therefore going to be necessary to get him out of range of such potential pollutants as mothers, sisters, pets and all the fuss of family life. Historian Peter Lewis, writing in *Manful Assertions*, tells us that Victorian boys had to be:

> ... removed from the home, because home is the site above all of compassionate love (but also of other 'feminine' qualities and emotions) which weakens resolve and impedes progress to manhood.[9]

In *The Making of Them*, I described in detail how the boys brought up to run the Empire would never be at home in themselves, would never really come home again and would find family life something that – understandably – they just did not understand. Here I want to take the argument in a slightly different direction and suggest that the very thinking learned in these places is not only not compatible for genuine success in the 21st century – let alone good leadership – but was already out of step a hundred years earlier.

Playing the game

In the 19th and until well into the middle of the 20th century, boys were educated in the classics so that they looked backwards, not forwards. The entire mindset avoided emotions and sexuality like the plague, as we have seen, but espoused a Spartan culture of the body that became more important than intellectual achievements and would enshrine imperial values in the uniquely British cult of 'Games.' As it happens, it is perhaps sport that has become our most enduring legacy to the rest of the world. But sport and 'games' are not quite the same thing. Games, in which boyishness is promoted, is not about exercise or having fun; it is a means of aspiring to the highest values of British Rational Man: strategic thinking, group loyalty and esprit de corps, in which the individual is less important than the team and the team less important than the ideal. Games rationalised the cult of personal sacrifice, already practised in the boarding house, to a messianic and uniquely British extreme, and it was this that gave those Super-Brits their extraordinary and baffling character and, I believe, resulted in an unacknowledged, normalised form of insanity and the direst consequences.

To recap: the most important outcome of these total institutions is that the boarding school survivor emerges as the ideal Rational Man. As such, he has unbending loyalty to his own kind, is bent on self-replication and is extremely skilled in promoting his interests. However, as Hyper-Rational Man, he is also extremely mentally challenged, which amounts to a kind of irrationality, for he has no skill in emotional, relational processes and, as we have seen, he is beset by fears of what he has disowned. Importantly, having normalised a level of irrationality, he cannot denounce genuine madness. Critically, he does not hold to the Socratic axiom, "know thy self", which, paradoxically, is the foundation of genuine reason. In particular, he does not know how maimed he himself is or to what degree, whether he is struggling to operate as a husband, engaged in so-called 'innocent' bullying (which I explained earlier), promoting hyper-conservative education policies or making a pointless last stand on a mud wall in Africa.

But he does know how to 'play the game.' It was the gesture of the pointless last stand that seems to have really got to Jeremy Paxman and finally stirred him up. Recognising Gordon of Khartoum as a figure of sublime folly, the news presenter stares wryly at the camera and suggests that the whole of the Empire, in the end, became a game. He then recites a chunk of Sir Henry Newbolt's famous and insidious poem, 'Play up! Play up and Play the Game,' the second verse of which refers to the 1885 Battle of Abu Klea in Sudan during the unsuccessful expedition to rescue General Gordon. The poem's full title is *Vitae Lampada*, taken from a quotation by the Roman poet Lucretius, meaning 'the torch of life.' It refers to the way in which a schoolboy, a future soldier, learns selfless commitment to duty in public school cricket matches:

> There's a breathless hush in the Close to-night
> Ten to make and the match to win
> A bumping pitch and a blinding light,
> An hour to play and the last man in.
> And it's not for the sake of a ribboned coat,
> Or the selfish hope of a season's fame,
> But his captain's hand on his shoulder smote
> "Play up! play up! and play the game!"
>
> The sand of the desert is sodden red,
> Red with the wreck of a square that broke;
> The Gatling's jammed and the Colonel dead,
> And the regiment blind with dust and smoke.
> The river of death has brimmed its banks,
> And England's far, and Honour a name,
> But the voice of a schoolboy rallies the ranks:
> "Play up! play up! and play the game!"

This poem, I propose, is very dangerous. It has similarities to Kipling's contemporaneous work, 'If,' which I alluded to in *The Making of Them*, because it seems to suggest a worthy idealism. Its mischief, I argue, lies in the fact that it seems to be attempting to seduce and brainwash the listener with its lofty purpose when in fact it confounds a profound spiritual truth with a grandiose ideal. The spiritual ideal (actually the subject of the Hindu classic the *Bhagavad-Gita*) is that non-attachment to the desires of our ego means that we sometimes may have to surrender to action – even fighting – without fear of outcome, simply because it is our lot. The ideal promoted in the poem, however, is that the notion of overriding loyalty, as learned at public school, confirms the bogus idea of the immature

Englishman's destiny to rule the world, and that his assumed superiority over his imperial subjects is God–given and God-decided. Such sentiments would rationalise pointless sacrifice, such as the Charge of the Light Brigade and other calamities, and absolve the decision-makers from attending accountability, as if it were all a great game.

The setting of the first verse is the renowned 'Close' at Clifton College, a prestigious public school in a smart Bristol district, built on an eminence high enough above the harbour that the smells of the slave-trader ships would not spoil the atmosphere of entitlement. Here in 1881 a confident and youthful Newbolt was head of the school. He happened also to be chums with Douglas Haig, who went on to Oxford, where he joined the Bullingdon Club, and later became famous for dispatching millions of young men to pointless sacrifice in the Great War, earning the nickname 'Butcher Haig.' That was the war in which schoolboys, pretending to be adults and trying to play the game, were unable to fully "rally the ranks." The slaughter was great and our civilisation still groans from the wounds.

Shell-shock and the Great Unmentionable

At the beginning of the 20th century, two things promised to undermine the Rational Man Project: the Great War and the discovery of the unconscious mind. In the end, the Project withstood the challenge – although at tremendous cost – yet an unexpected combination of these two seemingly disparate events provided an extraordinary window into the Project's strengths and weaknesses. The First World War had started as a great game – "it was all a mad hatter's tea-party, for a while," as D.H. Lawrence described it.[10] But what he called the "bruise of the false and inhuman war" spread as the killing and casualties continued.

The war produced an enormous, totally unforeseen epidemic of trauma in survivors, known as shell-shock. It did not diminish after the soldiers were far from the trenches. It was as if the war planted a destructive impulse in the soldiers' bodies, destroying individual expression of will, movement and often speech. Only one psychiatrist, William Halse Rivers, seemed to have any understanding of what was really going on inside the men and how they might be healed. Rivers was a student of Freud's brand new psychology. Psychoanalysis offered a conception of the workings of the unconscious mind, in particular how symptoms that were not permitted expression by society were re-expressed as physical symptoms by so-called 'hysterical' patients. Rivers maintained that the soldiers' neuroses did not result solely from the war experiences themselves but were "due to the attempt to banish distressing memories from the mind." In other words, the soldiers' attempts to dissociate from what they had experienced – for the sake of their own sanity – had produced a secondary problem.[11]

Instead of trying to forget what they had been through, Rivers encouraged his patients to remember their memories and share them with an empathic listener. This laid the foundations of treatment for all trauma counselling, as well as for what later became known as PTSD (post-traumatic stress disorder), which today's military have to take seriously into account. Rivers' story is movingly retold in Pat Barker's *Regeneration Trilogy*, in which she highlights the terrible double bind that he found himself in. If his patients recovered they would inevitably have to go back to the Front; in order to survive again they would have to practise more of the repression that Rivers had taught them to reverse.[12]

Another woman, Elaine Showalter, also turned to the story of Rivers and the shell-shocked soldiers. In her remarkable survey *The Female Malady: Women, Madness and English Culture 1830–1980*, she explains how sufferers of shell-shock had something in common with many women psychiatric patients of the time, in that their most common neurotic symptom was that they became, quite literally, dumbstruck. Hundreds of soldiers lost the ability to speak, as Showalter describes:

> When all signs of physical fear were judged as weakness ... viewed as unmanly, men were silenced and immobilized and forced like women to express their conflicts through the body.[13]

Today, in hindsight, we can easily understand that what the men had experienced in the trenches was beyond words, unspeakable. Nor was anyone interested in what they had to say, for they had been betrayed and sacrificed in an affair in which they had absolutely no voice, one that had been conducted at the highest hierarchical level by Field Marshall

Haig and his German counterparts. In this sense, their inability to speak was the greatest expression of truth that was possible. But Showalter mentions one other salient point. Although "the rate of war neurosis was four times higher among the officers than among the men," she tells us, the dumbness generally only affected the *enlisted* men. Showalter suggests that "for the public-school boys, the university aesthetes and athletes, victory seemed assured to those who played the game." These men were already trained to withhold their personal responses.

Rivers noted that the officers expressed their sickness differently because they had experienced the 'benefit' of public school education:

> The public schoolboy enters the army with a long course of training behind him which enables him to successfully to repress, not only the expression of fear, but also the emotion itself.[14]

In what is possibly the first ever serious psychological commentary on the problems of British educational elitism, Rivers saw that these officers had mentally organised their experiences differently from the regular soldiers. He understood that they were *already* practised in the art of dissociation, learned at school playing games. Dissociation, however, carried with it secondary problems which might be masked by their ability to present themselves in the way they had been trained to. Rivers realised that this level of defence was distinct and felt the need to write a paper on the differences.[15] In fact, without the dubious skill of dissociation, the war could not have continued, so futile were so many of the assaults that were ordered. The war's continuation relied on a belief in 'playing the game' whatever the cost.

The officer class would have to express its protest in its own way, for example in the famous war poetry of Brooke, Sassoon, and others, and also, I think, in the fashion for homosexuality amongst the intelligentsia, which, as I suggested in *The Making of Them*, became a widespread protest against the Edwardian order. I now think this particular phenomenon runs deeper than that, and that it was a protest against Rational Man's abandonment of love for one another. For the Rational Man Project survived: crazily, the project was not abandoned – we did not turn our back on it. It would survive throughout the century, despite another war, despite the 1960s.

But the war was not a game, however much history relates that once again a great slaughter had been "won on the playing fields of Eton." The Great War was surely the most pointless slaughter ever witnessed on the planet. It was Rational Man at war with himself in public, creating vulnerability and ignoring it on an immense scale, preferring to 'play the game' rather than feel the cost. It is as if the collateral damage was to innocence itself. For example, as the play *War Horse* reminds us, 80 million horses were also slaughtered, as well as an uncounted number of indigenous young men drawn from Britain's worldwide colonial dominions.[16] It was the culmination of rationality's hundred-year lurch down a profitable but desperate blind alley.

Since vanquishing Napoleon, Britain had led the world in many things, but this includes a consistent tearing away from love, empathy, openness about sex, the value of the experience of the body and the wisdom of instinctual nature. The war, and our inability to atone for it, created deep wounds that we still suffer today, a hundred years on. It also offered lessons that those in power still refuse to recognise in their consistent support of the Rational Man Project with its educational elitism and blind faith in the values of capitalism.

When the unconscious mind was 'discovered,' it was as if another new world had been found. Initially, Freud thought he had uncovered the systemic faults of modern civilisation. He found it full of repressed fear, of vulnerabilities that could not be acknowledged, of love, of longing, of sexual desire, of memories of the abuse of innocents. There are some who think that the amount of sexual abuse disclosed to him was too much for Freud to stomach and, in his desire to be accepted as a Rational Man of science, turned his back on it to produce what became known as the *Seduction Theory*. Others suggest that his concept of the *Death Instinct* played a similar role for the horror of the Great War, which was, again, too much for him to acknowledge.

The entire Rational Man Project had been like Herod's Massacre of the Innocents: during the previous century, it had butchered and exploited indigenous peoples and subjected women, children and all that was emotional to the realms of exile. Now it had squandered the lives of millions of young men, usually rendered poetically as 'the flower of youth,' although the reality was much harsher. There were many lessons to be learned that were too much for our civilisation to face. I see the collective psyche of the British still reeling from this, in the same way that Victorian England continued to reel from the shock of the French Revolution. We do not know how to heal from it. One of the signs of this is that we cannot acknowledge the need to kick our addiction to the same crippled officer class that we continue to elect. Our current Wounded Leaders would not have seemed at all out of place in 1895 or 1915.

There are others, mainly artists, who are able to feel this loss, this unfinished trauma. Here is how Doris Lessing, who died in 2013, described the ongoing wound of the Great War, in 2006 aged 87:

> The trenches of the First World War did not at once give up their horrors. My father, the old soldier, used to mock with 'the Great Unmentionable' – the soldiers' phrase for the general reluctance of the civilians to talk about the war at all. It took decades for the First World War to enter public consciousness; meanwhile it had become history, the story of fathers and grandfathers.[17]

Lessing was writing in an introduction to a new edition of D.H. Lawrence's infamous book *Lady Chatterley's Lover*, which she saw primarily as an attempt to heal the problem of the First World War and all that it stood for.

While England wanted to move on, occupied as it was with motorcars, semi-detached housing estates and metropolitan railways, Lawrence, with the sensitivity of a consumptive, was not deceived. "There's black days coming – for us all and for everybody," he put in the mouth of Mellors, the gamekeeper. Prophetically, Lawrence, who died in 1930 just as the Blackshirts began their rise to power, sensed that disaster would come again if we did not learn the lessons of the war, and for him they were psychological and not political lessons. For Lawrence – a man who, like Hardy, had navigated the perilous route across the British class divide by means of his wit and his mother's ambition – only a return to love, to tenderness, to sympathy and sexuality would do.

Lessing continues:

> … in the 1920s, there in France, in Belgium, the soil held millions of rotting corpses of mostly very young men, and if talk of the war was being channelled safely into war memorials and Remembrance Days, people who had been near to the nightmare would have had to remember. And against the horrors, the rotting bodies,

the senseless slaughter of the trenches, the post-war poverty and bleakness – against the cataclysm, 'the fallen skies', Lawrence proposes to put in the scales love, tender sex, the tender bodies of people in love; England would be saved by warm-hearted fucking.

Wounds to the deep emotional self

Today we tend to think of *Lady Chatterley's Lover* as being about sex, remembering as we do the obscenity trials of 1959 and 1960 and the ushering in, as Larkin sung of, the beginning of a greater awakening about sexuality. But to me it is not really *about* sex, although there are some extraordinarily open conversations about sex in it and some strong descriptions of lovemaking. The book deliberately describes a divided nation, and highlights the absence of tenderness and blind coldness of the upper classes. It depicts their retreat from the life of the body and how this, hand in hand with the profit-led industrialisation, had despoiled England's land, broken its people and "emasculated" (as Lawrence puts it) her leaders.

"Oh God," gasps his heroine, Connie, imprisoned in a marriage to a war-crippled baronet landowner. She is being driven out of her husband's estate and through the grim village, home to the miners employed in his colliery, who are seen "more as objects rather than men." Connie painfully reflects:

> What has man done to man? What have the leaders of men been doing to their fellow men? They have reduced them to less than humanness, and now there can be no fellowship any more! It is just a nightmare.[18]

Lawrence's remedy is simple enough, if too romantic for some: love. Love that embraces femininity, empathy and sexuality – this is his antidote to 'playing the game.' He condemns the class-divided society, the entitlement of its upper classes and, even more than the sex, this revolutionary attitude may have been the real reason the book was banned for so long. He advocates the return of the Instinctual Man, which is personified in Mellors as a kind of Green Man figure living at the edge of the woods in what used to be Sherwood Forest, the Olde England of Shakespeare, now surrounded by grim villages blackened with coal dust from the mines and the smelting pits of the industrial Midlands.

It is as if this passionate novel about a woman yearning for love will bring life back to England before Lawrence himself dies. Perhaps one of Laurence's finest achievements is to present, at the core of the book, the inner dialogue of a woman. He even pulls off a remarkable intimate exchange between two women, an enormous feat of empathy for a male writer, in which Lady Constance Chatterley and her husband's nurse, Mrs Bolton, who lost her husband down the pit, talk and weep together about loss, the memory of touch, the brutality of industrial work and the durability of love relations. It is an exquisite scene enlivened with a communality of feminine wisdom, as in the older woman's comment:

> When you come to know men, that's how they are: too sensitive, in the wrong place.

Ignored and objectified as she is by her crippled upper-class husband, Sir Clifford, and his effete friends, Connie begins to acknowledge that she is being damaged by the absence of sensitivity towards her from her husband. Clifford's maimed state represents both the reality of the ghastly war and, more importantly, a metaphor for the paralysed nature of the British upper classes, fed on a strict diet of entitlement and the Rational Man Project. For Clifford is not just physically wounded; like all ex-public schoolboys, he is internally crippled in his inability to love and receive love. He can only survive and maintain an illusion of control. He cannot and *will* not grieve. Lawrence clearly means him to be the classic representation of what I am here calling the Wounded Leader. Lawrence would have met many such men in England, and they would have considered themselves superior to him.

Unsurprisingly, their counterparts across the North Sea were as implicated in the tragedy that unfolded in 1914. Recent discoveries by the British historian Richard Bohr, who investigated royal archives in Germany, shine a new light on the man the British blamed for the war: 'Kaiser Bill.' A well-crafted TV documentary, first shown in November 2013, recounts the story of Wilhelm's difficult breech birth in 1869, during which his English mother (Queen Victoria's eldest daughter Vicky) nearly died, and which resulted in his left arm being paralysed.[19] As he grew, the people around him could not bear his crippledness so they applied all kinds of barbaric methods to re-stimulate the dead arm. Meanwhile, his mother increasingly distanced herself from the damaged goods that the young Prince represented. His unbearably traumatic childhood and mother's rejection may account for his sense of betrayal by England and his desire to construct a wave-ruling navy – one of his first undertakings when he became king at the age of 29 – to shake his fist at the whole world.

Psychoanalyst Brett Kahr sees Wilhelm's stigmatising disability, tortured childhood and lack of maternal warmth – including his refuted adolescent erotic overtures to his mother while away at school – as leading to the Kaiser holding personal grudges that led to the world's disaster, grudges that might have included an envy of the sort of fit young men who were sacrificed at war.[20] But psychohistory offers us a different view. Reflecting systemically on the story of this crippled leader, we see a crippled culture poised to implode dramatically because its values were unsustainable. We see the whole hyper-rational civilisation foundering on the shores of vulnerability, ignored by the feminine love so despised, crippled and unable to acknowledge it, a left arm (the receptive rather than acquisitive arm, controlled by the right-hemisphere, as we shall see in the next part) paralysed through its habitual dissociation.

And implode it did, with massive sacrifice of innocence, and it was unstoppable. For this was a family war: it was a war between cousins, just like those ancient epics that make up the foundation myths of our Indo-European culture, the *Mahabarata* and the *Iliad*. In these stories, conflict is shown as happening on an archetypal and symbolic level, even though it accounts for actual *lebensraum* battles happening at the time. The battle signifies how one paradigm inevitably has to give way to another, and perhaps illuminates why the Great War keeps its grip on us, because of the failure to dismantle and reconfigure the hyper-rational worldview.

So the Wounded Leader remains with us. This motif is one that we become aware of from time to time as it reoccurs in modern fiction. These days, the crippledness becomes more implicit than explicit, perhaps because of changing attitudes to the disabled. The best recent example is found in James Cameron's 2009 movie *Avatar*, which was badly reviewed but hugely popular. In the film, an avaricious mining operation from an Earth that has destroyed its greenery wishes to get rid of Planet Pandora's indigenous *Na'vi* people, who live in tribal conditions but in harmonious communication with their environment and with enlightened gender roles. Security head Colonel Quaritch, played by Stephen Lang, is highly developed in musculature and technological mastery but has no conscience. A hollow man, enlivened only by greed and hatred, he is finally killed by the heroine's second arrow to his heart.

Back to Lawrence: in *Lady Chatterley's Lover,* it is the coldness of the Wounded Leader Clifford that drives his wife into the arms of Mellors. Again, this metaphor is not just personal – it is systemic. It is the coldness of the whole Rational Man Project towards all that evokes vulnerability and love, towards the feminine. Connie stands for all these disowned qualities; her desperate case is typical of those who are not defended against them and who try to stand up for love. In my practice I have seen many such desperate cases: women or family members who have taken on the disowned characteristics and feelings of what cannot be felt by the dissociating survivor. As we would say today, Connie becomes increasingly depressed until she receives some tenderness from Mellors. I must quote at length to show how she begins to make sense of her husband:

> Clifford looked at Connie with his pale, slightly prominent blue eyes, in which a certain vagueness was coming. He seemed alert in the foreground, but the background was like the Midlands atmosphere, haze, smoky mist. And the haze seemed to be creeping forward. And it frightened her. It made him seem impersonal almost to idiocy.

> And dimly she realised one of the great laws of the human soul: that when the emotional soul receives a wounding shock, which does not kill the body, the soul seems to recover as the body recovers. But this is only appearance. It is, really, only the mechanism of reassumed habit. Slowly, slowly the wound to the soul begins to make itself felt, like a bruise which only slowly deepens its terrible ache, till it fills all the psyche. And when we think we have recovered and forgotten, it is then that the terrible after-effects have to be encountered at their worst.

> So it was with Clifford. Once he was 'well,' ... writing his stories and feeling sure of life in spite of all, he seemed to forget, and to have recovered all his equanimity. But now, as the years went by, slowly, slowly Connie felt the bruise of fear and horror coming

up and spreading in him. So it was with Clifford ... the paralysis, the bruise of the too-great shock was gradually spreading in his affective self. And as it spread in him, Connie felt it spread in her. An inward dread, an emptiness, an indifference to everything gradually spread in her soul.

Connie could be describing any boarding school survivor affectively traumatised by the Rational Man Project's fondness for educating its sons in the total institutions of the public school. Inevitably, his wife begins to lose any feeling except loneliness and starts to get properly depressed. Here was a man who had been sent back from Flanders in 1918, "more or less in bits." What was Clifford supposed to feel? Not being a real 'gentleman,' Lawrence, like Hardy, could still feel; unlike Hardy, who was desperate to become a gentleman, Lawrence was not ashamed to show that he could *feel* or to talk about feelings. This theme of feeling over time connected to wounds to the soul is one that profoundly occupied him, for Connie's thoughts also reappear in an important poem of his, 'Healing', which I have cited before in *The Making of Them*:

> I am not a mechanism, an assembly of various sections.
> And it is not because the mechanism is working wrongly,
> that I am ill.
> I am ill because of wounds to the soul,
> to the deep emotional self
> and the wounds to the soul take a long long time,
> only time can help
> and patience, and a certain difficult repentance,
> long, difficult repentance, realisation of life's mistake,
> and the freeing oneself
> from the endless repetition of the mistake
> which mankind at large has chosen to sanctify.[21]

Lawrence also knew something about the unconscious and psychoanalysis, so he could talk with authority about the "affective self" or "deep emotional self" and the nature of the wounds to the soul, and the time that the psyche demands. In fact, he wrote two essays on the subject of the unconscious and psychoanalysis. They have been largely ignored by literary critics for being too psychological and by psychoanalytic historians for being too literary, but they were nevertheless prescient on the errors of Freudianism and the importance of Jung.[22] More importantly, Lawrence wrote with unsurpassed authority about the danger of losing all ability to feel and how this could be institutionalised in British society, to its cost. He makes much more valuable reading than any psychoanalytic writer on the subject, I would suggest, except perhaps his contemporary, the ignored Scot, Iain Suttie, who was interested in the love and affection that passes between parent and child as the basis for society rather than internalised mental concepts.[23]

Connie's husband can express no feelings except exasperation, whether with his motorised wheelchair that won't take him uphill or with the colliers who look like they will go on strike again soon. Clifford is a rich man, a landowner, a mill owner but also a writer; yet in place of passion and belief he has wit. Perhaps it is the kind of wit we know all too well today from the Ned Sherrin show or the pages of the *Times* or the *Telegraph*, where anyone who believes in anything is lampooned, nothing can be taken seriously, nothing is changed – everything is at the playground level: "Only joking." Lawrence, putting his finger on how empty this style actually is, wrote that Connie's husband:

> ... seemed the most modern of modern voices, with his uncanny, lame instinct for publicity he had become, in four or five years, one of the best-known of the young "intellectuals." Where the intellect came in, Connie did not quite see. Clifford was really clever at that slightly humorous analysis of people and motives which leaves everything in bits at the end. But it was rather like puppies tearing the sofa cushions to bits: except that it was not young and playful, but curiously old, and almost obscenely conceited. It was weird: and it was nothing. This was the feeling that echoed and re-echoed at the bottom of Connie's soul: it was all nothing, a wonderful display of nothingness.

When will we ever learn?

Lady Chatterley's Lover opens with the line: "Ours is a tragic age, so we refuse to take it tragically." In this misunderstood masterpiece, Lawrence reveals the true folly of the Rational Man Project: entitlement covering emptiness, money and class together in a feudal hangover, the alienation of women and workers, and England ruined and "emasculated." I think this last, difficult word used by Lawrence needs unpacking. He is not, I think, proposing a new machismo, but rather that men might become less rational, that they might feel and love women and sex as an expression of the highest value, which for him is tenderness. This is the opposite to the mindset of the age, the machismo of the public school ethos disguising emotional crippledness, embodied in Clifford and still not rejected by us today.

Lawrence had one other exact literary contemporary, a German, who was also inspired by love, vulnerability and death, and also an invalid who died young: Rainer Maria Rilke. Rilke would have understood Lawrence's plea for "tender-hearted fucking," Rilke had a sense of the male's role in courting and honouring the female – and thereby the whole of life – as a sacred and healing way of returning to naturalness, to love, to the innocent life of the body, beyond the strategic retreat to the rational mind. Here is how Rilke expresses it:

> The terrible untruthfulness and uncertainty of our age has its roots in the refusal to acknowledge the happiness of sex. This peculiarly mistaken guilt separates us from the rest of nature, even from the child. The child's innocence does not consist in the fact that he does not understand sex, for that incomprehensible happiness, which awakens for us deep within the pulse of a close embrace, is already present – although it as yet undifferentiated – in every part of his body.[24]

Rilke, like Lawrence, died too soon. Lawrence's mission failed and his book was not made public until the 1960s. Britain did not learn the lessons he offered, did not make the "long, difficult repentance, realisation of life's mistake" that could have renewed her. This may have been because of "the great laws of the human soul: that when the emotional soul receives a wounding shock" you have to be able to go back into it and feel the impact, as both Lawrence and the shell-shock psychiatrist Rivers proposed.

Britain, however, wanted to move on. "Dark times are coming" morphed into the reality of the Second World War. After that was over, there was a brief moment of unity and renewal in Britain, a chance, out of exhaustion, to create a new unified nation that represented the reality of the common struggle that had been and the post-imperial age that was dawning. But it turned out to be a surface change only; what Lawrence brilliantly called a "mechanism of reassumed habit."[25] The Welfare State and the National Health Service were created, but the Education Act (1946) stopped short of abolishing public schools.

Lord Jeremy Hutchinson QC, interviewed by Melvyn Bragg for his BBC documentary Class and Culture, said that when Labour won the election after the war he had been convinced that what he called the "apartheid in education" would go.[26] "Clement Attlee could have done it," said Bragg "but he didn't. Perhaps he thought public schools would wither on the vine." Even though he graduated from Stowe through Oxford to the bar to the House of Lords (in contrast to Bragg's background, which he himself describes as being from "class mongrel" to "media class"), Hutchinson has absolutely no doubt about the problem:

> As long as 7% of the population go to public schools and have a separate and wonderful education, the class system will go on, it's bound to, we have class somehow in our genes in this country, it still goes on.

Attlee, Bragg explained, had assumed public schools would become less important as state schools increased in excellence. "Yet, if anything, they have become more dominant (look at the Cabinet)," commented Nigel Farndale, interviewer, journalist, and author of *Last Action Hero of the British Empire: Commander John Kerans*, when he picked up Hutchison's point in his review of the programme in the *Daily Telegraph*.[27] It sounded as if he may have been about to put his finger on the problem too but, unfortunately, Farndale is one of Lawrence's "modern voices"– too busy being amusing and playing games with the theme. It is exactly what Lawrence was talking about with Clifford's "lame instinct for publicity" and "slightly humorous analysis of people and motives which leaves everything in bits at the end." Here he goes, like so many of his kind, in his own "wonderful display of nothingness," having told us that the first TV critic of the Telegraph was in fact blind:

> I am happy to report that this thread of eccentricity continues. When the editor asked me to take over this column I said: "Sure, but I must warn you, I find 90 per cent of television unwatchable." As I discovered from the first episode of this documentary series, my taste in television has a lot to do with my being middle class.

Not finding this kind of stuff funny is, I believe, a test of sanity. For what Farndale could have pointed out but failed to, in opting for what Lawrence would have recognised as "obscenely conceited" puppy humour, was that Britain did not learn the lessons of either war by creating a real follow-through to support a society based on mutuality and empathy and an educational system to suit. Making mistakes is human, and understandable, but, the psychotherapist in me wants to say, continually failing to learn from them becomes pathological.

It has become a pathological problem. Britain did not learn from her mistakes but continued in the old Rational Man Project tradition: class loyalty, profit motive, 'tradition' and bustling public schools, now nicely called the 'independent sector.' Result: a society still divided and led by Wounded Leaders, Cameron and Boris and Co. leading us into the 21st century, with their crippled thinking.

It is towards this that we must now return our attention.

CHAPTER 10

Descartes' Mirror:

The dawning of the unconscious mind ~ The Brit and his neighbour
Losing Madonna and Child ~ C'est logique!
Great British irrationality and the pedant-bully
A question of faith ~ Christian Gentlemen
Moral: when 'rational' faith meets superpower

The dawning of the unconscious mind

If the First World War was the catastrophic culmination of the Rational Man Project, it was not its final act. The Great War is often said to have heralded the arrival of the modern age but from our perspective its legacy serves as a constant reminder that rationality has negative, 'shadow' aspects. These are principally based on a psychological trick, seemingly impossible to unlearn, created by the Project's ability to disown feelings and objectify persons, and leading to a moral abyss.

In hindsight, Freud's contemporaneous 'discovery' of the unconscious mind may be understood as an attempt to examine the shadow of the Rational Man Project and thereby take an essential step towards healing the Western world.

Even if initially focused on individuals, the great pioneers, such as Freud, Groddek, Adler and Jung – all hailing from the German-speaking world – knew that there was a major problem in European rational society. Each understood that the work of healing the collective psyche had to begin with individuals; that individuals needed to become accountable for those psychic processes with which they did not want to be identified, in order to heal the whole.

We will return to this notion of accountability, for it is a crucial one, but for now we turn to Rational Man's mind (particularly the British version) and its internal workings. In this chapter I will show that it was possible to develop a rational culture just across the sea that avoided some of the British pitfalls, and that some of these had already been set in motion historically. I shall then show how the Canadian treatment of their indigenous populations, as an extension of British colonial Rational Man policy, corrupted the leadership, as it continues to hinder progressive communal government policy in Britain today. I shall show that a profound irrationality, which is at the heart of boarding culture, is clearly at work inside Rational Man and that the consequences of this is not just undesirable but profoundly dangerous. But first: how did the British respond to the unconscious?

That the rational mind should have an unconscious dimension was – and remains – in itself either mysterious or problematic, depending on one's inclination. The 19th century saw an alarming rise in insanity, madness, hysteria or mental illness. The terms changed over time, but the real definition – which we might state as being 'that which did not fit into the Rational Man Project' – did not.

Right from the start, psychology wanted to establish itself as a branch of medical science, under the umbrella of respectable rational endeavour. But with the discovery of the unconscious mind we run into ever more irrationality, for how can science deal with something that cannot be located, let alone measured? Rational science depended on a measurer and his ability to measure; a classifier and the classified. And they were not to be the same person.

This is why Freud's self-analysis and Jung's journey into the unconscious were problematic research projects and marginalised psychotherapy from its beginning. Psychology struggled to come up with the measurements, even as Freud and Jung, both medically trained, did their utmost to be seen as scientists. Both broke all the rules in the beginning because they thought they could analyse themselves – a rational impossibility because it brought together the measurer and the measured. It is still a difficult notion within the profession today, where a view from outside the box is crucial. Even today, psychoanalysts, who are no longer required to be doctors, still cling to vestiges of the medical model, where there is an expert and an incompetent, by calling their clients 'patients.'

Psychology was to infuse the age but it was unable to really hoist itself into the mainstream of thought, chiefly because it was never a unified discipline. Endless schisms – as many schools of approach to the psyche as there are to God – did not help. And yet the new talking therapy seemed to work. Both men and women seemed to welcome outlets for what they had been repressing and a place where their emotional experiences could be counted as real. The new 'science,' if it was one, was needed, if never universally accepted. Though Britain welcomed an ailing Sigmund Freud to her shores (and subsequently a whole swathe of the inner suburbs of north-west London that nestle between the parks of Primrose Hill and Hampstead Heath would become known for their population of psychotherapists), the pragmatic British remained rather sceptical of the idea of unburdening their inner selves.

For British Rational Man, whose champion, as we know, is driven by inner fear and outer confidence and who employs the English language as a means of defence, psychology is a very frightening idea. English is riddled with terms of contempt towards psychology, or 'psychobabble,' as the tabloids call it. And, as we have seen, wherever the language of contempt or bullying appears in Britain we can be sure that the hand of fear is on the driving wheel. The Victorians had a horror of self-reflection, or 'navel gazing' as they contemptuously called it. It was supposed to be unhealthy and bad for the nerves – far better to take brisk exercise on some wind-blown moor. The military man has always mistrusted the psychologist; despite his obvious courage, he is scared of something he cannot see and fears he will be manipulated. His pet name is for the psychiatrist is 'trick cyclist.' The Jeremy Clarkson, 'stuff-and-nonsense,' 'take-'em-out'-and-shoot-'em' robust conservative style, beloved of the *Daily Mail* and *Telegraph*, favours a well-known tactic to protect itself from this fear: ridicule. Sometimes it is a warning about the advance of some 'monstrous regiment' of abhorrent psychobabblers – the ultimate horror for middle England.

And yet, there are more psychotherapy training programmes based in London than anywhere else on earth. Plus, historically, the British Renaissance psyche gave us Shakespeare, perhaps the first really psychological literature. Hamlet is familiar to us: a man plagued with self-doubt, internal conflicts and an inability to act decisively – the ultimate therapy candidate. We still love Hamlet and identify with him, even though we have since overlaid our national psyche with layers of the Rational Man Project. Shakespeare did cast him as a Dane, of course, but when we are told that "there is something rotten in the state of Denmark" we get the hint that Shakespeare may be referring to something going on closer to home. Perhaps he needed to encourage us to think outside the box?

The Brit and his neighbour

Groups – families, tribes, nations – often define themselves in comparison to their neighbours. So what about ours, the French, who birthed Enlightenment thinking and social revolution, whose Cartesian life is so evident? Do they manage introspection any better than we do? A brief look at them may help to see whether British hyper-rationality is really as unique as I am proposing.

In France the mindset is characteristically different to the British and has resulted in many projections from across the channel. French daily life, on the one hand, is richer because of an aptitude for domesticity and daily discipline; on the other hand, it is poorer as a result of habitual rigidity. My subjective experience, after 15 years of living in rural France, is that can be as hard to have a deep, subtle conversation as it is to get anything to eat outside the hours appointed for lunch and supper. This is never truer than when self-doubt creeps in. Amongst Anglophones, self-doubt is a habitual gambit that serves as an invitation to really talk, although it can also be just a style. Amongst the French, however, self-doubt seems simply to be an admission of failure and is not a welcome subject. Until they live in France, the Brits tend to think that the French are very emotional but this often turns out to have been a fantasy based on their own disowning.

With surprisingly modern psychological awareness, that extraordinarily wise Russian thinker Alexander Herzen – who, like today's postmodernists, was not afraid of generalisations – reckoned that the English tabooed any emotion below the diaphragm, whereas the French pretended to be full of feelings but were in fact thoroughly unemotional. For the Gallic temperament, Hamlet, plagued by self-doubt as he was, just did not add up. From his London base in the late 1850s, Herzen wrote:

> One would have thought that a people so capable of rapid comprehension as the French might have understood Shakespeare too. The character of Hamlet, for instance, is so universally human, especially in the stage of doubts and irresolution, in the consciousness of some black deeds being perpetrated round about them, some betrayal of the great in favour of the mean and trivial, that it is hard to imagine that he should not be understood; but in spite of every trial and effort Hamlet remains alien to the Frenchman.[1]

Hamlet's unending dilemma goes against the grain in rational France, where life can appear a gregarious, if superficial, affair, where everyone seems to hum to himself the pragmatic and phlegmatic mantra: *Pour chaque problème il y a une solution.*[2]

This is not to say that Brits like not knowing what to do. No, we prefer to 'get on with it.' We like gardening much more than sharing feelings. The British fear of self-examination – Hamlet notwithstanding – is consistent. The British are renowned for their self-deprecation; we can acknowledge self-doubt but, in general, we don't want to go very far into it. Because then we are back to 'navel gazing' and Rational Man still whispers in our ear that it's dangerous – never more so than if we have been educated as a boarder.

In these pages, I have been suggesting that the Strategic Survival Personality is the classic character grown in the Rational Man Project, hot-housed in the kind of schools we now understand were best suited to what I have called an industrial process, and uniquely confined to Britain and her colonies. I have argued that this classic poorly attached character, with his habitual self-protective avoidant or bullying style, became associated with a kind of national and well-loved character. For the strategic survivor, the greatest fear is that of exposure and that is precisely what self-examination represents to him. And worse, the fear will be heavily excited by any concerted external effort to penetrate his unconscious mind.

It is this anxiety that lies behind the extraordinary 'Calm Down Dear!' outburst by Prime Minister Cameron. The reader will remember that all he was actually meant to have done was bend the facts a little, told a tiny fib – no great sin in the world of politics, we might imagine, where everything is dressed in spin. But in his defensively organised survivor's brain, shut tight to his own unconscious mind, one discovery would mean that the whole house of cards could come crashing down.[3]

The strategic character, especially the one with a passive-aggressive manner, a defensive humour masking belittlement and an unconscious entitlement is, happily, not really to be found in France. This is what differentiates the two cultures. What saves the French and mollifies their fundamental rationality – although it does not reach in far enough to influence their insane bureaucracy – is their domesticity, their love of family. They wouldn't dream of sending their children away from the family to be educated, except for a couple of weeks for the summer *colonie*, a similar tradition to summer camp in the USA. An American writer, who spends part of each year in rural France, suggests that:

> The French are maternally oriented and have as their eternal heart the home and the rituals of table and family life, whereas somehow the British aspire to a kind of matricide in their institutions.[4]

It is a strong statement, and my friend is unwilling to be named. But if he is right, the implications are that the role of mother in the top half of British society has been undermined, broken or murdered and that this now continues from within the mother herself. Mothers in Britain, therefore, have lost their confidence in mollifying their rational non-emotional society. This awful idea begins to makes sense when you listen to the mother of one of the new eight-year-old boarders in Colin Luke's film, *The Making of Them*, confiding slyly and complacently to camera, in an interview that gave the film its name:

> I fell into conversation with a Frenchman I sat next to last night at dinner, and I just couldn't resist getting onto education, because the French have *such* different views on education – they cannot understand how we can *possibly* do what we do – how we can *bear* to send our children away: they should be coming into us *every* night and talking to us every night, how we mustn't lose touch with them, and how vital it is to see them *every* day. I *totally* disagree – I think it's the *making* of them, this sending them away. And, you know, I can see what happens, I can see them every three weeks – it's not a *drama* really.[5]

It may not be a drama for *her* but it will have affected her child for life. It will have forced him into survival mode and very likely given him a future mistrust of people and family connection, to say nothing of the opposite sex. When he grows up he may well have built in some unconscious misogynistic attitudes that slip out in his own equivalent of a 'Calm Down Dear' moment.

Nationally, the rupture from family and mother has given British rationality its unique character and is the essential point that in the end makes us so different from the French, as this mother demonstrates. It is a vital clue to understanding the *Entitled Brain*.

Losing Madonna and Child

In my earlier book, subtitled 'the British Attitude to Children,' I wondered how the loss of this maternal connection could so readily have occurred on this island. I imagined that pathways leading to the demise of the valuing of nurturing and dependence must have partly been in place before the Enlightenment and the Rational Man Project, in order to foster the breeding ground for these odd British attitudes. I speculated that the first blow might have fallen with the ripping out of the iconic images of nurturance and vulnerability when Henry VIII wrenched England away from continental Catholicism.

The immediate effects of this were stark and irreversible: the nationalisation of faith, the royal appropriation of monastic property and, most crucially, the tearing down of countless representations of the Madonna and Child and the *Pietà*. The absence of images of nurture and dependence will have had a profound effect on the generations who grew up only with the image of suffering man, represented by the crucifix that remained. Perhaps Shakespeare's return to the classics and paganism was an attempt to compensate for this patriarchal lurch. Certainly, the loss of the power and dignity of the universal image of Mother and Child and the rituals that accompanied it throughout the year, following the changing seasons with holidays devoted to the saints, is still palpable, I believe, in our society.

The legacy of this loss is not taught today in any of our schools. Nor would the likes of Minister Gove and colleagues be in a hurry to introduce it to reflect on the loss of parenting and childhood that the boarding child undergoes as mark of privilege. No, the British Empire and the way of life, with which we still identify, was built *over* this erasure and perfected, as we have seen, by means of the Rational Man Project. Imperial Britain had already got used to the absence of the nurturing feminine principle and came up with an ingenious and precise tool for bringing non-rational elements under its thumb, specifically its own children and the indigenous world. This was the cult of breaking children away from their roots, which Roman Catholic imagery might still preserve and somehow integrate, as in Latin America. Instead, the merciless and judgmental *inner Protestant*, who had the magic facility for making even great peoples feel inferior, was installed, as it were, as an operating system in their psyches. This was how the British Raj did the trick to the South Asian Indians as well as to her own people.

The transatlantic Indians – Native Americans – however, were more stubborn. Astonishingly, only a century and half ago, some of them were still rooted in a near Neolithic hunter-gatherer way of life. Others, like the Maya and Hopi, visited by C.G. Jung in the 1920s, had a settled farming life organised on celestial observations. Outnumbered by the British, and without their technological know-how, once they had been militarily vanquished, the Native Americans needed to be integrated if they were not to be massacred (as had happened in Tasmania). The new British educational invention, the boarding school – or 'residential school,' as it was called in North America and Australia – was a perfect way to finish off the job.

In Canada, a relatively late offshoot of the British Rational Man Project, evidence about these practices in the late 19th century as well as the early to mid 20th century has begun to emerge. In the spring of 2012, the Truth and Reconciliation Commission of Canada delivered its interim report on residential schools, entitled *They Came for the Children*, based on abundant records contained in the national bureaucratic storehouses. The records told of deliberate, considered government policy to separate indigenous children from their families in order to break their language, culture and religion – and thereby their will – in the name of socialisation and civilisation. What emerged as the key means for this was the residential school system partnered with the church. The commissioners summarised the evidence they found as follows:

Government and church officials often said the role of the residential school was to civilize and Christianize Aboriginal children. When put into practice, these noble-sounding ambitions translated into an assault on Aboriginal culture, language, spiritual beliefs, and practices. Residential schools were seen as preferable to on-reserve day schools because they separated children from their parents, who were certain to oppose and resist such a radical cultural transformation. The government's intent to break Aboriginal family bonds was clear from the outset.[6]

In the early years of these schools, one in six children did not survive. Whether they died of maltreatment, malnutrition or simply giving up the ghost can only be guessed – detailed records of this were, unsurprisingly, omitted. But it was not just the brutality that worked: it was the wrenching away of the children from instinctual and natural bonds, the life of the body, the culture of family. For this takes place in the context of love denied and is overridden by life-denying patriarchal ends. In fact, this was something very basic that the British Empire chose to ignore. The TRCC Interim Report again:

> Missionaries across North America commented on the close bond between Aboriginal parents and their children. A seventeenth-century missionary, Gabriel Sagard, observed, "They love their children dearly."[7]

The desire deliberately to sever the bonds of familial love was the ultimate mistake – indeed I would say 'crime.' It meant that a kind of covert genocide became normalised in the British colonies, although the French Canadians – of course – did not adopt the practice. The British loss of reverence for nurture and family became fully institutionalised overseas, as it was at home. This, I believe, has monumental consequences. It means that the mother's attitude in Colin Luke's film, quoted on page 212, and the treatment of 'savages' in the 1880s is a consistent psychohistorical entity. It means that ex-boarders will inevitably pooh-pooh the 'soft' areas of life, such us love, bonding and intimacy, as Utopian fantasies, because they cannot bear to bring the grief of what they have lost from out of their unconscious minds. No wonder they fear psychotherapists.

In the war against the despised and disowned indigenous or natural part inside of them, ex-boarders then settle for defensive belittlement as a way of life. It means that British ex-boarders can see themselves as world leaders but – like a Cameron in Europe – their brittle, unfulfilled characters leave them blind to the nuances of relationship. Psychohistorically, it meant that the Rational Man Project in Britain would ensure its continuity in the country's elite and fail to embrace the solution: compassionate self-reflection. For in self-reflection the observer and the observed may become one, the grief and repentance for crimes enshrined in culture may be acknowledged and a move can be made towards the ultimate reconnection, in which objects become subjects again. This can be the only remedy for hyper-rationality. Herzen puts the problem much more elegantly than I ever could:

> The impersonality of mathematics and the un-human objectivity of nature do not call forth sides of the soul and do not awaken them; but as soon as we touch upon questions of life, of art, of morals, in which a man is not only an observer and investigator but at the same time himself a participant, then we find a physiological limit, which it is very hard to cross with one's old blood and brains unless one can erase from them all traces of the songs of the cradle, of the fields and the hills of home, of the customs and whole setting of the past.[8]

C'est logique!

I want now to turn to a further problem that inevitabley occurs when rationality collides with the unconscious mind; this is a logical and structural problem. Logic is built in to Enlightenment thinking and, as every Frenchman knows, underlies a 'modern' approach to life. "C'est logique" is quoted in countless daily conversations in France, as a kind of proof. But the Age of Reason's logic, based initially on the rediscovered premises of Socratic philosophy, is only one way to approach the world. It benefited, as we have seen, from its heavy reliance on the process of differentiation and compartmentalisation. Philosopher Jim Danaher explains:

> Both Plato and Aristotle understood that we naturally encountered contradictions but we could eliminate them by thinking analytically and dividing things up into ever-smaller parts until all the contradictions disappeared. Socrates is a contradiction in that he is both a father and not a father. We can eliminate that contradiction,

however, by thinking about Socrates at one particular time or in relationship to one particular person.[9]

Here, readers may well be reminded of the dissociation and compartmentalisation process in its most basic form – thinking about something else. It is an everyday mental conjuring trick that, as we know, can become habitual and problematic. But Danaher continues:

> These are the qualifications that Plato and Aristotle ascribe in order to analytically break things down into ever smaller parts and thereby eliminate contradictions and give us clear and distinct ideas. In the modern era, Descartes took this a step further and convinced us that all clear and distinct ideas are true. This Cartesian thinking came to have such a hold on the modern mind that we eventually came to believe that only *clear and distinct* ideas were true. Consequently, analytic thinking came to be seen as synonymous with reason itself and ideas that were vague, ambiguous, or contradictory simply were not true. Modernity became obsessed with analysis and the elimination of vague, ambiguous, or contradictory ideas.[10]

Of course, there is nothing more "vague, ambiguous, or contradictory" than a psychology based on the premise of the unconscious mind – no wonder it is so challenging to rationality! It means that there may be unconscious motivations at play (better if they had been eliminated) in us all, alongside our conscious ones. This is why the *New Yorker* reviewer quoted at the beginning of this book baulked at a psychological approach that meant you might have "to subscribe to some fairly woolly assumptions, for instance, that a nation's child-rearing techniques affect its foreign policy."[11]

Thus the major goal of Aristotelian logic, upon which modern rationality is academically based, sets out very clearly to define and enforce its universe of reference, thereby avoiding paradoxes and contradictions and leaving us with "clear and distinct ideas." With that in mind, Plato and Aristotle introduced what have come to be known in philosophy as the Laws of Thought. These laws form the basis of Formal Logic, the epistemology upon which rationality is constructed or 'proven' – depending on your point of view. The pillars of the means of validating an argument rest on three sturdy foundation stones:

1. The Law of Identity, by which A always equals A
2. The Law of Non-Contradiction, which states that A never equals –A (pronounced '*not* A')
3. The Law of Excluded Middles, which states that one is permitted *either* A or –A but *not both* A and –A, for A and –A cannot exist at the same time.

This logic may seem simple enough but – especially in the case of the law of excluded middles, the great bastion of sane pragmatism – it runs up against the understanding of two further disciplines, which are close to philosophy but are not identical to it. These are psychology and theology, and they are based on altogether different logical systems, even if their practitioners tend to avoid pointing it out. Readers will recall that I have suggested that one of the Enlightenment's greatest strengths – the differentiation of disciplines – enabled specialisation and clear thinking, but specialisation, in which disciplines tend neither to talk to nor learn from one another, also became one of its greatest weaknesses.

The first discipline to clash with the logical structure of rationality was the one of newest, psychology, whose fundamental premise is that whatever the rational mind avoids has to be examined if it is to become whole again. *Depth psychology*, the branch of psychology I have been introducing in this volume, is chiefly concerned with the process of non-identification or dissociation and the storehouse of disowned material, the unconscious mind or the *subconscious*. Both unconscious and subconscious are challenging concepts for rationality, since the law of excluded middles specifically asserts that an 'I' and a 'not I' cannot exist at the same time. Depth psychology and its medical parent, psychiatry, on the other hand, are concerned with how the psyche manages and organises the 'not I' material alongside the 'I.' Practitioners generally seek to assist people with the reintegration of the 'not I' material that has been dumped in the unconscious or projected out onto another person. No wonder the pragmatic British tend to fear the 'trick-cyclists' who are pretending to be scientists but are acting right outside the bounds of rational laws!

Theology is the second branch of study that operates outside the laws of thought. Throughout all the world's religions, spiritual insights regularly arise in the form of paradoxes, especially in non-monotheistic religions. The idea that the soul is distinct and separate from its source is frequently considered to be the principal illusion to be seen through. In its place, the practitioner confirms an established paradoxical metaphor of 'somewhat distinct but not separate' – like a tree in a forest – as the fundamental metaphysical premise.

I remember when I first glimpsed the incompatibility of spiritual truth with rationality's laws. It was in 1969 and, having had enough of having rationality forced down my throat at the expense of emotion and sexuality at public school, I walked out of my Oxford philosophy class in vainglorious protest at having to swallow the law of excluded middles. I had been dabbling in Hinduism and it seemed to me that the Formal Logic Don must be wrong. Paradox was the key to unlocking the world's mysteries, I arrogantly said to myself at the age of twenty. I went on to read Oriental Studies but even then, elegantly translating the *Bhagavad-Gita* was apparently more important than its message. I discovered that the Rational Man Project had such a hold on thought processes that in the British education system, the outward form – in this case Sanskrit grammar – counted for far more than the inner essence: the profound teachings of the charioteer God Arjuna. I am afraid that the ensuing years have not yet caused me to change that view.

Great British irrationality and the pedant-bully

So far I have argued for the flawed nature of the Rational Man Project but I must now commit what in Britain counts as the worst of political sins: I am going to make a U-turn.

I want to propose that alongside the pragmatic, conservative, hyper-rationalism that characterises the British elite and their aspirant middle-class supporters is a series of habits and rituals that are founded in *extreme* irrationality. I will now mention three singularly British habits – almost drives – and suggest that these are profoundly irrational. They form part of the full profile of how psychologically stuck we are and, in particular, how these impede the emergence of healthy national attitudes that would lead to sound political leadership.

First comes sport – or better, the cult of 'games,' which we have already discussed. To sum up: the cult of games is intrinsic to public school life, whence it has been exported to the rest of the world, and recently overflowed into ritual ecstasy at the 2012 London Olympics. Its chief irrationality is that it is based on a bogus value system, that of team spirit and a uniquely British value known as 'playing the game.' It is not that these are wrong; but the lesson they afford is so readily taken out of context that it frequently leads to utter disaster, as in the sacrificial Charge of the Light Brigade, the ritual slaughter of the Great War and other follies. Besides, it tends to encourage partisanship over collaboration, which is a major fault in a shrinking world that now needs global perspectives.

The two other irrationalities are pedantry, which takes the law of excluded middles all the way to *logicum ad absurdum,* and a specific kind of religious faith that leaps over it altogether. Let us begin with pedantry, for the other is much more complex and even more controversial.

Making a virtue out of detail is a British middle class speciality. We are the masters of asserting how a word should be used, spelled or employed and pointing out when there has been the slightest irrational and rather foolish breach in these conventions. Such things matter a lot to the Brit, and many a foreigner has noticed how we can focus extremely seriously on the 'proper' way of doing some things, which to an outsider may be quite puzzling. We can get very upset over the slightest cruelty to animals, for example, while normalising the deprivation of the elite's children of a permanent home-life. The dynamic use of language and the ability to invent words such as the resplendent masterpiece 'chillax!' (meaning relax, chill out, take it easy), is seemingly enough to drive Mr or Mrs Disgusted of Tunbridge Wells to the brink of insanity. It is just not a real word, they would say, ignoring the English language's phenomenal dynamism.

This love affair with pedantry could legitimise itself through an appeal to rationality's truths, which, as we know, should be 'clear and distinct.' But its deployment is so obsessional, so keen for the word to look right, regardless of what it means, so partisan of the outer over the inner, that the British middle classes' resort to pedantry frequently enters the territory of madness. This madness has a purpose: to support hyper-conservative aims. For foreigners and the working classes will never, ever get it right and therefore deserve a regular mild put-down. In fact, when analysed, pedantry frequently reveals a bully beneath – but an innocent one, of course. It is 'clear and distinct,' in that when you have been hurt by it you will never forget it or fail to notice it when it occurs again. It can make you very nervous. However, naming it and stopping it is a different matter, because a pragmatic innocent excuse will always accompany the pedant-bully.

Readers may remember the 'kind' letter (quoted in Chapter 4) that pretended to alert me to the typos in the text of my first book and the number of sentences it took me to analyse the covert bullying and disowned vulnerability contained in it. I have much correspondence with many boarding school survivors who have heard about the treatment programme but may still be testing out the waters to see if it is safe for them to come in. I regularly come across pedantry defensively used and deployed with covert aggression but I now understand it as masked fear of vulnerability and dependence. What is surprising, though, is that it apparently never occurs to the writer that a psychotherapist who specialises in these matters might interpret his tone as aggression or bullying. Here is another recent example.

A man had filled in an application form and answered the question, "Why do you want to do this workshop at this point in your life?" by saying only that his wife thought he should. Given that places are limited and candidates' motivation to attend needs to be checked out, I wrote back in what I hoped was a tone that would be gently encouraging and rather family-doctorish, in order not to alarm him:

> It would help me if you could enlarge a little, on an email, in confidence of course, as to why you want to do this course now, as opposed to your wife's idea.

But this request turned out to be the last straw. I cannot of course quote his full reply, because I promised confidentiality. But I can say that his reaction was to withdraw his application, and his tactic was to make me feel a fool for stupidly asking him to combine "enlargement with brevity." Thus he gave himself a way out, for every fool ought to know that these two – enlargement and brevity – cannot coexist – by the law of excluded middles! He could not rationally be expected to put his precious, defensively organised psyche in the hands of such an exasperating fool, and so could now safely get on with his life. My interpretation is that he seized this as an excuse for the fact that he was dealing with yet another – in his mind – absurd demand from his wife. I wondered about the horrors of pedantic correction she would have to live with. In his use of hyper-rationality, he irrationally cut off his access to an avenue that may have led towards help and towards coming home to himself. Is this mad, or just sad?

As we saw in the case of the man who pointed out my typos, covert bullying is a way of getting equal and compensating for profound feelings of inferiority; additionally, it can be a way of compensating for profound feelings of loss that are not recognised. This is not just individual: it is systemic – deeply connected with the psychohistorical narrative I have been pursuing concerning hyper-rationality and imperialism. I sense in Britain an unconscious well of deep outrage about the loss of the natural self, the inability to safely be a child, the loss of what anthropologist Jean Liedloff calls the *in-arms experience*,[12] the loss of the indigenous self on which war was made over centuries. At the effect of someone's pedantic hostility you become irritated, because the anger and the grief that exists in unknown vast surging quantities amongst the English middle classes become displaced and dumped on you. You become all the disowned material: the aggression, the foolish child, the indigenous savage and helpless – just because you used the wrong word or letter or pronunciation. The pedant, however, retains the illusion of being calm, normal and right.

In the next chapter we will go on to see how this illusion affects the structure of ex-boarders' brains in a society where such a brain is not identified as impaired but normalised. But first, we need to consider the third irrationality: faith.

A question of faith

Religion and rationality are always strange bedfellows. Rationality, by definition, has a reliance on *a priori* knowledge, while religion has a fondness for the "vague, ambiguous, or contradictory," to use Danaher's words. The logical outcome of British rationality, I suppose, would be someone like Richard Dawkins, scientist, best-selling author of *The Selfish Gene* and a supreme master of the pedantic public school sneer. In his latest incarnation as a radical atheist his highlighting of the irrationality in Christianity can sometimes be amusing. One such hilarious passage in his 2006 best-seller *The God Delusion* is his commentary on the, admittedly hard to grasp, Roman Catholic doctrine of The Holy Trinity. Like a schoolboy who has just cut chapel, Dawkins mischievously cites the Catholic Encyclopaedia's failed attempt to explain it; in fact, it is something that cannot be explained. "Do we have one God in three parts, or three Gods in one?" he wonders, dripping heavy scented sarcasm all over that and many of the following pages.[13]

Philosophically, Dawkins is not on as sure ground as he thinks he is. He is guilty of category error, for throwing out the baby of spirituality with the bathwater of dogma. But a Dawkins cannot really help in such matters, precisely because he tries too hard to be amusing, to be mocking. Like a rational pedant with an axe to grind, like an intelligent Jeremy Clarkson, there is a toxic feel to his sarcasm. His pedantry is a further dimension of rationality's shadow, which turns up all over Britain, as we have seen, especially in ex-boarders. Simon Cohen, who at the time of writing was researching public school humour and its influence on British culture in general, calls Dawkins:

> ... the most sneering and imperious of public school boys. With him we have a pseudo-scientific justification of survival strategies. How more powerful can you make yourself than claim you have the purview of human nature?![14]

Dawkins cannot solve the problem of religion because he is too far inside the rational box to see its limitations. A less taxing way round the problem of religion is simply to believe or not believe. And here the British have a rather special attitude to religion as they have traditionally professed it: it is never quite apparent whether they do believe it, or whether it is a social convention they accept, rather like good manners. Besides, if you have been educated in one of those temples of rationality, the boarding public school, you'll have lines of the Bible and the Book of Common Prayer coursing through your head, impossible to remove, supplying a resonant stream of elegant words, ready for handy re-use. They are very useful should you want to humiliate someone, as Boris did with his "God and Mammon" utterance, for example. The reason for this is not piety but forced attendance. Not counting any religious education or conformation classes, a full ten-year stint at a British boarding school probably meant that you sat in chapel, listening to the lesson and Psalms, some 2,500 times. So in the end you become identified with the religion whether you believe it or not.

It is perhaps safer to assume that the British don't really believe and, as once was the case with matters of money, barely mention religion at all. It's not really polite in Britain, after all. However, sometimes the temptation is too much. I was once at an ex-pat Christmas lunch party in south-west France, seated next to two middle-class Englishmen, both self-confessed Christians, one a recent covert to the Church of England. Starving for interesting conversation, I decided to enquire what the notion of *salvation* meant to them. I was especially interested in what lay behind this conversion to Anglicanism. In fact, one of his family members had told me that it was simply a way for him to join in more with his Home Counties community, which seemed fair enough to me. There was a long pause. I realised the pair were not comfortable with the conversation. It was perhaps impolite, too private. Finally the more experienced believer spoke:

"It is a question of faith, I suppose," said he.

"Yes, that's it, a question of *faith*," agreed the new convert.

Is it faith that can get us out of the rational trap? We may believe, but the real issue is surely: faith in *what*? In what does a good Englishman really believe? Lord Noel Annan, in his remarkable book, *Our Age*, suggests that:

> Protestant Christianity set a so impossibly high standard of conduct that the cult of the gentleman had to be substituted to provide a realisable ideal.[15]

Therefore, Annan suggests, the English made things a little easier for themselves by socialising religion, putting the visibility of organisation and good behaviour before piety. This attitude to religion seems to have remained in place in Britain and it also has a specific tone because of the unique link of church and state, which obliges politicians to profess faith. The socialisation of religion is not necessarily bad: indigenous societies have done it regularly to good effect, especially in Central America. But it depends, of course, on what sort of society is promoted. One that regularly denies the value of bonds of attachment cannot possibly be a good spiritual investment by any competent religious logic.

I never imagined that I would want to quote the outspoken right-wing broadcaster, historian David Starkey, known as 'the rudest man in Britain,' but he may have got it about right on the topic of the British and religion. Here he tells Rachel Cooke of the *Observer* about this unique British religious attitude:

> The church made a lethal mess when Michael Ramsey was appointed archbishop by Harold Macmillan. It rediscovered Christianity, and that was fatal. Until that point, the archbishops had been the high priests of English Shinto: in other words, the church's job was really just to enable us to worship the monarchy, and by extension ourselves. That was sensible. But then it got cluttered up with all that nonsense about Christianity. The church has got to choose between being a national church or an international communion. It can't be both.[16]

Is Starkey suggesting that what the British believe in is *themselves*? That, skilled at self-deprecation, with self-doubt as their social passport, they contentedly bask in self-worship?

Odd, but it might have some advantages. It might be good for business, and that is very British. The first post-Christmas news in the nation of shopkeepers is kind of holy ritual – the sales performance of the department stores along London's Oxford Street. In Christmas 2013, apparently, John Lewis came top of the class, with House of Fraser a close second, while Debenhams came bottom.

Christian gentlemen

In imperial times, the preference for civilised Anglicised society over real religious experience had a wider implication. The Empire linked religion with global business enterprise, partly to make it feel that it was giving as good as it was getting. Christianity and 'civilisation' were the items exchanged for the raw materials and commodities manhandled by the Empire's enslaved indigenous inhabitants, converted into manufactured goods and sold back to the citizens of Europe. A colonial entrepreneur could feel good about the deal if the 'savages' were getting the wisdom of the Church of England into the bargain. The process was brilliantly conceived, for religion could be a major part of smashing the indigenous way of life while simultaneously easing the 'savage' up the next rung of the ladder to become a farm or factory worker, creating servants of the industrial revolution, poised for imperialism's next transmogrification into corporate power.

The establishment of residential schools, steeped in Christianity and with even more horrors than public schools but none of the privilege, was an essential tool in this process. These schools played a major role in the colonies, although not so much in Africa. Perhaps Africans took to Christianity more readily than American or Australian aboriginals, on whose lands most of the schools were built. In India, where missionary zeal fell mostly on deaf ears, boarding schools were only established for wealthy, high caste Indians who wanted to play the winner's game. Ordinary Hindus and Muslims could accept Jesus without embracing his cult. In Canada, however, the boarding school intervention was done very consciously, debated in Parliament and subject to reports that can be studied today. In 1879, the newly confederated government in the Federal Dominion of Canada appointed Nicholas Davin to investigate the boarding school system in the United States with an eye to establishing similar schools in the Northwest Territories. The Davin Report is a fascinating insight into how religion could be combined with rationality for the sake of the goal of taming indigenous populations. The Truth and Reconciliation Commission of Canada describes it thus:

> On the strength of his limited investigation, Davin recommended the federal government establish a partnership with the Canadian churches for two reasons. The first was moral. The type of education he was advocating would undermine existing spiritual and cultural beliefs, and it would be wrong, he said, to destroy their faith "without supplying a better" one; namely, Christianity.[17]

This would seem less noxious if it were a theological idea, a question of faith, based on a real belief that Christianity was the better religion. But, as we have seen, the British way was to combine religion with social cohesion and money. The Interim Report continues:

> The second reason was economic. Davin said teachers should be paid adequately, but by hiring missionaries, the government

would get "an enthusiastic person, with, therefore, a motive power beyond anything pecuniary remuneration could supply." Put more plainly, dedicated religious men and women would be attracted to residential schools, even if the pay were substandard.

In other words, with unfailing colonial pragmatism – after all, they were dealing with indigenous objects rather than rational persons – it might as well be done *on the cheap*! This was not an isolated case and was not confined to politicians or clergy, who are allowed, one might imagine, to be irrational sometimes. No, it was deeply embedded in the Victorian rational scientific viewpoint. Besides, according to the German historian Peter Wende, the whole of the British Empire was designed to be done on the cheap.[18]

In the TV documentary, *Empire*, Jeremy Paxman recounts the extraordinary case of the Anthropological Society of London, and it is worth revisiting that in the context of the pragmatic use of Christianity to promulgate colonialism.[19] The society was founded in 1863 by the explorer Richard Burton and a speech therapist, James Hunt. It was a breakaway organisation from the existing Ethnological Society of London, defining itself in opposition to the older society. According to its founders, who supported the Confederacy in the American Civil War, which was currently raging, it would concern itself with the "collection of facts and the identification of natural laws that explained the diversity of humankind."[20] The issue that most sharply divided the two groups was the "Negro question." Here is how Hunt addressed this august body in his opening speech:

> Whatever may be the conclusion to which our scientific inquiries may lead us, we should always remember, that by whatever means the Negro, for instance, acquired his present physical, mental and moral character, whether he has risen from an ape or descended from a perfect man, we still know now that the Races of Europe have much in their mental and moral nature which the races of Africa have not got.

Most of Hunt's listeners will have concurred – of course they did, because the major popular item of faith in Britain was that "the British, the British, the British are best." The imperial attitude was (and sometimes it seems like it still is) that Brits occupy a God-ordained place in the universe and were born to be leaders. It is admirable that Paxman pointes to this, but to me he is still far more timid here than in the newsroom. Why did he not refer to Cecil Rhodes? Rhodes was one of the classic figures in the inglorious late 19th century carve-up of Africa, a founder of a firm (De Beers) that still commands immense riches, and the man after whom a whole country (now called Zimbabwe) was named. In 1887, when he was 24 and still at Oxford, Rhodes was proud to put it this way:

> I contend that we are the finest race in the world and that the more of the world we inhabit the better it is for the human race.[21]

The new theories of Charles Darwin had not completely replaced God; instead they were co-opted in the public mind to include the Brit as the pinnacle of evolution. It was as if God had created the lower animals for the apes to evolve from; similarly, man, evolving from the primates, would flower in his finest natural progression: an English gentleman! This 'explained' the widespread belief that the Empire was given to us. Not only was this something to be taken on faith but it also clearly concealed a remarkable racism, even if the word had not yet been invented.

Such attitudes do not belong to such a distant past as we may think. When I was a child in the 1950s, people generally felt sorry for foreigners, without any sense of irony. When my family moved to Germany in 1956 we were hesitant to go to the dentist because, like everything else British, British dentists were 'the finest in the world.' This turned out to be nonsense: the Germans were already streaks ahead of us in everything; they already had showers and central heating and all kinds of 'mod cons', including state of the art dentists' equipment.

Moral: when 'rational' faith meets superpower

Sixty years on, the Camerons and Blairs still act as if they believe in Starkey's "English Shinto" – in British superiority; or if they don't, they seem to think it the only possible rousing battle cry. Here's Tony Blair in May 2007, making his long awaited announcement to resign as Labour leader and prime minister of the UK:

Britain is not a follower, it is a leader. It gets the essential characteristic of today's world: its interdependence. This is a country today that, for all its faults, for all the myriad of unresolved problems and fresh challenges, is comfortable in the 21st century, at home in its own skin, able not just to be proud of its past but confident of its future. This country is a blessed nation. The British are special, the world knows it, in our innermost thoughts, we know it. This is the greatest nation on Earth. It has been an honour to serve it.[22]

If this sounds a bit like 19th century jingoism, or a Second World War rallying cry, or Shakespeare's Henry IV at the walls of Harfleur, some of us – or some parts of our selves – may feel that it is charming. But others – or other parts of our selves – have a right to be perplexed and alarmed for the future. For Blair goes on to comment on what he well knows was his political downfall – being led in blind faith by the Bush administration into the Iraq war, on evidence that even at the time he must have been known to be faulty:

I ask you to accept one thing. Hand on heart, I did what I thought was right. I may have been wrong. That's your call. But believe one thing if nothing else – I did what I thought was right for our country.

We may be impressed by his faith, but *wilful* blindness – which this appears to be – is downright dangerous. In his love affair with being on High Table[23] and being wooed and wowed by the Queen, it appears that Blair fell into every trap set by, arguably, the most Machiavellian manipulation of truth through an appeal to faith since the late Middle Ages. If you bypass the discriminating equipment of the neo-cortex and cannot see through a faith-based approach you court extreme danger. The development of a Strategic Survival Personality means that you are realistically vulnerable to potential manipulation by others who might want to exploit you badly. Even though he must have known that the history of faith and warfare combined is not a happy one, Blair got completely caught napping.

How this trick can work – and, alarmingly, has worked – even in a sophisticated rational culture was revealed in an extraordinary statement made in confidence to the award-winning American journalist and senior national-affairs reporter for *The Wall Street Journal*, Ron Suskind. In a 2004 article in *The New York Times Magazine*, quoting by agreement an unnamed aide to George W. Bush (thought to be Karl Rove, Senior Advisor and Deputy Chief of Staff to former President Bush), Suskind wrote:

> The aide said that guys like me were "in what we call the reality-based community," which he defined as people who "believe that solutions emerge from your judicious study of discernible reality." I nodded and murmured something about enlightenment principles and empiricism. He cut me off.

> "That's not the way the world really works anymore," he continued. "We're an empire now, and when we act, we create our own reality. And while you're studying that reality – judiciously, as you will – we'll act again, creating other new realities, which you can study too, and that's how things will sort out. We're history's actors... and you, all of you, will be left to just study what we do."[24]

This chilling remark, expressed in blazing arrogant confidence, ranks for me next to the dangerous lunacy of General Haig and shows what great danger we are in if the British elite are not super-aware and do not stop being hindered by their sense of entitlement, their inflexible brains, their lack of emotional intelligence and their defensive personality structures.

Bizarrely, 'reality-based' and 'faith-based' communities are now recognised terms in the United States. By the end of 2004, the phrase "proud member of the reality-based community" began to appear in US media expressions as a profession of authority. The original source of the term has been ascribed to Bruce Bartlett, a domestic policy adviser to Reagan and a treasury official for the first Bush. Bartlett had told Suskind that the nature of the conflict that surrounded the 2004 US election was

> ... the same as the one raging across much of the world: a battle between modernists and fundamentalists, pragmatists and true believers, reason and religion.

Bartlett had apparently little doubt (let alone shame) about where Bush and his faith-based enemy Al Qaeda stood, adding that:

This is why George W. Bush is so clear-eyed about Al Qaeda and the Islamic fundamentalist enemy. He believes you have to kill them all. They can't be persuaded, they're extremists, driven by a dark vision. He understands them, because he's just like them. The whole thing about faith is to believe things for which there is no empirical evidence.[25]

It is not a question of intelligence; Blair is certainly no fool and, as the Democrat Senator Carl Levin told Suskind, Bush was "plenty smart enough to do the job." Levin paused:

It's his lack of curiosity about complex issues which troubles me.[26]

ACT IV

INSIDE THE ENTITLED BRAIN

Bad equipment for a Leader

This ain't no upwardly mobile freeway
This is the road to Hell.

Chris Rea, British singer/songwriter, born 1952

CHAPTER 11

New Science:
The brain heart connection

Reason's shadow unveiled

Curiosity about complex issues, apparently so challenging for George W Bush, is probably the human attribute best served by the Enlightenment.[1] The ability to be curious about the world, both inside and outside the brain, is evolution's extraordinary gift to *Homo sapiens*. Much loved broadcaster Alistair Cooke, who died aged 95 in 2004, used to say that curiosity was the chief secret to longevity. Professor Brian Cox, particle physicist and presenter of the BBC's marvellous 2013 documentary *Wonders of Life*, might be worth following in this context, for although he describes himself as middle-aged he radiates youthfulness and infects his viewers with his unbounded curiosity. Cox exhibits a different kind of boyishness from those young-seeming politicians we met in Chapter 5. His scientific analysis of life, featuring the human brain's ability to wonder, analyse and present a living synthesis, delights and enlightens our sense of being alive.

As far as we know, the human brain is unique in being able to create such a marvel of perception, reflection and synthesis. We do know that a systemic relational web within the brain and the entire nervous system, fronted by the evolutionary unique self-reflective neo-cortex makes it possible.

Like other vertebrates, our brain's division into two interlinked hemispheres further refines our quality of attention into two distinct but connected functions. These differences in attention – and thereby perception – have important implications for the study of hyper-rationality. In very general terms, one function provides a broad, systemically interconnected picture and the other provides a sharply focused distancing in order to study details more closely. Working together, the two halves of our brain are capable of much more than simply serving survival.

In the preceding chapters we saw that distancing themselves from objects of study, which the Enlightenment facilitated, had huge advantages for humans in terms of creativity, before the disadvantages of excessive distance and separation – such as over-reliance on dissociation, compartmentalisation and objectification – began to bite. It is hardly surprising, then, to discover that people who have spent their childhood in love-free institutions and trained to become hyper-rational have brains that are habituated to compartmentalisation, lack of connection and excess separation. In consequence, these brains become further moulded by these mental tendencies as they become chronic habits. Science has now shown that the functioning, and even the material structure of the brain, can be adversely influenced if a human being's inbuilt expectation of living in a web of connections gets overridden by environmental conditions. But it is uncanny to discover that the same specialisation and lack of dialogue that first benefited but now hampers science and academia can become replicated in the actual structures of the brain. Before we turn to the scientific evidence for this, we must briefly return to our historical survey to see how the shadow side of rationality began to be exposed.

The trauma of the Great War and the Great Depression that followed it resulted in a further cataclysm for the Western world. In the meantime, rationality had its first serious philosophic challenge with the discovery of the unconscious mind. It was not until the next huge shift in consciousness, which began in the wake of the Second World War and came to fruition in the mid-1960s, with existentialism, postmodernism, feminism and ecology, that the world began to take serious note of the problems of Enlightenment thinking and the Rational Man Project. In the new critique of rationality, unlike at the beginnings of psychoanalysis, politics and psychology finally became bedfellows and, as such, were at last able to point to the limits of rationality within the framework of a nascent discipline of psychohistory.

Both the British anti-psychiatry movement and French social theorists began to point out that, from the 18th century onwards, the definition of insanity included whatever was considered to oppose the hallowed Enlightenment principle of Reason. The 1960s counter-argument was that madness could be understood as a healthy response to the dominant super-rational discourse of society, whose consensus reality held individuals in a kind of a trance. So going a little crazy or listening to the potential wisdom of the insane began to be fashionable. French philosopher Michel Foucault added that madness had a function in that it had the power to signify the limits of social order and point towards uncomfortable truths. To the official upholders of reason, he suggested, madness had political significance and therefore needed to be silenced.[2]

During the 19th century, rationality's fear of the irrational began to acquire a more scientific name: mental illness. The mentally ill needed to be away from society, constrained and isolated, as if their malady were contagious. In the 1980s, Elaine Showalter proposed that despite psychiatry's obsession with hysterical women it was not until the mid-20th century that anyone began to consider that what they had to say might be worth listening to or that some women might be unhappy in their social role[3] Such psycho-political arguments found many adherents in academia and amongst the young, but were still slow to influence the mainstream.

In the late 20th century, excessive rationality began to encounter challenges from other directions, especially when the influence of Oriental philosophies began to take hold. One of the most thorough critiques of Enlightenment thinking comes from contemporary philosopher and mediator, Ken Wilber, whose *Integral philosophy* synthesises schools of learning from Eastern as well as Western traditions. Through painstaking scholarship, Wilber shows how the Enlightenment managed to split apart the main disciplines of human intellectual endeavour, which he calls the 'Big Three' – science, morals and art. These correspond to Plato's 'The Good, the Beautiful and the True,' Kant's three critiques of Reason and Karl Popper's 'subjective, cultural and objective worlds,' or the domains of I, WE and IT. In Enlightenment thinking, as we have seen, these were differentiated and made separate in the attempt to free thought from the merged state of the pre-modern worldview. In his 800-page opus *Sex, Ecology, Spirituality*, Wilber tracks the philosophical underpinnings of this separation and proposes that it is time to reintegrate the Big Three, a movement that in the fields of cutting-edge science and spirituality seems already to be underway.[4]

Differentiation – blessing or curse?

With hindsight, the Enlightenment is probably best understood as a movement of mass differentiation. Differentiation is a fantastically powerful thought process because it enables thinking 'outside the box,' the praises of which I have already sung, and something called *necessary distance*, a particular feature of left-hemisphere attention, to which I shall return to in some detail throughout this section on the *Entitled Brain*. Enlightenment thinking managed to get outside the box and explode with creativity: human curiosity and invention began to know no bounds.

Differentiation works wonders but, like all things: up to a point. The psycho-philosophical problems of an excess of differentiation are twofold. First, differentiation involves distance, so all kinds of processes of separation, for good or bad, get activated, and differentiation can turn into dissociation. When 'I' and the 'object of my perception' have sufficient but not excess distance, the benefits of clear-sightedness can prevail. But whenever they get separated too far, there's trouble. In particular, the risk of demonising the object that is thought about or perceived as separate may arise. The classic example of this in the history of ideas is René Descartes, peering out of his window with philosophical eyes, realising he cannot not vouch for the living nature of the bodies of people he sees walking down the street.

It was a fateful realisation, for seeing the 'Not-I' as dead matter became the accepted thinking style that supported the colonial project. Every *thing* outside him became some *thing* rational man could employ or reassemble as it suited him. In the end, it facilitated greed-drunk Western civilisation to overexploit the Earth, in the name of progress but without the self-reflective features of foresight or conscience. Such a stance went contrary to the ancient human awareness of being of the

Earth. It is virtually unthinkable from an indigenous or even Oriental mindset, in which being part of the web of life is *the* consistent principle in life. It becomes psychologically possible only when we disown our association with matter, or 'Mother Nature,' which then becomes a primary 'Not-I' and thereby an 'IT.'[5] Failing to notice living things happens to be a prime feature of left-hemisphere dominated brain activity, which we shall examine in greater detail below, and such a way of thinking became very profitable.[6]

This distancing and disowning is much more internally stimulating than at first appears, for it excites a vicious cycle. Readers may well imagine that such a mindset could be capable of stimulating a particular brain activity, whereupon, over time, this brain activity then automatically reproduces a worldview, in a potentially unstoppable perpetual cycle. The person or the culture then takes this re-stimulated worldview to be the truth. In mindset theory this is called an *excited mindset*. In practice, the excited mindset with excessive left-hemisphere dominated brain activity is a phenomenon of the Entitled Brain that narrows attention and context; it is one that dominates the Brtish political scene.

An example from daily political life:

This phenomenon explains why a hyper-conservative can have so much complacent confidence in his own viewpoint – like Tony Blair on Iraq. Similarly, Ian Duncan-Smith can spread alarm about the cost of housing benefits with eerie detachment from the causes or consequences: the wholesale sale of social housing after Thatcher and the disproportionately expensive private rental market in Britain.

The human brain's left hemisphere also has a penchant for seeing details, organising and labelling. This brings us directly to the second problem of excessive differentiation: compartmentalised thinking. In this case, although differentiation helps you get 'out of the box,' you may simply land back in another box, albeit a different one and possibly a disconnected one. The drive to separation that usefully encouraged specialisation now frequently results in the excessive isolation of disciplines. This has been noticed by historians of science, scholars and poets, in different fields, with considerable alarm. While it facilitated the accumulation of knowledge and skills, its downside has resulted in a crisis of compartmentalisation. Knowledge ends up suffering the worst effects of excessive bureaucracy, as it were. Science can pursue research or technical application without conscience, emotion or aesthetics getting in the way; politicians can sing the praises of growth, while ignoring sustainability. Those areas simply belong to different departments, which are not talking to each other. In consequence of compartmentalisation, an industrial civilisation can exploit the earth, its animals and its peoples in the unquestioned pursuit of progress without widespread acknowledgment of the exploitation, without *feeling* much about it, without much conscience and therefore ultimately without a sense of accountability.

An example from daily political life:

Those who oppose the unaccountable exploitation of the environment – for example, what's known as the Global Justice Movement – occupy a highly alienated, politically ignored and marginalised stance. Hence our inability to solve many of today's critical problems at a global level.

We have become habituated to these methods, but they would simply not be on offer under an indigenous, pre-industrial worldview. Being well aware of the dangers of romanticising, I would summarise this as a perspective in which everything is seen as connected, where man is not simply given the world for his use but is considered part of the whole creation. Take, for example, the Native American Plains' Indian blessing, "All my relations." This phrase is used at all kinds of everyday and ceremonial moments, rather like a Christian grace. It gives a taste of a pre-modern world defined by its inclusivity: humans, animals, plants and rocks.

Anglo-American observers of native customs from the 17th to 20th centuries remarked on the universal respect accorded to all life, including that which the eye of reason would see simply as inert matter, such as the land.[7] This attitude was described by the Canadian Truth and Reconciliation Commission's Interim Report of 2012 as "an ongoing set of mutual obligations."[8] Out of such a mindset a rich moral order might evolve, which has to do with mutual obligation and stewardship. It is one that Muscular Christianity (the imperial British version of religion) and the Rational Man Project, charging hand-in-hand, headlong down Progress Street, were unable to recognise in their hurry to put things into neat and separate boxes. It is one we might do well to rediscover today.

A new brain science

The good news for our time is that the coming together of the Big Three (to use Ken Wilber's useful phrase) has already started to happen, in terms of a movement towards interdisciplinary sciences and between science, philosophy, psychology, theology and art, as a correction to the Enlightenment trend of excessive teasing apart.[9]

One of the main areas where the reversal of that trend is most apparent and impactful is in the study of the human brain and nervous system. On the one hand, this is due to new technology, especially functional magnetic resonance imagers, commonly known as MRI scanners. These devices can detect which parts of the brain are active when someone is thinking a particular thought or performing a specific action, effectively allowing areas of the brain to become mapped. Philosophically, however, new attitudes within science began to arise earlier, out of the insights of quantum physics. After Heisenberg,[10] Einstein and Bohr, the separation of measurer and measured as clear and distinct entities became increasingly unreliable. In medicine and psychology, practitioners, theorists and researchers have been forced to acknowledge the ineffectiveness of the medical model to address the internal workings of the human mind, and in particular to heal its suffering.

The banner under which many allied specialists are coming together and pooling their knowledge is neuroscience. In this process, seemingly unlimited branches of neuroscience are being born. I will refer to a few of the principal examples of this trend, but I do not pretend to be able to provide more than the briefest and most partial summary of the work in the space available here. What is important for our story is that many of these developments are highly relevant to understanding how the hyper-rational Entitled Brain works, what its limitations are and how in the light of these developments we might think about leadership more creatively.

I start with Portuguese medical brain specialist at UCLA, Antonio Damasio. Damasio is a leading light in *cognitive neuropsychology,* a distillation of the complementary approaches of both experimental and clinical neuropsychology. Using techniques such as 'functional localisation,' brain specialists can see that if a specific cognitive problem can be found after an injury to a specific area of the brain, then the likelihood arises that this part of the brain is involved in its processing. As far as proven can ever be proven in science, and in particular in the science of brain and mind, Damasio is famous for conclusively proving that there is a neurological substrate to emotion that is critical to our functioning and that works as a mediator for what we used to think were the purely rational processes of the neo-cortex.

In his highly readable D*escartes' Error: Emotion, Reason, and the Human Brain,* Damasio recounts the story of Phineas Gage, a dynamite worker who in 1848 blew a good part of his brains out in an accident and survived – as did his brains, preserved for permanent display in a glass jar.[11] Remarkably, Gage recovered from his injuries and suffered no visible cognitive functioning problems. But because he had lost access to his emotional processes he started to behave inappropriately and make poor judgements that were finally to ruin his life. The story whetted Damasio's appetite, and he began investigating questions of emotion and consciousness by means of studying patients with brain lesions, strokes and other damage. This research led him into regions of metaphysics and human relationships normally well outside his field.

Damasio pursued his line of thought while he worked on many difficult cases, such as the patient he calls 'Eliot.' This man had a massive brain tumour successfully removed by surgery and, to all intents and purposes, made a complete recovery with his intelligence entirely intact. When he returned to work, however, his bosses found that he now got terribly sidetracked in small details and lost his inability to prioritise. He could reason like a computer but was unable to make any meaningful choices. Eliot ended up losing his job, his marriage and his home. It turned out that he had suffered a complete personality change and his life went down the pan, yet he seemed to show no feelings about this or anything else. On examination – by now Damasio was beginning to know where to look – it was found that surgery had severed the connecting circuits between Eliot's amygdala and his neo-cortex. This meant that rational parts of his brain were receiving no guidance or input from his emotional centres. In Eliot's case, there was no cure: he had become like a robot and lost his connection to his humanity.

As a scientist, Damasio underwent a fundamental revolution in having to acknowledge that what makes us human and conscious depends as much on emotions – especially for good decision-making – as it does on reflection, planning and insight, the more universally valued parts of activity thought to arise in the frontal cortex of the human brain. He began to suggest that:

> Nature appears to have built the apparatus of rationality not just on top of the apparatus of biological regulation, but also from it and with it.[12]

In this, Damasio began to challenge the specialised localised nature of brain processes, which had been the dominant model. But he also went on to question the very foundation of rationality itself, for one of reason's own Enlightenment benchmarks was that reason defined itself as 'not emotion.' His next book told the story of his further researches pertaining to the emotions' central role in brain processing and the making of consciousness.[13]

Damasio was not alone in coming to similar conclusions about the centrality of feeling. A very productive cross-fertilisation of neuro-imaging, brain chemistry and psychotherapy began to take root in American universities. Jaak Panksepp, at Washington State University, is the founder of the field of *affective neuroscience*. Through his work, insights from human brain imaging have provided an effective framework for a better understanding of how feelings of sadness/grief and playfulness/joy are created in the brain, and their impact on our understanding of the mind and its disorders.

Allan Schore, from the UCLA Center for Culture, Brain, and Development leads research in the field of *neuropsychology*. His contributions have influenced the fields of *affective neuropsychiatry*, trauma theory, developmental psychology, paediatrics, infant mental health, psychoanalysis, psychotherapy and behavioural biology. He is the author of *Affect Regulation and the Origin of the Self*, now in its 11th printing, and editor of *Interpersonal Neurobiology*. His latest work[14] links brain studies with John Bowlby's *Attachment Theory*.[15]

An entirely new understanding of the complexity and interrelatedness of the entire body/mind problem is emerging as neuroscientists, psychiatrists and psychotherapists come into dialogue and share their findings. Increasingly, the old view of the brain as an isolated 'command and control centre' governing the more inert matter of the subsidiary body is being dropped. The entire nervous system – and especially the heart – is being seen as interlinked in the evaluating, decision-making and motivating processes, previously thought to be functionally directed by the brain. The human being, equipped with both conscious and automatic dimensions, far from being like a machine, is once again being thought of as a network of interrelated processes, more governed by his or her emotions, love relations and imagination than science ever expected to find.

What does this new science mean for the thesis of this book?

Damasio's brain lesion work proves that emotions are essential for good decision-making. The new respect for feeling has begun to influence mainstream approaches to the brain. If we add the conclusions of the new neuroscientists to the traditional understandings of depth psychology, which sees feelings not simply as a way of discharging tension or expressing sentiment but as the main pathways that lead us to meaning and value, then our picture becomes broader.

A new respect for emotions has begun to influence mainstream approaches to the brain and the heart. If we add the conclusions of neuroscientists to the traditional understandings of depth psychology, which sees feelings not simply as a way of discharging tension or expressing sentiment, but as the main pathways that lead us to meaning and value, then our picture becomes broader.

The neurological breakthroughs are developments that ring very loud bells in our examination of leadership and the psychohistory of British elitism. We are now able to comprehend the structural problems for the Entitled Brain and see how it may be operating in a dangerous vacuum, cut off from its own self-originating sources of information, designed to regulate the organism.

We now have a sound, medically-informed platform for proposing that a Wounded Leader – such as an ex-boarder, who has had to chronically disown feelings in early life and has not deconstructed his Strategic Survival Personality – is unlikely to be capable of making good decisions.

An example from daily political life:

We are now in a position to wonder whether this is the science behind Will Hutton's non-partisan view, quoted in Chapter 7, that the political judgments of the British Tory Party "have, over the centuries, been almost continuously wrong."

The heart of the matter

Stephen Porges, Professor of Psychiatry and Biomedical Engineering and Director of the Brain-Body Center at the University of Illinois, is (at the time of writing) an energetic 69-year-old from New Jersey who loves to engage in dialogue with writers, psychoanalysts and body-psychotherapists on subjects such as the nature of love.[16] Porges is the originator of the *Polyvagal Theory*, which links the evolution of the autonomic nervous system to emotional experience and expression, especially facial gestures, vocal communication and congruent social behaviour. He suggests that over time a special connection evolved between the human brain and the enormous quantity of nerve tissue that supplies the heart and face, and that this demonstrates that humans are uniquely primed towards precision functioning in emotional bonding situations, within intimate pairings and social groups.

The principal channel for these connections is the *vagus* nerve system. The Latin word vagus means 'wandering', since it reaches into so many parts of the body. More than 85% of the nerve fibres in the mammalian vagus nerve system are *afferent* nerves, meaning that they send information *towards* the brain, rather than receive instructions from it, in order to communicate the state of the viscera to the brain.[17] Again we see the control myth of the brain under challenge – in fact, a large source of vagal messages comes from the grey matter situated at the top of the heart, which seems to be the principal conductor of this system. This brain-face–heart connection provides the structures for what Porges calls the *Social Engagement System* that links our bodily feelings with facial expression, vocal intonation and gesture and is critical for the self-regulation of the autonomic nervous system (ANS).

Porges' work provides many insights into symptoms observed in several behavioural, psychiatric, and physical disorders but what is most important for this study is his revolutionary insight, based on his lab research, on what happens when a person does not feel safe. Under the circumstances of threat or stress, we automatically fire the sympathetic branch of the ANS and shut down the activation of the afferent vagal system's messages to the brain and fire the 'flight or flight' response for which a huge boost of chemical energy is needed. But in response to an extreme threat of annihilation we may need to shut our whole system down, like a mouse playing dead, and conserve energy. For this we use the parasympathetic ANS response to take up the collapsed characteristics of a 'freeze' state.

Porges' work has demonstrated that when we are in the freeze state called *immobilisation* we have no access to the social engagement system, which is a later mammalian evolutionary development, but remain trapped within the confines of much earlier, so called reptilian defences. We are therefore unable to read another person's facial signals or indeed turn on our friendly bonding message system to give the right encouraging signals. Instead, we anticipate danger and resort to further flight, fight or freeze processes as critical self-protection modes. Here we may immediately recognise the ex-boarder.

The process works the other way as well: when you are with someone you love, says Porges, you hear them even in noisy environments because the muscles that control the middle-ear get extra stimulation and blood due to a strong connection to the vagus nerve system; but this only occurs in a safe environment. Otherwise, we automatically react by relying on our most ancient system of protection, our baseline response of hyper-vigilance for predators. Fight or flight responses take tremendous energy; freeze responses carry risks. When mammals resort to the third defence of immobilisation it is sometimes a fatal strategy, since it drastically lowers the heart rate, sometimes below critical limits. A quarter of the mice that play dead when a cat has caught them die of heart failure, says Porges. In fact, his initial motivating question was: "How do we turn off old defensive systems?"

In the evolutionary transition from reptiles to mammals to humans, nature developed a further range of processes designed to slow heart rate and fire the parasympathetic ANS. These new methods could allow the heart quick access to data through the vagal nerve in order to calm the whole organism down and avoid using the risky ancient defences, while still retaining them as possibilities. This compensating vagal system with its corresponding responsive muscles in the face, the ears and the eyes evolved to help promote safety, particularly when amongst other humans, by feeding encouraging messages back to the heart, as it were, to enjoy the possibilities of contact rather than go into fight or flight mode. It was a tremendous advance for humans to employ their big brains to *respond* rather than to simply *react*.

Porges suggests that those who inhabit a chronic self-protective state miss out on the benefits of this system and have much less ability to self-regulate by firing the parasympathetic system. Sometimes, people who have been abused may not be able to leave their trauma state, he continues. Distinctions between anger, fear and disgust, says Porges, are difficult for those who cannot or rarely feel safe – such as autistic people or trauma victims.[18]

Other trauma research suggests that sufferers of PTSD (post-traumatic stress disorder) tend to mistake anger for fear and then may themselves cause abuse because they are triggered into drastically protecting themselves. Clearly, Porges' work highlights the underlying mechanisms at work here.

One of the debates in which I am involved with my colleagues who are interested in the psychology of ex-boarders is whether we should be presenting this client group as suffering from PTSD or whether there may be a more fitting term. Much of what Porges is describing is applicable to traumatised soldiers, with whom ex-boarders have some things in common, but the latter have of course not been required to kill or be killed, so that the comparison is incomplete. Martin Pollecoff, who runs a free therapy service for British ex-servicemen called The Long Boat Home, suggests:

If it is not spotted before you leave the forces then on average it takes 13 years for ex-service personnel to be diagnosed with PTSD. By that time we are no longer dealing with a trauma. What you get then is a personality that has *accommodated itself to the wound*.[19]

Pollecoff's telling comment is exactly what we see with boarding school survivors. With Porges' understanding of immobilisation states, we can see how the brain and nervous system can go into a kind of chronic spasm state in which they misread both internal and external emotional states and see loving approaches as potential attacks. One of the common non-technical ways of describing this state is to say that such a person has a 'closed heart.'

Porges is not the only scientist to recognise how the heart's systems have been overlooked, especially in their central role in regulating the ANS. The Institute of HeartMath in California – not a university but a corporation that markets bio-feedback machines – is involved in developing a new branch of neuroscience called *neurocardiology*. In standard medicine, the heart is usually considered only a pump – albeit a vital one. "What I do every day is plumbing," admitted one top heart surgeon interviewed on a BBC documentary. "We're thinking of it like a fuel pump and the human heart is much more than that."[20] HeartMath founder, Doc Childre, a pioneer in the study of heart rate coherence, calls the heart:

> A highly complex, self-organized information processing center with its own functional 'brain' that communicates with and influences the cranial brain via the nervous system, hormonal system and other pathways.[21]

It is not surprising that the heart is beginning to receive more attention as the hyper-rational paradigm begins to lose its grip. It is a unique organ – the first of all our organs to develop in the womb, capable of synchronising itself with another's resonance, at first the mother's and later a lover's. It can live outside the body for an indefinite period given necessary supplies; it is the centre of the body's self-regulating system and it is entirely similar in both genders. Even an ailing heart is able to generate sufficient electricity to power its own pacemaker, according to electro-cardiologist Paul Roberts.[22] In contrast to the university research into damage and pathology,

HeartMath's research considers how the neural matter located at the top of the heart is involved in coordinating excitement levels in the body, and whether these autonomic functions can be influenced by subjects consciously creating positive or calm emotional states and learning to affect intentionally a steady rate of heart rate coherence. Director of research, Roland McCraty, explains:

> How do stress and different emotional states affect the autonomic nervous system, the hormonal and immune systems, the heart and brain? Why do people experience the sensation of love and other positive emotional states in the area of the heart and what are the physiological ramifications of these emotions?[23]

Of enormous interest is the fact that, while the flight-fight reaction is unconsciously set in motion by environmental triggers perceived by the neo-cortex, involving instant appreciation of sense data, the 'heart's brain' has an important role in modifying and mollifying the affects of this reaction by firing the parasympathetic side of the ANS.

The signals that pass along the nervous system are principally chemical and electromagnetic. Mostly, the heart communicates with the brain electromagnetically, and traditional rational science can monitor this – for the ensuing electromagnetic field of the heart turns out to be measurable! Astonishingly, this field also extends out from the body, apparently to a range of at least five feet and perhaps much further. One science journalist suggests that its range may be very extensive indeed and that the only problem in ascertaining this is that the right measuring equipment has not yet been developed.[24]

There is some speculation about what the purpose of this extending heart field may be. Some imagine that it is designed to monitor or affect the environment outside the person it serves – as cat lovers already know. Perhaps it is connected to Porges' social engagement system. But research here is in its infancy. Although these facts about the heart are well known, and a great deal of research has been carried out on the causes of stress and pathways of the downward oriented sympathetic side of the system, so far, little has been done on the afferent channels. Porges and HeartMath are pioneers in the study of what happens when the heart takes a leadership role and sends messages upwards into the medulla and outwards into the cortex, basically saying: "Chill out, relax, everything's going to be okay, calm down my dear self." In fact, we already know a lot more about what happens in someone's entire body – including their brain and ANS – when they get a message saying: "Watch out, this person is likely to trick you, catch you out and get you into a lot of trouble!"

How do the discoveries of the HeartMath Institute and Stephen Porges affect our thinking about British elitism?

These discoveries have huge significance when applied to ex-boarders with a long-term but unconscious sense of not being safe. The effect of being chronically and strategically on stress alert on their ANS functioning, unable to read facial signals or send friendly approaches, explains why ex-boarder clients report difficulties in distinguishing intimacy or attack approaches. In consequence, they interpret all approaches as threats, just to be on the safe side, which compounds their habitual loneliness.

In addition, discoveries like these could make us more compassionate to politicians like David Cameron or Jeremy Hunt when we spot them trying too hard to send the 'right' messages, visibly putting on their 'serious' or 'compassionate' faces or overreacting at threatening moments like the 'Calm Down Dear' incident. Now we understand more of the limitations of the Entitled Brain, cut off from its sources of vital emotional stimulus and inbuilt self-calming processes, we have further grounds to repudiate the kind of education that features love-free, hyper-rational institutionalisation.

Attachment and the brain

Alongside the distinguished researchers I have alluded to, there are several interdisciplinary thinkers who have been evaluating the recent evidence and attempting to make new syntheses of the information so far available. The two most prominent whom I wish to mention here are British. The first, Sue Gerhardt, an attachment-oriented psychotherapist and co-founder of the Oxford Parent Infant Project, has produced a major review of the work of Damasio, Panksepp, Schore and others. Gerhardt re-contextualised the research in terms of infant development and the growing of healthy brains. She presented her findings in the highly accessible *Why Love Matters: How Affection Shapes a Baby's Brain*, said by *The Guardian* to be "mandatory reading for all parents, teachers and politicians."[25] In her introduction, Gerhardt reveals herself to be one who has struggled with Enlightenment specialisation:

> As a teenager I wanted to study both literature and biology, but was told that I could not mix art and science and would have to choose between them. I chose literature and later became a psychotherapist, but the enforced split always struck me as something that diminished each discipline. This recent possibility of integrating them seems to breathe new life into them both.[26]

Gerhardt marshals evidence from different areas of research to show that babies' brains develop differently in the first few months of life, according to the amount and type of care they receive. The evidence suggests that when a child is demonstrably loved, the orbito-frontal areas of the prefrontal cortex are stimulated and interconnect more powerfully, developing a greater neural cell mass of grey matter. Gerhardt describes the chemistry of attachment and its disorders. She goes on to show that this positive development results in increased self-confidence combined with an ability to empathise with others. Conversely, neglect tends not to stimulate brain development and regularly leads to increased anxiety, insensitivity and aggression.

Allied to this research, Gerhardt might have referred to the recent discoveries concerning the hormone oxytocin, popularised by Rutgers University anthropology professor Helen Fisher[27] and developed by Sue Carter, an expert in *behavioural neuro-endocrinology* (who coincidentally is married to Stephen Porges). The role of the so-called 'love hormones' in childbirth, pair bonding, and orgasm has allowed us to understand the chemical substrate of love and attachment. Gerhardt, however, prefers to describe what we know from the research into the problems that result from this. She tracks how early life experiences set our baseline levels for serotonin and cortisol. Low levels of serotonin are connected with depression as well as violence. She describes how abnormal brainwave patterns in the frontal lobes and abnormal levels of cortisol are associated in adulthood with many mental problems from depression to eating disorders to alcoholism. But Gerhardt always grounds her scientific overview in the world of human relationships:

> What I discovered was that the attention that we receive as babies impacts on our brain structures. If we find ourselves cared for by people who love us, and who are highly sensitive to our unique personalities, the pleasure of those relationships will help to trigger the development of the 'social brain.'

The notion of a *social brain* was first proposed by British anthropologist Robin Dunbar[28] and is currently being implemented into an important RSA[29] think-tank, The Social Brain Centre,[30] directed by Dr Jonathan Rowson, which concerns itself with the application of these theories to socio-political structures. The social brain sits comfortably alongside Porges' social engagement system. It also helps us to think about the kind of brains that have not experienced enough of this loving activity. The Entitled Brain has not developed into a social brain – it is self-referring and isolationist.

Well-thumbed copies of Gerhardt's runaway bestseller sits on the office bookshelves of most counsellors, psychotherapists and psychiatrists, because it summarises evidence for principles, previously intuited as a basis for practice, that now turn out to be measurable. Its thesis is a basic one: loving relational activity is good for you. It has the power to build actual physical brain structure and its absence can create a cerebral deficiency that is extremely difficult to repair. Whilst pregnancy and the first two years of life is the time of most rapid growth, or most dramatic damage, growth potential is not limited to that period. The power of relational stimulation and bonding continues to influence brain structure and build ganglia throughout life, especially in mid-childhood. It appears also to extend into adulthood, so that some relational psychotherapists are now getting curious about scientific measurement, using MRI scanners to report on their clients before and after treatment to see whether measurable results occur in later life.

Why should the medium of close relationships, initially that of mother and infant, affect brain matter growth? If we consider the particular origins of human evolution, we can see good reasons why this should be so. A young human's brain is destined to grow disproportionately in physical size relative to the rest of the body. It is this brain, and the size of it, and therefore the kind of head that is needed to carry and protect it, that sets the human animal apart from all others. The large frontal lobes mean that the child's skull needs to be large – too large for it to be birthed safely; so human babies are born 'premature', as it were. In consequence, he or she is far more dependent on its caretaker for protection than other mammals: a foal or calf is on its feet and feeding, minutes after birth.

The evolutionary benefit of the big brain entails a huge environmental risk, since the human child needs to begin life in atmosphere of high empathy and protection. This best occurs close to the body that the baby was once part of, in the presence of whose cardiac rhythms he has already accomplished his most rapid growth, and under whose protection he is destined to begin developing the capacities of his beautiful brain. Hence the built-in expectations of dependence; and hence the medium of loving, stimulating, interdependent attachment that will compensate for the child's excess dependence, protect it from the outside world, and assist in growing actual brain cells.

What does Sue Gerhardt's summarising work tell us about the story we have been following?

We now know for certain that loving relationships have a vital role in building brains, and the lack of them has a corresponding disadvantage. For success is not guaranteed, either in infancy or in adulthood: not everyone has an ideal start – life, circumstances, the luck of the draw intervenes. There are also some cultures, such as the British, which have over-emphasised the values of independence at the expense of those of dependence and belonging. People who are sent away to school in early childhood are likely to miss out on some actual brain matter development, especially if they come from cold families to begin with. This is demonstrably a feature of the Entitled Brain. From a mindset that devalues dependence and fears intimacy, ex-boarders are hampered in developing loving relationships or finding reparative relationships, in which they can re-grow their brains. The Entitled Brain is therefore an *impoverished* one. As we have seen, building relationships between leaders is an increasingly required quality for today's political leadership, so a poorly or insecurely attached leader[31] is very unlikely to perform well, especially if his institutionalisation has been compensated for with a sense of social entitlement.

The Divided Brain

The second British contribution to the new awareness that I wish to refer to comes from ex-Maudesley consultant psychiatrist and Oxford professor of English, Iain McGilchrist, who has written what has widely been hailed as the book of the decade.[32] To recommend *The Master and his Emissary: The Divided Brain and the Making of the Western World* as an important work would be understating this book's significance. In view of its vast scope, I can only attempt to give the reader a sense of some of its insights as I perceive them.

Humans are not unique in having a 'Divided Brain;' it is a feature of all vertebrates. It is well known in anatomy and philosophy that two separate but communicating halves of the brain, with independent but harmonising functions, divide neatly down the left and right side of our skulls. What is new is our ability to track and measure the activity of the two sides. Here is philosopher Jim Danaher, whom we first met in the previous chapter:

> Since at least the time of the Greeks, we have known that the human brain is composed of both a left and right hemisphere. Today, our advanced technology has brought us to a much better understanding of the two hemispheres and the way they function. With functional magnetic resonance imaging, neuroscientists think that they are able to see how the different parts of the brain respond to different types of stimulus and thus involve different types of thinking. The consensus today is that we are naturally equipped with two very distinct abilities in terms of how to think about our experience. [33]

McGilchrist's book summarises the huge body of research on the hemispheric functioning and differences, and proceeds to make some startling conclusions in areas where even neuroscience has so far been afraid to tread. The author begins by explaining why the brain has twin hemispheres and what they 'do' in cooperation, explaining how the brain contains:

> ... mutually opposed elements whose contrary influence make possible finely calibrated responses to complex situations.[34]

Drawing largely on data from the observations of stroke victims, McGilchrist minutely describes what happens when the hemispheres fail to cooperate, when one side is damaged or, as in the case that his book's title refers to, the left takes over. He describes two fundamental 'takes' on the world, constructed through two different types of attention: the right side focuses on living things, providing context, implicitness, intuition, depth, connection; the left on representation, explicitness, inanimate parts and, consequently, division, will and control.

A simple way of thinking about this is to consider how birds, also equipped with twin hemispheres but without a self-reflective neo-cortex, use two types of attention on an everyday basis. I have just been watching one at our bird feeder. Mrs. Bird looks about from side to side, to see what's happening. Are there any predators? Where's the cat? Then she bends over, focuses right down and in to see whether the speck in front is a piece of grain or gravel. Then: peck, peck, peck. She looks up again, turns her head from side to side, once more looking round, satisfied all is still ok, that the cat hasn't moved. Again she seems to squint downwards; once more the pecking continues. The pattern goes on until she notices something in another tree, and off she flies. The process is one of obtaining a situational perspective for the sake of safety, followed by a clear honing in on the object of scrutiny, and then a return to the overview again – and so on. For us humans, equipped with brains able to think about ourselves, our world and even about our own thinking, there are considerable philosophic implications of these different types of attention deployed by the twin brains. Danaher again:

> We can analyze our experience and break it down into ever-smaller parts, or we can join the parts of our experience together into ever-greater wholes. Both modes of thought are within our power and both have a logic, which governs their reasoning. To prefer one mode of thought to the exclusion of the other is to limit our rational capacity and leave us 'half-witted.' Sadly, much of the Western intellectual tradition has done just that, focusing on the

'analytic' and neglecting the 'holistic.' We have come to associate reason itself with left-brain analysis.

Clearly, this over-functioning of the 'analytic', by which Danaher is referring to the left hemisphere, has great implications for our understanding of the Entitled Brain and its genesis in hyper-rational institutions. But McGilchrist's work takes us much further. He avoids making simplistic definitions, preferring to investigate the specific nature of this attention and its metaphysical implications. "The kind of attention we pay actually alters the world: we are literally partners in creation," says he. The world is actually *changed* by the nature of attention, which matches the findings of quantum science and philosophy since Heisenberg. McGilchrist's book reveals that there is a precise order to how the two hemispheres work: thought and language are born, as it were, on the right, then grow up, as it were, on the left, to provide the 'necessary difference' for self-reflection, before maturing on the right in a contextual value-driven synthesis, out of which choice can arise. What begins in the right has to be sent to the left for differentiation but is then returned to the right where a new synthesis can be made. This bicameral process has advantages for specialised functioning and is super-creative when cooperating in the manner intended.

McGilchrist's work allows us to understand how the principle that attention creates reality is affected by, and affects what goes on inside, the brain. We can now appreciate how constructs derived from perception would be severely limited if both hemispheres failed to work in a partnership that is absolutely crucial for optimum functioning and reality testing. For example, the left hemisphere tends to see things in a non-empathic stance, abstracted from a wider context. It then tends to reconstruct a virtual whole from its narrow context, and then self-refers. This narrowed-down context is now represented by the left as absolute truth. This property, I believe, has immense implications for our thesis, and we will return to it.

Educated at Winchester, the one pubic school dedicated to an explicit intellectual tradition, McGilchrist is a modern-day Renaissance man in both scope and erudition. His second chapter surveying the neurological data has no fewer than 535 footnotes! The breadth of his perspective on the history of Western culture is dizzying. But his book – 20 years in the making – is full of feeling and reads like an adventure story. What makes his work so different from any other published so far is that he has been prepared to extend his researches into how this human brain hemisphere issue has affected the collective aspects of humanity. He does this through his extensive knowledge of European history, art, philosophy and theology:

> My thesis is that the separation of the hemispheres brought with it both advantages and disadvantages. It made possible a standing outside of the 'natural' frame of reference, the common-sense everyday way in which we see the world. In doing so it enabled us to build on that 'necessary distance' from the world and from ourselves, achieved originally by the frontal lobes, and gave us insight into things that otherwise we could not have seen, even making deeper empathic connections with one another and with the world at large.

The second part of his book is a brilliant critique of rationality beginning with the Greeks, through the Reformation and Enlightenment, to the final triumph of capitalism. In the light of the history of Western art, literature and metaphysics, beginning with Homer, McGilchrist demonstrates that, on a collective level, the left hemisphere functioning has had a tendency to become over-dominant. He cites countless examples of this and notes the consequent counter-reactions, such as the Romantic period or the 1960s, when right hemisphere thinking attempted to address the balance. But after each new point of equilibrium, the left brain, to our general impoverishment, regularly seems to seize overall domination. In the myth referred to in his title, the 'Emissary,' the left hemisphere, which ought to be working for the whole, overthrows his imperial 'Master,' who represents the entire cooperative brain, functioning for the sake of the whole body organism.

McGilchrist continually points out the ability of and need for the two hemispheres to work together "… in two diametrically opposed directions at once – towards greater abstraction *from* the world and, simultaneously, towards greater empathic engagement *with* the world" (italics mine). He sees this ability as crucial to understanding the great advances that humans have made in terms not only of technology but also of consciousness. However, their joint functioning is predicated on the way they relate to each other: information is passed through the *corpus callosum* but they can only switch each other on or off:

The left hemisphere misunderstands the importance of implicitness
... because it can only say 'no' or 'not' to what it finds given by
the right.

This on-off approach to consciousness can easily lead to
over-conceptualisation and a loss of empathy. Its hand can be
seen in the violent excesses of the French Revolution, itself
an attempt to address the balance of self-interested hyper-
rationality (a feature of the left hemisphere) and the instigator
of the British Rational Man Project. A further example would
be the rigidity of postmodernism. In both cases, dedicated
activists pursued ideas of freedom and communalism, but
the resulting movements ended up becoming disconnected
from empathy and the reality of bodily life. Personally, I was
delighted to read McGilchrist's assertion that left-brain driven
materialism founders on the exclusion of paradox – precisely
what led me to desert my Oxford philosophy degree course in
the 1960s. I was struck by his observation that schizophrenia
and rationality have something in common. In terms of brain
functioning, they both employ excessive left-brain filtering.
I was reminded of Arnold Mindell's challenging statement:
"Rationality is an altered state."

*What does this add to our understanding of the Entitled
Brain and the shadow aspects of rationality?*

When the isolated left hemisphere is running the show,
the over-functioning of the 'analytic' gains prominence.
When we add in the left brain's non-empathic stance, and
its tendency to see things abstracted from wider contexts
and create a self-referring context as the only visible
truth, we have great implications for our thesis. The
Entitled Brain, already starved of bio-feedback, makes
its isolated experience and dominating tendencies into a
world-view that asserts itself as *The Truth*.

We will return to this, particularly focusing on the crucial
aspects of context and doubt. But first we must take one more
look at the problem of feelings in Wounded Leaders, in order
fully to understand the nature of their emotional starvation and
the kind of long-term brain functioning this encourages.

CHAPTER 12

Emotional Intelligence and Leadership

Military Man ~ The feeling of a nation ~ The angry island
Stress and the twin nervous systems ~ The panic and the chillax buttons
Conclusions: context, vulnerability and the brain

Military Man

The cold wind pressed on my face as I heaved my foot laboriously
into the next footprint in the frozen snow. It was January 2005.
I was enjoying the performance of my thirty-year-old hiking
boots, but it had been a challenge to get my aging body up to
the summit of this Pyrenean peak, and I was very pleased that I
had. The view was stunning and there, casually leaning on the
height marker, his handsome face stretched by a relaxed grin,
was our guide, Sandy, carrying a pack three times the weight of
mine, looking as if he had only been out for a stroll. Of course,
he was five years younger than me, but he was one of those guys
who looked like he'd been fit all his life. Stowe, Sandhurst, the
Guards, then 'Special Ops' and now a standby reserve, Sandy
was a military man from top to toe, but his personality was
enlivened by a Peter Pan cheekiness and an ex-boarder rebel
style. To him, my wife and I were two 'trick-cyclists' who had
managed to infiltrate the mission (an organised winter walking
tour), and suspicious figures of fun.

Sandy adored mischief. How he loved to shock the whole
group over dinner with his stories, embellished by his non-PC
humour, usually featuring some wickedly attractive "Daughter
of Satan" (or two) who had lured him into an erotic encounter
in which conclusion or escape generally involved rivers of
alcohol, cartons of drugs, and purloined military hardware. You
couldn't help fall under his spell, even if around him you felt

you had inadvertently fallen through some invisible trapdoor and landed in the lurid modern equivalent of a P.G. Wodehouse story. But it was also rather frustrating: it was hard to know when he was serious and when he was 'only joking,' and he seemed to be only joking most of the time. The demanding walks, however, were meticulously planned and carried out: nobody was left to feel they weren't a valued part of the squad. While the group instinctively knew we could count on him to get us out of trouble if it arose, his regular hints that at any moment he might have to reorganise his rucksack for the mountains of Kurdistan dispelled any doubt about the temporary nature of Sandy's availability.

Despite our many differences, Sandy and I got on well. His favourite remark to me – the person nearest to his own age but tainted with a dangerous degree of intellectualism – was "Thinking is not good for you – gives you headaches." Of course I enjoyed the joke with him, but I wondered what it meant. Was this classic military stuff, where thinking for yourself might imply a seditious tendency to be critical about orders? Was it typical boorish public school anti-intellectualism? What did he mean by 'thinking'? Was it his way of saying that *feeling* wasn't good for you? I suspected it was the latter. I knew that we British use a code about feelings, and I guessed I was supposed to know. But I had been a psychological observer too long to really get the hint.

Feeling and thinking are regularly mixed up in the English language. Frequently we answer the question "What are you feeling?" with something like: "I feel that ..." The use of 'that' betrays such a statement as mental proposition – a thought rather than a feeling. Besides, socially permissible 'feeling words', amongst Brits who are involved in neither the arts nor the therapy world, are rather few; mostly, one can say one is 'upset' or 'cross' – hardly ever sad or angry. Of course, we British are famous for our 'stiff upper lips' and this is not always a bad thing; combined with the wartime spirit, it has given us resources to endure tremendous hardship. But why should feeling be such a difficult subject for us? Must we accept that the British are culturally conditioned to normalise doing things without feelings, whether by means of repression or disowning, disavowing, dissociation, splitting off – whichever way we name it and to whatever degree it is done?

The feeling of a nation

We have seen how the British elite forgo feeling in order to bolster their Strategic Survival Personalities to their cost; the Entitled Brain, despite its ability to store rational information is in fact deprived of emotional information and taken up with compensating activities. The top-down nature of British society means that all strata are obliged to imitate the behaviour of the elite, even without knowing it. Feelings have therefore become universally rather dangerous in Britain.

In my profession, we tend to ask the "What are you feeling?" question rather a lot, and many ex-boarders simply do not have an answer. They are not, in this case, being duplicitous. Frequently they have dissociated from their feelings; they have successfully split them off and are really not sure of them any more. Often they will say: "Just let me think about it a moment." This is hardly surprising when we consider that their privilege is obtained at the expense of their inbuilt need to belong in the safe environment of home. The very first protective action a boarder has to do, as he tries to juggle his shame at his inability to be fully happy about his privileged education, is to get rid of the sense of being lonely and abandoned.

The symptoms of Boarding School Survivors are varied and complex; they include difficulties in relationships and parenting, workaholism, inability to relax, isolation, inauthenticity, a sense of failure and becoming a bully, as well as the expected sexual problems. But the principal effect of boarding is a problem with emotion. This is not only a survival tactic but also consciously encouraged by the traditions of the schools. The classic style is one of emotional retention out of a commitment to duty rather than to the self, except in terms of strategic survival, which is unconscious anyway. This fits the national character ideal, which is not expected to be emotionally 'intelligent,' to use that now famous and marvellously simple term invented by journalist Daniel Goleman in his 1995 survey *Emotional Intelligence*.[1]

In Britain, the great Western mental malaise is perhaps most refined: anxiously living in our heads, obsessed with the past, worrying about the future, self-obsessed but never really taking a deeply reflective view, not given to practise what in the next chapter I call constructive doubt. An American friend once put it to me rather bluntly: "The British are in their heads." Such an assessment may sound gross, but the extraordinarily dynamic

English language permits such a highly developed imagination that its practitioners often seem to be accustomed to living outside of their embodied experience. The very briefest survey of literature from the early 19th to mid-20th centuries, which happens to coincide with the great days of the Rational Man Project, would confirm a British retreat from emotions and an advance towards either pragmatism or the imagination during this period.

Asked on BBC Radio 4 to analyse another successful BBC TV period masterpiece, this time Jane Austen's *Pride and Prejudice*, Professor John Carey, a specialist on the socio-political aspects of British literature, makes an equally blunt appraisal: "In Victorian Britain, people's bodies aren't engaged; it's just their minds."[2] The eternal turning point of the English novel or play from the Regency period onwards – in stark contrast to the preceding period of emotional richness – is the inability to express feelings and the dutiful inappropriateness of acting on them. If we take into account Freud's early work on the conversion phenomenon, which demonstrated that civilised man suffers endless physical symptoms by allowing what has been repressed to govern him, there is little wonder that Britain needs such an enormous Nation Health Service.[3]

In this context, D.H. Lawrence's writing can be seen as a crusade to upset the literary order, which truthfully mirrored the conventions of daily life and its stifled emotion, in order to revitalise British life. But Lawrence failed, for he was a man before his time, and the theme of emotional constriction would continue much further into the 20th century.

Perhaps the most explicit statement about the emotional handicaps of the British middle classes was David Lean's 1945 film *Brief Encounter*, based on a play by Noël Coward. To the background of Rachmaninoff's *Piano Concerto No. 2*, the film reveals the restrictive "conventions of British suburban life, centring on a housewife for whom real love (as opposed to the polite arrangement of her marriage) brings unexpectedly violent emotions."[4] The two would-be lovers, memorably played by Celia Johnson and Trevor Howard, constrained by the unbearable conflict between their emotions and their sense of duty, are unable to consummate their desires. Torn apart by their feelings, they embark on a heart-wrenching journey of self-sacrifice, rationalised as "doing the right thing." *Brief Encounter* seemed to set the tone for the security-conscious late 1940s and 1950s, which were soon to be torn apart by an explosion of feeling.

It arrived innocently enough, with the pop music boom of the mid-1960s, the Beatles cooing "Love, love me do!" and Bob Dylan wailing "How does it *feel?*" Now the worm began to turn, if only for a brief period. Perhaps the best statement of the clash of emotional repression and the aspiration of expression of that time was Alan Ayckbourn's 1973 trilogy of plays, *The Norman Conquests*, all of which feature the same action, cleverly viewed from three different perspectives. Set in a rambling Home Counties village house, reminiscent of a vicarage, Ayckbourn's drama reveals an extended family dominated by an unseen elderly mother figure and entirely unable to operate at the level of their feelings.[5] The exception is brother-in-law Norman, a wonderful part played by Tom Courtenay in the original and Tom Conti in the television adaptation, who indulges his passion for seducing women by means of his own flagrant emotional dis-inhibition.

Oddly enough, one of the greatest experts on emotions in human history was English and came from somewhere near Birmingham, centuries before the British began the fashion for the stiff upper lip. Shakespeare, writing during the English Renaissance, the period that led up to the astonishing and hastily overlooked English radical revolution of the mid-17th century, inhabits a fully emotional landscape, centuries earlier than William James and Sigmund Freud and their struggle to reverse the Cartesian dualism and re-evaluate emotions. Even today, whenever anyone is writing about what feeling is, they tend to quote our bard and his company of tortured characters: Hamlet, Mr. and Mrs. Macbeth, and Othello.

But now, with the benefit of more than a century of psychotherapy and 20 years of advanced neuroscience, we are in a much better position to talk about feelings in an objective fashion than ever before. Daniel Goleman's work demonstrates that emotional 'availability' and authenticity are amongst the most important human aspects for a child to develop and for an adult to embody. Goleman's initial task was to show that the benefits of emotional intelligence far outweigh those of competitiveness and the so-called *Intelligence Quota* measurement – IQ. Assembling all the current scientific evidence for the primacy of emotion, he swept away any doubt that it might still be a secondary human function. Goleman's book, *Emotional Intelligence*, became a runaway bestseller and is now widely accepted as a milestone. Yet the reason for the success of the book is probably a devastatingly simple one, perhaps to do with the title, which Goleman borrowed from Eileen Growald, founder of the American Institute for the Advancement of Health. It was the fact that he dared combine the words emotion and intelligence together – as if they were not utter strangers. One effect was that IQ as a concept immediately began to loose its hold on the public attention. In fact, Goleman had challenged the great separating trend of the Enlightenment by bringing together two fundamental elements that the Rational Man Project had been at such pains to keep apart. Intelligence, as we know, apparently belonged exclusively to civilised Rational Man, and emotion to the messy domain of children, women, savages and foreigners in general – the dissociated world of objects.

Goleman's important survey represents an interdisciplinary milestone establishing that the primacy of emotions is now beyond dispute, but he was simply retelling a story that had been already established in the laboratory. Antonio Damasio's work, referred to in Chapter 11, shows without any doubt that the neurological basis of the decision-making process depends on full access to emotions. Neuroscientific evidence for what is called the *plasticity* of the brain – the notion that brain continues to develop and respond by growing more tissue – confirms that feeling and bonding create much more actual brain structure than does the absence of them. Psychologists and psychotherapists have long understood that emotional availability has to do with understanding the context of events and having congruence in our actions. Without proper access to feeling we cannot express and get our wants, or protect ourselves with healthy aggression. Even more fundamentally, if we are too uncomfortable with feelings it is hard to develop a proper balance between receiving and giving out, which may perhaps explain why the British middle classes tend to find expressing wants so difficult.

Returning to the complex national relationship with feelings, we know that Brits, abhorring emotions, do at times admit to being a little bit 'cross' or 'upset.' And yet, in our imaginations, we are profoundly attracted to Southern Europe, ostensibly for the weather and the food but also, I suspect, because people in Southern Europe appear to us more at ease with their feelings.

Earlier in the book we saw how hostile the British can be, how normalised bullying is, and how painful the hiding of feelings behind humour can be. But the most enduring emotional ignorance leads us back to where we started: it is the one most easily identifiable from outside the island – the practice of sending children away to school by the very people who can afford to keep them there.

Its continuation and normalisation relies, as we have seen, on two mental-emotional conjuring tricks: mothers must ignore their feelings of maternal attachment and children must dissociate from their inbuilt instincts. But we also realised that dissociating from identities like "I am the vulnerable one" in order to avoid the secondary feelings that might arise, creates a very dangerous situation in the psyche. Disowned identities and disowned feelings then *control* your life rather than guide it, because dissociating does not mean you are *in charge* of your feelings, it means these very disowned feelings unconsciously run your life and dominate you, without your knowing about it. This is especially difficult when the primary feelings of grief and anger that are congruent to a situation – like the abandonment of children – have been disowned.

The angry island

There is *one* category of emotion at which the British seem to be somewhat proficient. We do seem to be on fairly intimate terms with a kind of anger – perhaps better called exasperation – that is often misdirected, strangely unregulated and excessively expressed. Unfortunately, this kind of feeling behaviour, called *emotionality* by psychotherapists, does not help very much in making good judgements or calming our autonomic nervous systems – quite the reverse. These very base level emotions do not encourage awareness and choice but stimulate defensiveness and isolation.

And many Britons are literally dripping with exasperation, frustration and irritation. Personal experience of driving over the Channel in France leads me to value the safety-oriented courtesy of British road users. But I'd rather drive in France – at least outside of Paris – than on this side of the Channel because I know that if I make a mistake on British roads someone is far more likely to give me 'the finger' or hoot impatiently or barrage me with aggressive looks than in France, where they'd simply want to overtake me. Food writer and professional wit, A.A. Gill suggests that the English inhabit an angry island:

> The English are naturally, congenitally, collectively and singularly, livid much of the time. In between the incoherent bellowing of the terraces and the pursed, rigid eye-rolling of the commuter carriage, they reach the end of their tethers and the thin end of their wedges. They're incensed, incandescent, splenetic, prickly, touchy and fractious. They sit apart on their half of a damply disappointing little island, nursing and picking at their irritations.[6]

Although Gill conveniently excuses himself by being born north of the border, I think he has a good case; he goes further:

> Perhaps aware that they're living on top of a keg of fulminating fury, the English have, throughout their history, come up with hundreds of ingenious and bizarre ways to diffuse anger or transform it into something benign. Good manners and queues, roundabouts and garden sheds, and almost every game ever invented from tennis to bridge. They've built things, discovered stuff, made puddings, written hymns and novels, and for people who don't like to talk much, they have come up with the most minutely nuanced and replete language ever spoken – just so there'll be no misunderstandings.

Those who have been educated in hyper-rational attachment-deficit institutions tend not to get very openly angry, though readers might think they have every right to. But when they get scared, they can become very angry and frequently hostile. I have been there myself, sadly. How might a Wounded Leader deal with anger? Readers might expect their leaders, who have been to the finest schools and now represent them, to be more in charge of their feelings than the rest of the nation. They may wonder how good these leaders are at dealing with their own "kegs of fulminating fury."

We have already seen how David Cameron can lash out with very little provocation; time to revisit the 2012 'Plebgate' affair, in which a minister, Andrew Mitchell, was alleged by some reports,[7] now discredited, to have got very 'upset' with policemen and insulted them. Although the whole affair is currently shrouded in mystery and deceit, it reveals just how divided a society the British culture of elitism maintains. But whatever happened, we still haven't been told why the Minister was so stressed, so frustrated – or "cross" as the BBC's chief political correspondent Nick Robinson put it. In fact, Mitchell had just been promoted – would citizens expect him to be at Gill's "thin end of the wedge?"

One of the things that struck me in this extraordinary affair was the time of year – mid-September. It is back-to-school time for the public schools – state schools go back earlier – and ex-boarders regularly report sensing an unaccountable misery at that time of year. Their bodies tend to remember the rhythms of their years-long institutionalisation and register unaccountable dreads and longings, even if their minds have split off their feelings about it. Some, when they feel safe enough, will say they feel very stressed then. Did Rugby-educated Mitchell have those kind of unallowable feelings percolating through him while he was running late along Downing Street with his pushbike? Who knows? I am just speculating, but the affair and retaliatory excesses of the police that are now beginning to emerge reveal plenty of unacknowledged anger floating around.

Amongst all the emotions, anger is a particularly difficult one; it is one that requires mastering over a lifetime, and disowning it only makes this more difficult. Aristotle, no less, considered anger an issue that everyone needed to cope with; here is Goleman's paraphrasing:

> Anyone can be angry – that is easy. But to be angry with the right person, to the right degree, at the right time, for the right purpose, and in the right way – this is not easy.[8]

This statement reveals something fundamental to the business of emotions. It is that having emotions is normal, automatic and, as we are beginning to understand, central to human life; but mastering them is an art or a skill that has to be learned. Dissociation is not mastering – it is quite the opposite. Dissociation actually makes feelings *more* powerful than they need to be. Feelings should not be so frightening; they are short-lived, they come and go. Learning to recognise, tolerate and to become gradually at ease with and able to master emotions is achieved just like any other learning. In other words, emotional intelligence comes about through proper encouragement, imitation, role models, practice and experience. Hyper-rational training programmes, like boarding schools, omit such modelling and such exercise.

The goal is something like this: in order to be our best, we need to be in touch with our emotions and informed by them. We need to avoid the dangers of repression but not become dominated by our feelings, to be as Shakespeare's Hamlet proposes, "that man/That is not passion's slave."[9] And in this respect, in general, Brits are rank beginners in the mastery of their own feelings: mostly they have been taught to fear them. Not being taught how to recognise and embrace them but instead to run in horror from them, we have been very poorly served. Our emotional education has been abysmal, and the elite have had it worst: they have exchanged their birthright of feelings for a mess of entitlement – the compensating illusion of entitlement.

Back to Sandy, for Military Man is a prime case and maybe holds clues to the whole subject. A soldier is trained to ignore his emotions: he has to be. He must disregard the most primal feelings, those that lead to self-preservation, in favour of following orders, in favour of his commanding officer's objectives, in favour of his loyalty to platoon, squadron, regiment and nation. He is obliged to, or he could not function as a soldier. Imagine the scenario: the charge begins, the sergeant yells "At them lads!" but one of the soldiers refuses to move. "I just don't feel like it," says he. "It doesn't feel safe to me; I feel like staying put." These feelings are accurate and totally congruent, and we would probably all have them. He is absolutely right and is functioning as a normal human being – but not as a soldier.

The militaristic institutional boarding school culture, designed to mass-produce Rational Man, overvalues its prime survival tactic, the repression of feelings. It took its cue from the soldier's preparation for war and, as we have seen, the boarding-school culture went on to effect and influence our culture unrealistically in the typically British top-down fashion. The military suspicion of feelings came to dominate British life to such an extent that it is now seamlessly identified with it. If we want to educate whole human beings to become the best leaders they can be, making best use of the wonderful body-mind continuum that nature gave us, then this attitude will have to be jettisoned.

Stress and the twin nervous systems

If we British are not very good at feelings, we do get very tense or stressed; despite our famous sang-froid we are very 'good' at getting stressed and tense. What happens inside a prime minister when he gets tense? When he imagines that someone is really out to get him in the cut and thrust of Prime Minister's Questions?

What happens is the same thing that happens inside a soldier or any other vertebrate under threat of annihilation. Fear makes the heart beast faster and this engages the *hyperarousal* or the *acute stress response*, better known as the 'fight or flight' system. The activation of the sympathetic branch of the autonomic nervous system (ANS) primes the body for fighting or fleeing and directs the adrenal glands to produce an internal cascade of hormones: extra glucose, adrenaline and noradrenaline all gear up the body fats and muscles for violent muscular action. For the needed energy boost, a flood of cortisol suppresses the immune system and increases blood pressure and sugar. Ready to battle for survival, the heart and lungs both accelerate; the blood vessels leading to muscles dilate while in other parts of the body they constrict. Digestion slows down or stops, the sphincters cramp, the tear glands close, the bladder muscles relax and its contents can spill; genital erection is inhibited. There may be paling or flushing, tunnel vision and loss of peripheral vision, loss of hearing and shaking. If the body acts on this reflex and exercises violently the system can return to where it started, but the stress response is hard to process if it is not answered with activity. When the stress response is chronic it makes us ill, as illustrated by the title of an important book on the subject, *Why Zebras Don't Get Ulcers*.[10]

Luckily, to counterbalance the side effects of the stress response, vertebrates are equipped with a counterpart to the sympathetic branch of the nervous system: the parasympathetic. The function of the parasympathetic is to activate what is known as the 'rest and repair (or digest)' response, returning the body to homeostasis after the fight or flight response has run its course. We can activate this system when we have peaceful or loving feelings, feel safely attached, are in connection or in relationship, or when we do things in a collaborative way. Such internal states make the heart beat slower and send neural, electromagnetic and chemical signals all the way up the big vagus nerve afferent channels. These signals reach into the face, to all the myriad facial muscle cells, and onwards into the amygdala and the cortex, so that the eyes recognise relational symbols and the nearby motor nerves send signals into the whole muscle and movement system to relax rather than tense up. Thus we spread the good news and the good stuff into the whole body-mind continuum.

Engagement of parasympathetic rest and repair can be cultivated by intentionally calming the heart rate through breathing and other techniques, such as mental processing, to increase right-hemisphere activity for wider contexts – even when this is counter-intuitive in stressful situations. Such self-regulatory movements stimulate familiarity with the priming of the vagal nerve and the whole afferent system. At the time of writing, this is still cutting-edge material for the medical and mental health professions. The required research is still in its infancy because until very recently all scientific attention has been on the opposite branch of the system. This is understandable, since it is the over-operation of the sympathetic that habituates the body to pumping far too much cortisol.

Today we call the resulting strain 'stress' – a word that nearly everyone uses nearly every day. We live in a stress culture and normalise it, just as is done in boarding school. Normalised stress drives the entire 'rat-race' culture – a metaphor that is misleading because whenever rats do race they use up so much physical energy that their adrenal-cortisol system returns to a congruent state. Contrast this with the modern human world, where we are driven by internal pressure and fear in competitive work environments that keep us pumping chemicals that our bodies never use on the 8,000-meter sprints for which they prepare them.

The stress culture is taken for granted in the West and now, increasingly, it is spreading to the East and to what is left of the indigenous world. Western healthcare systems already have enough research to acknowledge the fact that the proportion of illness and premature aging that is caused by an excess of stress is growing – not to mention the obesity problem. Our world is growing people who do not know how to regulate themselves, at an alarming rate.

We have to learn how to extricate ourselves from the grip of stress, both individually and collectively, if we don't want our health systems to be endless overburdened. It ought to be possible. We humans have so many possibilities in terms of action, reaction and self-regulation when we follow and cultivate the inbuilt proper cooperation between the body's two partnership systems – the twin ANS and the two brain hemispheres. Long before the physiology of these twin systems was known, Shakespeare understood the profound duality in the body. The partnership model seems to extend throughout the body, and the bard saw society through a similar lens. He gave both nobility and commoners full rein in his historical plays and paired comedy and tragedy as partners in the story of life. In the following extract, Shakespeare describes how a human moves from parasympathetic rest to sympathetic action. Here is King Henry V, exhorting his troops "into the breach," depicting the nobility of the fight response, appropriately engaged, he insists, in this context:

> In peace there's nothing so becomes a man
> As modest stillness and humility;
> But when the blast of war blows in our ears,
> Then imitate the action of the tiger:
> Stiffen the sinews, summon up the blood,
> Disguise fair nature with hard-favour'd rage;
> Then lend the eye a terrible aspect;
> Let it pry through the portage of the head
> Like the brass cannon; let the brow o'erwhelm it
> As fearfully as does a galled rock
> O'erhang and jutty his confounded base,
> Swilled with the wild and wasteful ocean.
> Now set the teeth and stretch the nostril wide;
> Hold hard the breath, and bend up every spirit
> To his full height.[11]

Within the brain, the ANS is located in the medulla oblongata in the lower brainstem, sometimes known as the 'old' brain, to distinguish it from the evolutionary newer self-reflective neo-cortex. The ANS works automatically without conscious control, but we can wilfully affect, override and influence whether we encourage stress or rest, according to the perceptions and thoughts we prioritise in our attention. The issue of which system is the best one to fire at any given moment is key. Whether we move into 'action stations' or 'red alert,' as Military Man might say, or into 'chillax' mode, to use the word made famous by Cameron wearing his 'good old Dave' mask, depends on context;[12] or more correctly, it depends on how we assess the data perceived by the mind and put it into appropriate context, often at great speed.

The panic button and the chillax button

Metaphorically, we might say we have both a 'panic button' and a 'chillax button.' The skill is congruently determining when we are not in danger of being annihilated, learning when not to press the panic button but instead reach for the chillax button. Pressing the panic button is of course entirely appropriate in the right context – in times of war or being hunted, for example. But it is not appropriate in most everyday situations or even when one is actually hunting. For a hunter, the opposite applies: he has to be completely relaxed and alert and have as wide a context as possible. It is this mode that has been overridden over the last centuries; it could be reinvestigated and learned in order to override our inbuilt self-preservation systems for over-firing the flight or fight system that leads to bad decision-making.

Political leadership always involves dealing with stress. Stress is part of life, but too much or inappropriate stress makes life more stressful that it needs to be. Wounded Leaders tend not to be well resourced internally, so stress will get the better of them, as in the 'Calm Down Dear' incident related in the Prologue. Many leaders of our time demonstrate this: Cameron looks stressed at every interview and Andrew Mitchell seems to use stress as an excuse to be rude. Boris doesn't bother, which is why the public like him; he is able to power through on entitlement confidence and hide what I imagine to be a bully's attitude behind buffoonery. Perhaps Obama's mother gave him enough inner authority and guidance to give him a good sense of his heart and his right hemisphere, so he rarely looks as stressed as he might. This may contribute to his winning of such a resounding re-election victory, why most foreign leaders want to be close to him or photographed by him, and how he managed to charm the House of Commons and Russian Prime Minister Medvedev.

Learning to push the chillax button and fire the parasympathetic system is an important skill for anyone, and an indispensable one for a leader. Wounded Leaders have been trained only to cultivate an internally relaxed state in two distinct ways, both of which, I argue, are now redundant.

1. First, there is the *Way of the Soldier,* in which Military Man concludes that feelings are dangerous; only dissociation, compartmentalisation, courage, obedience to orders and clan loyalty can bring about right action. This has its advantages in a war context, but is very difficult to unlearn; 'Civvy Street' is littered with PTSD victims.

2. Then there is the *Way of Entitlement,* which we can see in Boris but was perfected in Victorian Britain. Here is Prime Minister Spencer Cavendish, Duke of Devonshire, whose home was Chatsworth, most splendid of all country mansions, giving his Pythonesque advice in 1895 to the young Winston Churchill about the problem of pre-speech nerves:

> I used to [feel nervous], but now, when ever I get up on a public platform, I take a good look around and as I sit down I say, "I never saw such a lot of damned fools in my life" and then I feel a lot better. [13]

In the *Way of Entitlement,* both dissociation and compartmentalisation are taken to extremes. The Entitlement Illusion successfully helped people rise above their fears by devaluing their own emotional decision-making processes in favour of an inner superiority perfected in the narrow-focused Entitled Brain. It is this that enabled the governance of the British Raj, and later Africa, to be achieved with only a handful of ex-boarder administrators. Gordon of Khartoum is its iconic exemplar. After the death of Steve Biko in 1977, the Way of Entitlement allowed white Apartheid leaders of South Africa to stay detached from the reality of how the rest of the world regarded what was happening in their country.

Happily, the new knowledge to which I have been referring both highlights problems and also offers some pointers towards health. In fact, we now know that we can train ourselves and our leaders not to push the panic button in various ways. Here are a few suggestions:

- A prime way is to learn to master our feelings, as we have seen in this chapter, so that we do not need to practise dissociation excessively and so we have full access to the emotional data we need for optimum decision-making.

• Next, we must learn to use the brain-heart system properly. As we saw in the previous chapter, biofeedback machines, such as those sold by the research institute HeartMath, can help us to monitor and cultivate the coordination of our heart rate, which is the main signal for parasympathetic firing. We can use these and other kinds of relaxation techniques for learning how to consciously prime our rest and repair system rather than unconsciously firing the fight or flight response.

• We can exercise our minds to cultivate constructive doubt over our initial panic perceptions and engage right brain activity. The world will always be imperfect and we must put things in context, sometimes saying to ourselves, "Come on, put this in perspective!" Much of this is common sense, but the next chapter explores the faculty of doubt in detail.

• We can do cognitive and therapeutic work to understand the things and reactions that cause us to panic. In the 'Calm Down Dear' example, in order to avoid a habitual hysterical reaction, Cameron would need to recognise in the threatening Angela Eagle problem the unconscious split-off archetypal feminine and his inevitable consequent misogyny.

• We can exercise our minds to cultivate self-reflection and an inner sense of time, using techniques that teach us to respond rather than to react. It is not unknown in Britain. Cricket lovers will remember that when the West Indian Brian Lara first arrived on the scene he created so much time that he could decide how to hit a fast ball in the milliseconds it took for that lethal ball to get near him. Alternatively, a trip to the British Museum will reveal some priceless examples of Buddhist sculpture stolen from the East. The point of these statues was not actually to be worshipped (as Victorian archaeologists who had been brought up with Christianity imagined) but to mirror a state of internal calm and alertness, the better for practitioners of meditation to learn it.

• We can do exercise for our hearts, not only on cardiac machines in the gym but also in the gym of life. The path of intimacy – learning to love – can't be done without heart; as it becomes a habit, it strengthens the afferent channels in the nervous system. Knowing that you are loved provides a secure base for life, as Bowlby said (Chapter 11). Loving even if you do not feel loved is a skill of leadership mastery, as Nelson Mandela showed, even if in another context he advocated armed struggle. The power of not being afraid of vulnerability strengthens our hearts and opens the gateways to intimacy.

Conclusions: context, vulnerability and the brain

Before proceeding to the final chapter, I will summarise some of our conclusions so far:

• We have seen how rationality helped humanity enter a new world of ingenuity. Hyper-rationality, however, with its fear of emotions, its left-brain domination and overuse of the psychological defence mechanisms of dissociation, objectification and compartmentalisation, created a trance that has wounded its adherents as it has the objects of its gaze. In the end, the fear of all vulnerable states, and the consequent masquerading of defence mechanisms as values, weakens rather than strengthens.

• An up-to-date education system ought to educate its pupils in the ways of cultivated brain balance and emotional intelligence, away from self-protection through the drastic use of defence mechanisms and the stress that results as a consequence.

• But first, the spell that has normalised these things needs to be broken; for as we have seen, when it is used defensively, normalisation is a powerful poison that prevents recognition from within 'the box.' We need a bigger picture.

One issue from Iain McGilchrist's monumental essay on left hemisphere domination, *The Master and his Emissary: the Divided Brain and the Making of the Western World*,[14] stands out for me above all others: the mother of all problems appears to be one of context. The classic tendency of the left brain's ability to focus unilaterally ignores the bigger picture (which belongs more to right-brain attention) and thereby misses the chance to work, as nature intended, in a creative cerebral partnership. Instead, the left, McGilchrist tells us, seizes a context and makes it into *The Context*. From this perspective, seeing wider contexts, admitting mistakes or pausing for reflective doubt becomes very difficult.

The main task in teaching young minds, then, seems to me to lie in putting facts, figures and feelings at the service of the bigger picture; in other words, training contextual thinking. Once again, we can look back to another, not so distant era, where this was recognised but not implemented. McGilchrist recalls a time at the end of the 19th and beginning of the 20th century, when the American pragmatist philosophers John Dewey and William James:

> ... began to signal dissatisfaction with the atomistic, rationalistic approach in philosophy and the abstraction that necessarily goes with it. Dewey wrote: "... neglect of context is the besetting fallacy of philosophical thought ... I should venture to assert that the most pervasive fallacy of philosophic thinking goes back to neglect of context ... neglect of context is the greatest single disaster which philosophic thinking can incur." [15]

If contextual thinking needs to be taught to philosophers, then I would argue that it cannot be dispensed with elsewhere and can even be introduced with huge benefit from an early age. Following the natural processes of the brain is surely the way to enhance learning and to make the acquisition of facts and skills stick. As all teachers know, children's brains have an enormous capacity for rational learning – one example is the way it is so much easier to learn several foreign languages at an early age than later in life. But to use this facility, children need to feel safe and contained in themselves, otherwise their minds will not be free to learn. Rational learning needs to be done in partnership with a grounding in an emotional intelligence that obviates the need for psychological defensiveness.

As we have seen by examining the flawed model used in Britain over two centuries, the consistent, chronic and unrecognised use of the defence mechanisms encourages individuals to run their lives from fear and compensated grandiosity – the Way of Entitlement. Putting fear at the centre of life has drastic consequences on chronic stress levels and impacts the ability to extract the proper benefit of the body's own healing, sensory and protection systems. Our exemplar of the flawed misuse was the Strategic Survival Personality, adopted *per force* and at speed by the privileged but abandoned young boarders in Britain. The Strategic Survival Personality, along with the bullying it uses to ensure its continuation and all the stress it acquires in keeping going as the centre of the personality, is organised entirely around the fear of being vulnerable. It makes a lot of sense in a context in which an attachment-deficit institution is your home, rather than a loving family, and in which showing your feelings is banned and keeping out of trouble is imperative. But it construes vulnerability as a thing to be avoided for life. Vulnerability, however, is an existential attribute – a central part of being alive and being human. All of us have to come to terms with this facet of life.

It turns out that vulnerability – or rather, the art of not being afraid to be vulnerable – is an incredible skill and one that needs to be taught from a child's earliest days. There is a deep paradox in the nature of vulnerability in that when an individual is not being afraid to be vulnerable, it makes them extraordinarily powerful. For example, Tony Blair would probably have been forgiven and re-embraced if he had had the courage and the self-reflection to say, "I'm sorry, I made a mistake about Iraq, I got it wrong." Instead, our political life is dominated by normalised bullying based on the fear of vulnerability. We despise the leader who is said to have made a U-turn. As in the example of Cameron's 'Calm Down Dear' incident, Wounded Leaders shy away from the power that arises in people when they are not afraid to be caught out. They cannot imagine that not needing to be run by the Strategic Survival Personality, not being afraid of their feelings, could be the royal road to acquiring genuine inner authority.

Learning the art of not being afraid to be vulnerable is therefore perhaps the greatest leadership challenge, for it gives a person command over his own life and takes the key way from his fear-driven Strategic Survival Personality. Unfortunately, this has not been culturally developed or supported – particularly in men – and undervalued in women. But it is not impossible to learn it or teach it. In some therapeutic trainings, it is something that is singled out for special attention. If schools were to adopt training of this sort from the start, there would not be such a hill to climb later on when we embark on the task of unlearning culturally normalised defences against vulnerability. In the metaphor we used in Chapter 6, this would be the way to put the Self in charge of life, rather than the ego. On the interpersonal level, vulnerability is the gateway to intimacy, the lynchpin of relationships – all relationship experts say something similar.[16] To choose to open yourself to another person is to take a risk and thereby give the other a gift: to say that you trust.

Teaching such skills would also mean helping pupils develop a good left and right brain balance, in ways that sometimes may be counterintuitive. McGilchrist suggests that the left hemisphere of the brain is ranged against vulnerability, and quotes Carl Kerenyi, the Hungarian philologist and mythologist, a collaborator with C.G. Jung. In the ancient world, according to Kerenyi:

> Vulnerability was an attribute of the gods, just as it is characteristic of human existence.[17]

It is this principle that became incorporated into Christianity and distinguished it from Judaism, even though its essence may have since been lost. McGilchrist proposes that vulnerability cannot be embraced by what he calls the "Promethean" left hemisphere, which seeks always to grasp, to acquire, to dominate. Physiologically, it has command over the right hand, which most of us use to get rather than to give. In Greek mythology, Prometheus is one of the Titans, the older demigods who preceded the Olympians, descendents of the Earth Goddess Gaia. Described by Kerenyi as "a cheat and a thief," Prometheus is credited with creating man out of clay and famous for defying the gods by stealing fire and bestowing it on humanity. As the enabler of progress and civilisation, he was much valued in the neoclassical 18th century, the forerunner of the Industrial Revolution. Known for his intelligence and as a champion of mankind, Prometheus became a figure who represented human striving, particularly the quest for scientific knowledge, the Faustian pact for ever-more information that conditions our world. "Under his tutelage, men became stealers of the divinity that lies round about them," says McGilchrist.

What does this signify? Untempered by the balance needed from the right hemisphere, from the knowledge that life involves give and take, the stealing attitude of the left hemisphere reinvents us as exploiters of life, of the earth, of other races, of other species. We lose the knowledge of being a part of a living whole.[18] Being alive, after all, means being interdependent and vulnerable, having trust in life alongside healthy doubt about ideas and fashions – including one's own – as we shall see in the concluding chapter. Only a heart that is not afraid and is allowed to take charge can be the centre of authentic leadership within a person.

The Rational Man Project runs on tremendous fear of what it has disowned – vulnerability, femininity and failure. It is compensated through grandiosity and is destined to run on a dangerous cocktail of excess adrenalin and cortisol. Today's world normalises the pressure on politicians, executives and workers to become increasingly 'competitive' that has been created by globalisation.

We have seen what a diet of fear and grandiosity can do to a society, to a person or to their partner. Relying on a hyper-rational training of the mind-body system, giving control to the 'emissary' rather than the 'master' and ignoring all promptings of the heart is normalised but disastrous – therein lies madness!

CHAPTER 13

No Doubt

Dubito Ergo Sum

Just after five o'clock on the evening of 11 May 1812, Spencer Perceval, Prime Minister to mad King George III, was entering the lobby of the House of Commons when a man stepped forward, drew a pistol and shot him in the chest. Perceval dropped to the floor and with the arrival of a surgeon a few minutes later was promptly declared dead. To date, he is the only attorney general to have been prime minister and the only prime minister to be assassinated. In the general atmosphere of fear at the time, described in Chapter 8, it was feared that the shot might be the start of an uprising. However, it soon became apparent that the assassin, John Bellingham, had acted alone and made no attempt to escape. The murder turned out to be an outrageous publicity stunt. Bellingham was a merchant with a grievance against the government for rejecting all his many petitions to be compensated for his ruination. This was due to his having been imprisoned in Russia as a result of the vagaries of government foreign policy. Bellingham was immediately brought to justice and, despite evidence that he was insane (which he strenuously denied), he was found guilty and hanged in public seven days later – the fastest execution in British legal history. By a curious quirk of history, his descendant Henry Bellingham, MP for North West

Norfolk, lost his seat in the 1997 Blair bonanza, in part due to the votes received by the Referendum Party candidate Roger Percival, a descendant of the assassinated Prime Minister.[1]

Spencer Perceval left 12 children, one of whom was John Thomas, a handsome and intelligent boy of nine – six years senior to his much more famous contemporary, Charles Darwin. John excelled at classics at his father's school, Harrow, but left at 16 and entered the army, becoming a Captain in the First Foot Guards. Of a serious disposition like his father, he practised temperance and took up religion. He was drawn to evangelical sects that encouraged the speaking of tongues, and this eventually began to consume him. At the height of his fervour, driven by spirit voices, he went AWOL in Dublin, where finally his brother found him. John Thomas had not slept for five days and was distraught. A 'lunatic doctor,' as they were called, was sent for, Perceval was declared insane and years of brutal institutionalisation followed.

By 1831, about the same year that Thomas Hardy's father had seen three men hanged for being in the vicinity of a hayrick protest burning, John Thomas Perceval was in his third madhouse, suffering the fate of those who became 'reason's opposite' at the time. The attitude to those with mental illness was a mixture of ignorance and fear. Insanity was that which was no longer rational, for it was not measurable, intelligible or curable. In Perceval's case it was exceptionally terrifying and despicable, for he was not one of the criminal classes but an English Upper Class Gentleman – the pinnacle of the Rational Man Project. Perceval was punished for this with three years of asylum confinement until, by his own remarkable efforts, he recovered his sanity. Extraordinarily, he managed to take notes during his brief visits to what Edward Podvoll, a psychiatrist in Boulder, Colorado who studied the case, called "islands of clarity." In 1840, Perceval published a full account of his fall to madness and recovery, entitled *A Narrative*.[2] Podvoll found this document of inestimable value; here he gives a flavour of it:

> It is impossible to describe the 'treatment' Perceval endured within the walls of the Brisslington madhouse. His own words about it are extremely painful to read. One outrage followed another. He was treated with shockingly cold ice baths and forced dunkings, cold vapour baths, and medicines that he called 'noxious fumigations,' and twice he experienced the treatment called 'bloodletting.'[3]

Here is how Percival himself describes the therapeutic programme:

> For nearly eight months I may say that I was never out of a strait-waistcoat; I used to be tied up in it, in a recess the whole day, on a wooden seat, for months and months, with my feet manacled to the floor, and in the presence of fourteen other patients. I twice required two severe operations, or was supposed to require; one, bleeding at the temporal artery; the other, having my ear cut open to let out extravasated blood ... I was bled till I fainted! I saw my blood taken away in basins full, and I did not know what to anticipate.

The long periods of isolation and restraint did indeed drive him to the depths of indescribable madness. Incredibly, he pulled through, obtained his release and devoted the rest of his life to furthering a better public understanding of mental illness and to the amelioration of asylum conditions. In the latter he had some small success, founding the Alleged Lunatics' Friend Society, but in the former he achieved very little.

However, in 1962, systems theorist and anthropologist Gregory Bateson republished Percival's two books about his asylum experience and in recent years Perceval has been hailed as the pioneer of the mental health advocacy movement. Podvoll, however, goes further and credits him with much more: that he actually found the way out from madness.

Perceval's discoveries are therefore critical for the study of both irrationality and, by extension, my argument is that they furnish a neglected vital key to understanding the nature and limits of rationality. Here is Podvoll's summary:

> For over a century, psychiatrists have tried in vain to identify the defect operating in the mind of people in psychosis, the aberration ultimately responsible for the peculiar 'psychotic logic' that induces their hallucinations and delusions. Perceval announced his own conclusion as to the nature of this psychotic defect on almost every page of his writings: a disturbance of the normal and intelligent function of Doubt.

The faculty of Doubt is in fact central to the original Enlightenment method but has been sorely neglected as a mental function in favour of Reason. Some scholars point out that René Descartes' original Eureka moment was not actually the oft-quoted phrase *cogito ergo sum,* which has gone down in history, but the longer *dubito ergo cogito; cogito ergo sum,* meaning: "I doubt, therefore I think; I think therefore I am." Writing in the *New York Times,* Ayaan Hirsi suggests that the original cautious values at the dawn of the rational awakening tend to be overlooked:

> Enlightenment thinkers ... argued that human reason is fallible. They understood that reason is more than just rational thought; it is also a process of trial and error, the ability to learn from past mistakes. The Enlightenment cannot be fully appreciated without a strong awareness of just how frail human reason is. That is why concepts like "doubt" and "reflection" are central to any form of decision-making.[4]

For Descartes, doubt was the key, as it was for Perceval. For the former, doubt pointed the way out from Christianity's stranglehold over the European mediaeval 'faith-based community' that had kept thought bound up until the Renaissance; for the latter, doubt led him out of the wilderness of insanity. However, in the ecstatic orgy of rational thinking that ensued, doubt got forgotten. It is astonishing that Podvoll chooses to credit an old Harrovian who had lost his mind for reintroducing forgotten doubt as the solution to psychosis.

For the purposes of our study, his insights offer a key element into understanding the delusional nature of hyper-rationality – why rationality can become, as Dr Mindell said, "an altered state."[5] Despite his evocative name, or perhaps true to it (*John Thomas* is an old euphemism for the penis, and, according to Jungian theologian Robert A. Johnson, Perceval, or *Parsifal,* is derived from 'Pure Fool,' the childish innocent who begins a search for the Holy Grail[6]), the apparent fool Perceval, all alone, abandoned as crazy, found, by dint of disciplined self-reflection and curiosity, that doubt was the tool he needed. Podvoll recounts how Perceval applied himself:

> He studied the natural function of doubt and all its permutations from the beginning to the end of his psychosis. This is not the doubt of indecision, hesitation, or ambivalence. Starting from his conversion to "power," he had begun to blind himself to a reflex, inherent in his own intelligence, that he called a flash of 'doubt!' that spontaneously interrupts a belief in the most solid perceptual world. It is a moment of clarity that happens in microseconds: It

is a moment of freshness of mind. In anyone, in an instant, it can spark even in the midst of a riveting nightmare, revealing it to be only an insubstantial drama of the mind.

For Perceval, it would appear and disappear during the most savage hallucinations. At every stage of losing his mind Perceval jokingly asked himself, "Am I only dreaming?" And in that moment, his insanity was interrupted. At the very first discernible moments of his insanity, Perceval 'doubted': "I felt it was either an awful truth or a dreadful and damnable delusion," and even when he was feeling suffused with a kind of liquid bodily pleasure he suddenly wondered, "Am I yet only imagining even when I am happy?"

Kidnapped by the emissary

Excited by Perceval's story, Podvoll's research led him to a handful other pioneers who had fallen into madness and managed to retain sufficient moments of memory and willpower to observe and record what was actually happening. Inspired, he pioneered an approach to working with psychotic patients based on two goals: first, encouraging their own doubt in their mental fabrications, which he called 'micro-operations,' and secondly, bridging the lost gap between body and mind by means of body-mind synchronisation techniques and exercises. Interestingly – and crucial for our study – the lack of doubt and the gap between body and mind, which are symptoms occurring in psychoses like schizophrenia, bipolar disease and megalomania, are also prominent in ex-boarders and many individuals who are heavily in the grip of what I have been calling hyper-rationality.

Before his book *The Master and his Emissary: the Divided Brain and the Making of the Western World* went viral, Iain McGilchrist was a practising psychiatrist who challenged previously held assumptions about psychosis.[7] Against the accepted convention that the minds of schizophrenic patients had too many extensive contexts – a right-brain hemisphere problem – McGilchrist demonstrated that they appear to be imprisoned, as it were, in a left-hemisphere trap. He shows how schizophrenics pay minute and precise attention to their hallucinations and inner voices, experiencing them to be true. In other words, they get stuck in a Podvollian 'micro-context' and believe it to be the truth. Podvoll's primarily tool was the encouragement of patients to make use of and cultivate their own doubting 'islands of clarity.' These are produced through the mental activity of doubt that arises at moments of increased right-hemisphere brain activity. This allows the mind to become curious about the bigger picture, as opposed to being overwhelmed by and trapped in the endlessly captivating but delusional movie that is running in the left.

Podvoll's work preceded the enormous amount of research that has now been acquired on the differences in brain hemisphere operation and our understanding of human beings' bicameral mind.[8] So we are now able to add in the neurological background to his rediscovery of the value of doubt. The relevant data are so numerous that I must refer the interested reader directly to McGilchrist's book, his voluminous online reference bibliography and the 535 footnotes to his second chapter, "What do the two hemispheres 'do'?" Meanwhile, what follows here is my own reading of his conclusions, and I must likewise refer those whose appetite is whetted to the original.

Arising from the immense collection of data that McGilchrist summarises is an increasingly distinct picture of the two attention types. Each has strengths and limitations. The right hemisphere takes in the reality of other people, whereas the left, with its sharper and narrower attention, is more attuned to recognise objects and dead matter rather than living things. The left hemisphere is competitive, frequently in denial of its own limitations, doesn't want to be bothered by conflicting accounts from the right, and can get lost in the detail. According to McGilchrist, as the left establishes context, it has a tendency to lose the *original* context: it takes the figure out of the background and makes this the *new* context. The right hemisphere's contexts, however, are more global, and it is therefore better placed to see the mental overload produced in a psychotic episode as delusions. The left's built-in disadvantage is in what McGilchrist calls its *grasping*: it tends to grasp a context and make it the only context and hang on to it for it dear life, as it were. These aspects of the left can result in a kind of narrow-mindedness and a tendency to dominate.

The left hemisphere's blinkeredness seems to arise from its ability to compartmentalise perceptions and its *in*ability to bypass contexts once seized upon that do not interface with reality. It means that under the sway of the left hemisphere subjects can become very single-minded, but sometimes their behaviour can end up being somewhat driven and irrational. In the psychotic patient, behaviour can become delusional and sometimes downright dangerous. In this way, the schizophrenic's overactive left-brain is what causes his awful isolation. The result is a madness of disconnection.

A further key feature of this disconnected problem appears to me to be a lack of internal energetic regulation in the person. Energy regulation is usually done by the neuro-cardiological system in communication with all aspects of the nervous system. But in a psychotic episode, the left hemisphere assumes command and control of the organism, and the brain then remains, as it were, isolated from the rest of the body's global reality. The brain becomes over-stimulated, flooded by a series of micro events and perceptions, which normally reside below the level of normal consciousness. At this point, the vagus-heart parasympathetic calming system will not be kicking in. As if on LSD, the person now relates to a unique self-centred reality, which feels real and conscious but is at the expense of any real relationship with other people, who have become objects. The person is under enormous internal stress, which he occasionally experiences as enjoyable excitement, as if they were on a roller-coaster ride. This speed of thoughts and processes, both unsettling and addictive, is what Podvoll considered the key feature of psychosis.

But Podvoll was an optimist. He firmly believed that if the patient can work for more islands of clarity and develop self-awareness through doubting the endless productions of his mind, whether paranoia or spiritual vision, he can become master of himself again and thereby take his place among the living. Self-awareness and self-examination also happen to be the key tools of Mahayanan Buddhist meditation techniques, of which Podvoll was a very serious student and therefore drawn to such solutions.

At the heart of Buddhism is the notion of the interdependence, connectedness and impermanence of all phenomena, from which awareness and an imperative towards self-reflection and self-regulation naturally arise. In the latter part of his life, Podvoll established a radically different kind of care facility, known as the Windhorse Project.[9] Even today, his hospices and halfway houses shelter recovering patients, who are taught elements of mindfulness and other Buddhist meditation techniques to relearn self-reflection, control of their minds and body-mind synchronization.

Podvoll's work, placing what I call *constructive doubt* as a central tool for basic health, repositions the value of rational enquiry, while McGilchrist's work shows how it functions within the brain. Healthy self-questioning requires the shutdown of the left hemisphere to allow the right to see the larger picture, the global context. In terms of mind, *global* means a breadth of both outer and *inner* contexts. Psychotherapists understand context always to be mediated by feelings, especially those sometimes called the *higher feelings*, said to involve the heart: healthy shame, grief, remorse, longing, empathy, compassion and so on. These feelings are often connected to the reappraisal of previous judgments or actions, a major function of constructive doubt. McGilchrist emphasises that the right hemisphere should not be known as the emotional brain because the left hemisphere does engage with emotions. However, there seems to be a difference in quality: the left seems to be more stimulated by the feelings of anxiety, terror and disgust than the right, and tends more towards action rather than reflection. The faculty of doubting self-reflection seems to be a kind of gatekeeper between the two brain hemispheres.

The way in which Perceval interrupted his insanity with moments of doubt shows how doubt allows the right hemisphere to introduce empathic global choices and send the proper tasks of discrimination and analysis to the left. This left–right–left cooperation is how the human brain is designed to function optimally, McGilchrist attests. Doubt may help balance the brain and so acts as the servant for the heart to become fully human again. Luckily, with the benefit of the new neuroscience, we are now in a far better position to evaluate the data about how the human brain works and what happens when chronic dysfunction or sudden traumatic illness strikes. Even though constructive doubt continues to be undervalued and under-applied, it provides the way out of the narrow limitations of the left-brain-only perspective. It has a vital function in solving the trap of micro-contexts, seeing the big picture in order to establish overarching contexts, as well as facilitating learning from mistakes and the expression of remorse and compassion. It is therefore a crucial tool for good internal leadership, which should precede being a creative leader in the outside world.

Madness and context

Readers may be wondering why we have been thinking about madness at this point. One reason is that the fostering of an excessively rational take on the world led to the greatest madness known to history, the First World War, during which rank dissociation meant that millions of innocent European youths were lied to and sacrificed, as borne witness by Siegfried Sassoon and the other war poets. Similarly, sending children away to grow up in attachment-deficit institutions could be called mad, since not one single theory of child development supports it. By extension, continuing to elect leaders who have been educated to become only partial human beings under a value system of 150 years ago, disguised by the trance of the Entitlement Illusion, might be called a form of madness. I could go on. Some readers may still dismiss these points as opinion or conclude that they raise more questions than they answer. We must bring constructive doubt to bear on this issue and ask ourselves: is sending children away to school sane or mad? To answer that it is British tradition does not suffice. Then we must further interrogate ourselves: is normalising it sane or mad? Is surviving it sane or mad?

The unilateral brain hemisphere functioning and disconnected situation I have been describing is not confined to doubt-free psychotics who have lost the ability to manage their lives. In fact, it is nearly identical to the extreme undoubting ex-boarder, a Complier type, who may be in a position of high responsibility without exhibiting symptoms of distress. Nor are the irrational blinkered contexts very far from the notion of the irrational British hyper-rationality that we examined in Chapter 11. At a certain point, extreme rationality and madness begin to resemble each other. This not simply my opinion: the renowned Belgian thermodynamicist and Nobel Laureate, Ilya Prigogine, who died in May 2003, was quite clear that extremes of rationality that no longer serve reflection inevitably turn into self-referring psychosis.[10]

We have seen how those who have had to forgo attachments, love and touch in early childhood in the competitive world of institutionalised rationality construct a brittle but functioning Strategic Survival Personality that frequently has a covertly aggressive, blinkered and pedantic perspective on life. Physiologically, such individuals regularly under-manage their self-imposed stress without the benefit of emotional intelligence of afferent heart-directed ANS activity, instead managing everything mentally by means of dissociation and compartmentalisation – left hemisphere talents. It would be extremely threatening to their commitment to survival if they doubted what they believed to be true (which would involve the right hemisphere) by acknowledging that they had significant problems to do with their emotions or relationships. Such acknowledgement would bring up fears of non-survival and with it an excess of anxiety.

The emotions of anxiety light up the ancient centres of the brain known as the *reptilian* brain, and direct the organism towards survival at all costs. In the hyper-rationally educated, such emotions – which are usually unconscious – easily go into overdrive. Seeing the narrow context and fearing annihilation, the anxious emotions re-stimulate the most primitive self-survival tactics at the expense of overarching contexts and other living persons. The Wounded Leader panics; disconnection, sacrifice and flight inevitably follow.

Signs of this out-of-balance left-hemisphere imprisonment are frequently exhibited by eminent British hyper-rationalist political heavyweights of a Rightist persuasion in their hostile attitudes towards whatever they consider 'soft.' The successfully managed, but over-contained anxiety of this position can be detected in their intonation and speech patterns: listen to Simon Heffer, John Redwood or Iain Fergusson, for example. This symptom is recognisable to psychotherapists practising the 'talking cure,' who usually interpret it as repressed anger leaking out (which is usually *also* the case). The anxiety can often be overlooked, however, because the person is functioning in a very limited reality, and their anxiety is masked by the sense of entitlement and a need for control.

Without the right hemisphere, the left flounders but seizes control; it attempts to eliminate doubt and banish the anxiety by dissociation and compartmentalisation, as we have seen. Philosopher Jim Danaher explains how this affects rational logic:

> What is so attractive about left-brain analysis is that it divides our objects of thought into ever-smaller parts that eliminate all contradictions and leave us with clear and distinct ideas. For example, take any paradoxical or contradictory phenomena and

begin to analyze it into its parts and the contradiction eventually disappears.[11]

The left can easily mistake its micro-contexts for *the context*, while omitting to use its major gifts, which are for "clear and distinct" ideas, for clarity, curiosity, doubt and useful compartmentalisation – especially doubt. Danaher again:

> Modernity became obsessed with analysis and the elimination of vague, ambiguous, or contradictory ideas. We fell almost completely under its sway and came to imagine that the picture of reality that such thinking provided gave us the best way to understand our world and our place in it. Today, however, we are able to see that from a very different perspective because of what we know concerning the human brain. We now know that as appealing as such certainty is, it merely represents one way that the human brain is capable of thinking. Instead of the moving picture of our actual experience, we are capable of ideas that represent snapshots, which make the distances, perspectives, and relations that we actually experience appear fixed and give us the kind of clear and distinct ideas that we crave.

We know from hundreds of studies that when the right hemisphere is knocked out by a stroke or other lesion, or is switched off by the left, there is no global context in which to ground insights and support its functioning in an independent manner. So the left-brain becomes, as it were, the dominant global superpower and objectifying colonial overlord – the 'Master' rather than the 'Emissary,' as McGilchrist frames it (see Chapter 12). It can then keep rising towards self-centred states such as entitlement, megalomania and paranoia, all of which have a secondary effect on perception and all of which are well-known features of hyper-conservative British elitism as they are of psychosis.

Politics without doubt

If the human brain thrives on doubt and self-reflection, human culture ought to value it. The Rational Man Project, however, considers doubt as a weakness and an enemy. Perhaps the biggest insult in British politics is to be accused of making a 'U-turn.' The project believes in progress but is opposed to change within the self; it would much rather eliminate the other, so it is often incapable of reform and cannot transform. George III's regime, for example, could not listen to the demands that led to the Boston Tea Party; it had to go out and teach the rebels a lesson. Mrs Thatcher's government could not reform the Greater London Council – they had to make it the enemy and then abolish it, eliminate, dissociate from it. Nor could they meet the miners' movement – they had to crush it, like Churchill in his time. In these over-reactions great harm was done, for, as psychoanalyst James Grotstein tells us:

> When innocence has been deprived of its entitlement, it becomes a diabolical spirit.[12]

It is not that this is wilful evil, necessarily; it is a way of acting from a severely curtailed perspective on the world learned long ago in childhood and if unchecked it can do harm. Besides, Rational Man can never be wrong; nor can he feel, so he is prone to bad decisions. Disastrously, because he cannot be wrong and he cannot feel he cannot grieve and cannot feel remorse; and so, psychically, we still cannot get over the First World War, as D.H. Lawrence predicted. It would be a U-turn.

A leader in the grip of the Strategic Survival Personality cannot therefore really think creatively if he can't doubt, because self-doubt would create internal anxiety that someone was going to attack him for making a U-turn. Given that he can't doubt, he can't think, according to Descartes. Given that he also can't feel, he can't make good decisions; given that he can't grieve, like Clifford Chatterley, he is stuck in an isolated and crippled prison of his own defensive personality structure, his false self, which has only transitory existence. He needs help, this is clear; but he doesn't need to be elected a leader. It's not good for him and it's not good for us.

Alarmingly, the above profile is not unique to a boarding school survivor: it is not unlike the profile of the sociopath – someone who has no conscience but has charm and acts as if he has feelings. Martha Stout, in her 2005 survey, *The Sociopath Next Door*, suggests that an estimated 4% of the US population are sociopathic, and such people tend almost invariably to be occupying positions of trust and power; they tend to be corporate executives, politicians, teachers, ministers, and even therapists.[13] And here it has to be said that modern Western societies, driven by relentless competition and the urge to buy and sell without self-reflection, seem to value sociopathy; those who want to achieve the highest positions have to accept an accelerated work ethic and hours their bodies would protest against if allowed free expression. Stout suggests that in rewarding sociopathic trends we are in danger of normalising sociopathy.

While the true sociopath is very hard to spot and operates with an extraordinary degree of cunning, the average hyper-rational man cannot deal with problems that involve a level of subtlety – for example, with a couched aggressor. Compartmentalising and projecting an outer veneer, which is a sociopathic trait, is socially sanctioned over years of rationality; but psychologically it is not actually robust – it is brittle. Such a leader is very bad at seeing who is bluffing and, if he is an ex-boarder and bluffing himself by running on his Strategic Survival Personality, he can easily be fooled. According to psychologist Lundy Bancroft, entitlement is the main feature of hyper-masculinity, which permits brutality in the name of order.[14] Only someone who is not a bully can spot someone who is, and an unrealistic sense of entitlement can cloud all judgement.

Politically, this is an everyday reality. For example, the so-called War on Terror, which lent validity to the aggressive ambitions of the Bush administration's neo-conservative agenda, was an alibi cunningly adopted by the Putin regime's ethnic cleansing in Chechnya. The aptly named (but surreal idea) war on an abstract concept – *terror* – works wonders; terror can become any revolt against any establishment. In fact, the early 21st century is crucially important for seeing the lack of discriminating doubt in action. Why did a leader with the intelligence and charisma of Tony Blair not spot the holes in the hype around the Second Gulf War, for example? Was it simply political expediency? That is certainly not what he says. Why, when he was used to Clinton's sophistication, did he seem to fall for Bush's grossness? Or was it habitual tunnel vision?

Leaders today must be on guard not to have a narrowed perspective lest they fall foul of a normalised global bullying that is run by vast global corporate powers, which former 'Economic Hitman' John Perkins collectively calls *the corporatocracy*.[15] Brilliant Blair fell right into the trap, and Cameron might have too, had it been laid in his time. He certainly looks charmed when he is next to Obama; perhaps his narrow vision would have made him similarly vulnerable to a desire to sit at High Table. The narrow focus of left-brain domination produces a brittle weakness in the end. In April 2012, actor Robert Redford, on a visit to Britain to promote creativity in filmmaking, certainly felt the need make a canny comment on Cameron's attitude to the film industry. After the PM suggested Britain should concentrate its funds on mainstream, "commercially viable" cinema, Redford's response was:

> I think that is a narrow view. I don't want to say it speaks of the man. That may be why he is in trouble. I won't get into the other reasons because it is not my business.[16]

Rationality's left-brain narrowing of context has a further problem: it is not accountable. The hyper-rational mind has to be matured in relationship, otherwise there is a danger of its owner becoming like Icarus, flying too high and being burned up by the sun. Up to a point, psychopaths do well in the system because they are not accountable, for accountability is based on connecting, communalism, mutuality, wholeness. The left-brain domination makes a lack of accountability much more possible through denial and compartmentalisation. This is one way, for example, that climate change can still be denied, despite the evidence.

Worse, the continued resort to dissociation has a circular effect. Dissociation trains the brain to overuse the left hemisphere, and then there is a secondary effect from getting used to left-brain thinking. This is probably the most harrowing of the mental conjuring tricks, for, as we have seen, the left-brain takes a context *out of context* and makes it the *new* context. As it makes a new context it invents a new terminology to suit, like the War on Terror.

This should not be passed over, for it is extremely dangerous because it normalises the operation of an atavistic, defensive, entitled, domineering, reptilian mind reinforced by rational logic. It can then turn this new context into a moral case for war, sacrifice and domination. The radical writer Noam Chomsky argues:

> The Iraq war is an instructive case. It was marketed to a terrified public on the usual grounds of self-defense against an awesome threat to survival: the "single question," George W Bush and

Tony Blair declared, was whether Saddam Hussein would end his programs of developing weapons of mass destruction. When the single question received the wrong answer, government rhetoric shifted effortlessly to our "yearning for democracy", and educated opinion duly followed course; all routine.[17]

Despite record numbers of protestors against it on the streets of the UK, participation in the Second Gulf War was a rapid *fait accompli* due to the Bush administration's ability to manipulate context and terminology, and thereby their allies, the so-called 'Coalition of the Willing.' In *The Greatest Story Ever Sold*, Frank Rich follows the steps of this conjuring trick in minute detail, sometimes playing it for laughs because the madness is almost too tragic to deal with. Big words and sure contexts were involved. For example, when the imagined 'Weapons of Mass Destruction' (known as 'The Smoking Gun') were never actually located, George W Bush asserted his authority by demanding: "Who's in charge of finding them?"[18] Bush could not say that they seemed not to exist – someone had to be to blame for not locating them, because he had based a war on the *idea* of them, and he wasn't going to do a U-turn in the build-up to that war.

Here, the brain's left hemisphere creates a micro-context through which it looks at everything; very rapidly, the idea, the hypothesis, turns into the truth. It is not a new manoeuvre in the psychohistory of hyper-rationality. For example, we can go back to Regency England, where we started this chapter.

In 1812, when Spenser Perceval was shot, the chances of a revolution were actually very slim. There were sporadic movements of landed peasants complaining about unemployment because of the introduction of machinery, but there was far less danger of the ferment of revolution spreading from France or America than the government wanted the nation to believe, and as has been taught in schools. Such teaching does not take account of the fear and grandiosity that conditioned the era. The British government overreacted to rather understandable concerns, just as they had done to lose their American colony, impulsively driven by survival anxiety in a limited field of context. With a left-hemisphere dominated mind you cannot see another person in their context, but you don't have to use doubt if you are in the Entitlement Illusion – you use the *Way of Entitlement*.

The Entitled Brain and British society

The years leading up to the turn of the 19th century and the Great War years, in which Queen Victoria's Diamond Jubilee was celebrated, are rightly called 'The Age of Privilege.' British elite society could hardly have been more self-confident than at that time. Though unsurpassed in elegance and assurance, from today's perspective the era seems like a Monty Python sketch, peopled with extraordinary actors like Gordon of Khartoum and Bertie Prince of Wales. In retrospect, we would think it quite mad. Its psychohistory confirms that many elements of unrecognised madness were, in fact, in place. The emotional atmosphere in the elite sections of the British scene was as self-assured and complacent as it had been anxious and suspicious a century before. And in 1895, the elite would have done well to be more afraid, for there was a bubble waiting to burst. Barbara Tuchman, an American journalist and historian living in the UK opened her elegant 1966 masterpiece *The Proud Tower: A Portrait of the World Before the War, 1890–1914* in this way:

> The epoch whose final years are the subject of this book did not die of old age or accident but exploded in a terminal crisis which is one of the great facts of history.[19]

In her first chapter, "The Patricians – England, 1895 to 1902," Tuchman explains how both Conservatives and Liberals subscribed to the belief in the necessity for a traditional entitled elite. Even Gladstone, the Great Radical, had said: "society cannot afford to dispense with its dominant influences." The universal credo of a 'superior fitness' bred in those whose families had owned the land for centuries was exactly opposite to that held across the Atlantic, in the colony needlessly lost through tunnel-visioned decision-making a century earlier. There, faith in the virtue of the self-made man sat alongside a suspicion that, as Tuchman puts it, "men of easy circumstances were more likely than not to be stupid or wicked, if not both."

And the US was not the only country where doubt was increasing. Just as had been the case a hundred years earlier, there were now more than murmurs of working class dissent: labour movements, trade unions, calls for universal sufferance, a desperate fury born of Irish impoverishment, and worse. There was organised Socialism backed by middle class intellectuals, who, unlike their counterparts in Britain, were not content to use their minds on witticisms, science or religion. In its most provocative ranks were those who preached a new idea: humanity could only be redeemed by getting rid of all forms of leadership and property rights – it other words, anarchy. The idea appealed to many individuals and loners, desperate by dint of poverty or alienation, who might strike anywhere with daggers, pistols or bombs. The danger was not only from dissenters. Even those who supported the Rational Man Project's aims were becoming a threat as the Empire's dominating success began to over-stimulate other nations. The US began its quiet mission to carve up surrounding territories in the Caribbean and the Pacific, while the Germans, French, Italians and Belgians joined in "a scramble for choice cuts of Africa."[20]

But the aristocratic government elected in Britain in 1895, an assembly of dukes, marquesses, earls, viscounts, barons and baronets who between them owned millions of acres of the country, were not overly troubled by doubt about their status or fear of the future. They saw it as their duty to hold onto Ireland and to permit a small inconvenience, out of noblesse oblige, in the form of the new death duties tax to be levied for the first time on landed wealth as it was handed down. For they were, as Tuchman writes, representatives of:

> ... that class in whose blood, training and practice over the centuries, landowning and government had been inseparable. Ever since Saxon chieftains met to advise the King in the first national assembly ... they had learned the practice of government from the possession of great estates, and they undertook to manage the affairs of the nation as inevitably and unquestionably as beavers build a dam. It was their ordained role and natural task.

The only commoners amongst the ranks of the government were enormously rich industrialists; today, following John Perkins, we might call them representatives of the 'corporatocracy' or, if they were Russian, 'oligarchs.'[21] The chief social movement of the century had been to widen and strengthen the middle classes enormously, both as a result of the prosperity brought by the Empire and as a means of extending it. In fact, the aristocracy were already a waning breed: many smaller landowners were struggling to maintain their properties as wealth transferred from the land to manufacturing in the industrial age. As we know, many of the aristocracy's former mansions became industrialised institutions for the 'hothousing' of young rational gentlemen, whose ties to family, femininity and vulnerability had been wrenched from them even before they reached their teens. This forced gentrification ensured that the social order in Britain was rigidly stratified, with a bloated middle class clinging to the values of the upper and despising and fearing the lower. The lower classes would soon be sacrificed in their millions in a war that, from some angles, appeared to be waged between the entitled elite and the lower orders, rather than nation against nation.

Today, the overtly patrician nature of our elite is less recognisable than in the late Victorian one described by Tuchman, and yet some of our Wounded Leaders would blend in with it seamlessly. Today's government is still a gulf away from the rest of the country, particularly from those at the bottom, who are increasingly less represented. Moreover, the thinking patterns and emotional intelligence of the current British government have more in common with its Victorian predecessor than with the bulk of the nation it represents. This is the Entitlement Illusion: the entitlement is still fully present, but the illusion means that they cannot feel it.

If many of today's Wounded Leaders do not care to notice the problem, some are not always at pains to disguise it. Hearken once more to London Mayor Boris Johnson, delivering the annual Margaret Thatcher Lecture in November 2013. In an attempt to shore up his support on the Tory right, Boris sounded the Imperial bugle: "We may not have many gunboats any more," he admitted but, hinting that the old spirit should not be forgotten, he rallied his troops by declaring it was "time we … persuaded the Eurocrats to stop trying to tell us what to do." [22]

Boris then outlined his economic and emotional policy by exhorting leaders to display their greed in order to promote economic growth, claiming that it was "futile" to try to end inequality. Not even the saving grace of *noblesse oblige* here from a man who had the same Eton, Oxford and Bullingdon Club education as those in the 1895 government. "The harder you shake the pack the easier it will be for some cornflakes to get to the top," he began amusingly. He continued:

I stress – I don't believe that economic equality is possible; indeed some measure of inequality is essential for the spirit of envy and keeping up with the Joneses that is, like greed, a valuable spur to economic activity.

Here we have pure Entitlement Illusion speak, without conscience, without healthy shame, without constructive doubt. For him it is The Truth – for the moment.

Bicameral brains and the Bullingdon Boys

Readers will now recognise this attitude as a sign of left-brain dominance, one of the Entitled Brain phenomena that gives the hyper-conservative so much complacent confidence in his own viewpoint, like Tony Blair on Iraq or Ian Duncan-Smith on welfare reform. The left-hemisphere-only perspective is rigid and self-assured; but it is also weak because of its blinkered focus, its short-termism. Boris may rouse the Right, but if he is elected he has to govern the whole; as with the bicameral brain, the emissary must in the end serve the master or there will be trouble, as McGilchrist is at pains to warn us.

In late 2013, business leaders were beginning to condemn the coalition government for its short-termism, exemplified by the mini-boom built on the back of further property inflation in the south-east, which business leaders knew to be delusory. But the Entitlement Illusion seals off this and any other wider perspective. As we have seen, Cameron seems to be untroubled by his extraordinary micro-context of belief, which states that he and his chums got where they are by virtue of hard work alone. Boris is not ashamed of his views on IQ elitism, which the Guardian's chief reporter Nicholas Watt has likened to Keith Joseph's 1980s version of eugenics.[23] Moreover, in trumpeting IQ, Boris uses an idea long since dismissed by professionals, an anachronism that does not trouble him; he does not refer to the more modern notion of emotional intelligence, either, in which, unfortunately, the elite to which he belongs score exceptionally low.

For heavens sake, don't breathe a word about emotions! In a 2012 BBC radio documentary, *A History of the Stiff Upper Lip*, one of the interviewees, conservative journalist Peter Hitchens, was able to condemn British emotional repression for its role in permitting the slaughter of the First World War. But next, he suggested that the "worm had turned" after the death of Princess Diana, which apparently released an "orgy" of feelings. Hitchens concluded by virulently venting his disgust that this had culminated in the excesses of popular 'junk' TV shows like The *X-Factor*, where both winners and losers loudly emote in front of their public.[24]

Whether such a view has any value is beside the point; my point is that such a perspective reveals itself as left-brained blinkeredness because it omits the social context in which those viewers exist. A psychohistorical view is needed to provide the systemic perspective: knowing the ecological nature of the psyche, which can only recycle and not throw away, we expect the despised emotions to be disowned and projected out. Next, they will have to turn up somewhere in the system. Instead of being accepted and mastered, which is what you have to do with emotions, the emotions were dumped in the psychic garbage bin only to turn up, predictably under-regulated, in a popular TV show. Hitchens distances himself from these unregulated emotions, so wherever they show up he will express disgust. In effect, the elite *need* the people to confirm their superior identity by default, need an undervalued state education system to affirm their belief in the private system, and so on. Thus the whole thing goes on and nothing ever really changes. As the documentary admitted in its pre-publicity:

> Archives from World War One to Princess Diana, and interviewees including Frank Furedi, Ralph Fiennes, David Starkey, Andrew Motion, Peter Hitchens, and Thomas Dixon suggest that results are mixed at best and that we haven't changed as much as we believe.

Because many things *have* changed, the emotionally immature and blinkered doubt-free state of elite entitlement is apparent in the case of the Victorian cabinet, but disguised in the leaders we have today. Or it might be truer to say *unrecognised within* the leaders themselves – this is the trance aspect of the Entitlement Illusion. Their self-assuredness may sound grand, but in fact it is very limiting; it is a weakness. A Boris or a Cameron may make aggressive noises but their partialness is weak and untempered, because they don't know what they are missing. For entitlement only gives one gear that has contributive value:

duty, leadership and work. Since these are at a cost of other human qualities, they become over narrowly focused, limited and eventually self-defeating. Here is one of today's CEOs interviewed in the film *The Making of Them*, revealing what he had discovered about his ex-boarder legacy:

> I think I came out really believing that work makes free, and that stuck with me for many, many years, to the point that it cost me the ability to parent my children, it cost me my marriage, it cost me, in fact, the quality of my career. On the one hand, you're prepped in this way to be part of the Establishment, to be successful, to be self-reliant and aggressive and all those things, but in fact, somewhere inside you, when it comes down to dealing with real relationships, with the real things in life, you are very, very weak and ill-prepared, and the tendency is to run away into work mode.[25]

The key to unlocking all of this is to recognise the fear that drives it. Fear runs the Strategic Survival Personality, and fear has the psychological ability of fanning entitlement, which can turn into extraordinary grandiosity, as we have seen. The CEO continues, revealing the grandiose detached style of the little boy inside him who has been running his inner world and therefore his family life:

> I can remember making a virtue of leaving home at five o'clock on a Sunday afternoon to catch the plane to go somewhere: I'm going back to the front, I'm going back my troops, I'm doing my duty.

Grandiosity severs the connection between power and responsibility. The psychodynamics of the Entitlement Illusion are built on this. They have been the major topic of this book, and now that we understand what psychological defences are called upon and what neurological pathways become occupied, we know what happens to this sense of entitlement when it is under stress. In Chapter 4, we saw how in chronic overuse of the defence of *projection*, disowned fear can turn up in another person, who then becomes fearful.

With the more intense and aggressive defence, *projective identification*, disowned fear now turns up in another person who becomes frightening. The principle is that when the original fear remains unconscious, it 'acts out.' In the Entitled Brain all these defences are employed and the original fear is sublimated into disgust for the vehicle that carries its disowned material; this disgust can then be expressed or acted on. Systemically, as we saw in Chapter 9, those who carry the disowned material of the British elite sit at the bottom of the social pile.

Earlier, we saw how an ex-boarder may be attracted to and marry someone who shows all the signs of being needy or vulnerable – qualities he is not safe enough to identify with himself, and has had to disown. Classically, as we saw, the spouse may begin to exhibit many symptoms of depression which the ex-boarder defends against. He can then remain the Functioning One – often over-functioning. Frequently, such a partner ends up fully depressed, unless and until the ex-boarder does sufficient therapeutic work to reclaim his covert but projected depression.[26]

From a systemic perspective, similar mechanisms can be said to operate on British society; here the working class becomes the marriage partner to the entitled elite, as it were. This unhealthy marriage confirms that Britain has not built a workable social democracy. The gulf between the elite and the people is too big. Apart from what they gather from 'junk' TV or from the builders when they have work done on their homes, the middle classes only really engage with the working classes in matters of strikes and football.

The view from across the channel is that, despite the enviable freedoms in Britain, the workers are hardly enfranchised. The French broadsheet *Le Monde* runs a feature called "Lettre du Royaume-Uni". In one edition, under the subheading "Surtout, n'en parlez pas" (it mustn't be spoken of), Eric Albert observes that in Britain there is never any sympathy shown towards strikers.[27] Instead, he is shocked by the tremendous sympathy towards anyone who has been inconvenienced by strikes. This ensures minimal media coverage of the strikers and their demands and, Albert observes, the British are used to it. He points out that there was no event to mark that a 2012 strike by doctors ever took place: "They have invented the invisible strike," he says. Even though that particular action was a middle class affair, the laws passed by Thatcher mean that there is no possibility for spontaneous action, no secret ballot and no solidarity strikes, thereby immobilising workers rights while maintaining them in law. Current police policy means that workers do not feel that they have the right to protest. As Albert comments, the public sector strikes against austerity of

November 2011 were the largest since the winter of discontent but were never followed up by any other action.

Football (sometimes called "a game played by gentlemen, watched by thugs," as opposed to rugby which is said to be the reverse) shows up our deep societal problems. Football in Britain is high-class entertainment today, because of the many foreigners playing alongside our boys in the leagues, but at international level it is another story. Despite having hugely talented individual players, our teams never seem to work. The accepted view in England is that the country's international team is painful to watch and support. People say: "Weren't they terrible? They're all millionaires and they still can't play!"

But this may not be the real problem – national footballers from all countries are rich these days. If I am right that the English working classes systemically carry depression because the middle and upper classes are defending against theirs, then the problem is bound to show up when they are confined to their own group. England international footballers frequently seem depressed when interviewed, even before the game. Their qualities often have more to do with determination than skill: the pundits call it 'heart' – but that's not what it is. Do they mean hard? Heart is actually something else. Perhaps they mean it in the ancient sense of Englishmen with hearts of oak; or perhaps they mean endurance, which is a quality of the heart because it takes a long-term view, and sometimes a dour one.

But the English players don't seem full of the joy the fans expect, that the pundits can sometimes generate, that you can feel in a stadium when the elation that a goal or a chance literally rattles your chest. It is more like a stubborn masochism. It works well in the Champions' League when you have a few such men playing together with more skilful and fluent foreigners; but a whole team of Englishmen is just too much of the same. It doesn't work and never has. England pulled it off once in 1966, when the team was still full of old-fashioned working men, but has never been anywhere near it since.

Actually, although the British can be very compassionate and warm, there is very little heart used in British discourse – hyper-rationality prevents it; most comments are ironic, speakers tend to be jokey, sour or 'Disgusted of Tunbridge Wells'. Many commentators, such as Hitchens or Simon Heffer, emit a closed-hearted malignity, which some people think is normal or even cool. But it isn't really; it is sad and pathological.

The heart is neglected in British society as long as the Entitled Brain is in power.

ACT V

EPILOGUE

For All my Relations

Native American Blessing

Epilogue: My Heart's in the Highlands

This book has been devoted to naming an elephant in the room. My arguments have pointed to problems and issues that have been previously ignored and need to be addressed. This will mean making some changes and, to close, I will name some of those I see as currently important. I may disappoint some readers by admitting that I don't have all the answers.

If British society were to turn away from the production of Wounded Leaders,[1] two important questions would immediately arise: what are the qualities that we really want in our leaders and what kind of education system might foster them? The first question, concerning the qualities of our leaders, is one for all citizens to reflect on as part of the existing democratic process. If people turn away from democracy as a result of apathy, it is a sign that we need a new politics and new kinds of leaders, not that we have a bad electorate. The second question – how to educate them – is arguably best left to educational specialists, but in this final section I scatter a handful of my own ideas and some stories as starting points for a conversation. My own educational preferences are drawn more from my time as both a student and trainer in psychotherapy and as a psychohistorian than from when I taught school as a very young man in India, or from what I learned at Oxford or public school.

The state of the nation

In this book, we have seen how a certain kind of leadership has been cultivated, replicated and normalised. If I have made my case, readers who have followed me so far will know what they don't want in their leaders; they will prefer them to have a better start in life in terms of good attachments, leading to the development of 'emotional availability' rather than privilege. They will perhaps prefer a universally wholesome education system, from which the most able rise by their own merits rather than by dint of their parents' income.

The current world situation demands leaders who are attuned to pursue what are called 'best-for-all' policies and such thinking arises most readily in a cohesive society, I would venture. I can find no better description of this wish than a short statement from the 1945 Labour Party Manifesto. At that time, when the nation had fought and suffered as one against forces of domination that called for a unified resistance, Britain was in no mood to continue on the course of internal divisiveness to which her sails had previously been set. The manifesto exhorted the exhausted Brits towards a vision of peace and communality, embodied in national ownership and universal care. It led to the landslide victory by Clement Attlee's party. Its principal act was the formation of the Welfare State, which we are currently considering dismantling. Here, in the simplest and briefest language, the manifesto set out its education policy values:

> The nation wants an educational system that will give every boy and girl a chance to develop the best that is in them. And, above all, let us remember that the great purpose of education is to give us individual citizens capable of thinking for themselves.[2]

Britain had splendidly pulled together to get through the Second World War, with women doing work normally reserved for men and the fate of the whole world considered daily by one and all. So people had been forced to think differently. For a brief moment, in a world where everyone's interdependence was taken as read and proven by the amount of blood spilled, it was taken for granted that a 'citizen' aspired towards best-for-all policies, that the adjective 'individual' referred to a capacity for outside-the-box thinking. It was the complete opposite of the every-man-for-himself thinking that British leaders learn as children and as espouse as a virtue in the post-Thatcher, predatory-capitalism dominated landscape of today.

In fact, most of the texts quoted in this chapter were written more than half a century ago. We may need to be reminded of the values that were retrieved when we last felt that the world was going to be engulfed by untrammelled ambition, and came face to face with the objectification of those who did not fit the required mould. It was in this spirit that in 2013 the filmmaker Ken Loach produced an astonishingly inspiring documentary of those times called *The Spirit of 45*. The film helps us remember a sense of community that is not so long gone and a set of values that seem to have been abandoned, both of which might be revisited in the context of the challenges of today.

Some who lived through the war and its aftermath must have had their hearts broken by experiencing a society now shaped by ruthless financial interests, led by men who seem to be centuries out of date, where the wrong things are kept and the right things thrown away. Universal healthcare, for example, is a mark of great humanity. A working, respected and invested-in National Health Service, the creation of those times, perhaps is something we should not be too quick to get rid of, even if it costs us. Universal healthcare cannot be done unplanned or on the cheap, as the British Empire was, according to the German historian Peter Wende, consultant to the 2013 *Der Spiegel* special on the British Empire.[3] If we choose to prioritise the NHS, governments will have to raise more in tax revenue. The way things are done in the US ought to warn us how not to do it. Here is a doctor, interviewed by Loach for his film, remembering the creation of the NHS, and still full of pride about it, making just such a point:

> If I were an American I would be ashamed to be part of such a rich country that can't afford to have generous ideas.[4]

But pointing the finger elsewhere is not enough. Labour's 1945 manifesto was very keen to get its own house in order, and rightly so. There is a plenty of dead wood to be cut out in our own garden. Asked how he felt about the state of Britain today, in an interview broadcast during the July 2013 'Proms' interval, the spy-novelist John Le Carré, who has seem many unpleasant sides of many nation-states, said:

> The most vexatious thing is how little different it is in so many ways. When I ran away from my public school, I was being told that I was the last generation, that was in 1945/46; and it was the Attlee government and we were going to have only one kind

of school in Britain, were going to be like other countries. I used to imagine that we would have no monarchy, that the class system would disappear, that there would somehow be a greater coming together of ordinary people, and actually looking back I never saw that happen. And somehow or other, in our own strange British way, we've kept the old order intact and just look at the constitution of our cabinet. I mean, when I was teaching at Eton I think 12 or 13 members of the cabinet were Old Etonians, and I thought this can never happen again. Now we have an Old Etonian London mayor, an Old Etonian prime minister and they're scattered across the cabinet just as they used to be.[5]

The BBC interviewer, presumably noticing something that looked like a feeling, followed this up with: "You look rather wry when you say that. Do you think that it is wrong?" To which the 82-year-old unambiguously replied:

I think that it is wrong to allow that structure to remain and then boast about equality of opportunity – that's ridiculous. I think a sober abolition, a sober integration of the educational system would be socially useful, I think it would make us all much happier. These poor people who are on the edge of being able to afford private education and then drain themselves of their money so that they can send their children to better schools, and so on, wouldn't have that agony. I mean I'm sorry for those people too. It isn't a socialistic perspective, it's a simple humanitarian one.

Before we consider what a "a sober integration of the educational system" would look like in practice, we must identify what we have discovered so far and see what values might be appropriate to guide an educational policy in these times.

Empathy: the new job requirement

In the previous chapter we saw how a "sober" view of vulnerability and the cultivation of constructive doubt could offer an antidote to the unbalanced Entitled Brain and a way out of the cul-de-sac of the Entitlement Illusion, constructed on the disowning and projection of vulnerability. In place of the fear of vulnerability, children could be taught to befriend and speak about their feelings in a creative and useful way. Contrary to the fears of radical alarmists, this does not detract from their ability to learn rational subjects at the same time. Quite the opposite is true. Thinking and feeling can go hand in hand. What might this look like in practice?

Some steps can be achieved very simply and cheaply. Time after time, the experience of training adults in psychotherapy has shown that the ability to learn is either enhanced (or prevented by its omission) by beginning a day's session with the brief opportunity to 'check in' on a personal, subjective, emotional level, combined with witnessing the check-in of others. Once emotions have been voiced and stories heard, students develop a much greater capacity for logical learning than in the absence of this practice. The cohesiveness built by the repetitive incorporation of such practices within the group stimulates both hemispheres of the brain while allowing each individual member to experience the safety, acceptance and containment that fosters the ability to "think for themselves." This practice is easily transferable to the classroom situation. As they become aware that the emotional realities of others are a constant backdrop to human life, students receive a cost-effective lesson in the acquisition of emotional intelligence, which we now know is a necessary condition for good decision-making.

The secondary benefit of such a practice is the practice of empathy skills, an essential component of relating to others. Depending on one's point of view, empathy and cooperation are either hardwired in humans or naturally arising functions; there is a mounting body of scientific evidence to show that it is as strong as the impulse to survive at all costs. Some readers may even imagine the Richard Dawkins' *Selfish Gene* view to be more a product of his Oundle and Oxford survival personality than the way the world works. Nevertheless, the cultivation of empathic skills does depend on the environment, for it is only possible to develop empathy naturally when you feel yourself loved, wanted and cared about. This is why those brought up in loveless conditions must first recognise their lack of empathic qualities and secondly be wiling to relearn them, before they can be effective in any people-dominated environment.

In the past, empathy has been seen to be a 'soft' art and one best left to women and artists, but increasingly it is becoming a known as a prerequisite quality for all interpersonal situations, including all workplaces, and especially healthcare and politics. Recently, empathy has started to be recommended by cutting-edge leadership development consultants even in the corporate world. In July 2013, the *Huffington Post* reported that empathy and relational skills will be amongst the most sought-after qualities by employers in the future:

> Fortune 500 companies hire consultants to measure the emotional intelligence (EQ) of their top executives and coach them on interpersonal skills. This corporate trend has been linked to an "affective revolution" in neuroscience. As researchers observe emotions and the physiology that drives them, and some even seek the neural basis of empathy, companies look to capitalize on the empirical measurement of emotions. Empathy is not just an ingredient for altruism anymore – it's a commodified skill. Dr. Cary Cherniss, a psychologist and long-time observer of emotional intelligence, published a study in 1999 suggesting that EQ proficiency contributes to the bottom line in any workplace.[6]

In the same month, George Anders, a contributing editor at Forbes and the author of four business books, wrote an article proposing that empathy will be, as his title states, "The Number One Job Skill in 2020."[7] These developments have not escaped the attention of some political leaders. On 7 April 2013, Scottish First Minister Alex Salmond delivered a remarkable address entitled "Empathy needed now more than ever" to the Princeton University Symposium on The Wealth and Wellbeing of Nations.[8] Salmond referred to a 1764 letter in which Adam Smith informed the Enlightenment philosopher David Hume that he was alleviating his boredom by writing a new book. This turned out to be the renowned *Enquiry into the Nature and Causes of the Wealth of Nations*, which introduced the concept of "the Invisible Hand" that was to provide universal "enlightened self-interest" and, as we now know, both liberated capital and inspired the doctrine that led to the excesses of Milton Friedman's disastrous free-market libertarianism.

Salmond, however, said he preferred to take his theme from Smith's earlier work, *The Theory of Moral Sentiments*, and cannily credited President Woodrow Wilson, a former Princeton Professor of Jurisprudence, with noting that *The Wealth of Nations* was never "meant to stand alone as the exposition of a complete system, it was only a supplement to *The Theory of Moral Sentiments*." Even former Premier Wen Jiabao of China carried a copy with him wherever he went, added the Scot, who reminded his audience that the father of economics had insisted that:

> What improves the circumstances of the greater part can never be regarded as an inconveniency to the whole. No society can be flourishing and happy, of which the far greater part of the members are poor and miserable.[9]

With his reference to the famous Scottish moral philosopher and pioneer of political economy, the First Minister squarely planted his seed-thought in the European Enlightenment tradition. One can imagine that he wanted to link his own political project and the founding of that august university. Next, Salmond triumphantly allied himself with the current President, Barack Obama, quoting him before he arrived at the Oval Office:

> There's a lot of talk in this country about the federal deficit. But I think we should talk more about our empathy deficit – the ability to put ourselves in someone else's shoes; to see the world through those who are different from us, the child who is hungry, the laid-off steelworker, the immigrant woman cleaning your dorm room. … We live in a culture that discourages empathy, a culture where those in power too often encourage these selfish impulses.[10]

Even if, today, many see Obama as a man who has had to lower his standards or who bit off more than he could chew, Salmond was convinced that he was right to prioritise empathy and assert that this quality would be necessary if humanity was to emerge from its current impasse. It must not simply be rhetoric but have political application, Salmond continued:

> People often see the lack of international agreement in addressing climate change as a failure of political will or initiative. It is. But it is also, surely, a failure of empathy, a failure of the fortunate to see, feel or imagine the consequences of inaction.[11]

In Scotland, he said, a sense of empathy would "…motivate us to take and use the powers we need to change the direction of the country." In order to make his point, and perhaps feeling a little vulnerable having stuck his neck out so far, Salmond, now referred to a recent experiment at the University of Chicago in which researchers found that, given the choice, rats would free other rats from cages even when there was no reward in it for them. Beginning to sound somewhat less convincing, Salmond suggested that if rats could choose freedom for other rats over cheese, the lesson was: "If rats can show empathy, then surely humans can show a bit more."

And here the First Minister brings us squarely back to earth, to the limits of Enlightenment thinking in which rational human beings were clearly the pinnacle of creation and ought to live up to that fact. It is a good Enlightenment Puritan argument and has some value. However, it does not yet embrace the big picture, because human beings have plenty to learn beyond the confines of rationality, as we have seen. It may even be that indigenous peoples and even animals – not included, as readers will remember, in the Rational Man Project – have much more to teach us than we think. Here's a story about someone who pursued such a radical idea.

Pre-rational emotional intelligence

J Allen Boone was a screenwriter working in Hollywood in the late 1920s. Quite by chance, and by dint of his curiosity, Boone discovered a way of communicating with animals via an unsuspected route: he achieved it by learning from an animal rather than by training it. His first teacher was a remarkable movie-star dog called Strongheart, whose lot it was to be baby-sat by Boone, and who was willing to coach his host in what Boone later called "dog-trains-man sessions." In the end, Strongheart took authority over most of the daily activities. Boone's last teacher was a humble housefly, whom he named Freddy; their relationship fascinated, dumbfounded and irritated some of his sophisticated Hollywood friends.

The training sessions took Boone into areas of instinctual empathic relationships with animals. He became convinced that animals had an immediate access to some interconnecting non-verbal, pre-rational empathic field in which they had an ability to assess the personality of human beings in a concise and precise way. His experience of being part of this field changed Boone's life for the better but left his logical mind utterly baffled. He needed to place this experience in the context of the "atomistic, rationalistic approach" to knowledge in which he had been brought up, so he scoured the limits of his world in search of an explanation. Nothing presented itself until he happened upon a 'desert rat,' an isolate called Mojave Dan, living rough in the wilderness that forms the north-eastern backdrop to the concrete jungle of Los Angeles. Here, drawn from a slim volume called *Kinship with All Life*, published in 1954 but still in print today, is how Boone described him:

> He loves the desert, and it is constantly revealing to him its deepest secrets. His 'family' consists of an assortment of dogs and burros; often wild animals became temporary members. Dan has practically no social or economic standing but he is rich in the kind of things that can never be taken away from him.[12]

Having put his question to this refugee from civilisation, Boone sat by his campfire for many a silent hour before the tersest of replies emerged: "If you want facts about a dog, always get them from the dog. If you want opinions, get them from the human." But Dan did share that he had noticed that rattlesnakes never bit Indians, though they often attacked white men. Boone set out to see if this was true.

> Almost everywhere I went there was a vicious and relentless warfare going on between white men and rattlesnakes; it was warfare to the death whether of the man or the snake. But I could find no such warfare between the Indians and the rattlesnakes. There seemed to be a kind of gentlemen's agreement between them. In all my journeyings in deserts, parries and mountains I never once saw a rattlesnake coil, either by way of defence or attack when an Indian walked into its close vicinity.

Finally, Boone understood that this must be because snakes can read a human's mental and emotional attitude towards his or her environment.

Presumably, the snakes encountered that dissociative, exploitative mindset, which we discussed in the central section of this book, dominated by left-brain activity, stress-evoked, 'flight or fight,' excessive cortisol systems rather than by the heart and its 'rest and repair' facility of the afferent system. Either instinctively or tangibly, perhaps by experiencing the magnetic field of the heart conditioned by the heart rate coherence coming from the rationally trained person's body, they know this attitude to be full of fear and hostility. They *feel* it, as a horse feels immediately if you are afraid.

Indigenous peoples, when they have been more or less left to themselves, have not dissociated themselves from the natural world, and instead practise an attitude such as 'All my relations.' In consequence, they don't give off this kind of alarm signal – not because they are 'better' or more evolved but simply because they have not been subject to hyper-rational education. There is clearly much to be learned from indigenous peoples. UCLA geography professor Jared Diamond's *The World until Yesterday* is a sober and easy introduction to traditional societies. After a lifetime of journeying in New Guinea, Diamond's book offers an approach beyond either denigrating or idealising indigenous peoples, understanding the limitations of what their societies offer and discovering just what people living in a near stone-age condition have to teach us.[13]

What is left of the indigenous world now has another challenge: how to survive the partial but consensual mindset of rationality without losing everything. All humans now have to find out how to move into a post-rational perspective, which will challenge us to our very cores because it is unknown. In the meantime, it may be time to rehabilitate the inner indigenous part of ourselves. We have somehow to make up for the catastrophic legacy of colonisation, with its slavery and its unquestioned exploitation. The hyper-rationally educated have still to learn empathy, as well as remorse and grief for the damage such one-sidedness has caused – interpersonally and politically. This was the lesson D.H. Lawrence wanted our civilisation to learn. I propose that there is still an indigenous part alive inside of each of us – you can see it in children before they go to school – and this could be encouraged rather than quashed. 'All my relations' could be a good learning mantra for children. It is crucially important: we live in one world, with other humans, animals and living things. We could learn not to let fear be our main teacher and reprioritise our willingness to cooperate and trust. Animals can teach us empathy and transparency, suggests Boone; children are naturally drawn to animals and could learn much from them.

Economics, emotions and relationships

In case readers are in any doubt, there is no suggestion here that we should be teaching our children to be naïve, either emotionally or politically. Quite the reverse: it is important, I believe, that our educational philosophy be very sharply focused indeed. In particular, we need to shed ourselves of the prevailing unchallenged and dangerous economic naïveté.

The current conception of economic management looks more like stress-driven half-hearted reactions to control a self-created monster than a concerted willingness to stimulate and regulate human affairs for the well-being of all. It is increasingly evident that current economics is far from anything approaching a "Theory of Moral Sentiments," as Adam Smith originally hoped. We can no longer deny that economics will never be a precise science, that prediction is often guesswork; we cannot go on ignoring that we have unleashed forces too great to control, that financial deregulation has turned freedom into chaos, that the gap between rich and poor is once again widening at an unsustainable rate. Smith's "Invisible Hand" has turned into a universal tyrant, as market forces are the dominant and uncontrollable deity that conditions all of our lives, everywhere, via unregulated international competition.

Even fairly elected democracies are now powerless. Former Greek prime minister George Papandreou tells of a crucial meeting of Eurozone heads of state that continued through the night and was forced to come to an untimely and half-hearted conclusion because of the alarm that the Tokyo markets were about to open, necessitating a hurried, cobbled together joint statement.[14] What is it that fuels this tyranny of the markets? Papandreou has no doubt of the scale of the problem. His context is:

> Our democracies are trapped by systems that are too big to fail, or more accurately, too big to control.[15]

This is surely right. From a psychological perspective, however, the markets themselves are run on a further tyranny. It is that of unacknowledged, unconscious emotion, and it is this that dominates us. We are, in fact, tyrannised by individuals' reactions to world events and a psycho-porridge of their combined hopes and fears. In other words, the markets are run on emotions clattering around inside rational educated left-brain dominated beings who have not been taught how to respect and regulate their emotions.

My small clinical practice in London, where I regularly see people who work in financial services, has shown me the extent of this unacknowledged, unregulated emotional tyranny. It not only affects the macro-context of the lives we all lead but also the micro-context of the lives its workers lead. I regularly come across cases where individuals tell me of their need to drink and dope themselves into oblivion every weekend in order to cope with the stress of long hours and competitive environments. I meet those who are bullied so badly at work in this atmosphere (which is of course normalised) that they unconsciously take it out on their partners at home. I see couples who have not spoken more than a few perfunctory words to each other since the last session a month before because they "have not had *any time*."

A particular set of emotions dominates this tyranny of market competition, which psychotherapists sometimes call the *lower emotions*. They include anxiety, fear of loss, greed, self-interest, competitiveness and hope of domination. These are all emotions that dominate the brain in a particular way, affecting the limbic system, the reptilian brain and stimulating the frontal left hemisphere. These areas run the basic survival instincts pointed to in Darwin's first (and partial) hypothesis, in which competition and scarcity were seen as the factors that dominate all life on the planet. The Hindus understood this as *Matsyayna* (the Law of the Fishes) where the smaller is eaten by the bigger, before wise regulation arises in humans.[16] But in itself, trade or business cannot be 'bad,' for it relies on many important values; it necessitates other emotions and tendencies, such as trust and cooperation, as well as other skills, such as empathically valuing the needs of others.

Here's a story illustrating the value of one of the positive emotions – trust – in the field of banking. It comes from *The New Yorker* and was written in late 2008, after the prime-mortgage market had collapsed. In December 1912, J.P. Morgan, founder of the now infamous global financial giant that bears his name, testified before the US Congress in the so-called 'Money Trust' hearings. Morgan was asked to explain how he decided whether to make a loan or investment:

He replied, "The first thing is character." His questioner skeptically suggested that factors like collateral might be more important, but Morgan replied, "A man I do not trust could not get money from me on all the bonds in Christendom." Morgan's point was simple but essential: systems of credit depend on trust. When trust is present, money flows smoothly from lenders to borrowers, allowing new enterprises to start, existing ones to expand, and daily business to move along without a hitch. When it's absent, we find ourselves in a world where lenders hoard capital, borrowers are left empty-handed, and the economy's gears grind to a halt.[17]

Trust, suggests the influential magazine – embracing wisdom in hindsight, as we all do – is then a crucial quality in all the affairs of men. Even the Russian dictator Joseph Stalin, for all his fear-driven psychopathic activity within his own borders, was known for his ability to keep his word amongst his world-leader peers. After Yalta, Churchill famously said that he would rather trust Stalin than de Gaulle, and a review by the veteran journalist Andrew Alexander of historical papers released recently by the Kremlin confirms that in international relations Stalin was a man to be trusted and one who consistently put his faith in the trust of others.[18] The ability to inspire and expect trust is a major component in relationships. This is exactly the point arrived at by *The New Yorker*:

> The fear that has overpowered lenders is not just about the current market chaos. It also reflects their lack of faith in the models and systems that they rely on to evaluate risk. For Morgan, that process of evaluation was all about relationships.[19]

Relationships are fundamental to human life, and skill in relationships must rank as one of the highest achievements for a human being. For relationship is never easy: intimate relationship frequently hurts or feels too difficult, after the early euphoric stages. Relating is a challenge; it demands effort. It means always including the reality, the feelings, the context and the needs of others, without leaving out or over-prioritising oneself.

The leader of today has to be instructed and practised in the art of relationship, since he or she (I'll stick to one pronoun) must be capable of empathy for those whose conditions he does not understand or those who do not understand him. Practicing constructive doubt, his head must not be prevented from sometimes ruling his heart, and vice-versa. He must have 'bifocal-vision', a twin-hemisphere grasp on the world: a sense of the whole, a sense of the details. He must have his social engagement system firing and his heart informing his ANS, so that he is not excessively governed by stress but alert for action. If he hails from the traditional elite, he must have stepped out of the Entitlement Illusion and be free of the confines of the Entitled Brain, so that he is not driven towards personal survival at all costs. He must have checked the domination of his Strategic Survival Personality so that he knows he belongs and can let love in – as well as appropriate criticism – without collapsing, and so he can relate to others as real persons and not objects.

So where do we go to learn how to teach relationships to the young, even when we may be struggling with our own relationships or when we ourselves have not experienced enough empathy coming our way for it to be obvious? It is not easy, because of the nature of relating itself and because we are not used to learning that comes from outside the scope of rationality. But we are not without resources. There are hundreds of pop-psychology books on relationships available (including one I had a hand in myself), full of advice and suggestions.[20]

The new body-psychotherapy pioneers like Willem Poppeliers show that using our hearts as the locus of organisation for intimate sexual and parenting relations, makes personification realistic and sexual regulation natural. Depth psychology teaches us that to be proficient in relationships (imperative for a good leader), above all, a person must be in relationship with *himself* and must have done sufficient work on his inner demons; he must eschew disowning and take back his projections; he must be sufficiently at peace with his background to feel that his parents did they best they could. The psychological shorthand for this process is to have done sufficient *inner work*. It is precisely this theme that Ricken Patel, Canadian-Asian co-founder and Executive Director of Avaaz, the most successful internet campaigning organisation in the world, recommended to a gathering of leaders at the 2013 Commonwealth Lecture at London's prestigious Guildhall in March 2013.[21]

There is also a body of psycho-spiritual wisdom to draw on, most notably the writings of influential theologian Martin Buber, who analysed the psychodynamics of empathic relating and came up with a potent formula to overcome the tendency towards objectification. Buber teaches that relationships must be rooted in personification, an *I–Thou* rather than *I–It* exchange.[22] Besides, there is a huge storehouse of ancient wisdom in all spiritual traditions, for example, the notion of *right relations*, a term used in Western interpretations of Buddhism to describe an attitude to personal relations and desire to reach out to embrace all life as non-separate, akin to the concept of 'All my relations' introduced earlier.

A *sine qua non* for the development of all these qualities is that citizens – and especially their leaders – should have had sufficient experience of being safe, loved, wanted and touched as children, as so many authorities now agree. The science and reasoning behind this has been better put than I am able to in the works of John Bowlby, Jean Liedloff, Sue Gerhardt, Alan Schore and others, whom I recommend to all parents, educators and psychotherapists. This knowledge is now no longer ignorable, because the nature of our childhood attachments affects us for much longer or more profoundly than we once thought – right into the physical development of our brains and immune systems. We can now soundly reason that the Entitled Brain is more of an impediment than an advantage, despite its occurrence in the *milieu* of privilege. From current geopolitical history, we see before our eyes how a sense of entitlement in people who have been abused causes intractable problems – witness the Middle East. Because, "when innocence," to re-quote the analyst Grotstein, "has been deprived of its entitlement, it becomes a diabolical spirit."[23]

My Heart's in the Highlands

When we feel the impact of the British Rational Man Project enshrined in the British Empire, we have to come into relationship with the values it supported and the influence of this even in today's world. Queen Victoria's son Bertie, who became Edward VII in the first year of the 20th century, had spent his long years as Prince of Wales as an ignored playboy; he was surrounded by beautiful women, including his Danish wife, and addicted to extramarital affairs. His entourage, like the more intellectual clique 'The Souls,' sought amusement at country house parties at which, after the day's racing, shooting or golf, wife-swapping enlivened the evenings.

Psychohistorically, it is as if Bertie was searching for something of the feminine after his cold mother had presided over an emotionally cold century. Lawrence might have understood. As a child, Bertie was a big disappointment to his parents for his lack of ambition and aggression, as his nephew, the future Kaiser Wilhelm II, was to his parents, on account of his physical woundedness. Neither lack of aggression nor woundedness could be tolerated in the robust age of Rational Man. At the beginning of the 20th century, King Bertie's indiscretions were tolerated – even his wife stayed loyal – and by the time he died he had become the most loved British monarch. But thereafter, in acute embarrassment, the monarchy retreated to secrecy, dissociation and compartmentalisation in sexuality, which, as we have seen, led to Mountbatten's devastating advice to Prince Charles.

Thinking systemically rather than individually, we might see Bertie's search for feminine warmth as a needed balancing act on behalf of the entitled but crippled elite. However, when the left brain takes over in sexuality it often traps men into thinking that they can grasp this by means of sex, by taking something that women have and men lack, out of a sense of inner emptiness. The left hemisphere is excellent at grasping, but the body has another reality, for the man's genitals are designed for giving, not taking. The heart, when it has been 'opened and awakened' (as taught by the new body-based psychotherapies PSTT and SGT[24]) is actually a man's most potent sexual organ.

We humans need our hearts to relate. Feeling, empathy and embodying values all involve the heart – this is what our own D.H. Lawrence was recommending, and indigenous peoples took as given. Through the Enlightenment thinking skills of separating Me from the Other, we facilitated the curious powers of creative rationality and got enormous benefit from it. But as feeling and experiencing increasingly became excluded from rationality, the more the data became like Plato's ghosts in the cave or Descartes' phantoms on the street. Reasoning depends on context, which involves a different kind of thinking, one that invites feeling, sensing and intuiting. So when we took rationality to extremes and replaced the 'necessary distance' with dissociation, we encouraged grandiosity and narcissism.

Narcissism is a regressive, narrow micro-context, which once more puts Me at the centre – an anti-evolutional return to the medieval mindset, with the earth at the centre of the universe and creativity held captive. But when we place the heart at the centre of organisation, we have the benefit of the liberating feeling of empathy, which makes the Other into Me, and narcissism becomes redundant.

Throughout the world, the human heart is frequently associated with place, with land. This in turn is either identified with – or the breeding ground for – soul, which gives meaning and binds individuals into a community. The poetic gives a form for this. The transcendent belief of some indigenous Americans is that there will come a time when the eagle and the condor will fly together again – when mind and heart will come together once more. Indigenous songs regularly celebrate their relationship with land, heart and soul, for pre-industrial cultures have their roots in a hunter-gatherer condition. Here, a harmonious relationship between man, the earth with its seasons and the animals that provide man's wherewithal for life are mutually interdependent in a delicate balance. This balance needs to be sustained through what Emile Durkheim called *participation ritual*, which provides the fundamental source of the "collective conscience" that in one's "day-to-day relationships of life" and in those celebrations of the collective "which bind [one] to the social entity as a whole."[25]

In 1929, after the third version of *Lady Chatterley's Lover* was published, amidst fuss and scandal, Lawrence wrote *A Propos of "Lady Chatterley's Lover."* This essay is an invocation to the past, a call to return to a time when we were in harmony with the seasons, with the great wheel of the year. But some traces of the vestiges of indigenous song or poetry in Britain can still be found, if we look for them. Here is an example of one; it comes from north of the border. Robert Burns has no problem knowing where his heart is – it's in the Highlands:

> My heart's in the Highlands, my heart is not here;
> My heart's in the Highlands a-chasing the deer;
> Chasing the wild deer, and following the roe;
> My heart's in the Highlands, wherever I go.[26]

To me, the poetic use of 'the Highlands' refers to both an actual place of beauty, wilderness and tradition in the north of Scotland, as well as to a hinted at psycho-spiritual realm. The latter is a 'high' location, a locus of priority, a place to think from, to make choices from, where the laws of nature still operate, where the innocent but not naive creatures run free, where men can chase their spirits, in order to learn from and be sustained by them. This is classic indigenous wisdom. Burns does not speak of *killing* but of going "a-chasing;" he is a searcher. His heart is not in the Lowlands, where the poor frighten the birds that have been bred to have their guts blasted out by the rich, who have just had a very good lunch.

In modern parlance, we might use a computer metaphor. "My Heart's in the Highlands" points to a higher operating system – a more powerful 'OS.' We know, as we become endlessly kidnapped by the need to update – to our cost – that an older operating system runs very nicely, thank you, until the data we are trying to deal with needs more sophisticated applications. Then we have to update or risk being left behind.

This book has shown that, despite their postion of privilege, the British entitled hyper-rational elite have been programmed from a very young age to run on a very inferior OS, as it were. Actually, we already have a higher operating system waiting to be uploaded: it is the brain–heart system. The brain, using both hemispheres in balance, without needing to have recourse to its more ancient structures (the so-called reptilian brain dedicated to fight, flight or freeze), sending useful messages to the heart, which then makes choices and sends commands, as it were, to determine how to self-regulate.

The joy of effective right-hemisphere functioning is that it gives insights that operate on a global and systemic level; it is designed to work in collaboration and cooperation. These are fundamental values that recent neo-Darwinian research is re-evaluating. Cooperation is now beginning to be viewed by many scholars as the overarching operating principle in nature, over and beyond the competitive survival principle, which became the leitmotif of organised Darwinism and was the perspective of Darwin himself. When the brain has both hemispheres working together and is in cooperative partnership with the heart, a human being is really 'in business.'

The architecture of politics

As education needs to change, so does politics, and there must be some structural changes here too. I don't mean changes to the make-up of parliamentary democracy, although we will have to insist on voting for differentiated policies rather parties. Britain can even manage without becoming a republic if it so chooses, for the benefit of the tourist industry, so long as we modify what we have, authentically and sensibly – or "soberly," as Le Carré puts it.

In this light, I maintain that we do need some big changes in style. The most important is to wrest our politics from the stranglehold of the public school and Oxford style, where someone always needs to be blamed and contemptuously attacked. The convention of politics in Britain is to blame first: the previous government is routinely blamed for all problems currently encountered. For example, the Care Quality Commission hospital problem (a scandal in the NHS during the early summer of 2013) is apparently the previous Labour government's fault. We take this for granted but fail to remark on the inbuilt surrealism. Even more outlandish, given the subject of this book, is that former Prime Minister Sir John Major can in one breath decry the stranglehold of privately-educated men:

> In every single sphere of British influence, the upper echelons of power in 2013 are held overwhelmingly by the privately educated or the affluent middle class. To me, from my background, I find that truly shocking.[27]

And in the next sentence, blame Labour for a "collapse in social mobility." Lest readers start doubting their own sanity, at this point, I can recommend a psychohistorical analysis, as pursued in this book, not to have all the answers but to provide a way to lay bare such fault and default reactions. The psychodynamics of it go something like this:

> 1. The blame is dissociated (or disconnected) from the actual problems; as an example, consider the understaffing that is being made worse by austerity regimes – just talk to anyone working in an organisation affected by this, such as the NHS.

> 2. The blame is isolated from a bigger picture, from any genuine over-arching value system, and compartmentalised. Earlier, we saw how Ian Duncan-Smith could comfortably attack the cost of housing benefits without reference to how the housing market

has been inflated by the sale of council houses, unrealistic mortgage offers and unregulated private rentals.

3. The blame is then projected, directed at the opposition, those with whom the politician has chosen not identify, even though cultural links between both sides of the House are overwhelming close.

4. The blame is de-linked from context: for example, changes were made to the NHS even before previous reorganisations had had time to settle in and bite.

5. The blame is normalised, so that politicians, media and public all become used to a faulty and static way of doing things, with a dynamism that remains solely superficial.

We have to ask ourselves whether it is honest, mature or effective to continue in this way. Such a politics is normalised, which is an effective defence; at the same time, voter turnout is at an all time low, demonstrating that, in the main, people have given up on politicians. A poll conducted by ComRes in the first week of November 2013 found that faith in politicians was at an all time low, with only energy company bosses viewed less favourably.[28]

I suspect that this is in large part due to the adversarial and dissociative way we conduct and report our debates. In case any reader is still in any doubt, here is how the BBC News reports an everyday parliamentary incident. It could be from any day of the year, but this one was from early summer 2013:

> Back benchers cheer the Health Minister Jeremy Hunt, pleased to see a Minister on the front foot.

Again, the hostility, normalised in the metaphor "on the front foot," which derives from cricket, that most aggressive way of playing the game,' is aimed at the Opposition; these, as I explained earlier, are psychological totems: the dissociated not-identified-with ones.

In order to change this, I suggest that a particular radical structural alteration is required, and this won't be universally popular. In a way, it will mean a return to the Guy Fawkes principle, but this time with the aid of our impressive home-grown architectural talent. We must have a new building to house our representatives – certainly a new House of Commons. We have to do away with the current set-up, where two sides are lined up opposite each other, positioned as adversaries, with members with greater influence at the front and those with less influence or with a tendency to be rebellious at the back. Parliament is not a public school or the Oxford Union – we have to remember this. It is the place where all the elected representatives of the people of the nation meet to discuss and take decisions. Like the beautiful new parliaments in the devolved regions and most other parliaments in the world, it would be better if it was circular or horseshoe-shaped. As in psychotherapy group sessions, business is better conducted in the round so that everyone can hear and see each other, every participant feels they are a full part of the whole and everyone, including those with particular hierarchical roles, occupies an equal position.

But we don't have to blow up the House of Commons – the Victorian building can still serve us, for example, as part of the capital's booming tourist industry. It could even rival Buckingham Palace as an attraction and earn its living in graceful retirement, perhaps as a museum for parliamentary documentary, honouring Britain's proud record of pioneering this form of government.

Interestingly enough, in the debate over the future of new towns and social housing – badly needed since Thatcher's Right to Buy finished off local authority housing – architects themselves are discussing some of the notions we have been considering, such as 'top-down' and narrow-wide brain balance. In a BBC radio documentary, *The Politics of Architecture*, broadcast in December 2013, leading architectural writer and critic Jonathan Glancey, investigating the forces that shape everyday architecture, declared:

> Unlike the politicians [he had interviewed] I think a top-down approach could work as long as it embraced wider views and didn't tip into arrogance. Let's aim high: let's build as beautifully and as intelligently as we can with and for everyone.

APPENDIX

A Future for Boarding?

In the West, individualism marks our societies, so there is a tension whenever the role of the state is discussed in education, as in other areas. Indigenous social units are smaller, and the welfare of the group is understood to depend on a web of relationships. Skilful childrearing is indispensible to the common good. In Chapter 9, we saw how the late 19th century native residential schools were designed to eradicate local customs in favour of the work ethic and rationality. These were thought to be the best modern tools for socialisation, they had been tried and tested at home and were seen as an invaluable way to create industrial social structure. The Canadian Interim Report, introduced earlier, discloses the attitude to childrearing that these schools attempted to replace:

> Because personal autonomy was highly regarded, scolding or disciplining children was not common. Seventeenth-century French colonists often commented that Aboriginal parents loved their children so much they were unwilling to deny them anything. The reality was more complex. Children were not indulged: they were taught their community responsibilities and trained in self-reliance and respect for others. For example, an Inuit child who asked for consolation might be comforted, but one who was having a tantrum might be left to cry. Given that the Aboriginal education system was intertwined so tightly with both spiritual belief and daily life, it is not surprising that Aboriginal people were reluctant to give their children over to others to raise.[1]

Oddly enough, even in Britain a century before the heyday of the boarding school system, no lesser authority than Adam Smith entertained doubts about the value of sending children out of the home. Here is what he said on the subject in 1759:

The education of boys at distant great schools, of young men at distant colleges, of young ladies in distant nunneries and boarding-schools, seems in the higher ranks of society to have done crucial harm to domestic morals and thus to domestic happiness, both in France and in England. From their parents' house the children may, with propriety and advantage, go out every day to attend public schools; but let them continue to live at home. That way of bringing up a child is the institution of nature; education away from home at a boarding school is a contrivance of man. You don't need me to tell you which is likely to be wiser![2]

Could the British follow the common sense and wisdom of their beloved father of economics and turn away from this practice? Could citizens take consumer action by boycotting these schools?

I am under no illusion about the great depth of the trance, and I am not alone in recognising this. Here is blogger Sally Fraser, having just attended her first Boarding Concern[3] conference and watched the remarkable BBC television film *A Very English Education,* in which director Hannah Berryman very subtly followed up on a handful of boys who had been filmed thirty-five years earlier in a documentary series that had sympathetically featured the boarding school Radley College:[4]

One ex-boarder, sitting with his ex-boarder mother, quietly explains that he would not send his own children to boarding school. His mother nervously points out that this is mainly because he can't afford it. There is a pause, before he gently and courageously asserts that no, even if he had the money he would not send them. The look on his mother's face is one of pure cold fear, and one I recognise from being on my mother-in-law's face ninety percent of the time since I came into her life. It says please don't let this be a lie, please, please don't let me have sacrificed my childhood, and my children's childhood, for something that was a lie. Well I'm sorry love, but you have.

Therein lies what will be the biggest obstacle to dismantling this archaic system. Not the greed or wealth of the institutions themselves, nor the society which needs an endless stream of emotionless workaholics and military men to perpetuate its hierarchies, not the class superiority and inferiority complexes which have been centuries in the making. There are many men and women who have to defend boarding schools, and the systems they rest on and support in turn, with everything they have because the pain of realising they might have been wrong, that they may have been wronged, and what they might have lost, is unbearable.[5]

Who could put it better than that? This why the British will probably not turn away from their addiction to boarding any time soon, at least of their own accord and why there will need to be some legislative changes to prise Britain out of its trance.

The psychological imperative we are presented with is that the developmental nature of children must be understood, respected and appropriately adhered to. This means that boarding in institutions has to be ended as a way of life for young children, and the habit of and fashion for it have to be broken.

Below I list some very basic suggestions of what needs to change as a starting point for such a conversation.

- **What some call 'early' boarding (under the age of 13) must be stopped.**

This will take some time, no doubt. At the time of writing, supporters of the watchdog organisation Boarding Concern were in dialogue with the veteran backbench Labour MP Barry Sheerman. Concerned about the issue, Sheerman was apparently preparing to table some parliamentary questions to the education minister. These were to be:

- What assessments has he made of the potential damage caused to children by 'early boarding'?
- What steps is he taking to ensure that vulnerable children do not suffer damage by boarding at a young age?
- Does he think that sending a child to boarding school at a young age can cause psychological damage to that child?
- What assessments has he made of establishing a limit on the age at which children can 'full board'?

- **Government, legal and health professions will have to work together in order to review and establish exactly what is covered by the responsibility of care enshrined in the words *in loco parentis*.**[6]

All fee-paying boarding schools in Britain do currently come under Ofsted inspection provision but are, in my view, inadequately regulated. One of the obstacles here is that

Britain is only just beginning to acknowledge the more evident problems of abuse, let alone the more difficult to quantify problems of neglect. Simon Partridge is one of the writers who recognises this cutting-edge issue:

> There is a growing consensus, backed by neuroscience and among traumatologists that neglect is even more damaging to the developing child and its brain than acute abuse. As Camila Batmanghelidjh [The Kids Company] put it when I asked her once: "Because abuse, however awful, has a beginning, a middle, and an end; for a child, neglect goes on forever."[7]

If the evidence of psychological harm from boarding and parental neglect is put alongside the many cases of physical, emotional and sexual abuse, which were historically put aside and normalised under the banner of 'character building', a bigger picture is revealed. As with nuclear power, expensive decommissioning costs would need to be taken into account, for many parents would feel justified in demanding their investment be returned to them, and many ex-boarders might be entitled to considerable financial compensation through the courts. Such a process has already been successful in the Canadian courts and led to their government commissioning an extensive C$60 million report on residential schooling.[8]

- **The reporting of child abuse has to become mandatory.**

Despite Freud's revelations, a century ago, of child sexual abuse in the Austrian capital and the dogged labour of many health professionals in the complexities of this pernicious crime since then, it has taken the dark legacy of the late Jimmy Savile, a once beloved celebrity, to awaken Britain to the horror of child abuse. As we now know from revelations coming from the Catholic Church, institutions like churches, care homes and boarding schools have tended to turn a blind eye to paedophilic behaviour, or even move the offender to other parishes or schools where they continued to abuse even more innocents.

A BBC *Panorama* programme broadcast on 4 November 2013 highlighted how this cover up has been assisted by gaps in the law and the lack of a mandatory reporting provision. This will need to be changed because in any 24/7 institution absolute vigilance should be required of the staff. As things stand, teachers and other authorities cannot at present be prosecuted in Britain (as they can in other countries) for failing to alert the police to known incidents of child abuse. The programme recounted that victims who have tried to prosecute or sue an institution that employed someone who abused them – or even groomed them over long periods – have been thrown out of court. The week after he left his role as director of public prosecutions, Keir Starmer QC said that failing to report allegations of child sexual abuse should be made a criminal offence in Britain. One wonders why he waited until he had left office to say:

> I think the time has come to change the law and close a gap that's been there for a very long time.[9]

• **The charitable, and therefore tax-avoiding and independent status of fee-paying boarding schools has to be reviewed.**

This was the starting point for MP Barry Sheerman, who was on a Commons Select Committee looking at the relevance of current Charity status, when he interviewed me at length in 2009 in the rarefied atmosphere of Portcullis House, before the MPs' expenses scandal intervened and caused the initiative to be scrapped.[10] It remains to be seen whether the questions cited above will actually be tabled. In the meantime the case for early boarding must be very difficult to establish.

In the light of the emerging evidence of the psychological problems of boarding and revelations of the widespread culture of abuse, boarding schools should be made to demonstrate in what ways attachment-deficit institutionalisation is good for children, and thereby charitable. No known theories of child development support it, excepting the 18th century German Poisonous Pedagogy discredited by Alice Miller in the 1980s, the beliefs of the 15th century Jesuit Ignatius Loyola or the 5th century BC Spartans.[11] Given the evident contradictions to all modern child developmental principles, the burden of proof should not be put on those who oppose a several billion pound industry backed by a substantial and aggressive lobby, but upon those who propose it.

And then what?

If all these suggestions were implemented, what would come next?

Here I will venture a suggestion that may surprise – even shock – my readers. I propose that there is a way to increase boarding *and* increase the common good. The first over-arching and self-evident principle is that boarding school for the young is disadvantageous and has to be stopped. We would then be left with an enormous resource in terms of schools – both buildings and teachers – and the challenge of getting on-side all those who have previously been making the private boarding system work as well as it has. My suggestion is simple: that the stock of boarding schools be recycled and used as sixth form colleges.

At 16, many children might benefit from a couple of years of residential education, especially if the regime at these schools were a wholesome one that acknowledged their separation rather than just keeping them busily avoiding emotions. At such an age, children are able to draw a real advantage from being in a group of peers rather than in a hierarchical system of younger and older children, which tends to encourage bullying. It might be a relief all round to get some of the 16-year-olds off the streets and away from the invasive culture of consumerism, whether of electronic products most can barely afford or the drink and drugs epidemic, to which we can longer afford to have our youth addicted.

Schools like this do in fact already exist in parts of Europe, although they have not been the focus of much attention so far in Britain because they do not have the glamour of elitism abut them. In rural France, the state provides weekly boarding in departmental capitals for older children to mitigate the problems of distance. Those attending such schools I spoke to appreciated the conviviality of town life and being amongst their peers and also loved to be back on the farm at the weekend.

In Denmark, there are 260 boarding schools spread throughout the small country in which teenagers – boys and girls together – can finish their secondary education. They are known as *Efterskole*, or 'after-school' schools. The Efterskole system is heavily subsidised by government but asks for parental fee contributions. It is based on the educational philosophy of

N.F.S. Grundtvig who wanted schools to provide more than simply vocational training. According to the schools' website:

> Each Efterskole is a self-governing independent institution and they all deal with both the educational and personal development of the students. They embrace a common educational focus on enlightenment for life, general education and democratic citizenship. Freedom of the Efterskole is assured by substantial state subsidies to both schools and students.

> The Efterskole has something to offer both educationally and socially, because the students live together. It can perhaps be said that the teachers who work at an Efterskole are not entirely ordinary. They are prepared to involve aspects of themselves other than the professional, so that the pupils have a positive relationship to the teachers.[12]

One such school was briefly featured on British TV in February 2114 when it was visited by the celebrity chef, Hugh Fearnley-Whittingstall, as part of a series wittily called *Scandimania*. "Hugh lands in Denmark, which the United Nations has declared the 'happiest country in the world'," said the programme notes, which described the Efterskole as "a boarding school where teenagers are taught how to be good citizens."[13] The Old Etonian seemed politely impressed but did not elaborate on how innocent and strange it must have felt to him after his own privileged abandonment. Nevertheless, the Efterskole could provide a useful model for Britain.

It goes without saying that entry to any new-style boarding schools would not be based on parental income. British governments would finally have to fall in line with others and provide a per-child subsidy for any form of education outside their immediate control. I would imagine that a selection of foreign entrants could help boost the revenue that government would have to supply. This is roughly how the Danes work it. Alternatively, those who could pay would pay. Such schools could become a kind of public-private partnership that centrist governments seem to favour.

Working these things out would be child's play, once we allow children to be children and let the "boys in the men who run things" finally come home again.

Notes

Prologue

1 The phrase comes from a line from *The Lady of Shalott* by the poet Alfred, Lord Tennyson, recycled by Agatha Christie as the title of a detective novel in 1962:

> Out flew the web and floated wide –
> The mirror crack'd from side to side;
> "The curse is come upon me,"cried
> The Lady of Shalott.

2 *Calm down, dear: David Cameron's 'sexist' taunt to Labour MP* by Andrew Porter and Laura Roberts, *The Telegraph* 28 April 2011.

3 *Labour fury as David Cameron tells Angela Eagle: 'Calm down, dear'* by Patrick Wintour, political editor, *The Guardian*, Wednesday 27 April 2011.

4 This and the following quotations were retrieved from Hansard, www.publications.parliament.uk/pa/cm201011/cmhansrd/cm110427/debtext/110427-0001.htm#11042772000005

5 Op cit, *The Guardian*, 27 April 2011.

6 Ibid.

7 *David Cameron's patronising putdown: was it a bad joke, or a sexist bullying?* by Aida Edemariam, *The Guardian*, Thursday 28 April 2011.

8 Brooks, L. (2011) *Calm down dear? Do me a favour David Cameron – language matters*, *The Guardian*, 28 April. For more about the Bullingdon Club, see the notes to Chapter 1.

9 Ed Miliband: We got it wrong on the 24-hour culture, by Mary Riddell, *The Telegraph*, March 11 2011.

10 Duffell, N. (2000) *The Making of Them: The British Attitude to Children and the Boarding School System*, London: Lone Arrow Press.

11 Cameron attempted to read a quote from the former Labour MP Howard Stoate backing the government's NHS reforms, claiming that Stoate had been defeated at the last election by a Conservative candidate when – as Eagle was pointing out – Stoate had in fact stood down.

12 Edemariam, A. (2011) Op Cit.

13 Duffell, N. (1996) *The best days of your life*, in *Human Potential*, Spring 1996.

14 Le Carré, J. (1995) *Our Game*, London: Hodder & Stoughton.

15 Duffell, N. (2005) *Surviving the privilege of boarding school*, in *Journal of the Mental Health Association*, Queensland, Australia.

16 Partridge, S. (2007) *Trauma at the threshold: An eight-year-old goes to boarding school*, in *Attachment* 1(3).

17 Retreived from www.bbc.co.uk/news/uk-politics-13207256

18 Duffell, N. (2000) Op cit.

19 Schaverien, J. (1997) *Men who leave too soon: Further reflections on the erotic transference and countertransference*, in *British Journal of Psychotherapy* 14(1).

20 According to one estimate, the cost saved by government is in the billions: "What would it cost the taxpayer to educate these children in the state sector? The average cost of educating a child of primary school age is £3,975. So that's £1.107 billion to educate the 4–10-year-olds and £2.273 billion to educate the 11–19-year-olds. That's £3.38 billion that HMG would have to find in additional revenue funding every year." Toby Young's speech to the Oxford Union against the motion: "This House Would Abolish Private Schools," 27 October 2011 (http://blogs.telegraph.co.uk/news/tobyyoung/100114147/should-private-schools-be-abolished/?utm_source=twitterfeed&utm_medium=facebook)

21 Unicef (2007) *An Overview of Child Well-being in Rich Countries*, www.unicef. org/media/files/ChildPovertyReport.pdf .

22 Herzen, A. (1991) *My Past and Thoughts*, Berkley CA: California.

23 Richards, K. (2010) *Life*, London: Weidenfeld & Nicolson

24 Freud, A. (1937) *The Ego and the Mechanisms of Defense*, London: Hogarth Press

25 Television documentary, *Boris Johnson: The Irresistible Rise*, BBC 2, first broadcast 25 March 2013.

Introduction

1 Thanks to Professor Andrew Samuels, from whom I have borrowed the form of this sentiment: see his video-blog at www.andrewsamuels.com/custom_coms/viewer. php?videofile=1101-boardingschools

2 From an interview with Anne McElvoy for BBC Radio 3 Nightwaves, played in the interval in the Proms 29 July 2013. Text from BBC iPlayer.

3 Duffell, N. (2000) *The Making of Them: The British Attitude to Children and the Boarding School System*, London: Lone Arrow Press.

4 Book review by Professor Pretuska Clarkson in *The British Medical Journal* 31 March 2001 (Vol 322, Issue 7289). BMJ 2001; 322:803.1 www.bmj.com/ content/322/7289/803.1

5 Schaverien, J. (2011) B*oarding School Syndrome: Broken Attachments – A Hidden Trauma*, in the *British Journal of Psychotherapy*, 27(2): 138–55).

6 I have published some brief definitions on http://woundedleaders.co.uk/what-is-psychohistory/

7 From Maurice Isserman's review in the *New York Times* on 19 June 2011 of *Witness to an Extreme Century: A Memoir*, by Robert Jay Lifton, New York: Free Press, 2011.

8 www.psychohistory.com

9 Interview with Lloyd deMause in *The Talk of the Town* in *The New Yorker*, authored by editors of the periodical, 5 December 1994.

10 Herzen, A. (1991) *My Past and Thoughts*, Berkley CA: California.

11 Monbiot, G. (1998). *Acceptable Cruelty* (original subheading was *Britain's Most Overt form of Child Abuse is Mysteriously Ignored*), *The Guardian*, 26 March.

12 Monbiot, G. (2012). *The Sacrificial Caste, The Guardian*, 16 January.

13 A new long-term study by Lisa Cameron of Monash University in Australia and co-authors, published online in the journal *Science*, January 2013.

14 Jung, C.G. 1989, *Memories, Dreams, Reflections* New York: Vintage.

Chapter 1

1 For those who are not familiar with cricket, a 'duck' means to be knocked out without scoring – a situation that carries considerable disgrace.

2 Dass, B. (1997) *It's Here Now, Are You?* New York: Broadway Books.

3 Clapp, S. (1998) *With Chatwin, Portrait of a Writer*, London: Vintage.

4 Michael Goldfarb, (2012) *The British Establishment: Who For?* http:// downloads.bbc.co.uk/podcasts/worldservice/docarchive/docarchive_20111025-1000a.mp3

5 Quote taken from Hibbert, C. (1997) *No Ordinary Place, Radley College and the Public School System 1847–1947*, London: John Murray.

6 The Bullingdon Club is a socially exclusive student dining club at Oxford University. The club has no permanent rooms and is notorious for its members' wealth and destructive binges. Membership is by invitation only, and prohibitively expensive for most, given the need to pay for the uniform, dinners and damages. *The Wisden Cricketer* reports that the Bullingdon was originally "ostensibly one of the two original Oxford University cricket teams but it actually used cricket merely as a respectable front for the mischievous, destructive or self-indulgent tendencies of its members." *The Oxford Proctor* concluded in March 2009: "So I am pleased to say that, except perhaps at the highest level of national politics, the Bullingdon Club this year has been quiescent." http://en.wikipedia.org/wiki/Bullingdon_Club

7 Goldfarb (2012) Op Cit.

8 A rather contemptuous word to describe a 'caring conservative' of liberal/ social-democratic persuasion, which came to prominence in the Thatcher years.

9 Goldfarb (2012) Op Cit.

10 BBC4, *The Grammar School: A Secret History*, Part 1, first broadcast 5 January 2012.

11 Duffell, N. (2000) *The Making of Them: The British Attitude to Children and the Boarding School System*, London: Lone Arrow Press.

Chapter 2

1 Schaverien, J. (2011) *Boarding School Syndrome: Broken Attachments – A Hidden Trauma*, in *British Journal of Psychotherapy*, 27(2): 138–155.

2 Laing, R.D. (1960) *The Divided Self*, London: Penguin.

3 The phrase emotional intelligence was coined by Daniel Goleman. Goleman, D. (1996) *Emotional Intelligence: Why it can matter more than IQ*, London: Bloomsbury.

4 Angela Lambert sadly died in 2007, not long after we had renewed our friendship at her cottage in SW France.

5 Lambert, A. (1991) *No Talking after Lights*, London: Penguin.

6 Duffell, N. (1990) *Turning Little Ones into the Old School: An Edifice that can Crush the Spirit*, in *Free Speech*, *The Independent*, 1 September.

7 Selections from these letters can be found in my book, published ten years later: Duffell, N. (2000) *The Making of Them: The British Attitude to Children and the Boarding School System*, London: Lone Arrow Press.

8 Duffell, N. (2000) Op cit.

9 Pullman, P. (1998) *His Dark Materials*, London: Scholastic.

10 A deliberate policy of isolating and shaming a person by their community colluding in not speaking to them, so the person begins to feel they don't exist.

11 Monbiot, G. (1998) *Acceptable Cruelty* (original subheading was *Britain's most Overt form of Child Abuse is Mysteriously Ignored*) in *The Guardian*, 26 March.

12 We have a strange relationship with what goes by the name of tradition in Britain. The best take on this, for me, is a 1983 film, *The Ploughman's Lunch*. Written by Ian McEwan, it highlighted the way countries and people rewrite their own history to suit the needs of the present. We bask in fake tradition and run a tourist industry off it. The House of Commons is a grand Victorian fake of a Gothic cathedral, trying to look like tradition. The odd British phenomenon of a state headed by a monarch who is also head of the church is the real and more suspect tradition. So is the lie of the English countryside, where early Medieval feudalism still shapes the field boundaries, while Scotland is still owned by a handful of men. Real tradition is something else: the wonderful BBC television programme *Italy Unpacked* in January 2013 took us to Milan's ethereal Gothic cathedral, where the same firm that built it still does the restoration work and where the accounts spanning more than 600 years may still be inspected.

13 For those readers unfamiliar with cricket terminology, I should explain that spin bowling is a technique of throwing the cricket ball slowly but spinning it, so that it rapidly rotates and bounces on the pitch in a devious way, thus making it difficult for the batsman to hit the ball cleanly. The pun on the political art of spin doctoring is fortuitous, since, as Wikipedia suggests, the techniques of spin include: cherry picking (i.e. selectively presenting facts and quotes that support one's position); non-denial denial; phrasing things in a way that assumes unproven truths; using euphemisms to disguise or promote one's agenda; and burying bad news (i.e. announcing one popular thing at the same time as several unpopular things, hoping that the media will focus on the popular one). The BSA, I suggest, has worked very hard in cultivating these arts.

14 More cricket terminology: a bouncer is a ball that is deliberately bowled very fast to bounce well in front of the batsman and then rear up high and unpredictably so that it may intimidate the batsman by threatening to catch him on the face or head. This form of bowling was invented in the 1930s by Douglas Jardine, whom I refer to later.

15 In an interview with Lloyd deMause, founder of the Institute for Psychohistory, the interviewer wrote: "To buy into psychohistory, you have to subscribe to some fairly woolly assumptions, for instance, that a nation's child-rearing techniques affect its foreign policy," in *The Talk of the Town, The New Yorker*, authored by editors of the periodical, 5 December 1994.

Chapter 3

1 http://mosaicfilms.com/about-mosaic-films

2 *The Making of Them*, directed by Colin Luke for Mosaic Pictures and broadcast on BBC *40 Minutes* in January 1994.

3 The film is available on YouTube, at www.youtube.com/watch?v=aatIB-yc7nQ

4 David Thomas, remembering his own school days, in a review of the television film *The Making of Them* in The Telegraph, 6 January, 1994.

5 Simon Partridge has pointed out that the idea of a double bind for boarders may not be strong enough and he proposes the term *Triple Lock*: Partridge, S. (2013) *Boarding School Syndrome: Disguised Attachment-deficit and Dissociation Reinforced by Institutional Neglect and Abuse*, in *Attachment*, July 2013.

6 Duffell, N. (2000) *The Making of Them: The British Attitude to Children and the Boarding School System*, London: Lone Arrow Press.

7 BBC Radio 4 *Open Book*: William Boyd talks to Mariella Frostrup, broadcast 12 February 2012.

8 Lambert, R. with Millham, S. (1969) *The Hothouse Society: An Exploration of Boarding-School Life through the Boys' and Girls' own Writings*. London: Weidenfeld and Nicolson.

9 See Weinberg, I. (1967) *The English Public School: The Sociology of Elite Education*, New York: Atherton; and Wakeford, J. (1969) *The Cloistered Elite*, London: Macmillan.

10 www.amazon.co.uk/product-reviews/0953790401/ref=cm_cr_pr_ http://www.amazon.co.uk/product-reviews/0953790401/ref=cm_cr_pr_

11 A rough game of tag in which children line up on one side of the playground with one or two in the middle who are the 'British Bulldogs'. On the command "British Bulldogs!" the non-bulldogs have to leave their line and attempt to gain the safety of the far line. The British Bulldogs then catch who they can by grabbing them and lifting them off the ground, whereby they are converted into British Bulldogs aswell. Doubtless a preparation for foreigner elimination and life in Parliament, but I remember it as great fun, played during halcyon schooldays before boarding.

12 Joyce, J., "Daniel Defoe" translated from an Italian manuscript and edited by Joseph Prescott, *Buffalo Studies 1* (1964): 24–25.

13 From *The Guardian*, 1 December 2011.

14 Some remarks about the British attitude to striking from the London correspondent of *Le Monde* appear in the final section, *Bicameral Brains and the Bullingdon Boys*, of the last chapter.

15 Ian Hislop's *Stiff Upper Lip - An Emotional History of Britain* www.bbc.co.uk/programmes/b01n7rh4

16 Gill, A.A. (2005) *The Angry Island: Hunting the English*, London: Weidenfeld & Nicolson.

17 Abridged from *The English Are So Nice* by D.H. Lawrence.

18 Poet Dave Shortt reckons this was the basis for Orwell's 'Doublespeak.'

19 *The Beano* is a British children's comic book that started life in the thirties and has had a surprisingly long shelf-life. It features various 'toff' (posh) kids as well as street urchins.

20 Quoted in the *Evening Standard*, 27 October 2011.

21 'Prolesville' is a snobbish public-school expression for a district where the common people, the proleteriat (or, to use the word that Andrew Mitchell apparently did not use, the "plebs") might live.

22 I later discovered it to be 'The Shard', a skyscraper at London Bridge, still under construction at the time of writing, and destined to be the tallest building in Europe. It is funded by a consortium headed by Qatar National Bank.

23 "Fagging was a traditional educational practice in British boarding private schools whereby younger pupils were required to act as personal servants to the most senior boys. While domestic servants were common in family households, the custom of fagging reflected household task distribution and taught pupils about service from both ends of the relationship. Under school rules, fagging might entail harsh discipline and corporal punishment, and it was sometimes associated with sexual abuse at the hands of the older boys. The practice of personal fagging faded away during the Seventies and Eighties but to some degree has been maintained in former colonies or replaced with systems that require junior boys to do tasks for the benefit of the general school community. In England, the word 'fag' became slang for a wearisome chore." Retrieved from Wikipedia, http://en.wikipedia.org/wiki/Fagging.

Chapter 4

1 In his 1960 article, *Ego Distortion in Terms of True and False Self* (in his 1965 book *The Maturational Processes and the Facilitating Environment*, pp. 145–146, New York: International Universities Press), D.W. Winnicott says that when a 'mother's adaptation' is not good enough (he is describing the very early years, but I believe the process continues into latency): "The process that leads to the capacity for symbol-usage does not get started (or else it becomes broken up, with a corresponding withdrawal on the part of the infant from advantages gained) ... in practice the infant lives, but lives falsely. The protest against being forced into a false existence can be detected from the earliest stages ... Through this False Self the infant builds up a false set of relationships, and ... even attains a show of being real."

2 In Roberto Assagioli's psychosynthesis, Winnicott's *False Self* is commonly known as the Survival Personality, and from 1988 I adapted this term to its specific character in ex-boarders.

3 *Born to Run* is a famous song and the third album by the American singer-songwriter Bruce Springsteen, released in 1975.

4 Corporal punishment was outlawed by Parliament in state schools from 1987. In private schools it was banned in 1999 (England and Wales), 2000 (Scotland) and 2003 (Northern Ireland).

5 Roger Clarke writing in *The Independent*, 29 April 1995.

6 Hickson, A. (1995) *The Poisoned Bowl: Sex Repression and the Public School System*, London: Constable.

7 Attachment Theory was principally the work of Dr. John Bowlby (1907–1990). Like Freud, Bowlby believed that mental health and behavioural problems could be attributed to early childhood. After the Second World War, Bowlby developed naturalistic infant observation at the Tavistock Clinic in London within the newly-created National Health Service. In the 1940s and 1950s he humanised and systematised Objects Relation Theory, the prevailing psychoanalytic discipline. Born into a prosperous family, the young Bowlby rarely saw his mother, who like many others of her class considered that parental attention and affection would lead to a dangerous spoiling of a child. Bowlby was brought up by his nanny, but lost her when he was four years old. At the age of seven, he was sent off to boarding school. In his 1972 book *Separation: Anxiety and Anger*, he revealed that he had had a terrible time and later said: "I wouldn't send a dog away to boarding school at age seven." Bowlby's Attachment Theory suggests that children come into the world biologically pre-programmed to form attachments with others, in order to survive. Bowlby was influenced by the biologist Konrad Lorenz who, in his 1935 study of imprinting, demonstrated that attachment was innate in young animals and therefore had survival value. In evolutionary terms, it would have been the babies who stayed close to their mothers who would have survived to have children of their own. Bowlby suggested that a child's attachment figure acted as a secure base for exploring the world and that the attachment relationship acts as the prototype for all future relationships.

8 www.theguardian.com/lifeandstyle/2011/sep/10/dom-joly-my-family-values

9 Looking back now to my first book, which summarised my work in the Nineties, I realise that I did not perhaps sufficiently give account of the extent of the dissociative or schizoid nature of the classic boarder's survival personality and how it

works in group or relationship situations.

10 For a fascinating account of wilful blindness in the wider world, especially in corporate culture, see Margaret Hefferman's (2011) *Willful Blindness: Why We Ignore the Obvious at our Peril*, London: Walker & Company.

11 Grosz, S. (2013) *The Examined Life*, London: Chatto & Windus.

12 McGilchrist, I. (2010) *The Master and his Emissary: The Divided Brain and the Making of the Western World*, New Haven & London: Yale University Press, is an extraordinary feast of information and conclusions recommended to anyone interested in such topics.

13 In this context, the work of the American psychotherapist Stephen M. Johnson is extremely helpful, since he shows how degrees of dysfunction can be conceived on a continuum between what he calls character style through character neurosis to personality disorder. This level of degree rating is both humanising and illuminating for therapeutic workers and opens up many more possibilities for understanding. See Johnson, S.M. (1994) *Character Styles*, New York: W.W. Norton.

14 Simon Partridge has alerted me, however, to the Apparently Normal Personality (ANP) described in a 2004 paper, *Trauma-related Structural Dissociation of the Personality*, by Ellert Nijenhuis, Onno van der Hart and Kathy Steele (available at the Trauma Information Pages website at www.trauma-pages.com/a/nijenhuis-2004.php).

15 Stern, D. (1985) *The Interpersonal World of the Infant*, New York: Basic Books.

16 Partridge, S. (2007) *Trauma at the Threshold: An Eight-Year-Old Goes to Boarding School*, in *Attachment* 1(3): 310–312.

17 Quoted from a letter kept by the mother of an anonymous correspondent of Hickson's, Hickson (1995) Op cit.

18 I refer the reader who wants to know more about the psychodynamics and origin of these theories, as well as the cultural phenomenon of the inner Protestant, to my book, *The Making of Them*.

19 At those scary but hopeful times when a breakdown might be inviting a breakthrough in the psyche it may be pointing to the need to abandon the defensive structure.

20 Shengold, L. (1989) *Soul Murder, The Effects of Childhood Abuse and Deprivation*, Fawcett Columbine; New York.

21 And therefore sometimes also in therapeutic relationships, if the therapist is getting really close.

22 Much more about this process can be found in Duffell, N .& Løvendal, H. (2002) *Sex, Love, and the Dangers of Intimacy: A Guide to Passionate Relationships when the 'Honeymoon' is Over*, London: Thorsons.

23 Grosz (2013) Op cit.

24 Most psychotherapists will hope their clients can 'achieve' this more healthy situation. Hence the success at that level of various therapeutic techniques like Gestalt, active imagination, voice dialogue, sub-personality work, etc., at Level I, but failure where Level II approaches Level III.

25 In psychotherapy, these may also be transferred to the therapist, showing up as feelings of incompetence that can seriously undermine progress unless the practitioner has the awareness, skill and courage to seize upon it.

26 Projective identification ought not to be missed in psychotherapy, because the skilful worker can understand it as an attempt to communicate by someone who has employed so much dissociation that communication in any other normal channels is no longer trusted. Such communications can be decoded by skilful and aware therapists but rarely by an intimate partner, for it is not their job.

27 Jones, E. & Asen, E. (2000) *Systemic Couple Therapy and Depression*, London: Karnac.

28 Real, T. (2002) *How Can I Get Through To You? Reconnecting Men and Women*, New York: Scribner.

29 Hickson, A. (1995) Op cit.

30 Probably some female readers will recognise some of these dynamics, which

are a cruel characteristic of hyper-masculinity, where sexual desire in men is blamed on women. From Genesis to the Taliban, it was she who supplied the apples and needs to be controlled, runs this popular and disgusting logic.

Chapter 5

1 Hunt's special advisor was suspected to have been a lobbyist for James Murdoch, the new British Prince of Darkness.

2 www.dailymail.co.uk/news/article-2207206/Andrew-Mitchell-Two-say-sack-Chief-Whip-police-pleb-storm.html

3 Ibid.

4 Bly, R. (1996) *The Sibling Society*, London: Hamish Hamilton.

5 http://movies.about.com/od/thequeen/a/sheen103106.htm

6 Peter Pan first appeared in a section of *The Little White Bird*, a 1902 novel written by J.M. Barrie for adults. Peter reappeared in a play called *Peter Pan*, or *The Boy Who Wouldn't Grow Up*, which later became a novel, *Peter and Wendy*, published in 1911.

7 Kipling, R. (1983) *Limits and Renewals*, London: Macmillan.

8 The film, *The Making of Them*, directed by Colin Luke for *Mosaic Pictures* and broadcast on BBC *40 Minutes* in January 1994 is now available on You Tube at www.youtube.com/watch?v=aatIB-yc7nQ

9 *The Special Relationship* is a 2010 American-British political film directed by Richard Loncraine from a screenplay by Peter Morgan. It is the third film in Morgan's informal "Blair trilogy", which dramatizes the political career of British Prime Minister Tony Blair (1997–2007), following *The Deal* (2003) and *The Queen* (2006), both directed by Stephen Frears.

10 Blair, T. (2010) *A Journey: My Political Life*, London: Random House.

11 *The Scotsman*, 1 September 2010.

12 Jeremy Hunt, who was Head Boy at Charterhouse, played this thankless role as Health Minister to Cameron.

13 *The Hutton Inquiry Report*, House of Commons, 2004.

14 http://en.wikipedia.org/wiki/Iraq_Enquiry

15 Adapted from a piece by Brian Wheeler, political reporter, BBC News: http://news.bbc.co.uk/2/hi/6506365.stm

16 Michael Goldfarb, personal anecdote.

17 Le Carré, J. (1986) *A Perfect Spy*, London: Hodder & Stoughton.

18 Transference phenomena, in which the unresolved feelings and thoughts about a major figure – usually a parent – became linked with a current relationship, usually therapeutic, were first noted by Freud and became the major methodological tool in psychoanalytic psychotherapy.

19 www.irishcentral.com/news/Tony-Blair-calls-his-Irish-mom-an-almost-saintly-woman-102249544.html#ixzz1lVUx4Xb1

20 Tim Walker in *The Telegraph*, 12 January 2012.

Chapter 6

1 Peter Allen, in Paris, Sky news website, 23 December 2011.

2 Hutton, W. (2011) *David Cameron's Act of Crass Stupidity on Europe*, in *The Observer*, 11 December.

3 Heffer, S. (2011) *Rise of the Fourth Reich: How Germany is using the Financial Crisis to Conquer Europe*, in the *Daily Mail*, 17 August.

4 Ibid.

5 Rawnsley, A. (2011) *This Abject Defeat for British Diplomacy is the more Striking because Mr Cameron's Demands were quite Modest*, in The *Observer*, 11 December.

6 Hutton, W. (2011) Op cit.

7 Hutton, W. (1996) *The State We're In*, London: Vintage.

8 Michael Goldfarb in *The British Establishment: Who For?* http://downloads.bbc.co.uk/podcasts/worldservice/docarchive/docarchive_20111025-1000a.mp3

9 See Chapter 1, section Who's the British Establishment for, actually?

10 Hutton, W. (2010) *The Only Way to Create a Fairer Society is to Start Talking*

about it, in *The Observer*, 10 January.

11 Hutton, W. (2011) Op cit.

12 Cohen, R. (2011) *The British Euro Farce, The New York Times*, 13 December .

13 Retrieved from www.independent.co.uk/arts-entertainment/tv/reviews/last-nights-viewing-jonathan-meades-on-france-bbc4-the-crusades-bbc2-6291546.html

14 *Blinded by a fanatical obsession to Brussels* by Simon Heffer, *Daily Mail* 12 December 2011, retrieved from www.dailymail.co.uk/news/article-2072887/Tory-fury-Cleggs-pygmy-insult-Britain-Lib-Dem-leader-accused-talking-nation-down.html

15 *A Conflict of Interest*, twelfth episode of the BBC comedy series *Yes, Prime Minister* first broadcast 31 December 1987, written by Antony Jay & Jonathan Lynn. Thanks to Andrew Mullis for this link.

16 Michael Goldfarb, published on globalpost (www.globalpost.com), 3 October 2011.

17 Cohen, R. (2011) Op cit.

18 Translation mine. *Der Spiegel – Geschichte 1/2013 Januar Das Britische Empire 1600–1947: Als England die Welt Regierte*. Original text: "Ohne Masterplan, vielmehr aus einer Kette von Zufallen sei das Empire entstanden, erläutert der Frankfurter Historiker Peter Wende im Gespräch mit den Redakteuren Norbert F. Pützl und Rainer Traub, der dieses Heft konzipiert hat. Ein entscheidender Gesichtspunk für die Briten sei gewesen, dass ihr Überseereich möglichst wenig kosten sollte. Dass London auch heute noch auf eine Sonderrolle in Europa pocht, liege daran, dass "im politischen Bewusstsein immer noch der Gedanke verankert sei: 'Wir sind eine Führungsmacht'".

19 Ashdown, P. (2011) *David Cameron has Isolated us in Europe and Diminished us in Washington's Eyes*, in *The Observer*, 11 December.

20 Rawnsley, A. (2011) Op cit.

21 Cohen, R. (2011) Op cit.

22 BBC World Service TV documentary, *Putin, Russia and the West, Part IV, New Start*, broadcast 9 February 2012.

23 Obama, B. (2006) *The Audacity of Hope*, New York: Three Rivers Press.

24 Unicef (2007) *An Overview of Child Well-being in Rich Countries.*

25 Reported by the London *Evening Standard*, 6 December 2011.

26 McGilchrist, I. (2010) *The Master and his Emissary: the Divided Brain and the Making of the Western World*, New Haven & London: Yale University Press.

27 Hutton, W. (2011) Op cit.

28 Ibid.

29 Ashdown, P. (2011) Op cit.

30 Annan, N. (1990) *Our Age, Portrait of a Generation*, London: Weidenfeld & Nicolson.

31 Michael Goldfarb interview with Stewart Maxwell in *The British Establishment: Who For?*

32 McIntosh, A, Roberts, R. & Williams, L. (eds.) (2012) *Human Ecology: Intercultural and Indigenous Approaches*, Farnham: Ashgate.

33 *David Cameron: Scottish nationalists want 'neverendum' not referendum*, by James Kirkup and Simon Johnson in the *Daily Telegraph*, 11 January 2012.

Chapter 7

1 Rawnsley, A. (2011) *This Abject Defeat for British Diplomacy is the more Striking because Mr Cameron's Demands were Quite Modest*, in *The Observer*, 11 December.

2 Hutton, W. (2011) *David Cameron's Act of Crass Stupidity on Europe*, in *The Observer*, 11 December.

3 Ashdown, P. (2011) *David Cameron has Isolated us in Europe and Diminished us in Washington's Eyes*, in *The Observer*, 11 December.

4 BBC TV, *Question Time*, 19 January 2013.

5 Germaine, G. (2006) *The Female Eunuch*, London: Harper Perennial.

6 Hickson, A. (1995) *The Poisoned Bowl: Sex Repression and the Public School System*, London: Constable.

7 George Melly, writing in the Foreword to Hickson (1995) Op cit.

8 Hickson (1995) Op cit.

9 Ibid.

10 Waugh, E. (1964) *A Little Learning*, London: Chapman & Hall.

11 www.chosen.org.uk

12 Unicef (2007) Report: *An Overview of Child Well-being in Rich Countries.*

13 The revolutionary new sexual psychotherapy of Dutch developmental psychologist, Dr Willem Poppeliers, is still little known in Britain. For a brief introduction see: Poppeliers, W. & Broesterhuizen, M. (2007) *Sexual Grounding Therapy*, Breda, The Netherlands: Protocol Media Productions. See also www. sexualgrounding.com

14 See Duffell, N. (2000) *The Making of Them: The British Attitude to Children and the Boarding School System*, London: Lone Arrow Press and Duffell, N. & Løvendal, H. (2002) *Sex, Love, and the Dangers of Intimacy: A guide to passionate relationships when the "honeymoon" is over*, London: Thorsons, and various articles available at www.genderpsychology.com as well as my forthcoming *Thinking About Sex.*

15 For a good description of the pressures on boarding girls see Lambert, A. (1991) *No Talking after Lights*, London: Penguin.

16 www.amazon.co.uk/gp/product/0953790401/ref=s9_simh_gw_p14_d11_g14_i2?pf_rd_m=A3P5ROKL5A1OLE&pf_rd_s=center4&pf_rd_r=11REK83RKTMR67PM8C8P&pf_rd_t=101&pf_rd_p=467128133&pf_rd_i=468294

17 Campbell, B. (1998) *Diana Princess of Wales: How Sexual Politics Shook the Monarchy*, London: The Women's Press.

18 Bradford, S. (1997) *Elizabeth*, London: Mandarin Paperbacks.

19 Dimbleby, J. (1994), *The Prince of Wales: A Biography*, New York: William Morrow.

20 William Boyd talks to Mariella Frostrup, *Open Book* broadcast on BBC Radio 4, 12 February 2012.

21 Campbell, B. (1998) Op cit.

22 *Sir Henry at Rawlinson End* was a surreal satire on the anachronistic attitudes of the British upper classes, more biting even than *Monty Python*, written by *Bonzo Dog Doo-Dah Band* member Vivian Stanshall in 1978 and made into a film in 1980, starring Trevor Howard as Sir Henry and Stanshall himself as Henry's brother Hubert.

23 Holden, A. (1994) *The Tarnished Crown*, London: Viking.

24 Campbell, B. (1998) Op cit.

25 Morton, A. (1992) *Diana: Her True Story in Her Own Words*, New York: Pocket.

26 Colditz was a famous World War II prisoner of war camp. Simon Johnson reported in the *Daily Telegraph* on 27 January 2013 that: "Queen Elizabeth, the Queen Mother warned against sending the Prince of Wales to boarding school in Scotland because she thought he would be miserable, according to a collection of her previously unpublished letters. Despite the Queen Mother's pleas, the Duke of Edinburgh ruled that his eldest son would attend his alma mater, located in rugged countryside near Elgin. But her concerns proved accurate after the prince described the inter-denominational school as 'Colditz in kilts.'"

27 Dimbleby, J. (1994) Op cit.

28 Morton, A. (1992) Op cit.

29 John Bowlby is the father of Attachment Theory. In the Forties and Fifties, Bowlby humanised and systematized Objects Relation Theory; both disciplines were formulated, not without reason I think, in Britain. See: Bowlby, J (1953) *Childcare and the Growth of Love*, London: Pelican, and also the radical work of Iain Suttie who influenced him: Suttie, I. (1935/1988) *The Origins of Love and Hate*, London: Free Association Books.

30 Le Carré, J. (1986) *A Perfect Spy*, London: Hodder & Stoughton.

31 Hyam, R. (1990) *Empire and Sexuality*, Manchester and New York: MUP.

32 Jean Liedloff has written compellingly about how the lack of what she calls

the 'in-arms experience' results in the epidemic occurrence of disowned exasperation in Western culture. See *The Making of Them* and Liedloff, J. (1986) *The Continuum Concept*, London: Penguin.

33 I have my wife Helena to thank for repeatedly pointing this out.

34 Keleman, S. (1994) *Love, A Somatic View*, Berkley, CA: Centre Press.

Chapter 8

1 Tomalin, C. (2006) *Thomas Hardy: The Time-Torn Man*, London: Viking Penguin.

2 From Doris Lessing's Introduction to Lawrence, D.H. (2006) *Lady Chatterley's Lover, A Propos of "Lady Chatterley's Lover,"* London: Penguin.

3. Tomalin, C. (2006) Op cit.

4 Originally published in 1894, this tragicomedy is set during a freezing Dorset Christmas earlier in the century. In the tale, the band – or choir – have played at various local parties before the church service and, having fallen asleep from the effects of the drink consumed there, are nudged into wakefulness by a younger member. Not realising where they are, they charge into a spirited version of a popular reel, The Devil among the Tailors, a hilarious mistake that finally allows the squire to get rid of them. Hardy, T. (1953). *Absent-Mindedness In A Parish Choir*, in *Life's Little Ironies: A set of tales with some colloquial sketches entitled A Few Crusted Characters*, London: Macmillan.

5 Readers may recall in this context the marvellous and obscure quote on this very topic from James Joyce, cited in Chapter 3. Joyce noted that the true symbol of the British conquest is Robinson Crusoe: "He is the true prototype of the British colonist ... The whole Anglo-Saxon spirit is in Crusoe: the manly independence, the unconscious cruelty, the persistence, the slow yet efficient intelligence, the sexual apathy, the calculating taciturnity." Joyce, J. *Daniel Defoe*, translated from an Italian manuscript and edited by Joseph Prescott, *Buffalo Studies 1* (1964): 24–25. I am still wondering why this had to be said in Italian, not English.

6 See Emile Zolla's wonderful account of this phenomenon as revealed through writing of the time, from the 16th to the 20th century. Zolla, E. (1973) *The Writer and the Shaman: A Morphology of the American Indian*, New York: Harcourt Brace Janovich.

7 The classic rational idealised/denigrated 18th century portrayal of the American Indian in literature could be represented by the famous lines from Alexander Pope's 1734 *Essay on Man:*

      Lo, the poor Indian! whose untutor'd mind
      Sees God in clouds, or hears him in the wind.

8 Stevens, L.M. (2004) *The Poor Indians: British Missionaries, Native Americans, and Colonial Sensibility*, Philadelphia: University of Pennsylvania Press.

9 *Canada, Aboriginal Peoples and Residential Schools: They Came for the Children*, Interim Report of the Truth and Reconciliation Commission of Canada, February 24, 2012. Available at www.attendancemarketing.com/~attmk/TRC_jd/ResSchoolHistory_2012_02_24_Webposting.pdf

10 Retrieved from www.abolition.e2bn.org/slavery_45.html

11 Rainer Traub, writing in *Sieg der Empörung* in *Der Spiegel – Geschichte* 1/ January 2013. *Das Britische Empire 1600–1947: Als England die Welt regierte.* (Translation: Outrage's Victory in the Spiegel History Supplement The British Empire 1600–1947: When England ruled the World.)

12 *Follow the Money: Investigators Trace Forgotten Story of Britain's Slave Trade* in *The Guardian*, 28 August 2013, reported on the research by Professor Catherine Hall and colleagues, at University College London.

13 Ibid.

14 Hochschild, A. (2005) *Bury the Chains: Prophets and Rebels in the Fight to Free an Empire's Slaves*, Boston: Houghton Mifflin Harcourt.

15 No wonder the reorganisation of the National Health Service is proving so difficult for the Conservatives. Any reorganisation would be hard enough, due to the size of the NHS, but it must be even more difficult for a government in which

so many members were institutionalised as children, because the NHS's hierarchical, structured separatism is very familiar to them, which means they do not notice it as an obstacle.

16 Mukherjee, S. (2010) *The Emperor of All Maladies: A Biography of Cancer,* New York: Scribner.

17 Dalrymple, T. (2001) *Life at the Bottom: The Worldview That Makes the Underclass,* Lanham, Maryland: Ivan R. Dee.

18 While compartmentalisation has its value for differentiation, depth-psychologists know a lot about its problems from their psychotherapy work with individuals. Compartmentalisation is particularly problematic when combined with disowning and projection, and even more so when it starts to pollute the systems in which an individual lives, such as their intimate relationships. As we saw when examining the Strategic Survival Personality – a hyper-rational structure – the tension of keeping things separate can put enormous strain on an individual, so that the defence mechanisms of dissociation and denial have to be deployed. These are used to manage and reinforce the separation, but the problem is that if they are unchecked they then add to and complicate the problem. The secondary effect, as we also saw, is that because of the ecological nature of the psyche, those things that have been disowned and become part of the 'Not-I' have the tendency to come back to haunt the disowner.

Here is a psychoanalyst, Thomas Ogden, describing (in a different context) how the compartmentalising of primitive feeling states works inside a tiny infant at the breast. Ogden's theoretical stance is Kleinian, which is known for a grim turn of phrase that tends to be extreme and pseudoscientific. But the reader should not be put off, for Ogden understands these phenomena very precisely. Here, he explains how a baby's conceptual switching from 'good' to 'bad' operates:

> In the paranoid-schizoid mode of generating experience, each time a good object is disappointing, it is no longer experienced as a good object – nor even as a disappointing good object – but as the discovery of a bad object in what had been masquerading as a good one. Instead of the experience of ambivalence, there is the experience of unmasking the truth.

Ogden, T. (1992) *The Primitive Edge of Experience,* London: Karnac Books. (Thanks to Helena Løvendal-Duffell for this reference.)

In other words, the dissociating mind ends up creating its own reality. Ogden says that in such a limited binary mental mode of operation the 'Bad Object,' though virtual, turns out to be experienced as true. It is then not the objective truth but the experience that holds sway. In our case, the thing that has to be not identified with turns out to really exist as a problem. It is devilish. In fact, it reminds me of how pre-modern monotheists needed the Devil as the embodiment of all they wanted not to identify with: so they created Satan and, lo and behold, he exists.

19 Taking measurements of the human skull was very popular in the 19th century as an activity of phrenology, a pseudoscience that tried to rationalise various biases – about the superiority of men over women or Europeans over Africans, for example. See Dick, L. (1995) *The Skull of Charlotte Corday,* London: Secker and Warburg.

Chapter 9

1 Jung, C.G. (1989) *Memories, Dreams, Reflections,* New York: Vintage.

2 *Empire,* BBC TV documentary in five parts, presented by Jeremy Paxman, first broadcast 27 February 2012.

3 Paxman, J. (2011) *Empire: What Ruling the World Did to the British,* London: Viking Adult.

4 Gott, R. (2011) *Britain's Empire: Resistance, Repression and Revolt,* London: Verso.

5 The term was coined and defined by American sociologist Erving Goffman in his paper *On the Characteristics of Total Institutions,* presented in April 1957 at the Walter Reed Institute's Symposium on Preventive and Social Psychiatry.

6 Goffman, E. (1961) A*sylums: Essays on the Social Situation of Mental Patients*

and Other Inmates, London: Pelican.

7 Simon Partridge, personal correspondence.

8 *Canada, Aboriginal Peoples and Residential Schools: They Came for the Children* (Interim Report of the Truth and Reconciliation Commission of Canada, February 24, 2012), available at www.attendancemarketing.com/~attmk/TRC_jd/ResSchoolHistory_2012_02_24_Webposting.pdf

9 Lewis, P. (1991) *Mummy, Matron and the Maids*, in Roper, M & Tosh, J. (eds.) *Manful Assertions, Masculinities in Britain since 1800*, London: Routledge.

10 Lawrence, D.H. (2006) *Lady Chatterley's Lover, A Propos of Lady Chatterley's Lover*, with an Introduction by Doris Lessing, London: Penguin.

11 Rivers, W.H. (1918) *The Repression of War Experience*, in The *Lancet*, 2 February.

12 Barker, P. (1992) *The Regeneration Trilogy*, London: Penguin.

13 Showalter, E. (1987) *The Female Malady: Women, Madness and English Culture 1830–1980*, London: Virago.

14 Rivers, W.H.R. (1920) *Instinct and the Unconscious: a Contribution to a Biological Theory of the Psycho-Neuroses*, Cambridge: the University Press. See http://psychclassics.yorku.ca/Rivers/appendix4.htm

15 Rivers, W.H.R. (1918), *The Repression of War Experience, Proceedings of the Royal Society of Medicine*; 11(Sect Psych): 1–20. PMCID: PMC2066211.

16 *War Horse* is a play based on a book for children by Michael Morpurgo. Adapted for stage by Nick Stafford, it premiered on 17 October 2007 in the Olivier Theatre at the National Theatre London and has been a huge international success.

17 From Doris Lessing's *Introduction* to Lawrence, D.H. (2006) Op cit.

18 Lawrence, D.H. (1960) *Lady Chatterley's Lover*, London: Penguin.

19 *Queen Victoria and the Kaiser*, Channel 4 documentary, 17 November 2013.

20 Brett Kahr, interviewed in the documentary *Queen Victoria and the Kaiser*, makes such a point, but the more relevant body-psychotherapy of Willem Poppeliers describes how and why growing boys have a right to a sexual response from their mothers (see Chapter 7).

21 Lawrence, D. H. (1930) *Nettles*, London: Faber and Faber.

22 Lawrence, D.H. (1920). *Psychoanalysis and the Unconscious*; and (1921) *Fantasia of the Unconscious*.

23 Suttie, I. (1988; first published 1935) *The Origins of Love and Hate*, London: Free Association Books.

24 Rilke, R.M. & Mood, J. L. (Ed.) (2004) *Rilke On Love And Other Difficulties: Translations and Considerations of Rainer Maria*, New York: Norton.

25 Lawrence, D.H. (1960) Op cit.

26 *Class and Culture*, BBC 2 TV documentary in three parts, presented by Melvyn Bragg. First broadcast 24 February 2012.

27 Nigel Farndale in the *Daily Telegraph*, 25 February 2012.

Chapter 10

1 Herzen, A. (1991) *My Past and Thoughts*, Berkley CA: California.

2 Translation: There's a solution to every problem.

3 It is also one of the main reasons ex-boarders make some of the most difficult clients to keep in psychotherapy, let alone to achieve results, because they have to want willingly to deconstruct the false self they have put up, to let down walls that were designed to keep them safe and prove that they are not the emotional, vulnerable innocent ones.

4 Personal correspondence.

5 *The Making of Them*, directed by Colin Luke for Mosaic Pictures and broadcast on BBC *40 Minutes* in January 1994.

6 *Canada, Aboriginal Peoples and Residential Schools: They Came for the Children* (Interim Report of the Truth and Reconciliation Commission of Canada, February 24, 2012), available at www.attendancemarketing.com/~attmk/TRC_jd/ResSchoolHistory_2012_02_24_Webposting.pdf

7 Library and Archives Canada, Humphrey Lloyd Hime, National Archives of

Canada fonds, C-000728.

8 Herzen, A. (1991) *My Past and Thoughts*, Berkley CA: California.

9 Jim Danaher, from *The Philosopher*, Volume LXXXXVIII No. 2 (www.the-philosopher.co.uk).

10 Ibid, italics mine.

11 Interview with Lloyd de Mause in *The Talk of the Town*, in *The New Yorker*, authored by editors of the periodical, 5 December 1994.

12 Liedloff, J. (1986). *The Continuum Concept*, London: Penguin. Jean Liedloff proposes that the lack of what she calls the "in-arms experience" results in an epidemic occurrence of disowned exasperation, which I pursue at some length in *The Making of Them*.

13 Dawkins, R. (2006) *The God Delusion*, London: Bantam Press.

14 Personal correspondence.

15 Annan, N. (1990) *Our Age, Portrait of a Generation*, London: Weidenfeld & Nicolson.

16 Cooke, R. (2012) *I can be a bit harsh*, in the *Observer Magazine* 22 April.

17 *They Came for the Children*, Op cit.

18 *Der Spiegel - Geschichte* 1/ 2013 Januar Das Britische Empire *1600 - 1947: Als England die Welt regierte*. (Translation: The British Empire 1600 - 1947: When England ruled the World.)

19 *Empire*, BBC TV documentary in five parts, presented by Jeremy Paxman, first broadcast 27 February 2012.

20 This quotation and the following were retrieved from http://en.wikipedia.org/wiki/Anthropological_Society_of_London

21 Flint, J. (1976) *Cecil Rhodes*, London: Hutchinson. Rhodes wrote this in a Confession of Faith (not published during his lifetime), which offered a vision of racist expansionism that was gaining ground before the First World War. To put the citation in context I have added here the full paragraph, which shows both the *lebensraum* and 'master-race' arguments, more usually thought to be German in origin, but in fact rather British of the time:

> It often strikes a man to enquire what is the chief goal in life; to one the thought comes that it is a happy marriage, to another great wealth, and as each seizes on his idea, for that he more or less works for the rest of his existence. To myself thinking over the same question the wish came to render myself useful to my country. I then asked myself how could I, and after reviewing the various methods, I have felt that at the present day we are actually limiting our children and perhaps bringing into the world half the human beings we might owing to the lack of country for them to inhabit, and that if we had retained America there would at this moment be millions more of English living. I contend that we are the finest race in the world and that the more of the world we inhabit the better it is for the human race.

22 Tony Blair's resignation speech, *Hansard* 10 May 2007.

23 'High Table' is where the top authorities – masters and senior prefects in public schools and their equivalents at Oxbridge Colleges – ostentatiously sit at mealtimes in 'Hall,' the dining room.

24 Suskind, R. (2004) F*aith, Certainty and the Presidency of George W. Bush*, in *The New York Times Magazine*, 17 October 2004.

25 Ibid.

26 Ibid.

Chapter 11

1 Suskind, R. (2004) *Faith, Certainty and the Presidency of George W. Bush*, in *The New York Times Magazine*, 17 October 2004

2 Foucault, M., Khalfa, J. & Murphy, J. (2006) *The History of Madness*, New York: Routledge.

3 Showalter, E. (1987) *The Female Malady: Women, Madness & English Culture 1830–1980*, London: Virago.

4 Wilber, K. (1995) *Sex, Ecology, Spirituality: The Spirit of Evolution*, Boston:

Shambhala. Wilber provides credible intellectual support for those who are interested in a world that can face the challenges of the future by means of reconnection rather than further disconnection.

5 The word 'matter' derives from the Sanskrit and Indo-European root word, *matr*, meaning mother.

6 Most remarks on brain hemisphere functioning are taken from the monumental McGilchrist, I. (2010) *The Master and his Emissary: The Divided Brain and the Making of the Western World*, New Haven & London: Yale University Press, to which I shall refer regularly in course of the next chapters.

7 Zolla, E. (1973) *The Writer and the Shaman: A Morphology of the American Indian*, New York: Harcourt Brace Janovich.

8 *Canada, Aboriginal Peoples and Residential Schools: They Came for the Children* (Interim Report of the Truth and Reconciliation Commission of Canada, February 24, 2012).

9 I would like to think that the varied themes of this current book are part of such an interdisciplinary direction. If some readers find its range and style unfamiliar, this may account for it.

10 Werner Karl Heisenberg (1901–1976) was a German theoretical physicist who was awarded the Nobel Prize for Physics "for the creation of quantum mechanics." In 1927 he published his Uncertainty Principle, upon which he built his philosophy, and for which he is best known. This states that any physical measurement perturbs the system being studied, so that pure objectivity is but an illusion. In particle physics, it means that space and time coordinates of an object can never be certain, but in the social sciences it means that an observer inevitably interprets what he studies through his own mindset. Retrieved from http://en.wikipedia.org/wiki/Werner¬_ Heisenberg.

11 Damasio, A.R. (1994) *Descartes' Error: Emotion, Reason, and the Human Brain*, New York: Avon Books.

12 Ibid.

13 Damasio, A.R. (2000) *The Feeling of What Happens: Body, Emotion and the Making of Consciousness*, London: Vintage.

14 Schore, A.N. (2012) *The Science and Art of Psychotherapy*, New York: Norton.

15 Bazzano, M. (2013) *Back to the Future: from Behaviourism and Cognitive Psychology to Motivation and Emotion*, in *Self & Society* 40(2).

16 *Love Code: The Chemistry of Intimacy* – a roundtable discussion with Stephanie Brown, Sue Carter, Elaine Hatfield, Dolores Malaspina, and Stephen Porges, filmed 27 September, 2008. http://philoctetes.org/past_programs/love_code_a_pathway_ to_intimacy

17 Porges, S.W. (2011) *The Polyvagal Theory: Neurophysiological Foundations of Emotions, Attachment, Communication, and Self-Regulation*, New York: Norton.

18 Lecture given by Stephen Porges and Sue Carter at the 2012 Cambridge Body Psychotherapy Congress, 13 September, and subsequent converstions with the author.

19 Pollecoff, M. (2009) in *Self & Society* Autumn 2009 and www. thelongboathome.co.uk. Italics mine.

20 *The Heart has its Reasons*, BBC World Service, 22 October 2010.

21 Childre, D & Marting, H. (1999) *The HeartMath Solution*, New York: Harper SanFrancisco.

22 *The Heart has its Reasons*, Op cit.

23 McCraty, R., Atkinson, M., *et al.* (1999) *The Role of Physiological Coherence in the Detection and Measurement of Cardiac Energy Exchange between People*. Proceedings of the Tenth International Montreux Congress on Stress, Montreux, Switzerland.

24 Braden, G. (2007) *The Divine Matrix: Bridging time, space, miracles and belief*, Carlsbad, California: Hay House, Inc.

25 www.theguardian.com/books/2004/jul/17/highereducation.booksonhealth

26 Gerhardt, S. (2004) *Why Love Matters: How Affection Shapes a Baby's Brain*, Hove: Brunner Routledge. See also her theory of how these issues can affect politcs

in Gerhardt, S, (2010) *The Selfish Society*, London: Simon & Schuster.

27 See the entertaining www.ted.com/talks/helen_fisher_studies_the_brain_in_love.html

28 The *social brain* hypothesis was proposed by British anthropologist Robin Dunbar, who argues that human intelligence did not evolve primarily as a means to solve ecological problems, but rather intelligence evolved as a means of surviving and reproducing in large and complex social groups. Retrieved from http://en.wikipedia.org/wiki/Evolution_of_human_intelligence#Social_brain_hypothesis

29 The Royal Society for the encouragement of the Arts, Manufactures and Commerce (RSA), an Enlightenment organisation now promoting 21st century enlightenment.

30 See www.thersa.org/action-research-centre/social-brain

31 One of the ongoing discussions amongst colleagues who are in no doubt about the problems of boarding centres on whether we yet have the right terminology. For example, should ex-boarders be described as sufferers of PTSD? Certainly some of their spouses might be. And which of John Bowlby's categories of attachment disorder would be correct, or is there another category still waiting to be named for them?

32 McGilchrist, I. (2010) Op cit.

33 Danaher, J. *Plato's Cave and the Bicameral Brain*, in *The Philosopher* LXXXXVIII(2), available at www.the-philosopher.co.uk/plato-and-bicameral-brain.htm

34 McGilchrist, I. (2010) Op cit.

Chapter 12

1 Goleman, D. (1996) *Emotional Intelligence: Why It Can Matter more than IQ*, London: Bloomsbury.

2 Professor John Carey is the author of Carey, J. (1992) *The Intellectuals and the Masses: Pride and Prejudice among the Literary Intelligentsia, 1880–1939*, London: Faber and Faber.

3 Interestingly, body-psychotherapy, which focuses on releasing emotions held in body tension, is seen as a very marginal branch of therapy. It derives from the work of the analysts Georg Groddeck and Wilhelm Reich who were practising in the early 20th century, although the therapy didn't arrive here until the 1970s. In Britain, it is almost always taught by foreigners, for it is much more popular in Holland, Germany and Denmark, where it has become synonymous with the very idea of therapy.

4 Retrieved from http://en.wikipedia.org/wiki/Brief_Encounter

5 Thanks to Tatiana Shuttleworth for pointing these plays out to me.

6 Gill, A.A. (2005) *The Angry Island: Hunting the English*, London: Weidenfeld & Nicolson.

7 www.dailymail.co.uk/news/article-2207206/Andrew-Mitchell-Two-say-sack-Chief-Whip-police-pleb-storm.html

8 Goleman, D. (1996) Op cit.

9 William Shakespeare, *Hamlet*, Act 3, Scene 2, text from *The Complete Works* (1958) edited by Peter Alexander, London: Collins.

10 Sapolsky, R.M. (2004) *Why Zebras Don't Get Ulcers: Guide to Stress, Stress-related Diseases and Coping*, New York: Henry Holt.

11 William Shakespeare, *King Henry V*, Act III Scene I, text from *The Complete Works* (1958) edited by Peter Alexander, London: Collins.

12 In an article entitled *"Chillax? Don't do it,"*, insists David Cameron over book claims he is most relaxed PM, the *London Evening Standard* on 21 May 2012 gently teased him for his fondness of karaoke, tennis, computer games and wine.

13 Tuchman, B.W. (1994) *The Proud Tower: A Portrait of the World Before the War, 1890–1914*, New York: Ballantine Books.

14 McGilchrist, I. (2010) *The Master and his Emissary: the Divided Brain and the Making of the Western World*, New Haven & London: Yale University Press.

15 Dewey, J. (1929) *Experience and Nature*, Chicago: Open Court.

16 Duffell, N. & Løvendal, H. (2002) *Sex, Love, and the Dangers of Intimacy: A*

Guide to Passionate Relationships when the "Honeymoon" is over, London: Thorsons.

17 Kerenyi, C. (1962) *The Religion of the Greeks and the Romans*, London: Thanes and Hudson. Quoted in McGilchrist (2010) Op cit.

18 McGilchrist (2010) Op cit.

Chapter 13

1 Retrieved from http://news.bbc.co.uk/2/hi/uk_news/politics/8375544.stm

2 Perceval, J. (1840) *A Narrative, Vol II*, London: Effingham Wilson.

3 Podvoll, E. M. (2003) *Recovering Sanity: A Compassionate Approach to Understanding and Treating Psychosis*, London & Boston: Shambhala.

4 Ayaan Hirsi, *New York Times Review of Books*, 6 January 2008, p. 15.

5 See the beginning of Chapter 9.

6 Johnson, R.A. (1989) *He: Understanding Masculine Psychology*, New York: Harper & Row.

7 McGilchrist, I. (2010) *The Master and his Emissary: The Divided Brain and the Making of the Western World*, New Haven & London: Yale University Press.

8 The term bicameral was first coined by Julian Jaynes in 1976. See Jaynes, J. (2000) *The Origin of Consciousness in the Breakdown of the Bicameral Mind*, Boston: Houghton Mifflin.

9 Podvoll embarked on this work after he had competed a twelve-year meditation retreat!

10 Prigogine, I. (1997) *End of Certainty*, New York: The Free Press. Viscount Ilya Romanovich Prigogine was noted for his work on dissipative structures, complex systems and irreversibility. Many see his work as a bridge between the natural sciences and the social sciences.

11 Jim Danaher, from *The Philosopher LXXXXVIII(2)*, available at www.the-philosopher.co.uk

12 Grotstein, J. (1984) *Forgery of the Soul*, in Nelson, M. and Eigen, M. (Eds) *Evil, Self and Culture Vol 4*, New York: Human Science Press.

13 Martha, S. (2005) *The Sociopath Next Door*, New York: Broadway Books.

14 Bancroft, L. (2002) *Why Does He Do That? Inside the Minds of Angry and Controlling Men*, New York: Penguin.

15 Perkins, J. (2004) *Confessions of an Economic Hit Man*, San Fransico: Berrett-Koehler. In his best-selling book, Perkins (a US boarding school survivor) bravely tells the story of his work as a highly paid consultant hired to strong-arm leaders into creating policy favourable to the US government and corporations – what he calls the "corporatocracy" – and of an epiphany that led him to "come in from the cold."

16 Singh, A. (2012) *Sundance Kid takes Cameron to task over 'narrow' view of film-making*, in the *Daily Telegraph*, 27 April.

17 Noam Chomsky on *Tom Dispatch*, part of the *Guardian Comment Network* at www.guardian.co.uk, 14 February 2012.

18 Rich, F. (2006) *The Greatest Story ever Sold: The Decline and Fall of Truth from 9/11 to Katrina*, New York: Penguin.

19 Tuchman, B.W. (1994) *The Proud Tower: A Portrait of the World Before the War, 1890–1914*, New York: Ballantine Books.

20 Ibid.

21 Perkins (2004) Op cit.

22 Watt, N. (2013) *Boris Johnson invokes Thatcher spirit with greed is good speech*, in *The Guardian*, 27 November.

23 Ibid.

24 *A History of the Stiff Upper Lip: Louisa Foxe goes on a journey through the archives*, BBC Radio 4. First broadcast 19 May 2012.

25 *The Making of Them*, directed by Colin Luke for Mosaic Pictures, first broadcast on BBC *40 Minutes*, January 1994.

26 In our Boarding School Survivors Workshops (www.boardingschoolsurvivors.co.uk) some people have found the courage to return to their partners and tell them "I am the one who is depressed," which promotes huge healing.

27 Albert, E. (2012) *Lettre du Royaume-Uni*, in *Le Monde*, 22 June.

Epilogue

1 The notion that Wounded Leaders were deliberately derived from an industrial production line interested BBC producer Mark Smalley and author, comedian and activist AL Kennedy, and I was invited to take part in a BBC radio documentary asking "Who's in control?" called *Production Line Living*, which was broadcast on 27 October 2013 as part of Radio 3's Free Thinking Festival. It can be downloaded from www.bbc.co.uk/podcasts/series/r3docs. The full interview is available on www.psychohistory.org.uk

2 1945 Labour Party Manifesto, retrieved from www.labour-party.org.uk/manifestos/1945/1945-labour-manifesto.shtml

3 Wende, P. (2013) *Das Britische Empire 1600 – 1947: Als England die Welt regierte* ("The British Empire 1600 – 1947: When England ruled the World"), *Der Spiegel – Geschichte 1*, January.

4 Ken Loach's 2013 film, *The Spirit of 45*, is produced by Dogwoof, www.dogwoof.com

5 From an interview with Anne McElvoy for BBC Radio 3 *Nightwaves*, played during the interval in the 'Proms' Concerts 29 July 2013. Text from BBC iPlayer.

6 Kielburger, C. & Kielburger, M. (2013) *A coveted job skill that you already have*, in the *Huffington Post*, 17 July, www.huffingtonpost.ca/craig-and-marc-kielburger/empathy-at-work_b_3606266.html

7 Anders, G. (2013) *The Number One Job Skill in 2020*, in *Forbes*, www.forbes.com/sites/georgeanders/

8 Alex Salmond, 7 April 2013, retrieved from www.snp.org/blog/post/2013/apr/empathy-needed-now-more-ever-fm

9 Adam Smith (1776) *Inquiry into the Nature and Causes of the Wealth of Nations*.

10 Retrieved from www.northwestern.edu/observer/issues/2006/06/22/obama.html

11 Salmond (2013) Op cit.

12 Boone, J.A. (1976) *Kinship with All Life*, New York: HarperSanFrancisco.

13 Diamond, J. (2012) *The World until Yesterday*, London: Allen Lane.

14 Retrieved from www.ted.com/talks/george_papandreou_imagine_a_european_democracy_without_borders.html

15 Thanks to John Bunzl for pointing me to this talk. I recommend readers to his website (www.simpol.org) for a comprehensive way of tackling these issues and to Bunzl, J.M. (2012) *Global Domestic Politics: A Citizen's Guide to Running a Diverse Planet*, London: International Simultaneous Policy Organisation. Look out for a forthcoming book on global thinking, a collaboration with myself.

16 Buhler, G. (trans), Muller, F.M. (ed) (reprinted 2001) *Sacred Books of the East: The Laws of Manu*, Richmond, Surrey: Curzon Press.

17 James Surowiecki writing in *The New Yorker*, 20 October 2008.

18 Alexander, A. (2011) *America and the Imperialism of Ignorance: US Foreign Policy since 1945*, London: Biteback Publishing.

19 Surowiecki (2008) Op cit.

20 Duffell, N. & Løvendal, H. (2002) *Sex, Love, and the Dangers of Intimacy: A guide to Passionate Relationships when the 'Honeymoon' is Over*, London: Thorsons; and (2012) 10th Anniversary Edition, London: Lone Arrow Press.

21 Ricken Patel, co-founder and Executive Director of Avaaz, in an address for the 2013 Commonwealth Lecture on the theme 'Opportunity through Enterprise', March 2013 at London's Guildhall. The full lecture is on www.youtube.com/watch?v=qHtMAVxS690

22 Buber, M. (1958) *I & Thou*, New York: Scribners. Martin Buber's *Ich und Du* was published in 1923 and first translated into English in 1937.

23 Grotstein, J. (1984) *Forgery of the Soul*, in M. Nelson and M. Eigen (Eds) *Evil, Self and Culture Vol. 4*, New York Human Science Press Inc.

24 See www.genderpsychology.com/cpd_programme and www.inter-psyche.co.uk/foundation.html

25 Retrieved from http://wiki.thearda.com/tcm/concepts/ritual

26 *My Heart's in the Highlands* is a song written by Robert Burns in 1789. In 1997 Bob Dylan released a song with this phrase as the refrain on his 30th studio album *Time Out of Mind.*

27 Harris, J. (2013) *John Major is right to be shocked about the public school elite's grip on Britain. The former Tory prime minister has a point: privately educated men dominate the Conservative party in a way unseen since the 1950s*, in *The Guardian*, 11 November.

28 Bienkov, A. (2013) *Energy Bosses Now More Unpopular than Bankers and Politicians*, politics.co.uk, http://politicscouk.createsend1.com/t/r-l-niudtdy-ydduldiikl-o

29 *The Politics of Architecture*, BBC Radio 4, first broadcast 3 December 2013.

Appendix

1 *Canada, Aboriginal Peoples and Residential Schools: They Came for the Children* (Interim Report of the Truth and Reconciliation Commission of Canada, February 24, 2012). Available at www.attendancemarketing.com/~attmk/TRC_jd/ResSchoolHistory_2012_02_24_Webposting.pdf

2 Adam Smith in *The Theory of Moral Sentiments VI: The Character of Virtue*, retrieved from http://en.wikipedia.org/wiki/The_Theory_of_Moral_Sentiments. Many thanks to Luis Vanderlei Bianco, a reader of *The Making of Them* from Brazil, for alerting me to this reference.

3 The watchdog organisation Boarding Concern was founded in 2002 (www.boardingconcern.org.uk).

4 *A Very English Education*, directed by Hannah Berryman, first broadcast on BBC2 on 27 October 2013.

5 Fraser, S. (2013) *We Don't All Get to be Prefects,* in the blog *Sally Fraser Writes...*, http://sallyfraserwrites.wordpress.com/2013/11/11/we-dont-all-get-to-be-prefects/

6 Academic work on this issue is available, for example, Freedman, B., Fuks, A. & Weijer, C (1993) *In Loco Parentis: Minimal Risk as an Ethical Threshold for Research upon Children*, Hastings Centre Report March–April, http://ftp.columbia.edu/itc/hs/pubhealth/p9740/readings/freedman.pdf

7 Simon Partridge, personal correspondence with the author.

8 *They Came for the Children*, Op cit

9 Keir Starmer QC, interviewed on *After Savile: No More Secrets?* BBC 2 *Panorama*, broadcast on 4 November 2013. The programme was introduced as "Why was it so easy for paedophiles like Jimmy Savile to get away with abusing children? In other countries evidence of abuse must be reported to the authorities. But here, turning a blind eye to child abuse in a school, or a hospital, or a church is not a crime. Reporter Sanchia Berg talks to victims, police and senior figures who are now calling for Britain to change the law and uncovers secret files which show that the government knew for decades that children's homes and schools covered up abuse. Head teachers and governors routinely moved abusers, sending them on with a good reference, rather than call the police. Even today, some head teachers still fail to act on reports and complaints."

10 http://en.wikipedia.org/wiki/United_Kingdom_parliamentary_expenses_scandal#Effect_on_MPs_and_on_the_political_structure

11 Miller, A. (1983) *For Your Own Good: The Roots of Violence in Child Rearing*, London: Virago.

12 Retrieved from www.efterskole.dk/~/media/Efterskole/Om%20efterskolen/English/Folder_UK_web.ashx

13 Retrieved from www.channel4.com/programmes/scandimania

Index